OXFORD STUDIES IN DEMOCRATIZATION

Series editor: Laurence Whitehead

. . . .

DEMOCRACY BETWEEN CONSOLIDATION AND CRISIS

OXFORD STUDIES IN DEMOCRATIZATION

Series editor: Laurence Whitehead

. . . .

Oxford Studies in Democratization is a series for scholars
and students of comparative politics and related disciplines.
Volumes will concentrate on the comparative study of the
democratization processes that accompanied the decline and
termination of the cold war. The geographical focus of the
series will primarily be Latin America, the Carribbean,
Southern and Eastern Europe, and relevant
experiences in Africa and Asia.

OTHER BOOKS IN THE SERIES

Democracy Between Consolidation and Crisis

*Parties, Groups, and Citizens in
Southern Europe*

....

LEONARDO MORLINO

OXFORD UNIVERSITY PRESS
1998

Oxford University Press, Great Clarendon Street, Oxford OX2 6DP
Oxford New York
Athens Auckland Bangkok Bogotá Buenos Aires Calcutta
Cape Town Chennai Dar es Salaam Delhi Florence Hong Kong Istanbul
Karachi Kuala Lumpur Madras Madrid Melbourne Mexico City Mumbai
Nairobi Paris São Paolo Singapore Taipei Tokyo Toronto Warsaw
and associated companies in
Berlin Ibadan

Oxford is a trade mark of Oxford University Press

Published in the United States
by Oxford University Press Inc., New York

British Library Cataloguing in Publication Data
Data available

Library of Congress Cataloging in Publication Data
Morlino, Leonardo, 1947–
Democracy between consolidation and crisis: parties, groups, and
citizens in Southern Europe / Leonardo Morlino.
(Oxford studies in democratization)
Includes bibliographical references.
1. Democracy—Europe, Southern.   2. Europe, Southern—Politics and
government.   I. Title.   II. Series
JN94.A91M67   1998   320.94'09182'2—dc21   97–48959
ISBN 0–19–828082–3

1 3 5 7 9 10 8 6 4 2

Typeset by Hope Services (Abingdon) Ltd.
Printed in Great Britain
on acid-free paper by
Biddles Ltd.,
Guildford & King's Lynn

To Emilia, Elisabetta, and Irene,
who made this possible

··············
Acknowledgements
··············

To write a book like the present one is to accept the challenge of synthesis and simplification. Even if synthesis is necessary for covering a broader ground and no theoretical step forward is possible without some simplification, a key question remains: to what extent are they acceptable and useful and to what extent, on the contrary, are they detrimental to a good analysis. Here, a sort of intermediate road was chosen in the belief that it was the best one. Whether this turns out to be correct will be judged by the reader. Here, I can only very gratefully acknowledge the precious help of several people during the years I was planning to write the book, and whilst I was doing so.

I began writing on this topic a long time ago, in 1981. In an unpublished paper, at the end of that year, I tried a speculative comparison between the Italian path to consolidation and the Spanish perspectives. A few years later, in 1986, two theoretical pieces were published in the *Rivista italiana di scienza politica*. During those years I already accumulated several debts. I particularly remember with gratitude the passionate debates with Julián Santamaria in Madrid and Philippe Schmitter, here in Florence. But the idea of going on to enlarge the comparative research in other qualitative domains came after my participation as a member of the Italian team in the survey conducted in the four Southern European countries in 1985, directed by Santamaria and Giacomo Sani and hosted by the *Centro de Investigaciones Sociologicas* in Madrid. The rich results of such a survey were never published in their entirety, and here also only a few data are analysed, in Chapter 3.

Only later, in early 1990, did I decide to write a book on the topic. A sabbatical year spent in the quiet, productive 'farm', as Stanford University (Calif.) is known by its aficionados, brought me to conceive this insane project, which again compelled me to conduct further empirical research in all four countries. I recall the rare, but intense discussions I had in 1990 with Philippe Schmitter and the simple, but effective help by Henrietta Grant Peterkin, the secretary of my host institution, the Center for European Studies at Stanford. I never had the opportunity to really express to her my gratitude for substantially improving my stay in Stanford; though many years later, I would like to do so now. In that year strong encouragement to write down and publish my work on Southern Europe in English came repeatedly from Kenneth Newton, then a fellow-member of the Executive Committee of the International Political Science Association (IPSA). To him as well, I take this chance to express my warmest thanks for that encouragement. Without his cordial, sympathetic pressure I would never have had the audacity to embark on this enterprise.

I think, however, that in the early 1990s the gymnasium where I was able to develop and strengthen my ideas and empirical hypotheses was the Committee on Southern Europe of the Social Science Research Council (New York). The profound understanding of Southern Europe, complemented by wisdom and professionality, of the chairpersons (Nikiforos Diamandouros and Richard Gunther), of the influential Juan Linz, and of the other members of the Committee (Edward Male-fakis, José Maria Maravall, José Ramon Montero, Gianfranco Pasquino, Hans-Jurgen Puhle, Geoffrey Pridham, Schmitter, Alfred Stepan, Sidney Tarrow, Manuel Villaverde Cabral) was extremely helpful for me. To all of them my deepest appreciation and thanks.

A short stay at the Hoover Institution in 1995 and a longer one at the Juan March Institute in Madrid in the same year gave me the possibility of discussing and basically improving the first chapter and the structure of the entire book with the suggestions kindly offered by Larry Diamond in the USA and by José Maria Maravall, Josè Ramon Montero, and Vincent Wright in Madrid. To all four I say thanks: to the American friend and the two Spanish ones for their precious, insightful comments and to Wright for the additional research he encouraged me to do (see the second part of Chapter 7), but also for taking an interest in a topic so far away from his field.

During the research I had the possibility of profiting from the collaboration of a few young colleagues. To Anna Bosco and Takis Pappas I owe much of the help in documenting the Portuguese and Greek parties. To Loris Koullapis, Giuseppina Merlini, Ignacio Molina, and Maria Ignacia Rezola, I am in debt for their enormous and essential contribution in analysing many years of the press in the four countries (see Chapter 7). Chiara Barlucchi assisted me in the computer analysis. Bosco and Jocelyn Evans scrupulously checked the bibliographical references. Michael Pretes and Evans pushed me to transform my *lingua franca* into readable English. To all of them my deepest gratitude.

Stefano Bartolini, Bosco, Maurizio Ferrera, Peter Mair, George Mavrogordatos, Angelo Panebianco, and Laurence Whitehead were so generous as to comment on either a few chapters or the entire first draft of the manuscript. I owe to them many improvements. I would particularly like to add special thanks and acknowledge my deepest appreciation to Whitehead not only for accepting me in the series he is the editor of, but also for his insightful, detailed suggestions. I'll never forget the hectic days at Nuffield College in Oxford.

After so much help, and so many suggestions and comments from which I profited, I feel even more obliged to take full responsibility for any mistakes and shortcomings the book may still contain.

The research projects which provided the foundations for this book and the related collections of data were financially supported by both the Italian Ministry of Education and the National Council for Research (Consiglio Italiano delle Ricerche). To these institutions and the scientific committees that believed in these projects, my grateful thanks. Without their support most of the research would simply not have been possible.

Some of the data and ideas expressed in Chapter 3 are taken from Morlino and Montero (1995) and Morlino and Mattei (1992); and some of the hypotheses on Italy in Chapter 7 from Morlino and Tarchi (1996). I thank again Franco Mattei, Montero, and Marco Tarchi for letting me use pieces of research conducted with them, and I take this opportunity to say how much I have enjoyed working together with them. Chapters 4 and 5 develop hypotheses that were anticipated in my chapter on parties, published in Gunther, Diamandouros, and Puhle (1995). Again I wish to thank these colleagues and friends for letting me use and build on my previous work.

L. M.

Florence
20 July 1997

Contents

........·····

List of Figures

........·····

·

List of Tables

······················

Introduction

······················

During the half of the twentieth century since the Second World War there have been several waves of democratization. At the end of the century in all of Europe, the Americas, and other areas of the world democratic regimes are no longer challenged as such. Such a rosy picture, however, has to be corrected and integrated by the internal challenges all democracies have to cope with in their real working. First of all, serious and sometimes overwhelming economic and social problems have challenged the newly installed institutions, or even the already existing democracies. In some cases this has provoked a crisis, also characterized by a deterioration of civil liberties and political rights, as, for example, happened in Latin America.[1] Thus, as democratization becomes more and more widespread, democratic institutions are fraught by the very problems they are supposed to solve.

If this is so, the relevant focus of democratization theory must be shifted. The central dilemma is no longer 'democracy versus authoritarianism', but if, how, and where democracy can be 'exported' and, more importantly, what takes place inside these regimes, also in terms of the emergence of new, often hidden, and subtle forms of authoritarian patterns. That is, the main questions no longer concern the conditions or factors that precipitate the collapse of democracy and bring about the setting up of an authoritarian regime. First, the questions become: what are the characteristic factors of democratic consolidation and internal crisis? What are the resulting democracies? And what are their distinctive features in terms of civil rights, forms of representation, and governing institutions? Second, how do these regimes actually work in terms of decision-making mechanisms, decisions made, and concrete policies enacted, and to what extent do these policies reflect important democratic values, such as accountability or responsiveness? Furthermore, it may be remembered that the second set of questions, concerning the 'quality of democracy', is related to the first set, as should appear evident in the conclusions to this volume.

This research aims at providing an answer to the first set of questions from a more specific perspective. It moves from the assumption

---

[1] On this topic see e.g. the excellent analysis by Diamond (1996).

that since in most countries—and, particularly, in those that form the empirical basis of this analysis—there is no alternative to democratic choice, the main internal processes of regime continuity and change can only be consolidation (or reconsolidation) and crisis. The outcomes can be very different—a strongly or weakly consolidated regime, a regime in crisis, or a hybrid result, but the processes at work can only be the two just mentioned: there is no longer space for breakdown and authoritarian installation.

Thus, research on democratic changes must focus on these two possible phenomena. How? The cases explored here suggest two basic questions, to which all others are related. The first one is: how is it possible that democratic consolidation takes place in countries where there are few or very few democrats, and contains in its traditions years or even decades of non-democratic rule? The second is: if external and internal elements allow some process of consolidation, is a subsequent moment or phase of crisis and adaptation bound to take place? That is, is there a moment when characteristics and elements of previous consolidation are bound to change with some consequent deeper or more limited crisis? These two questions oriented the whole research. The reply to the first one implies a greater attention not to consolidation as such, but to the process of the specific consolidations in each country; the second question can be solved only if it is connected to the first one, and several relations are taken into account.

This focus deserves some further qualifications. As the stress is on the processes,[2] not merely on the results of processes, the focus of the analysis must be on the actors—at élite and mass levels (whether individual actors, associations, agencies, movements, and so on)—and their involvement in the development, shaping, and maintenance of the relations between democratic institutions and civil society, namely, the people considered in their pre-political role. In fact, it is only possible to analyse a process effectively through the actions of élites and people. This means that institutional actors, party élites and other politically relevant élites, parties, and interest associations must be at the centre of the analysis. Who can consolidate or bring about the crisis of a regime if not élites or collective actors participating in the making of these processes? Who can organize, maintain, express and even

---

[2] An approach in terms of *process*—which has already been proposed at the beginning of contemporary political science (Bentley 1908) and later by systems analysis (Easton 1965)—or *processes* is largely accepted and fairly common in the present literature on political change and democratization, from Tilly (1975) to O'Donnell, Schmitter and Whitehead (1986). From the point of view of this research, not only should the regime be considered at the moment it became consolidated and stable or in crisis, but the development of the two processes should also be examined.

deepen attitudes of legitimacy or illegitimacy and dissatisfaction or discontent if not parties, groups, or movements?

The focus on actors may also be justified on two other grounds. First, most of the definitions of democratic regimes, as suggested by the literature, make explicit or implicit reference to actors and especially to the role of parties (and the party system), placing them at the centre of democratic processes and mechanisms. Some authors (see e.g. Barnes 1966) even point out that there may be a set of values, mass belief systems, or ideologies strongly present in society, but it is still the parties, with their organizations, that play an essential role in structuring, maintaining, and strengthening them.[3]

Second, taking a closer empirical perspective, parties, groups, movements, and a few élites still seem to lie at the heart of the events and the countries examined here. As also Malefakis (1995: 46) pointed out in sketching the common traits of Southern Europe, in this area 'modern political movements arose early', although they were unable to establish their hegemony and instability became a customary pattern. When more recently the role of parties (and party élites) in their representative functions is considered to be undermined, their great relevance has still to be stressed in the governmental roles they perform or as public office holders (see Mair 1995). After all, what are these institutions, as a set of rules with related constraints and incentives, without the people who give life to them?[4]

In the first chapter these issues will be addressed more systematically. Here, however, let it be emphasized immediately that in the analysis of processes the other key component is *time*: only through the passing of time and reconstruction of the stream of events is it possible to analyse the two processes. This requires examining data on the same variable or factor at different points in time; but it also requires the building of some funnel of causality in the examined processes.[5]

An analysis of consolidation and crisis and related questions is also relevant for Latin America, Eastern Europe, and other areas of the world. Here, however, the empirical basis for the research is provided by the four Southern European countries: Portugal, Spain, Greece, and Italy. At least one primary consideration is, therefore, in order. The processes of consolidation in Portugal, Spain, and Greece took place at

---

[3] And parties are defined in terms of élites. For example, a widely accepted definition of a party is: a more or less organized élite which takes part in (free or otherwise) elections in order to have their candidates elected to public office (see e.g. Downs 1957: 25, and Sartori 1976: 63).

[4] Diamond (1995), for example, stresses the relationship between institutionalization of the party system and the strength and durability of democracy.

[5] When possible, this is a better explanatory strategy than that which functions in terms of multi-causality, which does not admit any internal specification of time.

the end of the 1970s and during the 1980s, whereas the same process took place in Italy during the 1940s and 1950s, that is, in a different historical period, when ideological extremes and the Cold War were key aspects of the historical context in which that process developed. Italy also suffered a deep crisis later on, during the 1970s, and then again at the end of the 1980s, when an internal process of profound change began. During the same years relevant changes also occurred in the other three countries, but without the same far-reaching consequences. If, in spite of the different international contexts, there was some parallelism in the consolidation processes of Italy and the other three countries, and if in spite of a similar international context differences are evident in the consolidations of those three countries and the development of crisis, then the international factor cannot be placed in the foreground when analysing consolidation and crisis. When this factor is considered, it must always be analysed by stressing how it is transformed and 'translated' in domestic affairs—for example, in the structuration of cleavages of the country.

Given the differences among the four cases, the comparison conducted here will necessarily follow a middle road between the strategy of comparing the most similar systems and the opposite strategy of contrasting the most different cases.[6] The usefulness of such an analysis lies in having a broader view of the phenomena, with the similarities reinforced and emphasized by the differences. Thus, in the end, the potentially different roles of the institutions and actors analysed in the processes of consolidation and crisis should emerge more neatly.

With reference to the time span, when consolidation is examined, the 'point of departure' may be the moment when the installation is largely over. In our cases the approval of a constitutional charter may be considered such a moment: 1947 for Italy, 1975 for Greece, 1976 for Portugal, and 1978 for Spain. The final moment to be considered is a more approximate one. Thus, on the whole, the focus is on the first years after the installation as the core period of consolidation.[7] The following analysis of the four cases will clarify the reasons why the 'point of

[6] This is not the place to discuss the two comparative strategies in detail. See Przeworski and Teune (1970), but also Meckstroth (1975).

[7] The starting assumption is that the most important empirical features of consolidation take place ten to twelve years after the installation. With the lapse of time, consolidation may partially come to an end in some aspects, whilst continuing in others, which may also keep changing, and on the whole the process may go on until manifestations of crisis and change emerge. This makes the precise empirical indication of a final point of democratic consolidation, as a whole, more difficult and makes necessary this rather arbitrary assumption (which, however, should be submitted to subsequent empirical evidence) (see Ch. 2).

arrival' for Italy is the end of the 1950s, and for Portugal, Spain, and Greece, basically the middle 1980s or a little later.

When crisis, adaptation, and change are taken into consideration, the period will be 1990–6 both for Italy and for the other three countries. In Italy, the period really begins with the mobilization and protest of the 1960s, continuing to the end of the 1990s, with the interruption of a few years in between; for the other three countries, the period concerns the time when democratic stability is achieved and other problems emerge, the limits of previous consolidation become evident, and adaptation and change follow.

On the whole, the analysis will take place in three steps. The first will sketch the theoretical guidelines of the research with special reference to a definition of the concepts of consolidation and crisis, as well as contiguous terms that are part of the whole process of democratization: transition, installation, maintenance, and persistence. In the first chapter, the most important and alternative concepts will also be discussed, and the empirical notion of democracy, here assumed, will be presented. In addition, the main points of the research will be addressed in greater detail. The second chapter is very much related to the first one as it presents an empirical control and the measures of the two main processes described in the previous chapter.

With the second step, a key hypothesis of the research is explored: the main dimensions of consolidation concern consensus and legitimation, on the one hand, and some specific anchors, such as a few features of party system and party organizations, and the ways in which organized and non-organized interests are related to parties and state institutions, on the other hand. Thus, the focus will be on the process of consensus and legitimation at mass and élite levels, and with a closer attention paid to parties and democratic institutions. The problem is very simple: if it may be taken for granted that legitimation is indispensable in achieving democratic consolidation, how is such a process brought about? Is the lack of an alternative to democracy the key factor to be taken into account? And is consolidation still possible with limited legitimation? The third chapter will explore these problems. In particular, a basic distinction will be drawn between consensus at a mass level and support of political élites. The impact of memory on the collective political culture and the presence or absence of institutional alternatives will be considered, also to explain consensus and support. The relationships among legitimation and efficacy will come out as very weak during the consolidation phase, but it may be much more relevant later on.

The fourth and fifth chapters address the other problems related to the party system, the party organization, and the expression of interests. More precisely, do parties have an autonomous role in the process of consolidation? If so, what are the roots of such an autonomous role? What is the role performed by party organization in the process of consolidation and in the shaping of links with civil society? Or is it their ability to represent the interests of that society in the most effective way that brings about consolidation? Thus, the partisan organizational structures and the relationships among parties, interests, and the public sector of the economy during the process of consolidation will be analysed. Besides, which partial paths to consolidation emerge from this scrutiny?

The third step of research is opened by the first section of the sixth chapter. Here the lines of the previous analysis are drawn together by illustrating the models of consolidation in their entirety and pointing out the key explanatory factors of these models. The second part of the chapter will emphasize some additional characteristics of the models which are bound to change, and will begin sketching those changes, which are much more profound in the Italian case, and partial in the other three countries. In this chapter the mechanisms, patterns and unfolding of the crisis, and above all the intermediate, partial results will be considered. From this perspective, Chapter 7 will explore the main aspects of the Italian crisis and of the more limited manifestations of crisis in the other countries. They are the two different faces of the citizen reactions against political reality: first, the trend of dissatisfaction at mass level, in terms of attitudes; second, the behavioural manifestations of discontent and the perceived inefficacy for the problems people felt mostly and reacted against. This chapter will also try to disentangle the pragmatic reactions against democratic institutions, also related to corruption, by the more ideological ones grounded in differences of values.

The conclusion will come back to the main propositions emerging from the previous analysis. It will also speculate on the results of the research, in terms of the new directions those democracies are moving in. In the final remarks attention will also be devoted to the problem of the 'quality' of democracy in terms of accountability, and how it is related to the outcomes of consolidation and crisis.

PART I

The Theoretical Framework

Actors, Institutions, and Change

The Paired Concepts

A few years ago, inspired by classical sociologists, Bendix and Berger (1959) suggested that researchers should base their work on 'paired concepts', that is, on pairs of opposite concepts. The advantages are that one would be able to examine reality from a well-defined point of view, leading to greater in-depth analysis; that one could achieve a more complete overview of the phenomenon if the paired concepts were used together, as they should be; and, furthermore, that since the two concepts are at the extremes of an important continuum—for instance, tradition and modernity—one could perceive in greater detail all the nuances of the phenomenon being examined. In this book paired concepts will also be used, although rather differently. In order to discover some of the fundamental mechanisms underlying a democratic regime, with regard to changes in relations between institutions and civil society,[1] two opposite phenomena, consolidation and crisis, will be explored.[2] These can be seen as the processes that are most characteristic in the events of any democratic regime; and it will be seen whether and how the same factors are capable of describing and explaining the opposite processes of consolidation and crisis.

The purpose of this research is not to generalize from the specific cases:[3] Hirschman (1971) is right in stressing that the search for

---

[1] Apart from other considerations (see below) on institutions, I should emphasize that these are both government and representative structures. On the notion of civil society see this chapter, n. 71.

[2] Here I avoid dealing with the analysis of democratic installations in the countries under review. See the excellent four-volume work edited by O'Donnell, Schmitter, and Whitehead (1986). For an analysis of authoritarian crises and installations in the Southern European cases see also Morlino (1987).

[3] This is a particularly important point in the methodology of comparison. The most convincing theoretical position, also supported by empirical research, is that of Boudon (1984). According to him, it is only possible to formulate 'local theories', that is, empirically circumscribed hypotheses valid only for the cases and the period examined. But between the impossibility of generalizing from one or several cases and the opposite tenet there are different, intermediate, more interesting solutions. See below in the text.

generalizations can turn into an undesirable obstacle in the path of a research project. Nevertheless, by pinpointing the mechanisms that typify relations between civil society and the democratic regime in differing cases, especially with reference to the opposite phenomena of consolidation and crisis, I expect: (i) to focus better on certain problems that also deserve to be examined in other geographical areas or specific countries, from the viewpoint of the consolidation and crisis of Western democracies; (ii) to identify a set of concrete modalities by which these mechanisms make their appearance in Southern European democracies. Moreover, given certain specifications and possible modifications, the proposed notions and hypotheses might legitimately apply to other areas and other countries.

Given this premiss, this chapter begins with the definition of democracy with specific regard to its consolidation and crisis. These two processes will then be defined and related to similar processes and to the most important contiguous concepts. The subsequent focus on the dimensions and 'anchors' of consolidation and crisis will give a more precise idea of the avenues to explore in terms of actors and aspects. Finally, the theoretically alternative models of democracy that may emerge from the processes mentioned above will be presented.

Which Definition of Democracy?

The first of two preliminary problems is: how can a regime be defined as democratic?[4] The second is: in order to examine the change from one democracy to another democracy or the consolidation and crisis of a given democratic regime, how can one democracy be distinguished from another? In this section an answer to the first question is proposed, while the second question is considered at the end of the chapter, when consolidation and crisis have already been defined.

---

    [4] In the following pages 'democratic regime' will be used interchangeably with 'democracy'. The notion of regime is partially different from that suggested by Easton (1965: 193) as 'a set of constraints on political interaction . . . may be broken down into three components: values (goals and principles), norms, and structures of authority.' The present definition was already suggested in Morlino (1980: 67). The bulk of Eastonian definition is accepted, but the inclusion of values in this notion is criticized. Recently, these ideas have again been proposed by other authors in similar ways. See, for example, Fishman (1990: 428), who stresses the difference of the state by defining it as 'the formal and informal organization of the center of the political power, and of its relations with the broader society'; and Schmitter and Karl (1993: 40) whose definition is: 'a system of governance (that) is an ensemble of patterns that determines the methods of access to the principal public offices; the characteristics of the actors admitted to or excluded from such access; the strategies that actors may use to gain access; and the rules that are followed in the making of publicly binding decisions.'

A general definition of democracy will suffice.[5] Since Kelsen (1929), and later Schumpeter (1954), Sartori (1965), and Dahl (1971, 1986), liberal democracy has been defined as a set of explicit and pre-established rules for political participation, open competition, and the peaceful resolution of conflicts. These political arrangements are the result of compromise, the substantive outcome of which remains relatively uncertain (Przeworski 1985, 1986, 1991).[6] The main authors of such compromise are political intermediary structures, often linked to the various interests in different ways. Political intermediaries are important in so far as they play a leading role in the decision-making process and, more generally, in the functioning of a democratic regime.

The key role of intermediary structures and other actors in a democracy will emerge in the following chapters, as it may be considered a basic assumption of the whole analysis. For the moment, some important details to the just suggested definition will be added. First, the effective implementation of democratic rules may be a problem. These rules must be respected if there is to be a democracy: any regime calling itself democratic must address the question of 'legality'. Thus, if *de facto* powers have been granted to, or maintained by, the military or other actors, who can intervene and cancel the respect for those rules— or, indeed, if there are norms granting special powers to certain actors and these norms condition or limit respect for the fundamental rules mentioned above—then the regime cannot properly be termed democratic.[7] The same may be said when a power outside the country's borders substantially affects the inner workings of the regime.

Factors of this sort made Schmitter and Karl (1993: 45–6) add these two aspects to the definition of democracy: 'popularly elected officials must be able to exercise their constitutional powers without being subjected to overriding (albeit informal) opposition from unelected officials' and 'the polity must be self governing; it must be able to act independently of constraints imposed by some other overarching political system.' In short, the two elements are the absence of *de facto* powers and national independence. These cannot be considered defining aspects of a democracy, but they are essential conditions for the respect of fundamental rules without which a democracy cannot function as such. In

[5] On the several meanings of democracy see the illuminating essay by Collier and Levitsky (1994). The consciousness of the limits of any procedural definition is well expressed by Whitehead (1997).

[6] Przeworski (1991: 14) is particularly effective when he remarks that 'the decisive step toward democracy is the devolution of power from a group of people to a set of rules'. This explains the relative uncertainty that is mentioned in the text.

[7] On this point see below in this chapter where the role of the military and of other 'neutral powers' during the phase of consolidation and crisis is discussed.

this sense, democracy requires legality and independence if it is to exist in reality.

On the basis of the definition mentioned above, all the countries considered here can be termed democratic regimes. In all four countries the democratic structures and procedures were adopted after a period of authoritarianism, in some cases quite a long one: only seven years in the case of Greece (1967–74), but twenty-one, thirty-six, and forty-eight in the cases of Italy (1922–43), Spain (1939–75), and Portugal (1926–74), respectively. Democratic institutions have been in place since 1946 in Italy, 1974 in Greece, and 1977 in Spain.[8] As for Portugal, the situation is complicated by the role played by the army, at least until 1982. The constitutional reform approved in August 1982, and enacted by the end of September of that year, virtually eliminated the army's overarching role by abolishing the Council of the Revolution. Thus, according to the definition suggested above, Portugal is a quasi-democracy or a semi-democracy, limited by the political role of the army, from 1974 to 1982. In it, more than in the other countries, major adaptations during consolidation, interrupted by apparent indicators of crisis over a period of several months, may be observed (see Maxwell 1986*a*; but also below).[9]

The Two Processes

Once the general definition of democratic regimes is accepted, the focus on consolidation and crisis of these regimes is easier. In fact, it will necessarily concern the inner workings of the democratic regime and the mechanisms by which it is characterized. Consolidation, however, has been used in the common sense of the term—basically, the strengthening of the regime—and without a more precise definition by historians until recently. Only a few political scientists have attempted to define it. Rustow (1970: 358–61) deals briefly with the phase following the installation of democracy. However, he describes the phase in which

[8] As the main indicator of the beginning of the installation period the first free and competitive elections are taken.

[9] Let us not forget a second important aspect. At the very beginning, after the *coup d'état* of 1974, in Portugal there was an attempt to install a 'radical' and 'socialist' democracy, that is, a regime quite different from that encompassed by the definition provided above. Eventually, as said in the text, what came to be established and consolidated was a set of institutions that can be clearly defined as democratic. But again that implies that there were turning points and moments of crisis during the transition, installation, and subsequent process of consolidation. However, by 1982 the Portuguese democracy perfectly fitted the above suggested definition of democracy. If one has to point out a differentiating aspect with the other cases considered here, a larger public economic sector may be mentioned.

people become accustomed to living in a democracy as a 'habituation phase', rather than as a consolidation phase. This stage is character-ized by the extension of a democratic consensus to encompass other strata of society and by the selection of more democratically oriented leaders. The first author to adopt and analyse the concept of consolida-tion, although in a still unpublished work, was Linz (1974*a*). There have been later contributions by several other authors (Di Palma 1990*b*; Etzioni-Halevy 1993; Higley and Gunther 1992; Hirschman 1987; Linz 1982, 1988; Mainwaring 1992; Morlino 1981, 1986*a*, 1986*b*; Pridham 1990*a*; O'Donnell 1992; Maravall and Santamaria 1986; Schmitter 1985 and updated 1988; Whitehead 1989; Valenzuela 1992; Hall 1993; more recently, Gunther, Diamandouros and Puhle 1995, and Schedler 1997*b*).[10]

Linz is also one of the best-known authors on the topic of democratic crisis (Linz and Stepan 1978). But there are also historians who have dealt with the subject, such as Bracher (1971), and other social scien-tists (e.g. Binder *et al.* 1971; Almond, Flanagan, and Mundt 1973; Habermas 1975; Crozier, Huntington, and Watanuki 1975; Diamond, Linz, and Lipset 1989; Dobry 1986; Morlino 1979, 1981; Zimmermann 1983; and also O'Connor 1987, and several others). The list is long. Here their definitions and analyses will not be discussed. However, in this and later chapters, where necessary, explicit reference to their views will be made.[11]

By consolidation I am referring, first of all, to the years that follow the installation of democracy when all relevant institutions have been set up. As democratic installation may take place gradually and at dif-ferent rates, the process of consolidation may not begin at the same time within the different components of the regime. There may also be aspects of the consolidation process that happen much later, and go on simply because of the passing of time. But the core of the process takes

[10] Only where necessary the cited authors will be quoted again. A review of them is in Shin (1994: 135 ff.) and in Schedler (1997*a*), who for the first time well enucleated the main meanings of consolidation in the literature (avoiding democratic breakdown, avoid-ing democratic erosion, institutionalizing democracy, completing democracy, and deepening democracy). Schedler (1997*a*: 27) might also be right when affirming that 'any ambition to "legislate" the semantic field of DC into some imagery unity seems doomed to failure'. At the same time the clarification of the starting points of view, the related empirical definitions of consolidation, and the other contiguous concepts seem a neces-sary step in an empirical research (see below in the text). Of course, Schedler also proposes his definition of consolidation in another paper (see 1997*b*). Besides the above-mentioned works there are also contributions to authoritarian consolidation. For example, some of Stepan's hypotheses (1978, esp. ch. 3) on Latin America, and on Peru in particular, can be seen in this light, as well as some work on the consolidation of the Franco regime in Spain during the 1940s, such as Morlino (1981, chs. 1 and 6).

[11] A short but careful analysis of the notion of crisis as advanced by several authors is in Svensson (1986).

place right after installation, although at different moments and rates. This is so because consolidation coincides with a necessary 'breaking in' phase after installation. O'Donnell (1992: 18) captures this core element of consolidation when he characterizes it as a transition to the effective functioning of a democratic regime after the creation, or re-establishment, of democratic rule; and Whitehead (1989: 79) points out how previous uncertainties are overcome as the new 'procedures become better known and understood and more widely accepted'. Differently, a crisis may happen at any time, during or after installation or even consolidation, undermining the ongoing or preceding process.

Thus, *consolidation is the multifaceted process by which democratic structures, norms, and regime–civil society relationships are firmly established*.[12] This process implies the strengthening of the democratic regime to avert possible future crises. In more precise terms, if in a democracy well-defined relationships between governing and representative institutions and civil society are stressed, consolidation can be seen principally as the construction of (more or less) stable representational relationships between the government institutions that have just been set up, the emergent intermediary structures, and civil society itself. As will be pointed out later, these relationships are bound to go in two directions: from top to bottom, i.e. from the newly created institutions to the intermediate structures and to society; and, vice versa, from the bottom up, from society to the institutions.

Consolidation has two aspects: *adaptation* and *firm establishment*, or even 'freezing'.[13] These emerge during the process when the democratic institutions are 'at work', when a decision-making process has been set in motion; the electoral law affects the relationships and even the size of the main political actors, and distinctive dynamics are set. The two modes can be complementary, not simply alternative. Immediately after installation, because the new institutions have just emerged and relationships among the political actors are not yet defined, the day-to-day business of a democratic regime can run into difficulties both in the relations among the actors within the institutions, and in solving problems as they arise. As a result, there is adaptation, a *de facto* adjustment or a series of changes in the norms to adapt these to interests and to the actors working within the regime. Thus, in the more salient

---

[12] The different faces of the process are also stressed by Linz and Stepan (1996: 6) in their definition, where the behavioural, attitudinal, and constitutional dimensions are indicated as well as the interaction among five different arenas that reinforce each other: civil society, political society, state bureaucracy, rule of law, and economic society (see ibid. 7–15).

[13] 'Freezing' is a stronger establishment without the possibility of adaptation. This difference will be more evident in the second chapter.

aspects, partial and gradual change takes place in the actual functioning of the institutions during the process of consolidation. There can
also be a firm establishment during the process, namely, the settlement of a balance between actors and institutional practices is
achieved at the very beginning and remains unchanged for decades.
Obviously, either path leads to an identical result: persistence and a
stable democracy.

With respect to crisis, the main analytical problem is how to escape
the 'normality trap'. In other words, a definition of crisis that would
refer to an ideal or 'normal' state of democracy not in crisis is difficult
to give empirically. From this point of view, a simple definition, which
attempts to avoid such a trap, refers to the emergence of limits and constraints on the expression of civil and political rights, previously sanc-
tioned by the regime, together with limitations on political competition
or on the potential participation of the people. However, in addition to
a crisis *of* democracy, as defined above, there can be a crisis *in* the
democracy. In such a hypothesis *crisis* is *the process of decline in institutional efficacy*[14] *as well as divorce and change in relations among
civil society, parties, and government institutions.*

The two main dimensions of this second definition distinguish
between a crisis of efficacy and a crisis of legitimacy inside a democratic regime. Despite the differences in characteristics and origins, they
are inevitably related. In fact, if serious, the decline of efficacy—
because of economic crisis, widespread corruption, or the impossibility
of coping with important problems, and other reasons—will bring
about changes in the relations between civil society and institutions.
The opposite phenomenon may also take place, namely, those changes,
due to other or even to the same attitudinal changes or phenomena,
cause the decline of efficacy. This, however, does not entail any theoretical necessity of such a relationship, and on the contrary the two
dimensions and kinds of crisis are analytically different and may be
empirically autonomous: a crisis of legitimacy, not compounded by the
decline of efficacy; or, vice versa, a crisis of efficacy that the government
is able to contain without any consequence for the legitimacy of that

---

[14] On 'efficacy' related to stability and crisis there is a classic literature going from
Lipset (1959, ch. 3) to Linz (1978: 18 ff). The same aspect received attention even earlier
(see Barnard 1938: 19), and later in organizational literature and public policy research.
About the related notions of effectiveness and performance see Morlino (1985), where
'effectiveness' is more strictly related to the outcomes, which often are not clear or evident in the political reality. On performance as a wider concept Eckstein's definition (see
1971) is adopted. 'Efficacy' refers to the working of regime institutions, and the decline of
it to the gradual or abrupt, but clearly perceived worsening of the economic situation,
distributed resources, available public services, and so on, that is, the emerging institutional incapability/impossibility of solving the actual problems.

specific, existing democracy. In any case both phenomena should be considered in order to explore more deeply the internal crisis.[15]

An additional, important definitional element of crisis, especially that internal to a democracy, is the length of time: it does not necessarily take place in a short span of time. In fact, contrary to what could be suggested by the medical meaning of the term, which always makes reference to a sudden phenomenon of short duration, in most of the empirical cases a political or democratic crisis of the kinds suggested above takes time, and even a long time, to unfold. The main reason for this is simple and obvious: the actions and reactions of numerous vested interests to any change or adaptation take time to unfold.[16]

In this analysis the crisis inside democracy, with its dimensions and aspects, is more relevant. Thus, the second definition of crisis, that taking place inside a democratic regime, will be used and at the same time the crisis related to legitimacy, mainly because of a decline in efficacy, will be stressed. In fact, with the ever increasing and widespread acceptance of democracy, both in Southern Europe and in other parts of the world, it is also increasingly important to observe: (i) the mutation of a democratic regime into another with a reconstruction of the multi-faceted internal transformations, that is, through a more or less protracted critical process up to the installation of a new democracy; or (ii) a period of crisis and consolidation if the crisis intervened during the installation or a reconsolidation of the same regime, if some democratic consolidation had already taken place before the crisis; or even (iii) a long, protracted crisis and deadlock without any way out (see Figure 1.1 and below).

The main empirical aspects of this process are, on the one hand, the appreciable, perceived decline of efficacy and, on the other, *destabilization* and *destructuring* of relations of representation, mainly characterized by changes in the party system, in organized and non-organized interest groups, or in both. They can be observed in the mutation of one democratic model into another, in the period before the consolidation or reconsolidation, in the moments of protracted crisis, or even in the transition to an authoritarian regime.[17] In the first hypothesis the crisis will require a readjustment or *readaptation* of the relations already mentioned, with a profound change in the basic rules of the democratic regime, and might usher in the consolidation of a different type of democracy.

---

[15] But see also below, the section on manifest inefficacy.

[16] See esp. Chs. 6 and 7.

[17] On the transition to an authoritarian regime see Morlino (1981); on the other intra-democratic phenomena, see Chs. 10 and 11.

Here, on the whole, consolidation and crisis are conceived of as *processes*. In this way they can be analysed diachronically, and a more precise understanding of the democratic regime's dynamics and of the interrelationships of the actors involved is gained. A better and more precise reconstruction of events and of the role played by each of the political forces and leaders in the consolidation and crisis should also be achieved. Furthermore, this approach should help to explain why those actors who promptly accommodate themselves in the regime during consolidation (Rustow 1970: 358), or are able to take advantage of the critical changes under way, also gain the greatest benefit from the new institutional context, protecting their interests better or even being in a position to impose their choices.

From an empirical perspective it is also worthwhile envisaging consolidation and crisis in terms of the *outcomes* of a process: to what extent is the democratic regime consolidated, persisting, and more or less stable?[18] Does the crisis lead to the reconsolidation of the same democratic regime, to its demise and the establishment of another democracy, or to a gradual change and the creation of a political arrangement that is only partially different from the previous one? It is important to answer such queries, but this involves examining the results or outcomes of these processes. Furthermore, from a purely empirical point of view, there are aspects of the examined phenomena that may emerge suddenly. For some of them, it is virtually impossible to detect the ongoing development. It is only possible to see the partial outcome.[19] Finally, it is sometimes impossible to have the kind of quantitative time-series that allows the researcher to analyse the process in depth. Therefore, a number of other different qualitative data deserve careful scrutiny. In a consistent theoretical perspective they can be taken into account only if the achievements or the outcome of the processes, rather than the processes themselves, are stressed.[20] The two lines of analysis should be integrated.[21]

On the whole, crisis is considered here as the opposite of consolidation. Whereas the stabilization of patterns of representation, recurring modes of behaviour, and other features characterize consolidation,

---

[18] Clearly, here the question is also: when may the process of consolidation be concluded, and thus the outcome be seen and analysed? I will come back to this question later in the book.

[19] This will become more evident below when the empirical part is developed.

[20] These considerations will become much clearer when I deal with the empirical data, in the section on legitimation (process) and legitimacy (outcome).

[21] In an excellent review article, Kitschelt (1992: 1028) stresses the differences between the structure- and process-oriented approaches: a macro-quantitative or conceptually disciplined qualitative analysis with countries as units of analysis being the first one, and a descriptive diachronic reconstruction of individual cases being the second.

destabilization and destructuration of the same features are the recurrent features of crisis. Whereas accommodation and adaptation are the main features of a consolidating democracy, radicalization of domestic conflicts among the salient political and socio-political actors is the main feature of a democracy in crisis.[22]

These modes and dimensions sometimes take place in a more limited way. In other words, there is the possibility of partial consolidation[23] or partial crisis, namely, the possibility that these processes, and the related features, develop in specific domains of the democratic regime at a different pace than in others. Such a development may not be immediately related to the whole democratic consolidation or crisis, although in the long run consistent tendencies are very likely to appear. Actually, the problem mainly concerns the sector of interests: thus, for instance, could a strong sectorial consolidation or crisis at the level of interest groups, compounded by a weak party system, become so relevant for the regime as to influence or determine the whole process?[24]

Processes and Outcomes of Democratization

These definitions are better understood if they are placed among the other possible processes of democratization as well as matched with some contiguous concepts. The other three important processes of democratization are: transition, installation, and breakdown; while maintenance, persistence, and collapse or, simply, a change of regime are the outcomes of these processes. Furthermore, there is no fixed pattern that governs the succession of processes and outcomes, and the boundaries between these phenomena are often blurred. A newly established democracy can undergo a period of consolidation, or, alternatively, a political crisis, that may result in breakdown or reconsolidation and persistence. There may even be a change of direction within a particular process, or features of the two processes may be present at the same time. For example, when democracy was established in Portugal between 1975 and 1976, there was a change in the relative strength of the various civil/military alliances within the regime, a sub-

---

[22] Because of the opposition between crisis and consolidation it might also be beneficial to consider all the relevant empirical indicators of crisis when consolidation is analysed. Its very presence would suggest that no consolidation process is going on or, at the very least, it is a challenged and weak one. This point will be developed in the next chapter.

[23] This is what Schmitter (1988 and 1992) has in mind when he deals with *partial regime*.

[24] See Ch. 6.

sequent crisis of the institutional arrangement that had almost been installed, change with the establishment of another kind of democracy, and the beginning of a new, long process of consolidation. In addition, the setting up of a new democracy is not necessarily followed by consolidation, although this is a vitally important process. The crises and breakdowns of democracy that occurred in Italy and Spain during the 1920s and early 1930s, and in Latin America later on, are largely due to the failure of various governments to consolidate the new democratic institutions.

With these caveats in mind, the *transition* process refers to that fluid and uncertain period when new democratic structures are about to emerge, while some of the structures of the old regime still exist. Above all, it is not clear yet what regime is going to be installed—a democratic one, or even another form of authoritarianism, perhaps a less repressive one. Tilly (1978) might call it a situation of dual sovereignty, meaning that there is still ongoing competition or conflict for supremacy in the coercive-political arena between two different actors or coalitions of actors.

This process can sometimes be over very quickly, when the change comes after a breakdown of the previous authoritarian regime, in some cases with a *coup d'état*. When this does not take place, there may be a more specific process of *liberalization*, that is, 'the partial opening of an authoritarian system short of choosing governmental leaders through freely competitive elections' (Huntington 1991: 9). In such a case the transition may be a much longer one, and may not even lead to a democratic regime, but only to some relaxation of suppression.

In France, Italy, Spain, and Portugal, such a fluid, uncertain phase of transition is fairly short and it moves from the Vichy Republic, the breakdown of fascism, the death of Franco, and the captains' *coup d'état* up to the first competitive elections, in a period of one or two years. In the Greek case, this phase is even shorter: elections came a few months after the military handed power to a civilian government led by Karamanlis in July 1974. Thus, the transition is concluded when there are the first free, competitive elections.

Conceptually and empirically, the transition process is very different from consolidation: it is basically the difference between fluidity and firm establishment. However, in some Latin American cases, such as Mexico after the Reforma Política (1977), there was a clear attempt to consolidate or, rather, to 'freeze' the liberalization *octroyée*, namely, to stop the transition midway in its march toward democracy and to maintain that arrangement indefinitely.[25]

---

[25] On the Mexican liberalization as 'a precursor' rather than a substitute for an eventual regime transition see Whitehead (1995).

Installation[26] is characterized by the creation of new structures and procedures, as well as by other more informal mechanisms intrinsic to a democratic system already outlined above. Consolidation has none of this kind of 'creativity'. It is not a deeply innovative process. On the contrary, it is characterized by the firm establishment of structures and procedures that are intended to last. The passing of time plays a key role in the consolidation process, and the firm establishment of the essential democratic structures and norms is complemented by their adaptation to the real problems that the incumbent élites face. This is also a way of withstanding any crises or potential breakdowns that may occur over time.

In the four cases, installation can be considered completed at the regime level when the constitutional charter is approved and, for Portugal, when the constitutional reform made that country a democratic one in October 1982.[27] These cases have the theoretical advantage of drawing a distinction between transition and installation. A few authors overlook this distinction (see, for example, O'Donnell, Schmitter, and Whitehead 1986). Here it is maintained because of its meaningfulness in countries where there was a distinct, well-defined phenomenon of institution building, in some case protracted over a long period, despite the fact that installation usually already begins during the transitional phase and overlaps with it. Additionally, installation may be very different from consolidation in terms of forces and actors that made and supported the first process vis-à-vis those who were crucial in the second one. This will become apparent in some of the cases.[28]

Consolidation and crisis are neither *maintenance* nor *persistence*. The 'breaking in' period is basically over. The characteristic aspects are those of adaptation and continuity in a fairly unstable situation (maintenance) or in a more stable regime (persistence).[29] Maintenance or, in a simpler way, endurance is the result of a partially successful consolidation or of the containment of crisis, which may reappear at any moment. Persistence comes out of a successful consolidation or at the end of a reconsolidation. As the core of the consolidation process takes place during the first years after installation, without a solution of continuity, it turns either into maintenance, if only partially successful, or

[26] I prefer this term, but *instauration* or even *inauguration*, as suggested by some authors, are also acceptable.

[27] See above on this point, and the first section of the next chapter.

[28] See Rustow (1970) and next chapter with specific reference to Italy and Portugal.

[29] Let us not elaborate on the differences between either stability/instability or on stability/persistence. For completeness of the argument I only point out that stability is the expectation of persistence. Thus, from an empirical perspective they are two ways of looking at the same phenomenon. I will use the term 'persistence'. On the whole topic see Morlino 1985, ch. 6.

into persistence if highly successful. Therefore, if no crisis emerges, the consolidation continues and overlaps with persistence after the first years, if only because of the passing of time.

Matching consolidation and crisis with maintenance and persistence helps to answer a key question: when can we say that the consolidation process or the crisis is over? The best possible answer for the question is: when the opposite phenomenon, i.e. the crisis or consolidation, emerges and becomes prominent. If there is no crisis, then the core process of consolidation takes place imposing its own logic during the first years after installation: the relationships between regime and civil society are established and the institutions show their own internal self-reproductive dynamics. With regard to the empirical cases, this means that consolidation generally takes place in about ten or twelve years or at least three full parliamentary terms. If a crisis takes place, the other process is also over. The crisis may come during installation, immediately after it, or during an abortive attempt at consolidation.

In addition to maintenance, a period of crisis may be followed by *breakdown, change,* or *reconsolidation.* There are no strong differences between consolidation and reconsolidation as far as definition and indicators are concerned. However, the previous regime and the modes by which the regime changes affect the process. Therefore, consolidation and reconsolidation will appear different when factors related to the previous authoritarian or democratic experience are considered. Breakdown or collapse is the last step in the crisis, and the following change of regime is characterized by violence and discontinuity, and it usually takes place in a limited span of time.[30] The change concerns the transformation of a democratic regime into another one, always characterized by problems of continuity, vested interests, and cultural patterns established by the previous institutions. Of course, the change may also be partial as the result of a partial crisis. Thus, there may be a crisis of a specific democracy followed by the reconsolidation of the same regime; crisis and more or less gradual or partial change of democracy; and also crisis and breakdown, with the establishment of an authoritarian regime.[31]

Figure 1.1 shows the main processes just defined with reference to the possible sequences and outcomes. It should be evident from the figure that once a democratic regime is installed and there is no lethal challenge to the democracy, the most empirically relevant processes are consolidation or reconsolidation and crisis, which may also result in

---

[30] It may be recalled that on breakdowns there is the largest tradition of scholarly analyses, above all with reference to the 1920s and 1930s. See Linz and Stepan (1978), Morlino (1981), Zimmermann (1985).

[31] 'Collapse' and 'ruptura' are consideerd synonyms of breakdown.

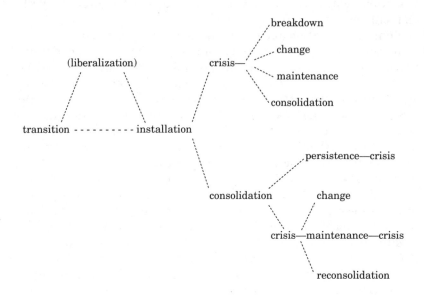

FIG. 1.1. *Processes, outcomes, and sequences in democratic change*

some forms of weak maintenance or partial change. At the same time, Figure 1.1 suggests that once consolidation has taken place, the crisis followed by breakdown appears as a more difficult event. Hence, there is a need to explain why the focus should be on those processes.[32]

A Few Contiguous Notions: A Short Excursus

Curiously enough, the term 'crisis' is more accepted and widely used[33] while the possible contiguous terms, such as collapse, breakdown, or

---

[32] On the contrary, when the problem is the change from democracy to authoritarianism, then the two most relevant processes are transition and breakdown. In fact, on these two phenomena Higley and his associates focus their attention. See Higley and Burton (1989) and Burton, Gunther, and Higley (1992).

[33] But there are reasons for that in the intellectual history of the word. Basically, they are the strong organic or functionalist paradigms behind the term; the diffusion of a Marxist wording in social science; and, perhaps, in comparison with 'consolidation' the higher interest of the phenomenon labelled 'crisis'.

ruptura, now have a more distinct meaning and different empirical references.[34] As for consolidation, there are other terms that might overlap in both meaning and empirical reference. This makes a short terminological excursus necessary. Reviewing it in comparison with a few contiguous concepts will also help to illuminate this notion.

Consolidation is neither structuration nor encapsulation. The first process is the key feature of the installation phase. In fact, *structuration* may be conceived of as the process of building new political structures. On the contrary, during the consolidation phase, recurring patterns of institutional behaviour are established and the same original constitutional model adapts to the new possible realities.[35]

The second concept, *encapsulation*, was coined by Etzioni (1964) with specific reference to international conflict. It represents a very interesting way of indicating the process of control and containment of conflicts. However, the term touches on both installation and consolidation, as far as it refers to both the construction and acceptance or compliance with those democratic rules aimed at the containment and control of internal conflicts. Such a feature emerges and becomes salient when interest groups are taken into account. In other words, encapsulation is a seminal concept despite not being immediately useful for the present analytical purpose.

Institutionalization[36] is the closest concept to consolidation. A key notion in sociological theory, it was transferred into the political realm by Huntington (1968). Following in Parsons's footsteps, Huntington proposes a definition that is at once too general and basically inadequate for the purpose of this study. In his words, institutionalization is 'the process by which organizations and procedures acquire value and stability' (ibid. 12). The very 'measures' of institutionalization (adaptability/rigidity, complexity/simplicity, autonomy/subordination, coherence/disunity) (ibid. 13–24) are not only criteria that would require a more rigorous operationalization, but would also be incompatible: they do not hang together. For instance, a form of institutionalization that displays simultaneously maximum adaptability and complexity and maximum coherence and autonomy seems virtually impossible. In addition, as rightly stressed by Di Palma (1990*b*: 41–2), some degree of

---

[34] A problem of definition might be raised so as to distinguish among these three words (but see above).

[35] When Schmitter (1985, 1988) defines consolidation as structuration, he has in mind both processes, installation and consolidation, which on the contrary should be distinguished (see above).

[36] The much debated analysis of what is an 'institution' is beyond the purposes of this chapter: different, contending positions are expressed by the traditional sociological approach, behaviouralism, rational choice theory, and neo-institutionalism in their works. For a few interesting observations see Sjöblom (1994).

incoherence and a weak institutionalization may not be detrimental to consolidation: this may be the price paid to 'give institutions a value of their own in the eyes of contrasting players' (ibid. 42).

Moreover, for the purposes of this analysis this notion still seems inadequate: on the one hand, it is too general as it applies to every institution, not only to the political ones; on the other hand, it is too specific, as a political regime is not only a set of institutions, but also encompasses non-institutional actors, informal rules, and several other aspects that would be incorrect to constrain in an all-institution approach. Of course, within a consolidation or crisis, this consideration does not exclude the analytical possibility of dealing with parties or organized groups, cabinet and parliament, civil service and judiciary as institutions, and therefore with its own problems of institutionalization and de-institutionalization.[37]

Thanks to the contributions of Linz and Stepan (1989), and above all of Di Palma (1990*a*), another term has gained currency and should be examined here: *crafting*. It describes four aspects of democratization: the quality of democratic rules and institutions; modes of decision-making, which shape the rules and institutions; types of 'craftsmen', i.e. the alliances and coalitions formed; and timing in the various tasks and stages of transition (Di Palma 1990*a*: 8–9). The principal merit of the concept is to underscore the enormous importance of institutions and how they are formed and moulded by political actors in a democratic regime. Thus, crafting plays an important role in the installation phase, and a more marginal one in consolidation. In this sense, it is useful to examine what the notion of crafting covers. To be more precise, after the creation of norms and institutions, there comes a moment when these norms and institutions must function and do the work for which they were created: it is precisely at this point that agreements and alliances are tested, the real position of actors and groups emerges, and it becomes apparent who will win and who will lose. If crafting covers all of this, then it would be better to distinguish between crafting as the moulding of rules during the installation, and crafting as concrete adaptation and implementation of these rules during consolidation or when the grounds for a crisis of the regime are being laid.[38]

---

[37] On this, despite the problems addressed above in the text, see the following chapters.

[38] In a previous contribution Di Palma defines 'consolidation as crafting the competitive rules so as to prevent essential players from boycotting the game' (1990*b*: 38). This definition may be interpreted as the problem of adapting previously defined rules so as to avoid the delegitimation of existing institutions. If this is so, this notion dovetails perfectly with my proposed definition.

This excursus, together with the preceding section, should have helped to gain a more precise and specific idea of the proposed definitions. If they are inserted into their specific 'semantic field', these notions acquire a more precise meaning: each definition must take into account contiguous ones and gain greater analytical precision from the comparison.[39] Hence, asking whether a minimal notion is better or whether a 'strong' notion is necessary—a question that has occasionally been raised with regard to the concepts examined here—is wrongly put. Once the semantic field to which these notions belong has been recognized and the terms within it defined, scholars should determine which empirical indicators derive from the proposed definitions[40] and what the specific aspects related to the two processes are.[41]

Legitimation and Consensus

It is still obvious that dimensions and modes of interaction among political institutions, party actors, and civil society are as diverse as they are complex, especially when several cases are being scrutinized. For example, a recent thoughtful review of the action of parties in achieving democratic consolidation enumerated twenty particular aspects that should be taken into consideration in at least three different domains, such as parties and state, inter-party relationships, and parties and society (see Pridham 1990*a*: 26–8). All considered, this means selecting those interactions that seem most relevant to the processes examined here, together with the results they yield in terms of democracy.

In this perspective three domains or sub-processes deserve closer attention. Two of them correspond to two opposite directions of analysis: the first one goes from civil society and parties to governmental

[39] Sartori (1975: 36) emphasizes this point very well when he says that 'no new stipulation is acceptable in isolation, that is without regard to the semantic, systemic, and/or theoretical field to which a given term belongs . . . We may equally say that each field of inquiry consists, basically, of a set of independent-interdependent terms. . .'

[40] See the next chapter.

[41] Thus, at least three terms have been mentioned so far: structuration or structuring, institutionalization, and also consolidation. To them stabilization may be added. For the sake of clarity, *consolidation*, as it has been defined above, is only used at the macro-level of the whole democratic regime; *institutionalization* is a complex and more general concept with different indicators and measures and it would make the analysis a more complicated one without any additional advantage; *stabilization* is simply the appearance of almost constant values in a given variable in a given span of time (see the next chapter for the empirical indicator and its use mainly with regard to electoral phenomenon); finally, *structuration* or *structuring* is the development of new organizations, especially in the relationships between civil society and the regime (see also the following chapters). For an analysis of these terms vis-à-vis consolidation see also Morlino (1991*b*).

institutions, i.e. a bottom-up direction, where parties are seen in their expressive function as a means of legitimation or as actors who create consensus and support for governmental institutions; the second from institutions and parties to groups or, in a broader sense, civil society, i.e. a top-down direction where parties are envisioned as public institutions for the political channelling of society, and even of societal control. If so, consensus and legitimation, on the one hand, and autonomy and control, on the other, are the two main dimensions of consolidation and crisis.

A third domain, however, must be added, and it intersects the previous ones: it concerns real social, economic, and political problems, the decisions made by governments on these issues and the reactions of the people, and the individuals who every day must cope with the difficulties of living and are not necessarily members of organized groups, associations, or parties. Their attitudes and behaviours, in addition to their electoral behaviour, are relevant to understanding and explaining the unfolding of a crisis, even more than of a consolidation.

The simple hypotheses which will be elaborated in the following chapters are: consolidation is the result of legitimation and control or autonomy; crisis comes out of delegitimation and collapse, or alterations, of that control, that is the anchors of previous consolidation, also because in the solution of social, economic, or political problems something went wrong, and negative reactions and detachment of people from that specific democracy and political leaders came out. How to better articulate these hypotheses, to give empirical support to them, and to show the absence of more empirically valid theoretical alternatives, will appear in the following chapters.

Legitimacy is a set of positive societal attitudes toward its democratic institutions, which are considered as the most appropriate form of government.[42] In other words, there is legitimacy when among citizens there is a widespread belief that, in spite of shortcomings and failures, existing political institutions are better than any others that might be set up. As Linz (1978: 18) has written, 'ultimately, democratic legitimacy is based on the belief that for that particular country at that particular juncture no other type of regime could assure a more successful pursuit of collective goals.' There are numerous alternative definitions of this slippery notion: however, this conceptualization seems a more convincing one, and it is shared by several authors, such as Lipset (1959), Almond and Verba (1963), and Linz (1978), among others.

---

[42] For a more detailed analysis of this definition see Morlino (1980). Here the reference is to *political legitimacy,* and the analysis consequently restricted to this aspect. It would be possible, however, to add two further dimensions: 'social legitimacy' and 'economic legitimacy'. On the latter, see Linz (1988: 65–113).

Legitimation or development and growth of positive attitudes toward political institutions is an important aspect of democratic consolidation, as far as it consistently entails loyal behaviour and support for democratic institutions. On the contrary, *delegitimation*, compounded by stronger conflicts and radicalization, may be a crucial feature of crisis. Even élite-oriented approaches to the study of democratic consolidation acknowledge the importance of this process (see Burton, Gunther, and Highley 1992; and many others). Furthermore, there are authors who attempt to avoid the conceptual and empirical traps that this concept contains, but eventually they cannot help referring to certain aspects of it. For example, Schmitter refers to 'contingent consensus' (Schmitter and Karl 1993) or support (Schmitter 1992); O'Donnell to actors who consider that the existing institutions 'will last indefinitely' and to 'procedural consensus' (O'Donnell 1992: 48–9); Valenzuela to institutions that 'are perceived by all political significant forces to be unambiguously the only means to create governments well into the foreseeable future' (Valenzuela 1992: 69); and Dogan (1988) places legitimacy and 'strains on legitimacy' at the core of the analysis, developed with others, on the main problems of contemporary democracies. The only author who clearly affirms that legitimacy is not a condition of regime survival is Przeworski with reference to authoritarian and democratic breakdowns (1986: 50). Later, Di Palma (1990a: 144) follows him by affirming: 'it is neither a precondition nor a necessary consequence of consolidation.' But then the first author recalls the 'organized consent' (Przeworski 1986: 53), and the second 'crafting a democratic agreement', and also consent, compliance, or support (Di Palma 1990a: 145).[43]

It only stands to reason, therefore, that most scholars recognize the role and salience of legitimacy, legitimation, and its opposite phenomena. Yet behind this apparent unanimity lie several problems that transpire from the works of the authors just mentioned.[44] Legitimation and its opposite are central elements in consolidation and crisis; indeed, this is very close to tautology: democratic institutions are consolidated because citizens see them as positive, or a crisis is engendered because, indeed, citizens have become highly critical of them.

Various analytical problems arise from this state of theory. The following are the most significant problems: there is the need for more accurate definitions of legitimacy and legitimation, which distinguish between attitudes and behaviours and also reveal the various degrees

[43] But see also Sartori (1993: 61–3).

[44] First of all, not only—as suggested by O'Kane (1993)—is this not a central concept in social science, but even focusing only on consolidation and crisis, it has to be complemented by other concepts and phenomena (see below).

of acceptance of institutions; furthermore, the distinction between legitimation of democracy *tout court* and that of a specific democratic regime is also needed; besides, it would be useful to determine the instances and time span of that acceptance vis-à-vis the analysed phases, including transition and installation; finally, it is necessary to take the analysis to greater depth, to go beyond legitimation and seek the explanations for those attitudes and behaviours. Most of these aspects will be considered in the course of the empirical analysis.[45]

Although the definition of legitimacy given above is acceptable and useful, it is worth considering a more attenuated version of the acceptance of the institutions that is often much closer to concrete reality at a mass level. To avoid any confusion, I call *consensus* all those attitudes of plain, often passive, acquiescence and acceptance of institutions by society, which merely registers the absence of any viable alternative.[46] It is not a matter of choosing, but of accepting what is there, even if it is perceived negatively. As Przeworski (1986: 51–2) suggests, what really matters is not the legitimacy 'of this particular system of domination but the presence or absence of preferable alternatives'. In other words, the consensus is grounded on the diffuse perception, at a mass level, that 'there is no other game in town'.[47]

Such attitudes and beliefs may remain unchanged, without being transformed into political actions. In other words, there is a problem of a difference and potential incongruity between attitudes and behaviour. If there is legitimacy and if it is translated into coherent behav-

[45] As suggested by Linz (1988), the analysis of legitimacy also concerns the socio-economic system, and not only the political institutions. This is a limitation of the analysis developed in this research, although this problem indirectly will be overcome by the inclusion of the perceived efficacy (see below).

[46] This notion largely overlaps the 'assent', suggested by Wright (1976: esp. 275–9): the 'assenters' 'are not active supporters of the democratic regime; rather they "go along", probably because no other sort of behavior ever occurs to them' (ibid. 276). There are two reasons for preferring the term 'consensus', rather than 'assent': (i) from a theoretical point of view, there is no true conceptual reason for a new word that may only add confusion to an already complex semantic field (see Sartori 1975);(ii) in a phase of consolidation or crisis, that is, of change, rather than of persistence and continuity, explored by Wright, people are more involved by those changes and the indifference exists, is widespread, but is empirically less relevant: greater attention should be paid to those who are in an ambiguous position that eventually gives them an attitude of passive acceptance of the regime. At the end they make the difference in terms of consolidation and a way out of the crisis.

[47] Here, a distinction between legitimacy and consensus is preferred, that is, between two kinds of positive attitudes toward political institutions where a difference of degree is also a qualitative difference. But see also the multi-dimensional solution in Morlino and Montero (1995). I think that the theoretical solution adopted here is better suited to both the qualitative and quantitative data considered in this book. The other solution, a multidimensional notion of legitimacy, is acceptable when quantitative data are analysed, as in the quoted essay. But see also McDonough, Barnes, and López Pina (1986).

iour, then there will be *support*, or actions that will lend support to the existing institutions. If there is consensus and the corresponding behaviour, this will entail *compliance* and *obedience*, though usually of a passive kind. In more concrete terms, there may be reluctance to criticize the institutions, together with their passive acceptance; there may also be habituation, routinization, and disillusionment with democracy as being able to solve real problems, such as unemployment, care for the elderly, health care, that is, what can be called 'democratic fatigue'.[48] In this case, there will be incongruity between the attitudes of the élites and the masses, as revealed in interviews and opinion polls, as well as in their behaviour. What prevents the translation of attitudes into behaviour is an important element with many facets and it deserves empirical analysis.[49]

The most obvious way to see whether there is consensus or democratic acceptance is through survey analysis. The absence of negative behaviours, such as episodes of violence and unrest, is also useful, but a consistent trend is hard to find, in terms of decline and growth with consolidation and crisis (see Chapter 3). Legitimacy and support are more difficult to discern at the mass level, by opinion polls[50] (in the first case) and certain forms of demonstrations (in the second), though the latter are rare. Indeed, the most decisive empirical aspect is the intertwining of the two phenomena: from the point of view of consolidation it is more important to note consensus and the absence of negative reactions at the mass level, and to observe legitimacy (or legitimation) and support at the level of élites; whereas in the case of a crisis, it is the opposite. In sum, for both consolidation or crisis the beliefs and actions of the élites are necessary, as well as decisive elements in a direction which is in favour or against the institutions, together with obedience or protest from the masses.

Expression of legitimacy and support is mainly in the hands of party leaders, who reveal this in public declarations and, less visibly, in their behaviour in parliament and in various other fora. However, they can also express illegitimacy, which is sometimes strengthened by mass protest. In this sense, an anti-regime group or party, created during installation and then firmly established during the following period, becomes an important actor in the analysis of legitimation. Such an actor may not change its negative attitudes and behaviours toward the regime for decades, or it may change them very slowly and gradually during the following decades, as long as a regime crisis does not

[48] On this see the analysis by Sartori (1993).
[49] For this point, see the pages of Chapter 7 on the Italian crisis.
[50] From these, however, it will be difficult to appreciate the trend because there are too few panels available. But on this, see the following chapters.

emerge. Although these considerations will be further developed later in this book (see esp. Chapter 3), let me recall here the very slow changes in the extreme left- or right-wing parties that took place in Italy and Portugal many years after installation.[51]

Legitimation and support are also in the hands of non-elective institutional actors, namely, the bureaucracy and the military. In fact, if the bureaucracy does not collaborate, consolidation will be more difficult, but it will be almost impossible as long as the military does not fully accept democratic rules and norms. On the contrary, signs of crisis, or even a full-blown crisis, are introduced with the so-called 'politicization of neutral powers',[52] with the entry into the political arena of the military or of the judiciary. This point is so important that some authors embodied it in the very definition of democratic regime (see above), and Chapter 2 will come back to it by analysing the role played by these actors.

There is another problem: considering the ambiguities and difficulties involved in gathering the empirical data mentioned above, is it possible to distinguish a process of legitimation for democracy, *lato sensu*, and one for a specific democratic regime? This must be done in order to analyse the passage from one democratic regime to another democratic regime, and it can be done through the detection of expressions of support or protest, at an élite and mass level. This is also possible in the case of attitudes, which can be evaluated by using surveys. In fact, embedded in the political culture of Southern Europeans there is a profound, first-hand knowledge of a different regime, even though this occurred at different times and with different duration and intensities. Above all, if a crisis exists or has existed, there then follows a very long political, public debate which may last for years, as in the Italian case. Thus, when a survey is conducted the respondents will usually have no difficulty in making those distinctions. On the other hand, when respondents in well-established democracies, who lack a non-democratic past and public discourse on the difference among democracies, are polled, their lack of any similar experience and notion means that questions about political alternatives to democracy are highly abstract and unrealistic. Finally, attitudes of consensus and obedience, or even compliance, cannot be empirically isolated, as they often spill over into and are indistinguishable from alienation and cynicism.[53]

The aim or object of legitimation and consensus, or of their opposite, is democracy *lato sensu*, or a specific democratic regime. In reality, atti-

---

[51] The electoral mechanisms, the logic of party competition, as well as some cultural attitudes entrenched in civil society contribute to this 'firming up' process.

[52] On this point see Linz (1978) and further developments in Morlino (1981).

[53] But on this, see also the empirical analysis in the following chapters.

tudes and behaviours of acquiescence, acceptance, or refusal also apply to the national community or, rather, to the country's recognition as a unit with that population and that territory. To question national unity, especially if its foundations are weak, because there is a diversity of language, race, or religion, is an element that is typical of radicalized party conflict during a crisis. In any case, this is yet another aspect in which parties can play an essential role either during consolidation (Spain) or in a crisis (Italy).

The third issue is timing and tempo, that is, the moment when legitimation appears and starts to grow. At a mass level, positive popular attitudes have begun to develop in the aftermath of the installation of new democratic regimes. In earlier stages of democratization, favourable attitudes of this kind, or behaviours associated with them, are not expected to be well rooted in civil society. While vaguely pro-democratic orientations may be widespread, support for a particular democratic regime and its key institutions will not have had a chance to develop. These attitudes are formed and strengthened during the consolidation period.

Obviously, the period of time required for the establishment of such system-supportive attitudes is expected to vary from one case to another. In some cases, positive attitudes develop quickly, while in others the process of legitimation is a longer one: it may take years, it may be interrupted by crises, and its content may be profoundly transformed by political changes carried out under the same regime. Most authors suggest that Italy falls into this latter category. What exists at the beginning of democratic transition and installation is some degree of refusal, reaction, and criticism of the preceding institutional structures: it is on this basis that positive attitudes can be built during consolidation. What takes place during the crisis is a range of attitudes rejecting the present institutions and, sometimes, the traditional actors.

The situation is different, however, at an élite level: on the one hand, in the case of the military, the bureaucracy, and, occasionally, the judiciary, the process of legitimation or delegitimation may be slow and gradual; on the other hand, for ruling party élites, acceptance and support are immediate reactions to the setting of the regime, and may endure for years, just as the opposition élites will express a more or less radical rejection at once, an attitude that will change only slowly. Evidently, between the two levels—élites and mass—there is a basic tendency toward mutual consistency; what changes is the time of the reactions, which is usually slower among the people.

The fourth issue is how to explain the formation and persistence or transformation of those attitudes and behaviours that are favourable or unfavourable to the newly introduced or already existing institutions. To a large extent, this is a classic question for this kind of research. The answers can be found by referring to preceding historical experiences, well rooted in the political culture of that country, as well as to the concrete working of the regime itself. As for the memory of an authoritarian past, which often, and above all with the passage of time, becomes less negative than might have been expected, it may be this very element that leads to a situation of 'no other game in town' and at a mass level is expressed in consensus and acceptance of the institutions.[54]

The concrete functioning of a democracy signifies, at the mass level, the 'perceived' efficacy of that regime. It is reasonable to assume that the satisfaction of basic demands through specific governmental actions can induce people to form, maintain, or strengthen their positive attitudes toward the democratic regime. Of course, popular perceptions of the capability of a regime for solving relevant problems are particularly sharp in new democracies, where the system-supportive attitudes described above may not have been deeply rooted in society. Thus, the perceived efficacy of a regime is among that set of attitudes which are fundamentally related to democratic legitimacy and recognition of its political institutions as the most appropriate form of government.[55]

If considered in behavioural terms, however, efficacy may or may not influence legitimacy. This issue was first raised by Lipset (1959) and Linz (1978, 1989). From a different perspective, some scholars have also raised doubts about the empirical possibility of distinguishing between legitimacy and effectiveness or efficacy (Muller and Jukam 1977). The high correlations that often result suggest an undetermined causal structure linking the two concepts (Loewenberg 1971). In this vein, opinions about the legitimacy of a regime are linked to judgements on the merits of incumbent authorities, perceptions of governmental efficacy, and/or the gap between respondents' ideals and political reality (see Weil 1989).

For several reasons, it is possible to distinguish analytically between legitimacy and efficacy as Greeks, Portuguese, Spaniards, and Italians have clear frames of reference when asked about political alternatives to democracy, the desirability of democracy in the abstract, and regime efficacy. Because of their personal experiences or collective memories, Southern Europeans are culturally and attitudinally equipped to sepa-

[54] This point is so important as to deserve to be analysed by itself (see below).

[55] Dahl (1971) emphasizes the salience of perceived efficacy. The efficacy here mentioned is that of the democratic regime, not the perception of 'personal efficacy'. See also the next chapter.

rate the legitimacy of a regime from perceptions of its efficacy, although the ability to make these distinctions will gradually decline as the passage of time makes the authoritarian experience more and more irrelevant to the collective memory of the country. In the 1980s, however, that memory was still vivid and alive, although to a lesser degree in Italy than in the other three cases and in earlier decades.

At the end of this brief excursus into the main theoretical problems posed by an analysis of legitimation, consensus, or their opposites, the question to ask is: how should legitimacy (and consensus) be measured? This question, too, has been addressed by scholars in many different, and sometimes contentious, ways.[56] Moreover, for some—because it is a value-loaded concept—its very nature precludes analysis using conventional indicators; for others, it is virtually impossible to detect empirically (see Schaar 1981; O'Kane 1993). The literature on this (and related) concepts is characterized by a remarkable gap between the relatively high level of theoretical and conceptual development and the weakness of the many empirical indicators that have been used to date (see also Weatherford 1992). In the following chapters a solution will be suggested using both quantitative and qualitative data in order to test the extent of inclusiveness in the achieved legitimacy and mass consensus: from a more *exclusive legitimation*, which is unable to incorporate consistently sectors of élites—sometimes very important in terms of economic influence, or simply numerical resources—to an *inclusive legitimation* where all political organizations are encompassed in the acceptance and support of democratic institutions; and from a narrow consensus where at least a political alternative is present in the minds and values of people to a large consensus where acquiescence is widespread and any regime alternative has disappeared (see Chapter 3).

Autonomy and Control

I have just indicated that after installation, attitudes and behaviours favourable to the regime have not yet come into existence, even though the process of consolidation has begun. Also, when a crisis has started, thanks to the manifestation of widespread negative attitudes of delegitimation, the effects on the institutions may still be extremely limited. Thus, in more explicit terms, are legitimacy and consensus, and their opposites, the only aspects central to the processes under review? Otherwise, would it be possible to imagine some degree of

[56] See e.g. Weil (1989), Weatherford (1991), and more recently Rose and Mishler (1996).

consolidation—though not mere maintenance (see above)—with an extremely limited legitimacy? And can one conceive of the absence of a serious democratic crisis in spite of a definite process of delegitimation? Or even a decline of efficacy without any impact on legitimacy?

Such questions lead into less familiar territory. On this the suggestion is to explore a second, top-down direction taken by the analysis of consolidation and crisis. It basically concerns the emergence, shaping, change, or dissolution of 'anchors' that hook or even control civil society in general, as well as various specific sectors of it. This metaphor gives a better idea of the asymmetrical relationships that are involved when the top-down direction is considered.[57] Moreover, 'anchoring' implies the possibility of limited change and adaptation as the boat moves on the water without exceeding certain limits. Thus, parties, and party élites especially, are no longer seen as the expression of civil society and the representatives of the various interests in the decision-making arena and of their accommodation; instead they acquire their own vested interests in self-maintenance and self-enhancement, possibly becoming institutionalized, and try to develop different forms of penetration, regulation, or even control of society, but some adaptation, flexibility, and limited change is always maintained.[58]

How, and in what way, does this come about? The most obvious answer is to consider the classic division of the twin circuits of electoral and functional representation. In concrete terms, the former implies an analysis of parties (and party élites) in competition among themselves. Electoral competition begins and is defined—in more or less stable and visible forms—by specific modalities and characteristics, during the electoral campaign and elections, between one election and the next, and in parliament.[59] My main hypothesis, which is grounded on the classic analyses of party organization and elections,[60] suggests that, above all in highly ideologized contexts, competition forces parties to develop more efficient and functional organizations, to run effective electoral propaganda, to be present and active even in the inter-electoral period, and to create and project a well-defined image for the electors, also through their parliamentary activity. After some elec-

---

[57] This is one of the reasons this metaphor has to be preferred to the more classic notion of 'linkage' (see Lawson 1980, 1988; see also Luttbeg 1974). In the latter, there is a symmetrical relationship where an accordance with demands of people to élite decisions is envisaged. And this is not the case.

[58] This could be labelled the 'partyness of society' (see Katz 1986: 31–71). With reference to party government approach, here a partially different path is followed (see below).

[59] The notion of party competition is in Strom (1989, 1990, 1992).

[60] Among other authors, Huntington (1968: 461) should be recalled: 'organization is the road to political power, but it is also the foundation of political stability'; and a little further on, 'he controls the future who organizes its politics.'

tions, among the non-intentional side-effects of competition, parties may acquire some measure of direction over civil society, through the stabilization of party 'supply' and of its leadership (also at a parliamentary level), and through the organization of the parties themselves and the formation of collective identities (see also Mair 1991). One must not forget that these are also, to a large extent, due to the application in successive elections of the same norms, which are drafted in any democracy to regulate party competition. These include the public financing of parties, the setting of limits and constraints on electoral propaganda, the existence of higher or lower thresholds for access to electoral competition and allocation of seats, and the electoral formula adopted. To this end the analysis of other rules and institutions must be added: those rules and institutions that allow parties and party élites to perform better, such as the constitutional rules that set up the connection between government and parliament or the standing orders that regulate the internal working of parliament, and so on.[61]

In any democracy the very dynamics of party institutions tends to strengthen those institutions and, to some extent, edge them towards implicit forms of direction over civil society. It is important to consider these aspects because it helps one to understand how left-wing parties, born with subversive and anti-regime objectives, ended by channelling, freezing, and integrating a potential for protest that would, otherwise, break into threatening manifestations for the democratic institutions. In short, one begins to understand the paradox of 'negative integration'[62] on the left, which is an essential element in the consolidation of the regimes examined.

Because of its very characteristics, especially its sensitivity to political, social, and even technological changes,[63] party competition may change the role and salience of party organization, or of other, more or less effective, forms of direction of civil society; but it can also initiate a phase of real destructuration—as well as a profound renewal of the political class—which will 'liberate' civil society and trigger a phase of crisis and change. The limits and characteristics of competition, in a more or less radical form, and of destructuration, will determine the results of the crisis.[64]

Factors of anchoring also come from the functional circuit, which requires examination of relations with civil society, various economic

[61] See also the following chapters.

[62] This is the well-known term used by Roth (1963) in referring to the Social Democrats during Wilhelmine Germany.

[63] The obvious reference is to the role of the media, which was profoundly changed when television became widespread.

[64] On the specific indicators and measures required for a more detailed analysis of these phenomena, see especially Chs. 2 and 7.

and non-economic élites, business associations and trade unions, as well as other agricultural, industrial, and service associations, and people at large. In the functional circuit, one can hypothesize that the parties' capacity for direction or even control depends on a few aspects at a state level, as well as on the rules of the regime, the type of party system, the parties, and a few aspects of society. For want of a better word, and considered as a whole, this is called the *autonomy* of civil society in its manifold aspects—economic (mainly business), intellectual and media élites, as well as interest associations and other kinds of associations—toward the state institutions or the party élites and parties or, from the opposite point of view, the *control* of party élites through political institutions over civil society.[65] Two more precise features of this dimension may be taken into account. They concern the links of party élites and parties with: (i) organized associations, such as business élites, unions, and also religious associations and other structured interest groups in the policy-making; and (ii) non-organized, but active élites, such as large or small, but widespread, private business, intellectuals, or even only individuals in a *clientelistic relationship*; and, if there is, also (iii) organized interest and government at the same time in *corporatist arrangement*.[66]

On patronage and corporatism there is a large literature, and nothing has to be added here (see Chapter 4). However, another important way of looking at relationships and links between parties and economic élites, unions, and other economic associations is to examine whether parties and the party system as a whole are able to perform a '*gatekeeping*' role towards the groups, that is, the role performed by the incumbent and opposition parties (or by the party system) in controlling the access of interest groups and élites to the decision-making arena, in settling the priorities among different demands and possibly in trying to solve problems that may affect the everyday life of citizens.[67] Consequently, for interest associations and other élites, party intermediation may become the best way to protect their interests.

[65] The problem of autonomy and control is developed with its normative implications for democratic regimes by Dahl (1982). Whereas the definitions of those notions parallel those suggested by this author (see ibid. 16 ff.), here the purpose is only an empirical one.

[66] It is well known that the realm of organized and unorganized interest groups as well as of movements may be complex, rich, and multifaceted. Here, however, it is far from necessary to take into account the whole set of interest networks and relationships. It is only relevant to consider the organized and unorganized interests that are more relevant for consolidation and crisis as well as for the basic characteristics in the actual working of a specific democracy. For a terminological analysis of interest groups (and movements) see Jordan (1994). Specifically, on democratic consolidation and the representation of social groups see also Schmitter (1992).

[67] See also Morlino (1991a) for a more detailed analysis of this notion and its empirical application to Italy.

Besides, the notion of gatekeeping concerns only the party system, not the judiciary, the bureaucracy, or the army; and, more importantly, gatekeeping is not the only role parties may perform vis-à-vis interest groups.

It is possible to sketch at least four scenarios for such a relationship between parties and groups, with or without a direct role for the public sector. The first, *dominance*, or, in a stronger form, *occupation*, envisages the situation where the party system to a large extent dominates civil society in general, and interest groups in particular. The groups, although bearers of their own clearly identifiable and fixed interests, are mainly ancillary organizations for the parties, which have very solid autonomous sources of power in terms of ideology, internal organization, and large membership. This is the case for unions[68] and other associations, but it is also true where very weak business élites are subordinate to parties. There may also be 'the presence of mechanisms of recruitment and nomination and of organizational activity and decision-making within the group in which exponents of the party have absolute supremacy, and where the interests of the group are subordinate to those of the party' (Morlino 1991*a*: 21). Moreover, there is a large or very large public sector of economy, and all positions in that sector are filled by party appointments.[69]

The *symbiosis*, that is, the third scenario, defines 'that situation in which party and group mutually strengthen each other in their respective spheres of activity. In this sense they are in a position of exactly equal standing in which the one needs and depends on the other. In the Western European experience, one finds a symbiotic relationship between the Catholic parties and the Catholic mass organizations. More clearly, the relationship between Socialist and Social Democratic parties and labor trade unions is characterized by symbiosis' (Morlino 1991*a*: 22). Symbiosis is also characterized by ideological identity; recruitment in the same cultural environments; mutual exchange of

[68] In the specific relationships between parties and unions, the *conditioned domination* or 'recognized protection', if the perspective of the trade union is stressed, may be envisaged, that is, 'a situation in which the trade union manages to have its own sphere of autonomy, albeit limited, but is obliged to rely upon the party for its own maintenance, its organizational structuring, and also in order to make its interests heard. Consequently, there is neither a perfectly symmetrical relationship nor an absolute party pre-eminence, but rather . . . a conditioned domination of the party or rather recognized protection on the part of the trade union' (Morlino 1991*a*: 22). Still, in the relationships between parties and trade unions, especially Social Democratic parties and worker trade unions, another possibility is *symbiosis*, a situation in which 'party and group mutually strengthen each other in their respective spheres of activity . . . they are in a position of exactly equal standing in which the one needs and depends on the other' (Morlino 1991*a*: 22). In the Western European experience, there is also a symbiotic relationship between the Catholic parties and the Catholic organizations.

[69] Daalder (1966: 75) regards this as the most important aspect of these relationships.

personnel from union élites to party leaders and vice versa; mutual help in the various activities and form of participation, such as militants and middle level unionists who commit themselves to electoral campaigns; and also participation of party activists and militants in union mobilizations (demonstrations, strikes, and so on).

The fourth scenario, *neutrality*, foresees no definite dependency between groups and parties. Interest groups are more or less organized and politically active, with their own economic and social bases and resources. Similarly, parties have their autonomous power bases and also maintain control of the decision-making process, which mainly resides in the opportunities that the rules of the democratic regime give to party élites and in the characteristics of the party system. Basically, parties are able to perform a gatekeeping role: groups and people are compelled to appeal to parties and party leaders to promote and protect their interests. The essentiality of the parties (and party élites) is emphasized by their ability to perform their institutional role as problem-solver by choosing or accommodating different conflicting interests, in coping with the main issues and problems existing at the moment, and also in having their decisions accepted by most of the people who are affected by them. Groups are in a more independent position vis-à-vis parties. They are not ancillary organizations and they enjoy a measure of autonomy in civil society.

In the case of neutrality, no especially strong relationship is established or exists between a group and a particular party. 'Groups find it more convenient not to establish privileged relations with any party. To increase the probability of success of their actions they apply pressure on the various parties with respect to the various situations and instances, thus forming a multi-party appeal. They do not have the undoubted advantages of a privileged relationship with the party in government, but neither do they suffer the disadvantage of being linked to the same party in opposition. . . . At the empirical level, neutrality means total autonomy for the groups and allows them to establish relationships with one party or more parties for a limited duration and defined in terms of the issue. Above all, they are able to establish relationships in the decision-making arenas when particular issues relevant to the group are under discussion' (Morlino 1991*a*: 23–4). In particular, business groups are in a more independent position vis-à-vis parties and, in spite of their possible links with parties, unions also have their own domains and autonomy. However, because of several empirical cases of this sort there may be different, stronger, or milder forms of neutrality in connection with the factors that will be indicated below.

In the fifth possibility, *direct access*, parties (and party élites) are bypassed in the actual performance of the representation process.

Interest groups and business élites outbid parties because of personal relationships with parliamentary members, ministries, and the bureaucracy, or in other ways. Parties have very weak autonomous bases and sources of power and they are unable to achieve stronger ones. No kind of gatekeeping role is performed. The concrete possibility 'for direct and unchecked access is such that when it is necessary the group manages to put itself in immediate and direct contact with the central or local ministerial bureaucracy, in order to be present in the decision-making arenas of government and parliament . . . with its own reliable personnel. In a situation of this sort the party is . . . secondary and unnecessary in the carrying out of the functions of representation and . . . for the protection of the group's own interests' (Morlino 1991*a*: 25). In such a hypothesis there is substantial political irrelevance of the parties, which are also non-ideological, weak organizations with a highly volatile electorate, so that a group manages gradually to penetrate the decision-making arenas which are relevant for it and to penetrate the bureaucracy itself. 'In this perspective the most important outcome that a group can obtain is to succeed in getting the delegation-direction of policies relative to its own sector of activity from the government or parliament by means of apposite laws, a guaranteed presence in ministerial commissions or in various other ways' (ibid. 25).[70]

There are obvious connections between the aspects sketched here and the existence of a more or less articulated civil society[71] with

[70] There is also the hypothesis of *indirect access*, which 'represents a group that completely conditions the party at the level of appointments and recruitment within the party itself and at the electoral level, as regards its own activity in the decision-making arenas, or in the various other forms. In short, the party is the expression of the group and nothing else' (Morlino 1991*a*: 24).

[71] Here, by 'civil society' is meant the totality of citizens seen in a pre-political moment, with their individual preferences, interests, and choices as well as their voluntary associations, groups, and activities disciplined by legal rules. Such a definition makes the concept empirically useful, as it points to a public sphere, where there may be few or several organizations as well as implemented legal norms. However, the problem of autonomy vs. control must always be seen within this legal framework that makes the society 'civil' and at the same time qualifies the autonomy mentioned above. A more circumstantial definition, which also distinguishes civil from political society, can be found in Farneti (1971). An excellent short analysis of the notion of 'civil society' from liberalism to Marxism is in Etzioni-Halevy (1993: 80–1). But the literature is very large. See, for example, Pérez Díaz (1987: 18 ff.; and 1993: 76 ff.), Bernhard (1993), Diamond (1994) and the special issue of the *Journal of Democracy* (3; 1994), Peeler (1995), Rubinstein (1995), Shils (1991), Schmitter (1993), Thomas (1994), and also the theoretical and empirical analyses in Keane (1988) and Fine and Rai (1997). On the possibility that the focus on civil society blurs and relegates to the back of the stage the crucial role of élites and their autonomy, see Etzioni-Halevy (1993). However, when necessary, this empirical problem will be overcome with specific reference to the different kinds of élites. Of course, here no side is taken on the different contending ideological positions on this topic.

different kinds of autonomous, non-political élites as well as networks of associations, including interest groups: they are two sides of the same coin. Besides, it is not particularly difficult to check empirically the existence of civil society: an active and participating public, different kinds of élites, together with independent press and TV networks, a rich tapestry of associations, more or less highly organized, in other words, a high level of associability. If so, the relationship with party élites will be one of neutrality or of direct access. On the contrary, if civil society is poorly organized and without autonomous resources, then the dominant scenario is probable.

Furthermore, if salient features concern the factors that may account for party control over society or its autonomy, and the crucial aspect related to economic and social pluralism is taken for granted, other political and social factors should be taken into account to explain such control and its milder different forms. They include:

1. At the state level, the size of the public sector or of state intervention in economic affairs, and the restriction of the market; with the consequent possibility that all positions in that sector may be filled by party appointments and that party élites may—and, actually, do—develop special relationships through the allocation of economic resources;[72]
2. At the regime level, the rules that contribute to the role of parties vis-à-vis groups and élites, such as the centralization of the decision-making process and governmental control of that process;
3. At the party system level, a specific system such as the predominant one;
4. At the party level, a few internal characteristics that help strengthen the role of parties, such as strong internal party cohesion, perhaps with a developed organization or a strong leader;
5. At the socio-cultural level, the diffusion of strong ideologies that give parties a prominent position in public debate.

On the other hand, a limited public sector, a decentralized process of decision-making (where, for example, there is room for interest representation at the parliamentary level), a heterogeneous multiparty system, high internal party fragmentation and poor organizational structures, and strong de-ideologization, may give room for an autonomous civil society, if it exists.

This reference to links between parties and interests, their related features and their principal explanations is clearly due to a research

[72] It is also well known that a democratic model with neutral institutions, such as an independent judiciary, is another way of protecting civil society and making it more autonomous.

choice. In my view it is justified at a theoretical level, as I did above, but also at an empirical level, as should come out of the specific cases.[73] However, it may not be able to capture all the tangled relations among political élites, regime institutions, and civil society that exist in all modern societies. This seems particularly true when the maintenance or crisis of established relationships is explored. The way out, which is more clearly suggested in the next section,[74] is to integrate this analysis by scrutinizing the manifest inefficacy.

By putting all factors together, two opposite patterns result: control in the case of party dominance, a large public sector, limited space for private interests and a dependent, poorly articulated civil society; and autonomy in the case of party neutrality or direct access, a vital and complex civil society, and almost no public economic sector. Of course, the most empirically relevant and interesting cases are in between the two extremes. Such intermediate possibilities envision a situation of semi-control, where the political élites prevail and influence civil society that is partly dependent on them, also because of the existence of a fairly important state-owned economic sector, or semi-autonomy, where neutrality or direct access is complemented by a relatively autonomous society, again in spite of a sizeable public economic sector.[75]

Manifest Inefficacy and Negative Reactions

Party organization, clientelism, forms of corporatism, and different modalities of gatekeeping are the main anchors that can overlap and in

---

[73] In addition to the empirical solutions sketched here, see its implementation in Chapter 4. The research problem raised in the text could also have been formulated in terms of stabilization and change of party systems. On this problem there is an extensive, large literature, that would have suggested an exploration of the impact of political institutions (electoral laws or other aspects), the persistence and transformation of the electorate (especially the actual working of the process of political socialization), the persistence or change of social cleavages, values, and issues and of the related party organization (on these factors see e.g. Ware 1996: 217 ff.). Of course, to follow all directions of research would have been impossible. Despite the obvious limitations, the choice made here seems an almost compulsory way to reach more parsimonious theoretical hypotheses on consolidation and crisis; but they need the empirical support. See again Chapter 4.

[74] Because of its salience a short section must be devoted to this point. See below.

[75] Recall Etzioni-Halevy (1993), who underscores the role of autonomous élites with regard to political power both in the first examples of democratic installations and in the consolidation of democracy. A hypothesis to be shared if—as Etzioni-Halevy does (see ibid. 103–6)—the intimate relationships between certain élites and democracy, which is made possible by their existence, is stressed. This author also includes in her analysis the autonomy of judiciary and bureaucracy.

this way characterize and strengthen the process of consolidation.
When focusing on the crisis of a specific democracy and its maintenance, rather than on consolidation, some aspects cursorily mentioned
above have to be stressed. These largely concern the reactions and
behaviours of civil society. No doubt these aspects are also related to
the two basic dimensions of legitimation and autonomy vs. control that
are mirrored by the tranformations or dissolutions of these anchors.
But they also point out the impact of existing social, economic, or political problems as well as the impact of the decisions made by the government on the population. In this vein, they may play an autonomous
role in the crisis of a specific democracy or part of it. Eventually legitimacy and consensus are mainly related to élite integration and absence
of viable political alternatives, and autonomy and control to the relations between parties and interests, but immediate perceptions and
reactions of civil society are also important to get the meaning of a specific, partial crisis.

Briefly, I shall define these additional factors as *manifest inefficacy*
and the related *dissatisfaction*. The main reason for choosing the negative dimension of the two phenomena is that only these features are
relevant for impeding consolidation or bringing about a democratic crisis. If these phenomena and the related aspects are not present, there
is no evident, appreciable crisis to analyse. With regard to consolidation, legitimation and the extent of autonomy should emerge as the key
aspects: the absence of manifest inefficacy and negative reactions are
much more relevant than the opposite, efficacy and positive reaction,
also because negative behaviour and attitudes are more commonly
seen and easier to detect.

Manifest inefficacy is the apparent, clearly perceived incapacity for
solving or coping with salient issues by institutions and governmental
élites. *Dissatisfaction* is the expressed or assumed negative reactions of
citizens to problems, decisions, or non-decisions to salient issues. The
following considerations should be borne in mind:

1. The open, manifest perception of incapacity is indirectly displayed by the presence and discussion of the issues in the press
   over a wide span of time.
2. Despite the perceptions and analyses, a problem may remain
   unsolved, and even possible decisions do not succeed in solving
   the problem. In other words, an objective inefficacy is included in
   the definition.
3. The salience of the issue or problem is suggested by the number
   of people involved, and by the critical nature of the problem for
   the existing democracy and society. This should be empirically
   examined.

4. The responsibility for the inefficacy is imputed to the state and politicians at different levels. This is the effect of a widespread belief in Southern Europe that the 'state should solve all kinds of problems'.
5. In the event of no public reaction the malaise is also registered because of its possible consequences in terms of changing electoral behaviour or the unfolding of a threshold effect, that is, such a malaise remains covert for years and then abruptly bursts out through different kinds of negative reactions.
6. Several kinds of negative reactions, from mild protest to terrorism, have to be considered.
7. Of course, there are negative reactions (unexpressed malaise) because either no decision is made and the problem remains, or, conversely, an unsatisfactory decision was made.

As a consequence of the definitions, there are at least two principal forms of dissatisfaction: (*a*) expressed, behavioural negative reactions or dissatisfaction with a perceived, manifest inefficacy (expressed dissatisfaction); (*b*) passivity, obedience, and simultaneously unexpressed dissatisfaction, malaise, fatigue, and alienation because of perceived, manifest inefficacy (covert, unexpressed dissatisfaction). Although they are not exhaustive in terms of the possible dimensions of dissatisfaction, both of these consequences are important and should be detected. The reasons for dissatisfaction (and, first of all, inefficacy) are economic, political-ideological, or more generic. These reasons must also be analysed. In order to detect empirically the aspects related to this domain, two directions of analysis may be pursued. The first reflects attitudes and indicates the dissatisfaction with the functioning of the four democracies, on the basis of survey data, during the period scrutinized here. The second is the extent of behavioural, manifest inefficacy and the negative reactions to the democratic institutions. An important point for the deepening of the analysis is also to check the consistency or inconsistency between attitudes and behaviours, and its possible explanation. The empirical analysis of the two aspects, however, will be developed in the third part of the book.

Which Types of Democracy?

There is still a theoretical issue to address before concluding this chapter. The outcomes of the processes illustrated in the previous sections are persistence, maintenance, or others (see Figure 1.1). But the results of those processes may also be seen in a different, substantial perspective: what kind of democracy has been consolidated or transformed and even disrupted by crises, in each of the four Southern European countries? Not to lose part of the actual contents of politics it is essential to see which democratic regimes eventually managed to consolidate after installation, and which entered a crisis, if any, later on. The theoretical guidelines for such an answer, with an indication of the crucial variables and respective models of democracy, may be immediately suggested, whereas it is neither possible nor necessary, here, to undertake a systematic analysis of the various types of democracy.[76] It will suffice to take a look at those forms that are most relevant to the cases examined.

As to the institutional aspects, over the last decade there have been various important scholarly contributions (Powell 1982; Lijphart 1984, 1992; Linz and Valenzuela 1994; Sartori 1994; and others). One lesson to be derived from these writings is that electoral law[77] and rules for government form a 'system' with many facets and they coexist and interact with the institutional arrangements concerning executive and legislative powers. Thus, with some simplification and choice, the two macro-variables stemming from this literature may be classified and combined as follows:

a1. Presidential institutions and majoritarian electoral system;
a2. Semi-presidentialism and majoritarian electoral system;
a3. Semi-presidentialism and proportional electoral system (PR);
a4. Semi-parliamentarism and reinforced proportional or majoritarian system;[78]
a5. Parliamentarism and PR;
a6. Presidentialism and PR.

In semi-presidentialism, a concept developed by Duverger (1980), the head of state is elected by the general population and the prime minister must maintain the confidence of the parliament. This diarchical arrangement has the consequence that the power of the president is weakened or nullified by an opposing, powerful, and cohesive majority in parliament.[79] Semi-parliamentarism is a chancellor democracy where the prime minister and his or her cabinet play a much stronger role vis-à-vis parliament. The best-known example of the first case is the Fifth French Republic, whereas the United Kingdom is a commonly

[76] The principal work is still that of Lijphart (1984), with his later additions (esp. 1994).

[77] On this topic see Duverger (1950); Rae (1971); Bogdanor and Butler (1983); Grofman and Lijphart (1986); Taagepera and Shugart (1989); and Sartori (1994).

[78] On the notion of semi-parliamentarism, see Sartori (1994, ch. 6). By reinforced or corrected proportional representation is meant an electoral system with multi-member districts, high electoral thresholds, and, on the whole, a low extent of proportionality (on this see Gunther 1989).

[79] This feature is important for Portugal. See below.

cited example of the second case. The specific institutional arrangement where presidentialism and PR for the election of parliament are
in place together—the most recurring institutional solution adopted in
Latin America (see Jones 1995)—is also worth pointing out.

There is a third, particularly relevant, characteristic which can help
to give a better definition of the institutional model, *stricto sensu*. This
is the extent of decentralization in the allocation of power among the
central government and the peripheral authorities. The classic main
variables that should be taken into account are: the equal representation of the local units of whatever size at the central level through a
specific chamber; the autonomy of local units in several domains; and
the fiscal autonomy of local governments. Forms and modes of decentralization may be found in each of the four types sketched above.

The second set of features that defines a democracy is given by the
party system. Some authors clearly state the historical and logical connection between political parties and democracy (see, for example,
Pomper 1992) or even define democracy in terms of parties (see Sartori
1993: 41). As intermediate institutions—which are at the same time
vote-seeking, office-seeking, and policy-seeking[80]—parties (and the
party system) can be seen in a variety of moments and functions: for
instance, in their efforts to achieve (electoral) consensus and support at
a mass level; or when they fill governmental and parliamentary posts,
or accept office in local government; or when they formulate policies
that are supported by themselves as incumbent parties and resisted by
the parties in opposition; but also in their relationships with the
bureaucracy, the military, and the judiciary, still at an élite level.[81]

The number and relative size of parties, some of their specific organizational aspects,[82] and the composition and homogeneity or heterogeneity[83] of the party coalition supporting the cabinet, are the main
features that define the party system in a democracy. A simplified
typology may be suggested:

  b1. Cohesive predominant party system and one-party cabinet;
  b2. Dominant party with a strong leader, one-party cabinet;

[80] This is the efficacious partition proposed by Strom (1990), on the basis of the most
common objectives pursued by such institutions, according to the classic literature on the
topic.

[81] From a more societal perspective the parties may be seen in their classic function of
the 'transmitters of social demands' and as the 'delegates' or 'representatives' of civil society to govern the political system by satisfying those demands (Pizzorno 1980: 13 ff.).
Subsequently parties tend to acquire some autonomy and achievement of their own
interests (ibid. 14).

[82] Particularly, the extent of internal cohesion and the role of the leader(s) within
them.

[83] That is the policy distance among the parties which support the same cabinet on different issues.

b3. Bipartism and one-party cabinet;

b4. Homogeneous multipartism and coalition cabinet;

b5. Heterogeneous multipartism and coalition cabinet.[84]

It should be obvious that behind each case competition exists in different forms and to a different extent, influenced by the various institutional rules with respect to the threshold of access to the political arena, especially the electoral one, the difference between the main parties in terms of votes and seats, the size of electoral volatility in the party systems for different reasons, and some characteristics of electoral law or parliamentary decision-making process.[85]

There is, however, another set of factors that is relevant for a better understanding of what a democratic regime is. Despite the fact that these features are not usually considered when a typological analysis of democracy is proposed, their salience should be suggested. In fact, on the one hand, they express more substantial elements of democratic regimes with social and economic implications; on the other hand, they strongly connect the typological analysis with the very processes of change I analyse, as they emerge as the characterizing elements of consolidation and crisis (see above), and even of installation. They concern the dimension autonomy/control, which was described above and is so important in the processes of consolidation and crisis. By such dimensions I might also refer to certain aspects of party government, e.g. the 'partyness of government' or the 'party governmentness' (Rose 1969; and, more recently, Wildenmann 1986 and Ware 1992), even in such developments as gatekeeping, and more peculiar aspects of welfare.

The overall picture is shown in Table 1.1, where all the main variables are listed. In terms of democratic models, the combination of the three sets of variables might yield several different democracies. However, here it is more important to point out a few majoritarian models only. In fact, in the geopolitical area under discussion, these appear to be the most recurrent models. First, there is the *majoritarian democracy*, or, in the words of Lijphart (1984), the 'Westminster model,' which is the result of the combination of semi-parliamentarism and reinforced PR or a majoritarian system, bipartism and one-party cabinet and autonomy; but a majoritarian model might also be the result of the combination of presidential institutions and a majoritarian elec-

---

[84] Such a typology is largely inspired by the well-known work by Sartori (1976).

[85] The notion suggested by Strom may be adopted for both the dimensions he proposes: political contestability and situational competitiveness. Briefly, the first dimension is given by the threshold in the access that the parties have to the electoral arena; the second dimension by the salience of party strategies, the 'payoff variability', that is, the variation in payoffs to each player across his set of strategies, and the 'player indeterminacy', that is, the equivalence of payoff distributions across players (see Strom 1992: 35–40)

TABLE 1.1. *The most salient factors in democracy: a typological proposal*

A. Governmental institutions	B. Party system	C. Civil society/ politics
a1. Presidentialism & majoritarian electoral system	b1. Cohesive predominant party with a strong leader & one-party cabinet	c1. Autonomy
a2. Semi-presidentialism & majoritarian electoral system	b2. Bipartism & one-party cabinet	c2. Semi-autonomy
a3. Semi-presidentialism & PR	b3. Homogeneous multipartism & coalition cabinet	c3. Semi-control
a4. Semi-parliamentarism & reinforced PR/majoritarian system	b4. Heterogeneous multipartism & coalition cabinet	c4. Control
a5. Parliamentarism & PR		
a6. Presidentialism & PR		

toral system, bipartism and one-party cabinet, and autonomy. That is, a strong, autonomous civil society sets the limits and constraints of a majoritarian institutional arrangement that stresses the assets of decisional efficacy.

In addition, there are the models which might prove to be more relevant here: *plebiscitary democracy* and *strongly majoritarian democracy*. The former is the result of presidential institutions and a majoritarian electoral system or proportional representation for the Assembly, a very common solution in Latin America (see Diamond 1996 and Jones 1995); multipartism with high heterogeneity or a dominant but poorly organized party, and a strong leader; and a society that may be controlled or quasi-controlled in its main sectors. The latter model is the combination of presidential institutions and a majoritarian electoral system or semi-presidentialism/semi-parliamentarism and a majoritarian electoral system, a cohesive dominant party and one-party cabinet or homogeneous multipartism and a coalition cabinet, and the control of society, without any check or constraint imposed over the political institutions.

The fourth empirical model of a majoritarian democratic regime is the *weakly majoritarian democracy*. The main features of the model are: parliamentarism and PR system or presidentialism and PR; a cohesive dominant party and one-party cabinet or a dominant party,

TABLE 1.2. *Empirical models of democracy*

Majoritarian Democracy
a4. Semi-parliamentarism & reinforced PR/majoritarian system; or
   a1. Presidentialism & majoritarian electoral system;
b2. Bi-partism & one-party cabinet;
c1. Autonomy.

Plebiscitary Democracy
a1. Presidentialism & majoritarian electoral system; or
   a2. Semi-presidentialism & majoritarian electoral system; or
   a4. Semi-parliamentarism & reinforced PR/majoritarian system; or
   a6. presidentialism & PR;
b1. Predominant party, strong leader, one-party cabinet;
c4. Control; or
   c3. Semi-control.

Strongly Majoritarian Democracy
a1. Presidentialism & majoritarian electoral system; or
   a2. Semi-presidentialism & majoritarian electoral system; or
   a4. Semi-parliamentarism & reinforced PR/majoritarian system;
b1. Cohesive predominant party & one-party cabinet; or
   b3. Homogeneous multipartism & coalition cabinet;
c4. Control.

Weakly Majoritarian Democracy
a3. Semi-presidentialism & majoritarian electoral system; or
   a4. Semi-parliamentarism & PR; or
   a6. Presidentialism & PR;
b1. Cohesive predominant party & one-party cabinet;
c2. Semi-autonomy; or
   c3. Semi-control.

Proportional Democracy
a4. Parliamentarism & PR;
b3. Homogeneous multipartism & coaliton cabinet;
c1. Autonomy; or
   c2. Semi-autonomy.

Conflictual Democracy
a4. Parliamentarism and PR system; or
   a6. Presidentialism & PR;
b4. Heterogeneous multipartism & coalition cabinet;
c4. Control; or
   c3. Semi-control.

---

strong leader, and one-party cabinet; but there is the possibility for the relative, more or less strong, autonomy of civil society that puts limits on the institutions.

Among the non-majoritarian models, a continuum may be established between two polar situations: *proportional democracy* and *conflictual democracy*. The former is characterized by a basic consistency among the three levels: in a parliamentarian system, elected by PR, a fairly homogeneous multipartism is accommodated and a coalition cabinet is the most obvious result, while the autonomous groups in the society are largely present through unions and other associations. In conflictual democracy there is no such consistency: parliamentarism or presidentialism and a PR system are complemented by a heterogeneous multipartism, and above all there may be some party control of civil society, and this is the only way in which such a democracy can actually work. Growth toward a more autonomous society would mean problems and probable crisis within this model. A more detailed analysis of the cases will empirically implement some of these models, as suggested by Table 1.2.[86]

Where to Go from Here?

Adaptation and firm establishment, destabilization and destructuration or even readaptation, consensus and control/autonomy, manifest inefficacy and negative behaviours are the main features to explore in the processes of consolidation and crisis: these are the composite dependent variables. At this point the first empirical check should be through which indicators and measures the two processes may be detected. A curious aspect of many writings on these themes is that by taking for granted the two phenomena the authors overlook or 'forget' the basic need for its simple and immediate empirical identification, which is also a prerequisite for any successive analysis and explanation. The empirical identification of the two processes will be suggested in the next chapter.

[86] See Ch. 6 for its empirical developments.

Indicators and Measures

Some Questions and A Few Problems

How to empirically detect the phenomena to be studied is strictly related to their definition. This may appear to be an easy task, yet it is not the case for consolidation and crisis. Analyses[1] may be clustered in three different positions: (i) the precise empirical detection of the two phenomena is considered a superfluous exercise, when not a waste of time; (ii) the analysis must consider the empirical conditions or explanations and examine them; (iii) examining only the effects or outcomes of consolidation and crisis, disregarding the processes. Problems and flaws are inherent in each of these positions. The main consequence of the first one is that, if there are not precise indicators, it is possible either to affirm or to deny the existence of the phenomena in the same specific cases; and it is even easier to refuse them at a more conceptual and general level. Besides, a greater freedom is *de facto* possible in the same conceptualization of the phenomena: there is more room for 'minimalist' and 'maximalist' conceptions.[2]

The consequence of the second and third, more meritorious, positions is simply to ignore the problem. For example, the presence of anti-system parties is, first of all, an important indicator of a lack of legitimacy rather than of a lack of consolidation (Burton, Gunther, and Higley 1992: 7–8). It is not an independent indicator of consolidation, but rather of one commonly considered condition or explanation of the phenomenon. By the same token, civil order or political violence cannot be considered as independent indicators of crisis, rather they make reference to legitimacy (or illegitimacy).

Third, when some empirical indicator is devised, looking at the outcomes rather than at the processes is the most recurring way of avoiding some measurement problems. But, in this vein, the suggestion by

---

[1] See the authors quoted in the third section of Ch. 1.
[2] As, for example, took place in the debate on consolidation (see Ch. 1).

Huntington on the 'two-turnover test'[3] is not acceptable as a test of consolidation. In fact, in addition to considering only the outcome, it is also too demanding and at the same time it pays exaggerated attention to the myth of party alternation in government. According to this test, only Greece would have been defined as a consolidated democracy in the early 1990s, despite its high political radicalization;[4] Portugal would have been so defined after the 1995 elections and Spain after 1996 election (see below); Italy never would have been, and would not be for many years to come.[5] An exceptionally rigorous test, which does not consider the development of the process, does not allow for differences among democracies, and leaves out countries persisting as democracies for half a century (e.g. Italy), is not a useful one.

It is true, however, that there are no ready-made solutions, and when looking for simple measures to implement in several cases, rather than in very few ones, the problem is much more difficult to solve because of the complexities in both phenomena as well as their ambiguities and possible overlapping with the contiguous processes. The difficulties encountered in defining the end of each process[6] is an additional illustration of these problems. Here, four guidelines will be followed: (i) in some cases the opposite indicators are useful for detecting consolidation and crisis, in others this is not entirely correct: an indicator is much more preferable in checking for one phenomenon than is its opposite in checking for the other one; (ii) since the process is emphasized, different quantitative or qualitative values at different moments are necessary for each indicator, at least to be able to discern some emerging trend; (iii) a *per differentiam* procedure seems the best way of empirically analysing the phenomena, that is, by establishing a difference between installation, consolidation, and crisis; (iv) looking for only one indicator of a multidimensional, complex reality, such as each democratic regime, is too ambitious, if not impossible; a different path will be followed, and different dimensions and domains will be analysed.[7]

[3] 'By this test, a democracy may be viewed as consolidated if the party or group that takes power in the initial election at the time of transition loses a subsequent election and turns over power to those election winners, and if those election winners then peacefully turn over power to the winner of a later election' (Huntington 1991: 266–7).

[4] See below and the following chapters.

[5] France only became consolidated during the 'cohabitation' of the 1980s. Japan would not pass the test, let alone almost all the Eastern European and Latin American countries.

[6] But see the solution suggested in Ch. 1, which refers to the end of consolidation, when manifestations of crisis are not present, widespread, and consistent, and to the end of crisis when there is either breakdown or reconsolidation; as well as the implementation of these criteria at the end of the present chapter.

[7] The notions of partial consolidation and partial crisis, mentioned in Ch. 1, also point to this direction of analysis.

The domains to consider include: the working political institutions, the elections, the party system, and the political élites. Thus, the empirical indicators and related values will be explored in the regime, electoral, partisan, and élite domains. However, a multi-dimensional synthetic proposal as well as a simplified measure of consolidation and crisis is suggested; and at the end of the chapter, a more precise indication of the empirical units of analysis provided.

The Regime Domain

The phases of transition and democratic installation are characterized by choices, at both the élite and mass levels,[8] about the main governing institutions. They are symbolically concluded when the parliament has approved the Constitutional Charter, as happened in Italy in December 1947, in Greece in June 1975, in Portugal in April 1976, and in Spain in October 1978. In Spain the citizens also expressed their support for the new regime by approving its basic democratic institutions in a successive referendum on the constitution (6 December 1978). In Portugal the minimal requisites of a democracy were achieved when the Constitutional Reform of August 1982 was enacted and the civilian control of the army was formally stated (see below). Thus, from 1976, when the constitution was approved, to 1982 the regime was a hybrid polity, where the consolidation of pluralism had been set in motion, but the different factions of the army—as a consequence of the coup of 25 April 1974—still controlled the open, competitive interplay among the civil actors within the existing institutions. This means that in Portugal a partial consolidation began and overlapped with the setting up of additional, but key, elements to complete the democratic installation.

The early years of possible consolidation are especially distinguished by the change of politics from the great symbolic declarations and enthusiasms of transition and installation phases into the day-to-day necessities of effective institutional functioning: politics becomes 'business as usual'. Conversely, during the years of crisis, politics is above all democratic 'fatigue' rather than the effective functioning of institutions, and politics is again no longer 'business as usual'.

Therefore, to detect empirically and understand better the unfolding of the two phenomena the focus must be shifted to important specific features mainly concerning the interplay among the key political institutions of the regime at both the domestic and international levels.

---

[8] This second level is more evident when there is a referendum that approves the élite institutional choices.

These indicators reflect the establishment and adaptation as well as the collapse and change of institutional routines, even given the non-implementation of existing rules. In such institutional relationships the achievement of an appropriateness[9] and internal consistency of institutions or the emergence of an opposite trend have to be included. However, establishment of patterns or, conversely, breaking of them are also relevant in determining which democracy has been actually consolidated or in crisis. When additionally specified that some element is empirically more effective in detecting consolidation and another element in detecting crisis and, however, more than one institutional indicator is needed before deciding if there is consolidation or crisis, the qualitative and quantitative indicators required include the following dimensions for the entire period analysed in the four countries:

1. Institutional role of the head of state vis-à-vis the prime minister, the parliament, and the public;
2. Duration and party composition of the cabinet;
3. Balance of power between the government and the parliament in the legislative activity: cabinet dominance, equilibrium, or parliamentary dominance;
4. Relationships between local and central powers;
5. Neutrality, or neutralization vs. politicization of the army;
6. Role of the judiciary;
7. Establishment, adaptation, or breaking of the 'rules of the game': majoritarian vs. consensual rule in the electoral system;
8. International alignments.[10]

[9] Given the existing political forces and their goals the appropriateness is the consistency between those forces and the institutions. This definition parallels March and Olsen's notion (1989: 23 and *passim*), but here institutional adaptation and change are stressed rather than the opposite, that is, how institutions shape actors and situations.

[10] Other indicators of consolidation could be the set of laws, bills, and more specific norms that give roots and implement the basic constitutional rules, as well as the several sentences of Constitutional Courts, that particularly in Italy, Spain, and Portugal repeal laws, existing in the previous authoritarian regime. (In Greece the most important laws of the previous military regime were repealed by Karamanlis's cabinet between September 1974 and June 1975.) Furthermore, during the crisis, what can be seen is the lack of implementation of existing legal norms or the proliferation of new rules less and less consistent with the previous ones. Thus, a long list of laws and Constitutional Court declarations, not difficult to gather, would be the result of looking at this kind of indicator of consolidation and crisis. However, they sometimes carry ambiguous meanings just in terms of consolidation or even crisis. Consequently, the other ones, suggested in the text, are preferred.

The head of state

The change in role of the head of state may be an excellent indicator of a process of consolidation through adaptation or of crisis. In the process of consolidation, such change brings about a higher consistency between the actual role of political actors and the existing rules. Such a phenomenon took place in both Greece (1986) and Portugal (1982), but not in Spain, where the monarchical arrangement makes any change of this sort more difficult, or in Italy, where the change has rather to be analysed within a process of crisis (see also below).

In Greece, the constitution of 1975 had been approved without the vote of the opposition parties, and particularly the Socialists of PASOK. They mainly opposed the so-called 'superpowers', granted to the head of state by the constitution, which had made him very similar to the French president despite not being directly elected.[11] The constitutional revision under the PASOK government in 1985–6 and a new pro-Socialist president, Sartzetakis, changed most of chapter 2, section B, part 3, of the Greek constitution concerning the powers of the head of state.[12] Basically, his discretionary powers regarding the dismissal of cabinet, calling its meeting and its chairing, or issuing bills on the organization of the state, were repealed; those on the appointment of the prime minister, the dissolution of parliament, the holding of referenda on national issues, the granting of amnesty, the proclaiming of a 'state of siege' were amended and transferred to the parliamentary majority and, consequently, in most cases, to the prime minister.[13]

In Portugal, the revision of 1982 follows a long political debate, unfolded also in the press, and it is more complex and substantial than

[11] This was also emphasized by the president of the Committee who drafted the constitution and was immediately elected head of state (on 20 June 1975). See Tsatsos (1988: 75).

[12] In particular the following articles were changed: 32 (para. 1, 4), 35 (1, 2, 3), 37 (2, 3, 4), 38, 41 (1, 2, 4), 42, 44 (2, 3), 47 (3), and 48. At the same time art. 39, which had created the Council of the Republic, and art. 43, para. 3, were repealed. The Council of the Republic was formed by the head of state, the former presidents of the republic, the prime minister, the former prime minister, the speaker of the parliament, the leader of the opposition, but never met between 1975 and 1985, except the first time to define more precisely its functioning. As a matter of fact, its task of controlling the head of state became superfluous when his powers were restricted. At the same time, ten years after the democratic installation the critical advisory role it could perform appeared useless. Finally, this body was not able to establish any political role for itself. For the Constitutional Chart see Oberdoff (1992: 163 ff.); for a balanced appraisal of the 1975 Constitution in terms of continuity-discontinuity in Greek institutional history and the impact of the 1986 revision see also Diamandouros (1995).

[13] From a juridical perspective, a good thorough analysis of such a revision is conducted by Perifanaki Rotolo (1989). See also Katsoudas (1987) for a cursory analysis.

the Greek case.[14] The change-adaptation concerns: maintaining the presidential powers of dissolution of the parliament, appointment and dismissal of the prime minister, who is no longer politically responsible toward the president, but only toward the parliament; abolishment of the Council of Revolution; and creation of a Council of State, a Constitutional Court, and a Superior Council of National Defence. The mix of changes and maintenance of a few powers gave to the president, still directly elected, a different autonomous power of guarantee. At the same time, the addition of other norms[15] strengthened the role of the Assembly, also vis-à-vis the president; and through the Assembly the new constitutional arrangement gave more centrality to the prime minister, who can now ask for a confidence vote from the Assembly, and overcome the presidential powers if supported by a parliamentary majority.[16] This actually took place after 1985 and, above all, after 1987 with the dominant role of the Social Democratic Party (see below). In this vein the constitutional revision is a key step in a longer adaptive process, where a higher institutional consistency is gained through the expulsion of an independent military power and the acquisition of a major role for parties, namely, representative institutions expel a non-elective body (the army) from the constitutional design and in this way also weaken the president, directly elected, but constitutionally linked to the Council of Revolution.[17] The second step will actually come when a strong parliamentary majority is formed, and the weakened powers of the president are largely 'disactivated'.[18]

[14] A very large number of articles were changed, added, or abolished, not only those of part 3, section 2, chs. 1 and 2, on the president, with the addition of ch. 3 on the Council of State, and sections 3 and 4 on the parliament and government, but also those on the Council of Revolution, which were repealed, and on the other bodies that were created. On the whole, the new text has 300 articles, rather than 312 and the law of Constitutional Revision 237 articles, which refer to the corresponding changes, additions, and repealing. See studies on the 1976 Constitution by De Vergottini (1977), on the new text of the constitution, Oberdoff (1992: 289 ff.), and the analyses by constitutionalists, such as Miranda (1990), Gomes Canotilho and Moreira (1991); and also specifically on the changes of the powers of the head of state, De Caro Bonella (1983).

[15] For example, with the enlargement of legislative competence for the parliament (arts. 167–8) or the transfer of competence on emergency state and siege state on the same body.

[16] The revision of 1982 leaves the president without autonomous powers in governmental activity, and also his power of dismissing the prime minister (art. 198/2) or his veto powers (art. 139) are limited and the range of discretion narrowed.

[17] Therefore, such a constitutional revision put an end to the anomaly of the military political presence in the Portuguese constitution, and since 1982 it makes it possible to consider Portugal a democracy, rather than a democratic hybrid (see above, also Ch. 1 and below, this section).

[18] This is common in semi-presidentialism. See how Duverger (1980) sketched this model, and the successive analysis by Sartori (1994: 121–40). It may also be recalled here that the Portuguese president maintains less power vis-à-vis the French one: basically, even when he could be supported by a parliamentary majority, the president has no

The exceptional intervention of the head of state in countries with no strong presidential characteristics can be soundly taken as a clear, evident indicator of crisis, be it either only short term and temporary or larger and deeper. Thus, in Italy more than in Portugal, a few cabinets, appointed by the head of state without a clear parliamentary supporting majority may be recalled, respectively, in 1992–6 with President Scalfaro (see Table 2.1) and during 1978–80 with President Ramalho Eanes (see Table 2.4). In addition, in Italy, the public declarations of President Cossiga (1991–2), aimed at reforming the key governmental institutions, which at the same time were delegitimating the existing ones, should also be mentioned. In Spain, the intervention of King Juan Carlos on the evening of 23 February 1981, against the army officers who had launched a coup, to maintain the democratic allegiance of the other officers, is also a key moment during a phase of disenchantment and crisis (see the following chapters). Also the intervention of the Greek head of state to dissolve the parliament twice in a few months (1989–90) and to call three elections in ten months is within the constitutional rules, but it is at the same time an apparent symptom of serious problems of governance (see below).

Duration and composition of the cabinet[19]

If properly understood and cautiously taken,[20] these two aspects of the relationships between cabinet and parliament may usefully indicate stable or more fluid, changing patterns in those relationships. And, therefore, they indirectly point to consolidation or crisis. As an indicator of the extent of cabinet control of the legislature, changes of cabinet in the four countries reveal the emergence of precise patterns. The clearest case is Portugal (see Table 2.3), where in the first two years of

autonomous power of legislative initiative, that is, he is not the head of the executive as in France. It is also interesting to stress how a semi-presidential arrangement has weaker constraints than others. The main side-effect of this is the variability in the actual working of this institution in connection with the personality or the political strategies of the president. For example, Mário Soares, elected twice in 1986 and 1991, has performed his role in a different way during the two terms, being much more 'interventionist' during the second term, when the party leadership was stronger than previously. This goes against the analysis that political scientists usually suggest. On the presidency of Soares see the excellent article by Braga da Cruz (1994).

[19] In the following tables, the order of presentation of data per country is a choice of the author on the grounds of population, according to the most recent census data (Italy: 57.1m.; Spain: 38.4m.; Portugal: 10.4m.; Greece: 10.3m.). It should be remembered, however, that Spain is much larger than Italy (505,000 vs. 301,000 sq.km) and so is Greece than Portugal (131,000 vs. 91,000 sq.km).

[20] We may recall how the change of cabinet is a traditional indicator, and there is a large literature about it beginning at least with the analyses on cabinet instability in Weimar Germany and other countries during the 1920s and 1930s.

the new regime (1974–6), there are six cabinets, one every four months; in the second period (1976–81) there are seven, i.e. one every twelve months; and in the most recent period (1981–95) five cabinets, i.e., one every three years (34.2 months). Similar patterns are immediately established in Spain and Greece. In the former country there have been nine cabinets in the twenty-one years since Franco's death, or seven cabinets in nineteen years, one every three years or so (32.6 months), if the transitional cabinets are excluded; and in the past fourteen years a cabinet overlapped with the whole legislature, even if a few important reshuffles were made (see Table 2.2). In the latter country, if the two first, short transitional cabinets are excluded, there are eleven cabinets in twenty-one years, with a duration very close to the Spanish one (see Table 2.4).[21] The opposite pattern of parliamentarian dominance is established in Italy, not immediately, but from 1953 onwards: fifty-five cabinets in half a century show that.

The explanation of such patterns and their timing is not a direct goal of this analysis. However, in Spain such patterns of stability and executive dominance are accounted for by the limited number of parties as well as the constructive vote of no confidence (art. 113 of the Constitutional Charter) and other norms of the constitution and of standing orders of Cortes. In Greece, this takes place because of an even more limited number of parties (see below) and milder constitutional norms to strengthen the cabinet.[22] Thus, if despite these structural and legal elements changes of cabinet take place, then they are even more meaningful. In fact, in Spain the only change of cabinet amid a legislature takes place with the resignation of Suárez at the end of January 1981, when there were very serious problems inside the governing party, which virtually disappeared within a year, and it was as much a prob-

[21] A more precise analysis of the actual working and dynamics of the Greek executive is in Koutsoukis (1994: 270–82). Spain follows similar lines that characterize a chancellor democracy; for example, in the autonomy of ministers in their fields and the coordination only with the prime minister when economic resources are not involved or the bills suggested by the minister do not affect the competence of other ministers.

[22] Mainly, the requisite of the absolute majority of all MPs to approve a motion of no confidence vis-à-vis the absolute majority of present MPs for the confidence (art. 84.6). The Portuguese constitution follows the same lines as the Greek on this. In fact, art. 195.4 and 198.1 f require the absolute majority of MPs 'em efectividade de funções' to reject a governmental programme or to approve a motion of no confidence. The expression, effectively incumbent MPs, may only be understood within the constitutional tradition of Portugal. In any case, it is fully equivalent to the Greek requisite of all MPs also as a consequence of a curious constitutional routine established in Portugal. The MPs who cannot participate in a parliamentary session, even if temporarily, e.g. for a day, appoint a substitute. Such appointments are recurring, so that at any moment all MPs are effectively incumbent or in office. For a thoughtful analysis of this routine and the related data see Opello (1986: 295–8). In all three countries the parliamentary standing orders (the texts are published by the Diário da República for Portugal and the Official Bulletins for the other two countries) basically confirm the constitutional norms.

TABLE 2.1. *Change of cabinets in Southern Europe: Italy, 1945–1996*

Leg.	P. Minister	Date	Duration	Party support
T	Parri	VI/20/45–XI/24/45	5	DC,PCI,PSI,PLI,PDL,Pd'A
T	De Gasperi I	XII/10/45–VII/1/46	7	DC,PCI,PSI,PLI,PDL,Pd'A
T	De Gasperi II	VII/13/46–I/20/47	6	DC, PCI,PSI, PRI
T	De Gasperi III	II/2/47–V/13/47	3	DC, PCI, PSI
T	De Gasperi IV	V/31/47–V/12/48	11	DC,PLI,PSLI,PRI (min.)
I	De Gasperi V	V/23/48–I/12/50	20	DC,PLI,PSLI,PRI
I	De Gasperi VI	I/27/50–VII/16/51	18	DC,PSLI,PRI
I	De Gasperi VII	VII/26/51–VI/29/53	23	DC,PRI
II	De Gasperi VIII	VII/16/53–VII/28/53	1	DC (min.)
II	Pella	VIII/17/53–I/5/54	5	caretaker
II	Fanfani I	I/18/54–I/30/54	1	DC (min.)
II	Scelba	II/10/54–VI/22/55	16	DC,PSDI,PLI (min.)
II	Segni I	VII/6/55–V/6/57	22	DC,PSDI,PLI (min.)
II	Zoli	V/19/57–VI/19/58	13	DC (min.)
III	Fanfani II	VII/1/58–I/26/59	7	DC, PSDI (min.)
III	Segni II	II/15/59–II/24/60	12	DC (min.)
III	Tambroni	III/23/60–VII/19/60	4	DC (min.)
III	Fanfani III	VII/26/60–III/2/62	19	DC (min.)
III	Fanfani IV	II/21/62–V/16/63	15	DC,PSDI,PRI (min.)
IV	Leone I	VI/21/63–XI/5/63	4	caretaker
IV	Moro I	XII/4/63–VI/26/64	7	DC,PSI,PSDI,PRI
IV	Moro II	VII/22/64–I/21/66	18	DC,PSI,PSDI,PRI
IV	Moro III	II/23/66–VI/5/68	27	DC,PSU,PRI
V	Leone II	VI/24/68–XI/19/68	5	caretaker
V	Rumor I	XII/12/68–VII/5/69	7	DC,PSU,PRI
V	Rumor II	VIII/5/69–II/7/70	6	DC (min.)
V	Rumor III	III/27/70–VII/6/70	3	DC,PSI,PSDI,PRI
V	Colombo	VIII/6/70–I/15/72	17	DC,PSI,PSDI,PRI
V	Andreotti I	II/17/72–II/26/72	1	DC (min.)
VI	Andreotti II	VI/26/72–VII/12/73	12	DC,PSDI,PLI
VI	Rumor IV	VII/7/73–III/2/74	8	DC,PSI,PSDI,PRI

Leg.	P. Minister	Date	Duration	Party support
VI	Rumor V	III/14/74–X/3/74	7	DC,PSI,PSDI
VI	Moro IV	XI/23/74–I/7/76	13	DC,PRI (min.)
VI	Moro V	II/12/76–IV/30/76	3	caretaker
VII	Andreotti III	VII/29/76–I/16/78	18	DC (min.)
VII	Andreotti IV	III/16/78–I/31/79	10	DC (PLI,PRI,PSDI,PSI,PCI)
VII	Andreotti V	III/21/79–III/31/79	1	DC,PSDI,PRI
VIII	Cossiga I	VIII/5/79–III/19/80	7	caretaker
VIII	Cossiga II	IV/4/80–IX/27/80	6	DC,PSI,PRI (min.)
VIII	Forlani	X/19/80–V/26/81	7	DC,PSI,PSDI,PRI
VIII	Spadolini I	VI/28/81–VIII/7/82	13	DC,PSI,PSDI,PRI,PLI
VIII	Spadolini II	VIII/23/82–XI/13/82	3	DC,PSI,PSDI,PRI,PLI
VIII	Fanfani V	XII/2/82–IV/29/83	5	DC,PSI,PSDI,PRI
IX	Craxi I	VIII/4/83–VI/27/86	35	DC,PSI,PSDI,PRI,PLI
IX	Craxi II	VIII/1/86–III/3/87	7	DC,PSI,PSDI,PRI,PLI
IX	Fanfani VI	IV/18/87–VII/9/87	3	DC,IND. (min.)
X	Goria	VII/29/87–III/11/88	7	DC,PSI,PSDI,PRI,PLI
X	De Mita	IV/13/88–V/19/89	13	DC,PSI,PSDI,PRI,PLI
X	Andreotti VI	VII/23/89–III/29/91	20	DC,PSI,PSDI,PRI,PLI
X	Andreotti VII	IV/16/91–IV/24/92	12	DC,PSI,PSDI,PLI
XI	Amato	VI/28/92–IV/22/93	10	techn.
XI	Ciampi	IV/29/93–I/12/94	8	techn.
XII	Berlusconi	V/10/94–XII/22/94	7	FI, AN, CCD, LN
XII	Dini	I/17/95–IV/20/96	12	techn.
XIII	Prodi	V/18/96–		PDS,PPI,RI,UD,Verdi (RC)

Notes: Under *Leg.* and *P. Minister*, the data refer to the number of the legislature (T means transitional, C refers to Constituent Assembly), and the name of the head of the cabinet. As for *date*, the beginning date for each cabinet is when it is sworn. When not officially indicated, the end date has been conventionally considered the day before the elections. The *duration* is in months, and more than 15 days means an additional month. With *party support*, the parties that support each cabinet are indicated, even if the support is minoritarian; *caretaker* refers to a cabinet which is formed by party representatives, without a parliamentary majority, and appointed to perform only urgent, current affairs; *technical* refers to a cabinet filled by technicians, who are not party representatives, without a parliamentary majority, but which usually enjoy the confidence of the head of state; it could also be defined as a *presidential cabinet*. When party support is indicated in parenthesis, this means that it is outside support, namely, the supporting party does not have its own ministers in the cabinet.

Source: Italian press.

TABLE 2.2. *Change of cabinets in Southern Europe: Spain, 1975–1996*

Leg.	P. Minister	Date	Duration	Party support
T	Arias Navarro	XII/4/75–VII/1/76	7	techn.
T	Suarez I	VII/7/76–VII/4/77	12	techn.
C	Suarez II	VII/4/77–III/30/79	21	UCD (min.)
I	Suarez III	III/30/79–II/25/81	23	UCD (min.)
I	Calvo Sotelo	II/25/81–XI/30/82	21	UCD (min.)
II	Gonzalez I	XII/1/82–VI/21/8	43	PSOE
III	Gonzalez II	VII/23/86–X/28/89	39	PSOE
IV	Gonzalez	XII/5/89–VI/5/93	42	PSOE
V	Gonzalez	VII/9/93–III/2/96	32	PSOE (CiU,PNV)
VI	Aznar	V/5/96–		PP (CiU,PNV,CC)

Note: see Table 2.1.

Source: Spanish press.

TABLE 2.3. *Change of cabinets in Southern Europe: Portugal, 1975–1996*

Leg.	P. Minister	Date	Duration	Party support
T	Adelino da Palma	V/15/74–VII/9/74	2	MFA,Ind.,PCP,PS, PPD,MDP,SEDES
T	Vasco Gonçalves	VII/18/74–IX/30/74	2	MFA,Ind.,PCP,PS, PPD
T	Vasco Gonçalves	IX/30/74–III/26/75	6	MFA,Ind.,PCP,PS, PPD
T	Vasco Gonçalves	III/26/74–VIII/8/75	4	MFA,Ind.,PCP,PS, PPD,MDP
T	Vasco Gonçalves	VIII/8/75–IX/12/75	1	MFA,Ind.,PCP,MDP
T	Pinheiro de Azevedo	IX/9/75–VII/22/76	10	MFA,Ind.,PCP,PS, PPD
I	Soares	VII/23/76–XII/8/77	16	PS (min.)
I	Soares	I/23/78–VII/27/78	6	PS,CDS
I	Nobre da Costa	VIII/9/78–IX/14/78	1	techn.
I	Mota Pinto	X/25/78–VI/7/79	7	techn.
I	Lourdes Pintasilgo	VII/31/79–XII/1/79	4	techn.
I	Sà Carneiro	I/3/80–XII/9/80	11	AD
II	Pinto Balsemao	I/9/81–VIII/14/81	7	AD
II	Pinto Balsemao	IX/4/81–IV/26/83	21	AD
III	Soares	VI/9/83–X/28/85	29	PS,PSD
IV	Cavaco Silva	XI/6/85–VII/18/87	20	PSD (min.)
V	Cavaco Silva	VIII/17/87–X/5/91	50	PSD
VI	Cavaco Silva	X/28/91–IX/30/95	47	PSD
VII	Guterres	X/28/95–		PS (min.)

Note: see Table 2.1.

Source: Portuguese press.

TABLE 2.4. *Change of cabinets in Southern Europe: Greece, 1974–1996*

Leg.	P. Minister	Date	Duration	Party support
T	Karamanlis	VII/26/74–X/7/74	2	ND
T	Karamanlis	X/8/74–XI/21/74	1	caretaker
I	Karamanlis	XII/14/74–XI/19/77	35	ND
II	Karamanlis	XI/28/77–V/6/80	29	ND
II	Rallis	V/9/80–X/17/81	17	ND
III	Papandreu	X/21/81–VI/1/85	43	PASOK
IV	Papandreu	VII/26/85–VI/17/89	47	PASOK
V	Tzannetakis	VII/2/89–X/7/89	3	ND, Syn.
V	Grivas	X/12/89–XI/4/89	1	caretaker
VI	Zolotas	XI/22//89–II/12/90	3	ND,PASOK, Syn.
VI	Zolotas	II/13/90–IV/7/90	2	caretaker
VII	Mitsotakis	IV/11/90–X/9/93	42	ND (DIANA) (min.)
VIII	Papandreu	X/13/93–I/15/96	27	PASOK
VIII	Simitis	I/22/96–IX/22/96	8	PASOK
IX	Simitis	IX/23/96–		PASOK

Note: see Table 2.1.

Source: Greek press.

lem of delegitimation as of democratic institutions. There was also almost a month of power vacuum that culminated with the attempted *coup d'état* on 23 February. Similarly, in Greece, behind the four short cabinets between 1989 and 1990 there is the uncovering of corruption, strong ideological and radical party conflicts, and serious economic problems. Again the cabinet change is a good indicator of a possible or existing crisis, and even more so if there are constraints on such changes.

The analysis of this indicator may also be useful when the opposite pattern exists. In fact, despite parliamentary dominance, periods of even shorter cabinets may again emphasize difficulties and problems for the existing regime. In Italy, this is so in 1953–4, 1968–70, 1973–6, 1979–83, and even in 1994, when several reasons, such as the weakening of Christian Democracy, policy differences among allied parties, protest, mass mobilization, and terrorism, created problems for the heterogeneous, conflictual, incumbent coalitions.[23] Conversely, in other moments, such as 1947–53, 1954–7, 1963–8, and 1983–7, a higher governmental duration points to phases of consolidation, persistence, or even reconsolidation.

[23] It is well known that the low duration of cabinets does not imply changes and instability of policies when—as often happens in Italy—the incumbent parties and the ministers remain the same from one cabinet to another.

TABLE 2.5. *Legislative activity: Italy, 1948–1996*

(A) Legislative activity[a]

	I legislature 1948–1953	II legislature 1953–1958	III legislature 1958–1963	IV legislature 1963–1968	V legislature 1968–1972	VI legislature 1972–1976
Gov.	63.1	39.2	29.5	26.4	17.8	19.4
Par.	36.9	60.8	70.5	73.6	82.2	80.6
(N)	(3,728)	(4,129)	(5,213)	(5,592)	(5,097)	(5,719)

(B) Legislative output[b]

	I legislature 1948–1953	II legislature 1953–1958	III legislature 1958–1963	IV legislature 1963–1968	V legislature 1968–1972	VI legislature 1972–1976
Gov.	88.8	74.7	73.2	69.3	70.3	75.8
Par.	11.2	25.3	26.8	30.7	29.7	24.2
(N)	(2,314)	(1,894)	(1,793)	(1,766)	(841)	(1,122)

(C) Governmental vs. parliamentary efficacy[c]

	I legislature 1948–1953	II legislature 1953–1958	III legislature 1958–1963	IV legislature 1963–1968	V legislature 1968–1972	VI legislature 1972–1976
Gov.	87.3	87.4	85.3	82.9	65.1	76.5
Par.	18.9	19.1	13.1	13.2	6.0	5.9

Notes: [a] Percentage of legislative initiative, per origin. [b] Percentage of approved bills, per origin. [c] Percentage of approved bills out of proposed ones.

Source: Parliamentary data banks.

Finally, in the gradual nature of the Portuguese process, the first moments of harsh conflict with the key role performed by the Movement of Armed Forces (MFA), that had launched the coup and broke down the authoritarian regime, and the conflict among the parties is apparent in the six transitional cabinets in two years. And the decline of fluidity came about with the party agreement that brought the constitutional revision of 1982 and the expulsion of the open constitutional role of the army in the polity.[24]

Balance of legislative power between cabinet and parliament

The relationships between cabinet and parliament may be seen from the opposite perspective of parliament. This may be done by looking at the main activity of every parliament, that is, the law-making process, again in terms of firm establishment of patterns and routines or of their breakdown. Among the several, different perspectives according to which such activity can be analysed, there are three indicators that specifically point to those relationships, namely, the legislative initiative, the legislative output, and governmental efficacy. The first indi-

---

[24] An additional analysis of cabinet change from different perspectives would be possible and useful. As a meaningful indicator of consolidation and crisis, however, the above considerations should be enough.

VII legislature 1976–1979	VIII legislature 1979–1983	IX legislature 1983–1987	X legislature 1987–1992	XI legislature 1992–1994	XII legislature 1994–1996
27.4	21.3	18.1	12.5	7.4	5.9
72.6	78.7	81.9	87.5	92.6	94.1
(3,650)	(5,032)	(5,683)	(8,018)	(4,609)	(5,254)

VII legislature 1976–1979	VIII legislature 1979–1983	IX legislature 1983–1987	X legislature 1987–1992	XI legislature 1992–1994	XII legislature 1994–1996
85.1	76.9	79.6	69.6	74.8	11.3
14.9	23.1	20.4	30.4	25.2	88.7
(665)	(961)	(789)	(1,065)	(314)	(248)

VII legislature 1976–1979	VIII legislature 1979–1983	IX legislature 1983–1987	X legislature 1987–1992	XI legislature 1992–1994	XII legislature 1994–1996
56.5	68.8	61.0	74.0	68.9	9.0
3.7	5.6	3.5	4.6	1.9	4.5

cator is the percentage of bills introduced by the government in comparison with those introduced by MPs. The second refers to the bills that are passed, according to its origin (governmental vs. parliamentarian). The third considers the percentage of success among the governmental bills and the parliamentarian ones.[25]

Italy is the most extreme case of the establishment of parliamentarian dominance. As Table 2.5 shows, the predominance of individual parliamentary activity is such that the law-making process is the integrated result of both parliamentary and governmental activity, and in the parliamentary side the same governmental party is present (see Morisi 1992: 36 ff.). Taken together, the three indicators of Table 2.5 stress that: since the end of the 1950s the representative role of MPs is strongly dominant; a bit earlier, since the second legislature, a high percentage (about one-fourth/one-third) of legislative output has parliamentary origins; governmental efficacy has been fairly strong for about thirty years (1948–76), but later it is still acceptable only because of the increased adoption of decrees, which became a stable pattern in the way of governing (see Table 2.9). The breaking of such patterns dramatically emerges in the most recent legislature (1994–6): the representative role of the executive is close to nothing; the parliamentary

---

[25] Although not exactly in this way, the reference to this sort of indicator is recurring in the literature on the field. See e.g. Liebert and Cotta (1990).

TABLE 2.6. *Legislative activity: Spain, 1977–1996*

	Constituent A. 1977–1979	I legislature 1979–1982	II legislature 1982–1986	III legislature 1986–1989	IV legislature 1989–1993	V legislature 1993–1996[d]
(A) Legislative initiative[a]						
Gov.	68.4	60.9	65.1	47	43.2	44.3
Par.	31.6	39.1	34.9	53	56.8	55.7
(N)	(228)	(555)	(315)	(266)	(317)	(287)
(B) Legislative output[b]						
Gov.	92	98.4	92.9	91.5	85.2	84.9
Par.	8	1.6	7.1	8.5	14.8	15.1
(N)	(112)	(244)	(197)	(118)	(128)	(119)
(C) Governmental vs. parliamentary efficacy[c]						
Gov.	66	71	89.3	86.4	79.6	79.5
Par.	12.5	1.8	12.7	7.1	10.6	11.3

Notes: [a] Percentage of legislative initiative, per origin. [b] Percentage of approved bills, per origin. [c] Percentage of approved bills out of proposed ones. [d] For the V legislature data refer to the years 1993–1995.

Source: Congreso de los Diputados, Dirección de Estudios y Documentación.

TABLE 2.7. *Legislative activity: Portugal, 1976–1995*

	I legislature 1976–1980	*II legislature* 1980–1983	*III legislature* 1983–1985	*IV legislature* 1985–1987	*V legislature* 1987–1991	*VI legislature* 1991–1995
(A) Legislative initiative[a]						
Gov.	41.6	26.3	18.2	11	20.4	18.1
Par.	58.4	73.7	81.8	89	79.6	81.9
(N)	(919)	(540)	(654)	(501)	(999)	(729)
(B) Legislative output[b]						
Gov.	64.3	69.1	22.4	22.9	36.4	34.7
Par.	35.7	30.9	77.6	77.1	63.6	65.3
(N)	(308)	(97)	(352)	(140)	(508)	(334)
(C) Governmental vs. parliamentary efficacy[c]						
Gov.	51.8	47.2	66.4	58.2	90.7	87.8
Par.	20.5	7.5	51	24.2	40.6	36.5

Notes: [a] Percentage of legislative initiative, per origin. [b] Percentage of approved bills, per origin. [c] Percentage of approved bills out of proposed ones.

Sources: I and III Legislature, Opello (1986); and *Diario da Assembleia da Republica*. II Legislatura, Divisao de Documentaçao da Assembleia da Republica; IV, V e VI Legislatura, *Diario Assembleia da Republica*, various issues.

TABLE 2.8. *Legislative activity: Greece, 1974–1995*

(A) Legislative initiative[a]

	I legislature 1974–1977	II legislature 1977–1981	III legislature 1981–1985	IV legislature 1985–1989	V legislature June–October 1989	VI legislature November '89 –March 1990	VII legislature 1990–1993	VIII legislature 1993–1995
Gov.	*	87.2	93.1	89.7	61.9	41.5	83.1	*
Par.	*	12.8	6.9	10.3	38.1	58.5	16.9	*
(N)	*	(733)	(449)	(400)	(21)	(53)	(373)	*

(B) Legislative output[b]

	I legislature 1974–1977	II legislature 1977–1981	III legislature 1981–1985	IV legislature 1985–1989	V legislature June–October 1989	VI legislature November '89 –March 1990	VII legislature 1990–1993	VIII legislature 1993–1995
Gov.	99.9	100	100	100	100	100	99.7	100
Par.	0.1	—	—	—	—	—	0.3	—
(N)	(744)	(491)	(342)	(314)	(9)	(15)	(286)	(92)

(C) Governmental vs. parliamentary efficacy[c]

	I legislature 1974–1977	II legislature 1977–1981	III legislature 1981–1985	IV legislature 1985–1989	V legislature June–October 1989	VI legislature November '89 –March 1990	VII legislature 1990–1993	VIII legislature 1993–1995
Gov.	*	76.8	81.8	87.5	69.2	68.2	91.9	*
Par.	*	0	0	0	0	0	1.6	*

Notes: [a] Percentage of legislative initiative, per origin. [b] Percentage of approved bills, per origin.
[c] Percentage of approved bills out of proposed ones.
* data not available.

Source: Parliamentary data banks.

TABLE 2.9. *Growth of law-decrees and of non-ratification, per legislature: Italy, 1945–1995*

I	II	III	IV	V	VI	VII	VIII	IX	X	XI	XII
29	60	30	94	69	124	167	274	304	470	522	690
28	60	28	89	68	108	136	170	136	190	118	113

Note: The figures of the first line represent the law-decrees presented by the cabinet during each legislature. In the second line there are only the ratified decrees.

Source: Data Bank of the Italian Senate.

output is overwhelmingly predominant (89 per cent vs. 11 per cent) (Table 2.5); both governmental and parliamentary efficacy are the lowest since 1948 and a great many decrees are not passed (see Table 2.9).[26] In fact, even the Italian way of circumventing the parliament, through the law-decrees, seems to be at a dead end. On the one hand, in the most recent legislatures the decrees became the prominent way of the legislative activity for the government; on the other hand, as stressed by Table 2.9, a declining percentage of decrees were ratified: 44.7 in the IXth legislature, 40.4 in the Xth, 22.6 in the XIth legislature, 16.4 in the XIIth legislature.[27] As a way of comparison of two extreme cases, let it be enough to mention that in Greece during the 1974–95 period the law-decrees numbered about 150, and all of them were ratified.[28]

A pattern of equilibrium seems routine in Portugal. On the one hand, since the early 1980s the representative role of parliament has been predominant; and the legislative output is even higher than the governmental one: a routine according to which 'parties preferred to negotiate certain laws in Parliament' rather than to impose on the parliament a governmental initiative, is established (Braga da Cruz and Lobo Antunes 1989). On the other hand, since 1987 governmental efficacy has been much higher than the parliamentary one (see Table 2.7); there has been a recurring adoption of decrees during the

[26] In the last legislature 109 out of 652. The rate of conversion in previous legislatures was: 118/522 in the XIth leg., 190/470 (Xth), 136/304 (IXth), 170/274 (VIIIth); while in the VIIth it still was 136 out of 167 and in the VIth 108 out of 124.

[27] As shown by Fedele (1996: 155), even during the Berlusconi cabinet 52.3% of governmental legislative activity was formed by law-decrees. The actual role of such decrees in Italian politics has been analysed by Cazzola and Morisi (1981).

[28] The figure was given to me by Professor Alivizatos, whom I warmly thank. According to the Greek constitution (art. 44.1) the decrees are called 'acts of legislative value'.

technical cabinets of 1978–80;[29] and the broader size of output with a parliamentarian origin is accounted for by the sectoral content of that output, the so-called *bagatelas*.[30] By looking in detail, it would be possible to see ups and downs within the routines discussed above, but no clear breaking of them.

Although in different degrees, Spain and Greece achieved fairly similar patterns of executive dominance (see Tables 2.6 and 2.8), the representative role of parliament is developed more in Spain than in Greece, but much less than in Italy or Portugal; an overwhelming part of legislative output has governmental origins; governmental efficacy has been very strong in Spain since 1982;[31] and the parliamentarian efficacy is almost zero in Greece. However, in Greece the role of MPs is reaffirmed through the establishment of the practice of amendments proposed by MPs belonging to both the incumbent party and the opposition. This is *de facto* a safety valve for an otherwise overwhelming dominance of government vis-à-vis the Voulì. As for the content of them, such amendments have sometimes nothing in common with the discussed bill. The result is the approval of catch-all laws. Yet in Greece two additional, salient patterns are the recurring legislative delegation to the cabinet and the very short time in passing bills. They again emphasize the strongest governmental dominance among all four cases (see Alivizatos 1990: 141).[32] Contrary to Spain, in Greece there was a short period when some of the main patterns were held off. This happened in 1989–90, when there is even a level of activity by MPs that is higher than that of the government (see Table 2.8). This again stresses the moment of crisis in Greece at the end of that decade.

A more detailed analysis of the legislative process would illuminate other patterns in the actual working of the four parliaments and in their relationships with the cabinet.[33] In all cases, however, the role

[29] See the data in Braga da Cruz and Lobo Antunes (1989: 364).

[30] See the related data in Opello (1986: 313). The Portuguese term is translated in Italian as 'leggine' and it is a phenomenon largely present in the Italian parliament also.

[31] In Spain, a closer comparison between legislative output and governmental efficacy suggests that up to 1982 governmental bills had a previous parliamentary consent: see in Table 2.6 the high percentage of governmental output vis-à-vis the relative lower governmental efficacy up to 1982. In fact, during this first phase the Suarez cabinet agreed to several bills with the opposition, and this fact brought a few scholars to label such a period as a consociationalist one (see e.g. Capo Giol 1992), and the following one as a 'majoritarian parliamentary system'. Actually, as noted in the text, there was no established routine until 1982.

[32] In a private conversation Professor Alivizatos called attention to the persistence of these parliamentary practices, which he had already previously discussed (see Alivizatos 1990). I take this opportunity to thank him for his indispensable help in collecting the data on Greek legislative activity (Table 2.8).

[33] In the Italian case, even a distinction of more precise phases is possible, within Parliamentary dominance, as suggested by Di Palma (1987: 193–201).

performed by incumbent and opposition parties is very strong. That is, it makes necessary the reference to parties and party systems. In two of them, namely, in Greece during 1989–90 and Italy since 1994, there is a clear, apparent breakdown of previously existing routines. This implies that the institutions, once established, oppose strong resistance to change, so that if a change of patterns becomes apparent, then there is also a clear indication of crisis.

Relationships between local and central powers

With reference to Portugal and Greece, although both constitutions confirm a unitary state, a broad discussion on decentralization is at the core of Portuguese political debate in the late 1990s, and some decisions in this direction have been implemented in Greece. However, the most interesting and controversial aspects come out in the other two countries.

In Spain, a difficult process unfolded with starts and stops, and even attempts at going back. Title VIII of the constitution, with its different routes to autonomy,[34] set up complex mechanisms and, consequently, as a side-effect, gave much room to ambiguity. This implies that the way the regionalization was implemented and the emergence of actual patterns of functioning are even more salient in this case. Thus, there is a long phase of installation: it had already begun in 1977 with the pre-autonomies and ended in 1983, when all statutes had been approved between 1979 and 1983; the first elections were held in the seventeen regions between 1980 and 1983, and unicameral parliaments, executives, presidents, and high courts of justice were set up. Consequently, it was possible to see the beginning of consolidation in some regions (Catalonia, Basque Country, Galicia) while there was still the installation of the new institutions in others. In terms of patterns of consolidation and more precise indicators of them, a few aspects should be mentioned. First, the declaration of the partial unconstitutionality of LOAPA[35] in August 1983 meant at least the 'freezing' of an asymmetric regionalism, where powers and competence among the regions are differently allocated, even among the first three 'historical regions' with deeper traditions and different languages and cultures. Second, the process of devolution of powers, one of the most important indicators in this process of consolidation, is very slow and precisely

[34] For details, see Leguina Villa (1982), and Maldonado Gago (1995).

[35] The acronym means 'Organic Law for the Harmonization of Autonomy Process'. The law was approved in 1982 to implement a 'pacto autonómico' reached by the Socialists and the then incumbent party, the Unión de Centro Democratico (UCD) (see below). On the LOAPA see De Blas Guerrero (1992).

characterized. As Shabad recalls (1986: 112), by June 1985 300,000 functionaries of the central government had been transferred to the regions and by the end of that year 'all but a few regional governments had received the full measure of competencies granted to them by their Statutes of Autonomy'. In the same year a law for financing the autonomous regions was approved. But by February 1992 another 132,000 civil servants changed administration,[36] by 1993 several additional tasks were transferred to the regions, and by 1994 a new system for transferring financial resources to regions came into effect.[37]

Thus, the core of the process took place within the mid-1980s, but on the whole the process has been going on for more than a decade. This is additionally emphasized by the role that the Constitutional Court performed in the LOAPA case and hundreds of other conflicts raised by the central government vs. the regional governments, and vice versa.[38] By 1993 such legal conflicts had sharply declined. However, curiously enough, during these years this conflictual behaviour was complemented by several agreements between the central government and regional leaders or between leaders of national parties, but above all it was complemented by hundreds of intergovernmental committees appointed for a negotiated devolution of powers. By the mid-1990s, in any case, the whole process is not settled and concluded. Basque terrorism still keeps the process open with radical independentist demands.[39]

In Italy, contrary to what the constitution foresaw, there was no implementation of regional governments until 1970, and a slow transference of powers to the fifteen new institutions later on, until the mid-1970s. The enactment of such a decentralization was one of the first effects of the crisis which exploded in the late 1960s.[40] During the core years of consolidation all the established patterns shaped a unitary state. In the second half of the 1980s, a social and political demand for additional decentralization, even in its more radical expression of inde-

[36] This figure is indirectly suggested by Heywood, who gives a number of 432,186 functionaries who had 'changed masters' between 1982 and 1992, with another 40,000 new recruits still at the regional level (Heywood 1995c: 156).

[37] As suggested by *El País* (see Anuario 1995), the share of expenditures decided by the regional governments is still growing: actually it tripled in twelve years (1983–95).

[38] During the 1981–93 period the conflicts between the central government and Comunidades Autónomas show the following trend: 49 (1981), 51 (1982), 68 (1983), 101 (1984), 131 (1985), 96 (1986), 101 (1987), 92 (1988), 60 (1989), 32 (1990), 18 (1991), 32 (1992), 12 (1993). See, Sánchez de Dios (1995: 154).

[39] Even the recent electoral results (see below) with the partial victory of a rightist party and the need to form a cabinet with the support of regional parties (see Table 2.2) reopened the process of the allocation of powers and related resources between the centre and the main represented peripheries.

[40] Putnam (1993) has written the reference book on the actual working of Italian regions.

pendentism or secessionism, again emerged and became a key issue in the political debate up to the point of being included in the programme of the centre and leftist parties, and not only of localist formations, such as the League. In spite of no salient decision on the issue until mid-1996, the new strong political demand again displays the crisis of the unitary conception of the state. How it will unfold still remains to be seen.

Relationships between the army and civil institutions

From my perspective the two processes can be seen through the more or less gradual establishment of civilian control over the army or, on the contrary, the emergence of an autonomous political role for the army. Of course, in each country different episodes that point to the first direction or the opposite one can be traced. The best qualitative indicators of the two phenomena seem to be: (i) the disappearance or appearance of military institutional prerogatives; and (ii) the related level of 'contestation' or conflict between civilian authorities and the army, or even inside the civilians or the military on issues that involve civilian supremacy.[41] Thus, civilian supremacy is established when the army no longer takes political initiatives, the military is completely outside the political arena, and no contestation emerges against the civilian authorities and the decisions made by them, even if they limit or set constraints on the army. The opposite phenomenon encompasses the emergence of military prerogatives and conflicts against civilian authorities who may try to control military initiatives in the political arena.

In Southern Europe, the Italian case never had these phenomena. First, during the democratic installation and consolidation civilian control was immediately established because of the Italian tradition of civilian supremacy; the previous fascist regime hammering home that tradition—the defeat in the war, and the formation of a fascist army— later on implied an obvious self-purging of officers who adhered to that army. Thus, from the beginning there was no necessity of establishing civilian control. Later on, in terms of crisis there were episodes that could be considered manifestations of an autonomous role of the army. However, even in the two most important episodes of such a kind (in

---

[41] 'Military prerogatives' are the peculiar property according to which 'the military as an institution assumes they have an acquired right or privilege, formal or informal, to exercise effective control over its internal governance, to play a role within extramilitary areas within the state apparatus, or even to structure relationships between the state and political or civil society' (Stepan 1988: 93). On 'contestation' and conflicts the suggestions and the analysis by Stepan (1988) and Agüero (1995) are followed.

1964, when General De Lorenzo was preparing a *coup d'état*, and in 1970, when a similar, less serious attempt was conducted by some troops in Rome), civilian control was very apparent.

In the other cases, on the contrary, there were three different processes of establishment of civilian control that can be inserted in the larger process of consolidation, but no opposite phenomenon and, in this vein, no crisis can be traced. The most interesting case of the three is the Portuguese one where—let it be recalled—a young group of captains had launched a successful coup on 25 April 1974. Here, the process of achieving civilian control was gradual. It lasted about a decade (1976–86), and the analysis of the two indicators emphasizes it well. In 1979 the parliament was still attacked by an officer for refusing the proposed military budget, but since 1980 there is no longer a military officer as Minister of Defence. Since 1981 the president of the Republic is no longer the Chief of General Staff. After a basic constitutional revision approved in August (see above), on 30 October 1982 there was the last meeting, with some debate, of the Council of Revolution, the key body through which the soldier-authors of the new regime attempted to 'protect' their hybrid creature. In November 1982, the law of National Defence was eventually approved despite being vetoed by President Eanes, and civilian control was openly declared and shaped through it. The implementation of the law raised conflicts, but also accommodations, especially since 1983, and then civilian solutions. With the 1985 elections Eanes *de facto* accepted the civilianization of his political designs by forming a centrist movement, which received good results in those elections (see below). By 1986, with the election of the Socialist leader Mário Soares the president of the Republic is no longer a military officer.[42] As of now, the process of establishing civilian control is basically concluded. This list of episodes leaves out several aspects and events, such as the transformation of the size of the armed forces (from 282,000 people in 1974 to 83,000 six years later, and 63,000 in 1986) with a drastic reduction of the related budget (Graham 1993: 65 and 77) or the structuring of the Ministry of Defence at the end of the 1980s (ibid. 67–8). It, however, clearly gives a sense of civilianization of the regime.[43]

---

[42] A simple chronology of events, through the press, would suggest such a list. But at this point there is also a large literature that helps such a recollection. See e.g. Bruneau and Macleod (1986) and Graham (1993) among the best contributions on the topic.

[43] This is not the place in which to pay due attention to the explanation of the achieved civilian control over the army. However, if the agreements among the parties and the division inside the army are usually suggested, then the role played by moderate, democratic officers should be stressed. In other words, the belief in the legitimacy of the same structure they created deserves to be considered as a key aspect of explanation.

Although the same indicators are useful in Greece and Spain to see the civilianization of those two democracies, such a process is relatively shorter in both countries. It is basically explained by the crisis in Cyprus that accelerated the breakdown of the military regime in Greece, and the role of civil leaders in the Spanish transition from an authoritarianism where the army was already playing a secondary role, but also by the internal divisions of military vis-à-vis the popular and electoral support to civilianization and democracy.

In particular, in Greece military prerogatives were quickly eliminated and the potential and actual conflicts with the military became a way to establish civilian supremacy, skilfully affirmed by Karamanlis in a few years. The resolution of the parliament in January 1975, where the event of 21 April 1967, was simply declared an illegal *coup d'état*, was the first step in denying the future possibility of the army undertaking political initiatives; the constitution of June 1975 formally states that the president of the Republic is the commander-in-chief of the armed forces, but the real command is in the hands of the prime minister and the Minister of Defence; the key law of 1977 eliminated the post of chief of the armed forces and created the Supreme Council of National Defence, chaired by the prime minister, with five cabinet members and the Chief of Defence Staff, with the actual responsibility for defence policy and the appointments of top officers; the reform of the military academy and the elimination of background investigations to enter the army came with the PASOK government in the early 1980s, when civilian supremacy is already clearly affirmed.

There is virtually no conflict surrounding the budget, in percentage the highest among all NATO allies, not only among the four Southern European countries,[44] and both Karamanlis and Papandreu, prime minister and Minister of Defence in 1981, were very sensitive to the professional demands of the military, and maintained their sympathies by pursuing a nationalist foreign policy. But deeper clashes took place between 1974 and 1976 when Karamanlis, always protecting the military from open and harsh criticism, was able to remove the tank units from Athens in August 1974; and later on, when he (1) reshuffled the top officers, by appointing loyal officers in the different armed forces (also security forces); (2) dismissed or compelled to resignation and retirement most of those involved in the previous military regime;

[44] For example the military budget as a percentage of GDP is 7.1 in 1985 against 6.6 in the USA (see Stepan 1988: 78–9). Such a high budget is accounted for by the continuous international tensions with Turkey and, later, also along the northern border with the new independent state, Macedonia, resulting from the break-up of the old Yugoslavia. The whole set of data on military expenditure during these years may be seen in the official statistics published in *World Military Expenditures and Arms Transfers* (various years).

(3) defeated the coup attempts, even the most serious one in February 1975 with about forty officers involved; and above all (4) initiated criminal prosecution against the Junta military leaders, who were arrested and sentenced to death, later changed to life imprisonment, in August 1975, and concluded several trials concerning torture. Other important trials were concluded with prison sentences during 1975–6.[45] It may be added that the neutralization of the army also had other characteristics to gain some extent of consensus even among the army officers not so close to the new government: particularly, programmes of retirement allowances, medical care and housing must be recalled.

In Spain the establishment of civilian supremacy is characterized by initial ambiguity[46] and later reactions to the decision of eliminating military prerogatives. Thus, in spite of the caution of civilian leaders, and particularly of every government up to González (see above), contestations are not avoided, and the sub-process is only basically concluded in 1984. As pointed out by Agüero (1995: 127 ff.), during the transition and the democratic installation at least four governmental decisions on the Ley para la Reforma Política (1976), the legalization of unions (1976), the legalization of the Communist Party (1977), and the *estado de las autonomías* recognized by the constitution (1978), brought about military reactions, such as resignations, strong antigovernmental declarations, several unpunished manifestations of officer misbehaviour, and more covert pressures on the government.

At the same time there were a few steps to limit, if not to eliminate, army prerogatives. They mainly included: (1) a decree to set rules and limits to the syndical and political activity of members of armed forces on active duty (February 1977); (2) the creation of a Ministry of Defence with the elimination of the three previous ministries of the three armed forces (July 1977); (3) the attempts of Gutiérrez Mellado to reorganize the armed forces (1977–9); (4) the reorganization of the eleven intelligence services existing during the Franco regime (November 1977); (5) the distinction set up in the constitution between armed forces and

[45] Of course, Karamanlis was enormously helped and supported by many people, and particularly by the relatives of the victims of torture and murder or disappearance. They also denounced to the judges the officers involved, bringing them to initiate criminal prosecution and compelling Karamanlis to act accordingly against the Junta leaders. The most important trials, broadcast by television, had a very strong delegitimating impact on the military and additionally helped the firm establishment of civilian supremacy. For details on this, see among others Psomiades (1982), Danopoulos (1984), and Veremis (1987).

[46] At the beginning there is such an ambiguity because the army with its presence in the previous regime takes a position of 'wait and see'. Later on, faced with the negative reactions to governmental decisions, the ambiguity is the result of the governmental decision by Suarez to postpone the more definite elimination of prerogatives and civilian control. See also below in the text.

police, with separate tasks in keeping public order (1978); (6) the Reform of Code of Military Justice in November 1978, but implemented almost two years later; (7) for the first time since 1936 the appointment of a civilian leader to the Ministry of Defence (April 1979); and (8) at least two other important laws (1978 and 1980) to restructure the organization of the armed forces and its independence from the government, with the additional creation of a Junta de Defensa Nacional and a Junta de Jefes de Estado Major.[47]

Despite the cautious attention of Suárez, the great capabilities of his minister, Gutiérrez Mellado, and the key positive role performed by King Juan Carlos to secure the loyalty of armed forces, military discontent and the occasions of contestation increased, also partly because of terrorist activities, the related issue of autonomy in the Basque Country and Catalonia, economic problems, and the divisions inside the governmental incumbent party, the Unión de Centro Democrático (UCD). A few conspiracies were revealed, such as the Jativa conspiracy (1977), the Operation Galaxia (1978), and another plot in 1979. Thus, the well-known coup attempt by Colonel Tejero (23 February 1981) came as no surprise amidst a governmental crisis (see Table 2.2): during those months, even the military press debated the reasons and possibilities of military intervention. The counter-intervention of the king, the cohesive civilian reaction, and divisions within the armed forces were at the roots of that failure. But military discontent, lack of discipline, and conspiratorial activities continued. During 1981–2 the new Calvo Sotelo cabinet took other initiatives to limit military prerogatives and to establish civilian supremacy: (1) the appointment of civilians to various offices in the Ministry of Defence, and for the first time a civilian Under-Secretary of Defence; (2) a law on the criteria of development and planning of the armed forces; (3) another law on retirement and new mechanisms for career development; (4) the reorganization of the Military Intelligence Service; and (5) the formal statement against the sentence that condemned Tejero and others, stating that a civil court should have the last word on important crimes such as the attempted coup of 1981. However, civil control was largely achieved when, after the large Socialist victory of October 1982, the Ministry of Defence was again reorganized in 1984 with the transformation of the Junta de Jefes de Estado Major into an advisory council and the creation of the chief of the joint chiefs of staff, a post directly

[47] The first Council was chaired by the king, and formed by the prime minister, the Minister of Defence, seven other ministers, and the components of the second Council. The Junta de Jefes took a much greater importance than expected and became a powerful channel for military demands, actually working against civilian supremacy. See Agüero 1995: 251–9.

subordinate to the Minister of Defence. The Socialist government also carried out a policy of modernizing the armed forces, reducing military on active duty, cutting the budget and also improving living conditions as well as other decrees to implement the 1984 reform. Other important decisions were made in 1986–9 regarding the modernization of the army, additional reduction of personnel on active duty, and criteria for career advancement.[48] As noted, however, by 1984–5 civilian supremacy had been basically established.

Finally, on this issue one additional observation is worth stressing. In all three countries the process of civilianization had a noteworthy acceleration immediately after a failed *coup d'état*: this happened in Spain after 23 February 1981; in Portugal, especially after 25 November 1976; and in Greece, after 24 February 1975. That is, in a situation of initial, growing civil control of the political arena, the *coup d'état* provoked strong, immediately negative reactions by party élites as well as a unification of those élites to cope with the military threat. At the same time, it revealed the poor organization of those attempts, mainly because of the division in the army, part of which even reacted negatively and stepped in support of civilian leaders. Thus, it is not difficult to explain why that attempt accelerated the mentioned process of civilianization.

Political role of the judiciary

This dimension can only really be relevant when crisis is analysed. As for consolidation, it is enough to mention a pattern that already exists in our countries, and was characterized by no distinct political role for the judiciary. For crisis the point is much more relevant. To overcome a debate that often seems to be deadlocked, on the politicization of the judiciary and the general political function of judges[49] I will first provide a few theoretical clarifications.

The recent phenomenon of the judicialization of politics has been rightly emphasized (see e.g. Vallinder 1994 and Tate and Vallinder 1995), but for the purposes of this analysis I will only consider the specific political role of the judiciary. This is the role that is relevant for democratic crisis, which is more precisely a crisis of a specific democratic arrangement, and not of democracy *per se* (see Chapter 1). Such a role stands out clearly when a judiciary decision has an apparent

[48] For other data, analysis of the legislation, and different detailed comments see, in addition to Agüero (1995, esp. 340 ff.), the special issue on the military of *Revista Española de Investigaciones Sociológicas* (36: 1986) and Bañón Martínez and Barker (1988).

[49] See especially Morisi (1994). Of course, it is on purpose that such a debate mainly unfolded in Italy. See below in the text and Righettini (1995).

impact on interest representation, party competition, and the actual functioning of institutions.[50] Such an impact should be empirically detected: in fact, the same decision by either a prosecutor or a judge may or may not have political impact: above all, if a potential political decision takes place in a context of destabilization and destructuring of representative relationships, then it has that impact; if it is the opposite, the potentiality is not transferred in actual political influence. As Huntington (1968: 194) sagaciously put it when analysing military involvement in politics, the reasons are political rather than military. Likewise, the reason for a political role of the judiciary is primarily political. If correctly rephrased and obviously discarding a parallelism with the supremacy of civil powers,[51] the same indicators of military political involvement can be adopted (see above). Thus, first, there is the emergence of judicial prerogatives when the institution, or part of it, plays a role openly and clearly outside the existing laws, often with open invasion of other's competencies, and with its decisions it influences the relationships among the state, intermediate structures—mainly parties—and society. Such a role may emerge without the clear, declared intention by a judge. Second, contestations between the other political institutions and the judicial sector emerge.

Because of the doubts and uncertainties that such an indicator may eventually leave open, (i) the privileged sector where it can be fruitfully applied concerns the inquiries regarding political corruption; and (ii) an additional, sound rule is to complement this analysis with that of other, different indicators of crisis. Concerning corruption, despite many inquiries on this matter that are recurring in Spain, Greece, and Italy (see Heywood 1995*a* and 1995*b*, Koutsoukis 1995, Partridge 1995, and Della Porta and Vannucci 1994), in the last country the indicators of such a political role are more clearly detected. In particular, between 1992 and 1994, but also later on, several judiciary inquiries, such as the well-known 'Mani Pulite' ('Clean Hands'), had a direct impact on the political arena up to the point of eliminating from political competition a party, such as the Socialist Party,[52] and several national political leaders. The conflicts between institutions and the judiciary took place on several occasions, such as, for example, in 1992 between the president of the Republic and the Supreme Council of the Magistracy,

[50] On the necessary distinction between a general political role performed by every judiciary and the specific role that is relevant in a democratic crisis see also Cazzola and Morisi (1996: 9–13).

[51] On the contrary, the tradition of independence of the judiciary in the European legal systems is well known (see Guarnieri 1992). Even in Spain Pinkele (1992) shows the existence of some room for independence, which became relevant in the following change of regime.

[52] On this see the section of Ch. 6 on the Italian crisis.

or in 1994 between Prime Minister Berlusconi and the Milanese prosecutors of 'Mani Pulite', or in 1996 between the Roman prosecutors and the Milanese ones.

Though to a lesser extent, in Spain and Greece the inquiries on corruption had a political impact, if for no other reasons than because of its presence in newspaper headlines. From 1990 to 1996, Spanish Socialist leaders have been involved in a series of investigations, such as the Juan Guerra case, the Grupos Antiterroristas de Liberación (GAL) affair, the Roldán case, and several other cases of illegal fraud or bribes. In Greece a few inquiries have had a political impact at least since 1987, with the 'corn case' involving a Socialist Deputy Minister of Finance, and in 1988 with the Koskotas case that concerned even the prime minister and the charismatic leader of PASOK, Papandreu, and other ministers of his cabinet, as well as in several other cases where another prime minister, Mitsotakis, and a number of politicians were prosecuted (see Chapters 6 and 7). At this point, to a lower extent in comparison with Italy, but more than in Spain, scandals and inquiries had become a common, recurring theme of party competition with an unavoidable political utilization of magistrates, with several conflictual episodes taking place between politicians and prosecutors.

Establishment, adaptation, or change of the 'rules of the game'

If according to the political tradition of the country the electoral system is considered as a 'rule of the game',[53] then the change or even a simple and partial adaptation of that system may be an indicator of crisis. Conversely, a system that goes on unmodified for decades points to the opposite reality, consolidation, or at least maintenance. When, on the contrary, the electoral system is a 'rule of government',[54] then its change is not a salient indicator for any of the processes under scrutiny. This point can be well analysed by looking at Italy vis-à-vis Greece, rather than at the other two countries, where, as in Italy, the electoral system appears to be a rule of the game, but unlike Italy there is no basic change and only marginal aspects are added or changed.

In Italy, there has been for decades a highly proportional electoral system that has definitely been considered a basic rule of the game, especially since the early 1950s when an attempt by the Christian Democratic government to change it into a more majoritarian system

---

[53] This term simply means a rule that refers to 'how the electoral or institutional game is played,' and as such it is recognized by everyone and *de jure* or *de facto* is also not possible to change it without large agreement.

[54] That is, the country has a tradition of changing the electoral law with the purpose of manipulating the likely results according to the interests of the government.

with the addition of a majority premium, was defeated by the mobilization of the entire left and centre-left parties and opinion. In spite of being a simple provision to provide more stability to cabinets, since then that attempt became well known as 'legge truffa' or 'swindle law', as the propaganda of the opposition labelled it, and the electoral system definitely remained a rule of the game. Thus, only a referendum, with its powerful direct appeal to a discontented electorate, was able to change the electoral system in a partially majoritarian direction. More precisely, the referendum of April 1993 approved the omission of few key lines in the existing electoral law. As a consequence the law changed its way of working and the parliament was compelled to approve new electoral laws for the Lower Chamber and Senate in early August of the same year.[55] In March 1993 the electoral laws for local elections were also changed.[56] In different, complex ways all these laws are mixed, and particularly those at the national level are only partially majoritarian.[57]

[55] It may be recalled that in spite of the opposite indications of some governmental party a previous referendum of June 1991 had approved the abolition of casting more than one preference vote on the electoral ballot, changing in this way a fairly important aspect of Italian proportional representation.

[56] The new law created a system consisting of single-member constituencies, within which a majority is required for election. If no candidate in an electoral district receives a majority, a run-off election is held between the two candidates receiving the most votes on the first round. In municipalities with over 15,000 inhabitants, the new system also provided for direct election of the mayor. The result was a drastic and immediate shift towards a bipolar distribution of mayors in various towns and of seats in municipal councils.

[57] In contrast with the relatively pure proportional representation system used over the preceding four decades, the new law allocates three-quarters of the seats in both houses on the basis of a plurality (single-member) electoral system. The remaining quarter of the seats are allocated on the basis of proportional representation to partly compensate those parties which have not received representation on the first (plurality) segment. In Senate elections the voter has one vote to cast, and a party that elects a senator through the single member/majority segment of the ballot has the votes that were cast for its victorious candidate subtracted from its total in the calculations of seats to be allocated in the proportional representation segment. In elections for the Chamber of Deputies the voter has two votes: one for the single-member district and another for the proportional list at the constituency level. In calculating the seats to be allocated to each party, the votes cast for the proportional representation lists are considered and the votes received by the second place candidate in the single-member constituency are subtracted from the total of the proportional votes won by the party of the candidate who has gained the seat in the single-member constituency. The remainder following this subtraction is the basis upon which the allocation of the proportional representation seats is calculated. In addition to the majoritarian biases inherent in all single-member district systems, a 4 per cent minimum nationwide vote is established by law as a prerequisite for receiving representation through the PR segment for the Chamber of Deputies; for the Senate, there is no legal threshold, but since the allocation of PR seats is calculated at the regional level, there is a *de facto* threshold of about 10 per cent (actually, it can be either much lower or much higher) of votes cast for receiving PR seats. The proportional representation segment of the vote softens the impact of the plurality system somewhat.

In Greece since 1922 it is a rare exception to find an election run under the same electoral system.[58] In addition, the system adopted by Karamanlis in 1974, a so-called 'reinforced' proportional system, which was very similar to the previous system existing before the authoritarian parenthesis (1967–74),[59] was debated by the opposition. Before the elections of 1977 and 1981, two decrees marginally changed the previous law;[60] a law of 1982 repealed the vote of preference, again reinserted in 1989; in 1985 a new electoral law was approved with the repeal of the high threshold existing up to that year;[61] and in 1989 still another law was approved with 288 seats allocated through (*a*) a first distribution reflecting votes won in each of fifty-six differently sized constituencies; and (*b*) a second distribution reflecting residual votes pooled together in thirteen major constituencies.[62] In 1993 another law reverts the situation back to 1985, by (*a*) changing a basic feature for the calculus of the second distribution, no longer on the basis of residual votes, but again on the basis of all votes—that is, a majoritarian drive is again introduced; (*b*) setting for the first time a new nationwide threshold of 3 per cent to be allowed to participate in the first allocation of seats; and (*c*) giving an advantage to the third party against the second one in the final proportional allocation of seats.[63] On the whole, Greek governments accepted the Hagenbach-Bischoff formula, but its tradition of the electoral system as a rule of government is strongly reaffirmed by all the adaptations approved in more than twenty years.

Thus, the Italian change is a limited transformation toward a majoritarian system, while the Greek ones indicate the adaptation of a sys-

[58] On Greek electoral history see Clogg (1987).

[59] Both the systems applied the formula of Hagenbach and Bischoff. The main aspect of it is the proportional allocation of seats in two or three different distributions. The basic difference between the two systems was the threshold to be admitted to the second distribution of seats for a single party (17% in 1974 against 15% in 1964).

[60] See, on the electoral rules of the 1974 and 1977 elections, Vegleris (1981: 21–48); on those of 1981 Clogg (1983: 190–208).

[61] See the previous note. For details on the 1985 electoral law, see Perifanaki Rotolo (1985: 669–85).

[62] The remaining 12 (non-constituency) seats are the so-called 'state deputies' and, since 1974, are distributed between parties in direct proportion to their total votes nationwide. As with the 1985 law, there is a very low threshold for participating in the second distribution (at least more than 1%) to get 1 seat; the constituencies remain 56:5 single-member districts, 33 with 2–5 seats, 15 with 6–9 seats, 3 with 21 (Athens central), 32 (Athens suburban), and 12 (Thessaloniki) seats. In contrast to the previous 1985 law, there was no third distribution of seats and the major constituencies were no longer 9, but 13. For details on this law see Perifanaki Rotolo (1990, 143–65). The key meaning of the changes are to get a higher degree of proportionality to allow third parties to be in the Voulì.

[63] The main purpose of the law was to bar from parliament the Muslim minority or minorities with locally rooted votes and put a difference between the first and the second party, also by giving room to the third party. I would like to thank very much Prof. Ilias Nicolacopoulos for introducing me to the intricacies of this law.

tem that is already a majoritarian one in a stronger or weaker direction. In this sense, in the Italian politico-institutional context the changes of electoral rules clearly point to the strong will of the electorate (and élites, as well) to change a key rule of the game, and in this sense it is an important indicator of crisis, especially if complemented by other indicators. In Greece the opposite is the case and the continuous adaptation of the system has no meaning in terms of consolidation and crisis, even if one of the most important changes is introduced in a year such as 1989 when other institutional indicators point to a manifestation of crisis. The objective meaning of the changes/adaptations is to maintain the electoral system as a rule of the government, rather than a rule of the game, shared by everyone.

International alignments

Even in the external-internal linkages a process of consolidation or one of crisis can be seen. With consolidation, the first useful indicator is simply the negotiation and conclusion of international agreements: the same process of establishing open and formal international links consolidate already existing relationships, largely because of the participation at different levels in the formulation of successful agreements and to related decisional bodies. Thus, for Italy between the end of the 1940s and the 1950s there is participation in the NATO alliance and the creation of the European Community with five other European countries; for Spain, Portugal, and Greece there is the change from a position of international isolation or semi-isolation to specific, strong alliances: for Spain, the adherence to NATO in 1985, through a referendum, and the accession to the EC in 1986 after a long period of bargaining; for Portugal, already in NATO, the accession to the EC in 1986, also after a long phase of negotiation; for Greece, again in NATO since 1981, an immediate request of entry into the EC in June 1975, the conclusion of negotiations in 1979 and entry in January 1981.[64] Therefore, on the whole, 1956, 1986, 1981, and 1986 are the years when the international alignments are established respectively in Italy, Spain, Portugal, and Greece.

A second, also important, indicator is the development of formal or informal networks and interests around those international alignments. Networks and related interests actually strengthen them. More precisely, the relationships between the national government or regional governments and the European institutions, the transnational or foreign, but European, interest groups and the national

[64] On the accession of the Southern European countries to the EC see the two excellent articles by Pridham (1991) and Whitehead (1991).

ones, or even transnational parties and partisan élites, who are present in the European Parliament, and the national or regional party élites, the relationships between the NATO officers and the army officers of the country, all of these are some of the established networks that give strength to international alignments. More specifically, the substantial financial aid going to the agricultural sector in the four countries is one example of such a network: at this point most large, medium, and small landowners would be unable to survive without the large repertoire of financial support in all sectors of agriculture coming from Brussels. In this sense strong links are established for years to come. Above all, this second indicator—perhaps more salient than the first one as the aim is to trace consolidation—does not indicate a definite moment when those networks and links are firmly established. Three to four years after accession to the EC seems to be the right time to establish those relationships, when all the facets of belonging to the EC have unfolded their consequences for the government, the bureaucracy, the associations of interests, the parties, and the people who receive advantages from the European financial aid system.[65]

For Southern European countries, there is no trace of possible changes in these international alignments, and in this sense there is no indicator of crisis. However, some malaise or uneasiness emerges because of the constraints that being in Europe puts on economic policies. In all four countries, but particularly in Italy, in the mid-1990s some leaders and political forces made cold or even negative declarations on the problems caused by belonging to the European Community, and particularly the constraints set up to enter the group on the new single currency. Likewise, those constraints and the expected consequent policies are also felt by people in these countries. At the same time, for other politicians and citizens such external constraints are the best guarantee of healthier economic policies. Thus, eventually no one dares to cast serious doubts on the international alignments of the four countries.

Table 2.10 summarizes the main indicators of institutional consolidation and the years when the related patterns seem to be established. They are retrospective indicators as only in the following years is it possible to affirm with reasonable empirical confidence that the suggested patterns were effectively established at the different levels. Furthermore, mentioning the timing of these more specific processes is a largely approximate exercise, which only tries to grasp the core aspects. It is, however, a necessary one in terms of defining more pre-

---

[65] On the impact of the entry of Southern Europe in the EC, and indirectly on the framework and interests created, see Francioni (1992), Almarcha Barbado (1993), Da Silva Lopes (1993), and Theofanides (1989).

TABLE 2.10. *Consolidation: the institutional domain*

	Italy	Spain	Greece	Portugal
Head of state: role adaptation	no	no	1986	1982
Cabinet: pattern establishment	1953	1982	1974–6	1981
Executive/legislative patterns	1958	1982	1974–6	1981
Establishment of local powers	1975	1985	no	no
Civilianization of army	no	1984	1981	1986
Settlements of international alignments	1956	1986	1981	1986

cisely the units of analysis along the time dimension, a decisive feature when a process is analysed. In the case of Italy three main indicators put the *terminus ad quem* of consolidation at the end of the 1950s by also showing that giving a precise date would be incorrect. At the same time, Table 2.10 shows that essential characteristics of Italian politics, such as the regions, were implemented in 1970, but established with their basic features in the middle of that decade. For Spain, the main point of arrival of consolidation is the mid-1980s if the civilianization of the army is stressed, as implied by the proposed definition of democracy (see Chapter 1). At the same time, when the local powers are considered, it may be pointed out that the basic aspects of Spanish decentralization are settled in 1985, but the process is really never concluded in the remaining decade (and it even seemed to be set in motion again, and a new, stronger decentralization was achieved after 1993). As for Italy, 1986 for the settlements of Spanish international alignments also gives a simple indication. In the same vein, for Greece the end of core consolidation is 1981, and the relationships between legislative and executive power and those of cabinet duration were immediately established, lasted until the beginning of 1989, and resumed as before at the end of 1990 (see also Table 2.11). In Portugal the *terminus ad quem* is 1986 with the civilianization of the army. This year and the following one is the key moment for consolidation as also the executive/legislative patterns, established in 1981, became even stronger in 1987.

The institutional indicators of crisis point to the years or phase when the suggested phenomena emerge and continue (Table 2.11). In this vein, for Spain and Greece two moments of crisis are detected during the consolidation process and later. They are respectively 1979–81 and 1989–90, and they are overcome later on. But in Spain the process of consolidation was not concluded yet, whereas in Greece it was basically so. Thus, in Greece, after a few years from the end of core consolidation

TABLE 2.11. *Crisis: the institutional domain*

	Italy	Spain	Greece	Portugal
Head of state: exceptional intervention	1992–6	1981	1989–90	1978–80
Cabinet: pattern change	no	no	1989–90	no
Executive/legislative patterns: change	1994–6	no	1989–90	no
Politization of army	no	1979–81	no	no
Change of electoral system	1993	no	no	no
Political impact of judiciary	1992–6	1990–6	1987–95	no
Changes of international alignments	no	no	no	no

there are distinctive signs of crisis, and in Spain only some political impact of the judiciary points to some phenomenon of this sort. A deeper crisis only emerges in Italy in 1992–6 with three indicators that point in that direction. On the whole, however, the institutional indicators are largely inadequate to detect and describe the processes of consolidation and even more so of crisis in the four countries. Other indicators are needed. At the same time the information given up to now does not allow one to reach more precise conclusions on the kind of democracies that are consolidated and may fall in a critical situation.

The Electoral Domain

Within this domain the phenomenon of anticipated elections cannot be fully included among the acceptable indicators of crisis. Such elections may take place in moments of crisis and deep conflict, but also for other reasons.[66] In fact, in our countries holding an election before the term has expired is a recurring phenomenon, but the reasons usually are other than an impending crisis: in Italy since 1976[67] there have been six anticipated elections out of seven; in Spain, since 1982, three out of five; in Portugal, since 1979, five out of seven; and in Greece, since 1977, five out of eight.[68] Moreover, during the last twenty years in Italy anticipated elections were not held only in 1992, and that is when seri-

[66] Such as the simple strategic calculus of the incumbent party or coalitions or some extent of partisan conflict that, however, cannot be defined as critical.

[67] That is, since the first anticipated elections.

[68] More precisely, in Italy the elections were anticipated in 1976, 1979, 1983, 1987, 1994, and 1996. The other anticipated elections are: for Spain in 1982, 1989, and 1996 (but not in 1979 when the elections were anticipated because of the obvious dissolution of the Constituent Assembly); for Portugal, 1979, 1980, 1983, 1985, 1987 (again not in 1976 for the same reason as Spain); for Greece, in 1977, November 1989 (in June of that year another inconclusive election was held), 1990, 1993, and 1996.

ous aspects of crisis had already openly emerged (see the previous section, esp. Table 2.11, and below).

This indicator, however, can be partially used when elections are very close to one another. This is the case in Greece with three elections in less than two years (in June and November 1989 and in April 1990); but also of Italy with three elections in four years (1992, 1994, and 1996); Portugal with two elections in two years (1979–80) and later three elections in four years (1983, 1985, and 1987). Even in this sense, however, this is an indicator to complement the other ones. Besides, the opposite situation, that is, elections held at the right time, cannot be included among the indications of consolidation for obvious reasons: recall Italy in 1992 and a situation of stalemate that brings the legislature to its 'natural end', but actually a crisis is going on.

Although not exhaustive, the analysis of three other aspects appears best suited to see if and when important components of the four Southern European democracies became established or entered a crisis. They are the stabilization or destabilization of electoral behaviour, the identification of patterns of party competition or its change, and the stabilization or destabilization of the leadership. These features give at least a first picture of relationships between parties and civil society.

Electoral stabilization involves the establishment of relationships between parties and the public and among the parties themselves. Following the initial phase of democratic installation, which is most commonly accompanied by considerable fluidity, mass behaviour may begin to follow more predictable and recurring patterns. In an opposite way, a phase of discontent and malaise, and detachment from present leaders and parties, may result in a change of those patterns with a higher fluidity. The key indicator of stabilization/destabilization in voting behaviour is *total electoral volatility* (TEV) (see Bartolini 1986, and Bartolini and Mair 1990). To this another qualitative indicator can be added only for consolidation, namely, *critical elections* (see Key 1955). As the stabilization or its opposite proceeds, a trend of declining or increasing volatility is expected: there will be a progressive shift from high electoral fluidity and uncertainty to more predictable patterns of voting behaviour, or vice versa. In addition, when critical elections occur there is a realignment of voting patterns, but also a relative freezing of those alignments.

In the case of consolidation, the decline of TEV and critical elections indicates that party–voter relationships have become more stable; that parties have established definite images; that the range of effective electoral competition is restricted to only some sectors of the electorate; and that a possible party system crisis is unlikely. In the case of crisis, the growth of TEV suggests that party–voter relationships are more uncertain, unstable, and in some cases changing; that parties are losing their appeal vis-à-vis the voters and that new actors are likely to emerge. In other words, the presence of these phenomena indicate either that a more stable party system is emerging or emerged or, on the contrary, that the party system is moving towards electoral destabilization or is already unstable. Let it also be stressed that the importance of these indicators lies in the possibility of building time-series and explicating the trends of the processes to be analysed.

Electoral volatility

Although it is not a particularly sensitive measure,[69] Figure 2.1 shows very neatly when there is higher fluidity, the phase during which voting behaviour is basically stabilized and the point at which the growth of voting instability begins. The most puzzling case in this regard is Portugal, the only country with no previous experience of mass democracy. The average TEV score between 1975 and 1983 was only 11 per cent, even after excluding the 1980 election, held a few months after the election of 1979. If the 1980 election had been included, the average TEV would have been even lower, but with a less consistent trend. With the elections of 1985, 1987, and 1995, however, there was a substantial increase in TEV, but also a basic restructuring of the party system (see Figure 2.1 and below). To place these figures in comparative perspective, it will suffice to note that the average TEV for all Western European democracies over the past decade was 9.2. Accordingly, the Portuguese figures were close to the average of consolidated countries over its first eight years of electoral competition. The most reasonable explanation for this paradox seems to be that until the early 1980s parties were not the main actors: the game of politics was also played in other arenas, and neutralization of the military had not yet taken place (see above and Table 2.10).

The other three Southern European countries are more convincing in terms of a steady decline of TEV in the first years subsequent to installation and of a later increase in it. Thus, Italy shows the clearest declining trend during the 1950s[70] with subsequent stabilization up to the

[69] There are also a few other measures of volatility, such as area volatility or interblock volatility and major parties volatility, that complement TEV and help to achieve a more precise appreciation of the phenomenon of the aggregate vote instability. See Bartolini and Mair (1990), and how all these measures were applied to Italy in Morlino (1984).

[70] It may be worth stressing that during the same decade in France there is the opposite trend and in 1958 the crisis and change to the Fifth Republic. TEV are the following: 5.7 (1946), 20.0 (1951), 20.2 (1956), 26.2 (1962), but 19.2 in 1962 and 4.0 in 1967 (Bartolini and Mair 1990, Appendix).

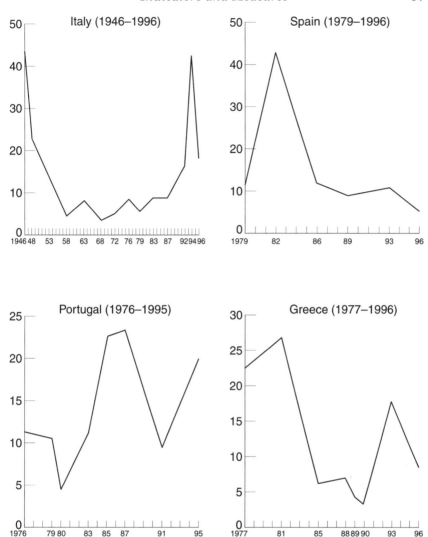

FIG. 2.1. *Trends in total electoral volatility*

Notes: The total electoral volatility is the sum of the absolute value of all changes in the percentages of votes cast for each party since the previous election, divided by two. This figure also refers to the last pre-fascist election in 1992. Two elections were held in 1989, one in June and the other in November.

Source: My calculations based on official data.

1990s, when there is an enormous increase to 16.2 (1992) and 41.9 (1994), and then again a sharp decline (17.7 in 1996). Spain and Greece had an upsurge of TEV in their third elections, in 1982 (42.3) and 1981 (26.7) respectively. That is seven or eight years after the beginning of the transition. In both countries the stabilizing trend is very apparent, and in Greece Figure 2.1 also reveals the opposite trend of higher fluidity after 1990 (17.7 in 1993).

TABLE 2.12. *Trends in inter-block volatility*[a]

	Italy		Italy	Spain	Portugal	Greece
1946		1972	1.1			
1947		1973				
1948	12.9	1974				
1949		1975				
1950		1976	5.4		6.6	
1951		1977				13.7
1952		1978				
1953	4.6	1979	0.7	1.0	3.2	
1954		1980			1.7	
1955		1981				23.5
1956		1982		7.4		
1957		1983	0.3		7.8	
1958	1.0	1984				
1959		1985			0.5	3.4
1960		1986		2.6		
1961		1987	1.1		15.5	
1962		1988				
1963	1.3	1989		1.7		4.7/0.5[b]
1964		1990				2.2
1965		1991			1.2	
1966		1992	5.2			
1967		1993		1.7		4.2
1968	1.4	1994	5.8			
1969		1995			13.8	
1970		1996	6.6	0.9		2.7
1971		1997				

Notes: [a] Inter-block volatility, or area volatility, is the sum of the absolute value of the difference between the percentages of votes cast for the right and centre (as one bloc) and the left, divided by two.   [b] Two elections were held in 1989, one in June and the other in November.

Source: My calculations based on official data.

Critical elections

This indicator complements the previous one on consolidation, but not on crisis: it can better display the stabilization of party alignments, rather than their change and destructuration. In fact, a critical election that inaugurates a phase of new, higher fluidity seems empirically more difficult to determine and, above all, does not necessarily imply an effective crisis of relationships between parties and civil society. The data on TEV presented in Figure 2.1 suggest that critical elections occurred in Italy in 1948, in Spain in 1982, and in Greece in 1981. These realignments are reflected in peak TEV scores in those years, followed by a marked decline. In Portugal, an electoral realignment occurred quite late in 1987, and is likely to have recurred in 1995. The dominant position achieved by the Social Democrats in 1987 was solidified by an equally impressive victory in 1991, but removed by the result of 1995 and the partial Socialist victory with its large plurality.

A second way of identifying critical elections is to analyse the inter-block volatility (I-BV) or area volatility (AV). If the salience of the left–right cleavage is taken for granted in all four countries, this is a good way to count the percentage of voters shifting across the divide between the left or centre-left and the centre-right or right. Table 2.12 presents data relating to this shift. It confirms that realigning or critical elections occurred in Italy in 1948, Spain in 1982, Greece in 1981, and Portugal in 1987 and 1995, particularly insofar as the highest I-BV scores were produced in the same years as the peak TEV scores.

The extent to which the 1987 election had a lasting impact in realigning the Portuguese electorate is confirmed by the extraordinarily low I-BV score produced by the next election, four years later. Prior to that critical election, Portuguese electoral politics was dominated by a few parties that managed to maintain their relative positions with the electorate despite high levels of governmental instability, frequent changes in party leadership, and even changes in some basic aspects of the democratic regime itself, including significant revisions in the constitution (see previous section). When President Eanes created the Democratic Renewal Party (PRD) in 1985, the electorate responded by giving it a surprising 18.5 per cent of the vote: latent discontent and protest had found a voice. It is most noteworthy, however, that in that year of high TEV (22.5), there was virtually no I-BV (0.5) (see Table 2.12). Eventually, the PRD proved to be a 'flash party'. Its electoral support fell to 5 per cent in 1987 and to 0.6 per cent in 1991. Given the high level of I-BV in 1987 (15.45 per cent, most of it from the centre-left to the centre-right) (see Table 2.12), a basic realignment of the party system occurred.[71]

The Spanish electorate has exhibited relatively high levels of TEV, with the critical elections of 1982 representing an enormous redistribution of voters among parties (42.3 per cent of TEV score), but extraordinarily low levels of I-BV: even in the party-system realignment of 1982, there were far fewer voters who crossed the divide between left and right (7.4 per cent) than in any of the other critical elections with lower TEV scores examined here (Italy: I-BV 12.9 per cent vs. TEV 22.8 per cent; Portugal: 15.5 per cent vs. 23.2 per cent; and Greece: 23.5 per cent vs. 26.7 per cent) (see Figure 2.1 and Table 2.12). Spanish voters may be prone to shifting their allegiances from one party to another, but such shifts occur almost exclusively within the boundaries of the various blocs, and this gave a special systemic stabilization of votes for a long time.

The opposite pattern emerges from an examination of comparable data for Greece. Virtually all of the total volatility manifested in the 1981 critical election was in the form of I-BV: with a TEV score of 26.7 per cent, only 3.2 per cent of these votes did not shift across the left–right cleavage. The explanation is largely mechanical and makes reference to the paucity of parties: given that most Greek voters cast their ballots for one of two parties, any substantial shift must involve moves from left to right, or vice versa. In the other countries, a shift of voting may take place within the right or left camps, without involving I-BV.

Party System

The third relevant domain concerns the establishment or destruction of definite patterns of partisan competition: the party system assumes or loses its main characteristics. The index of party fractionalization (PF), the 'effective' number of parties (ENP), in addition to the qualitative analysis of emergence or non-emergence of new parties and movements, of the number and size of parties, and to other systemic features, should provide the best available indicators to find out if patterns of competition among parties are established and may remain stable for some time or are changing.

---

[71] It may be recalled that from its beginning the PRD had not only a leftist component, but also a more moderate one.

Party fractionalization and 'effective number of parties'

An implicit rank ordering in terms of stabilization and destabilization of the party system is reflected in the index of party fractionalization. Following a decline in fragmentation in 1948 (from 0.79 to 0.66 in 1948) the configuration of the Italian party system remained stable at about 0.74/0.76 for about twenty years (1953–72) (see Table 2.13). Later on, the index declined and grew again, but it jumped in 1992–6. In Greece, the index has been relatively frozen around 0.61/0.63 since 1981, with a 0.60 only in November 1989 for the second election in the same year, and a curious jump in 1996 (0.67). Spain and Portugal have had ups

TABLE 2.13. *Index of party fractionalization*[a]

	Italy		Italy	Spain	Portugal	Greece
1946	0.79	1972	0.76			
1947		1973				
1948	0.66	1974				0.64
1949		1975			0.73	
1950		1976	0.72		0.75	
1951		1977		0.77		0.73
1952		1978				
1953	0.76	1979	0.74	0.76	0.69	
1954		1980			0.68	
1955		1981				0.63
1956		1982		0.66		
1957		1983	0.78		0.73	
1958	0.74	1984				
1959		1985			0.79	0.61
1960		1986		0.72		
1961		1987	0.78		0.66	
1962		1988				
1963	0.76	1989		0.75		0.63/.60[b]
1964		1990				0.62
1965		1991			0.64	
1966		1992	0.85			
1967		1993		0.71		0.62
1968	0.75	1994	0.87			
1969		1995			0.68	
1970		1996	0.86	0.69		0.67
1971		1997				

Notes: [a] The index of party fractionalization was calculated using Rae's formula: $F = 1 - \sum_{i=1}^{n} p^2_i$ where p is the share of vote attained by each party in the elections.

[b] Two elections were held in 1989, one in June and the other in November.

Source: My calculations based on official data.

and downs, but, with some exceptions (ten points of difference in Spain between 1979 and 1982 and 13 points in Portugal between 1985 and 1987) the differences between one election and the subsequent one was relatively or very limited (4 to 1 point) (see Table 2.13).[72]

An analysis of the 'effective' number of parties (ENP) (Figure 2.2) suggests a similar picture: in Italy a relative freezing of the party system with strong growth since 1992; an even stronger stabilization in Greece thanks to a more manipulative electoral law with a growth to 2.4 in 1996; a recent stabilization in Portugal; but a lower degree of stabilization in Spain. In this country, the dramatic change of 1982 is mirrored in the lower number of parties (from 4.2 in 1979 to 2.9 in 1982). Later, in the second half of the decade, the situation becomes less unstable, but the difference with Italy or Greece is still evident. In Portugal the change of 1985 is recorded by this measure, and again there is a subsequent stabilization and a clear reduction in the number of parties in 1987, 1991, and 1995: from 4.2 to 2.2, 2.2, and 2.5.

No new parties and movements vs. their emergence

The usefulness of both indices is limited if they are not integrated by a qualitative analysis. The indices, in fact, mask differences among the countries and changes over time. The reference to new parties or movements also encompasses the possibility of party splits or party fusion, which should no longer occur in consolidation and on the contrary may often occur during crisis, and of course in the installation phase. Indeed, during installation of a new democratic regime a large number of new parties can be expected to present lists for the first one or two elections. At a certain point, however, at least the regime's electoral system should begin to contribute to party-system stabilization. To be sure, the differing electoral systems will have varying impacts on the prospects for the viability of new parties. In this vein a crucial variable affecting the extent of stabilization is the level of the threshold set by each electoral system. These diversities notwithstanding, there will be

[72] PF is calculated on the basis of votes received by each party. If the same calculus is done with reference to the seats (the seat fractionalization) and a difference is made with vote fractionalization, this is only useful to point out more clearly the impact of the electoral law, with particular regard to Greece. In fact, only in this country does a distinct impact emerge: the adaptation of the voting behaviour has a clearly decreasing trend. A stronger 'reinforced' PR brings about a declining gap between votes and seats. In all other cases the picture is basically the same as that suggested by Table 2.11. In Greece between 1974 and 1990 there is a consistent reduction of the difference among the two indexes: −18 (1974), −16 (1977), −11 (1981), −8 (1985), −4 (June 1989 and Nov. 1989), −4 (1990). This trend supports the hypothesis of the gradual adaptation of the electorate for a 'useful' vote. Of course, the index of seat fractionalization is lower than the other index because of the reductive impact of electoral law.

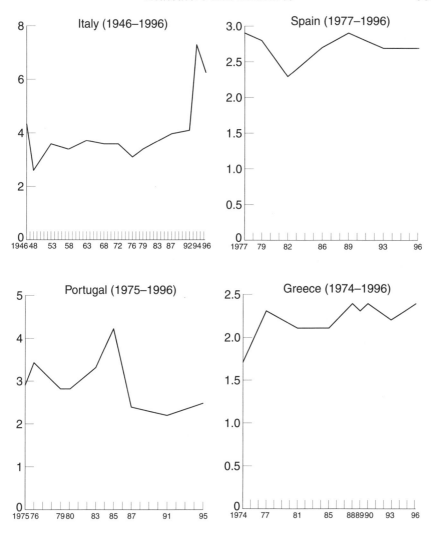

FIG. 2.2. *Effective number of parties*

Note: ENP is based on the formula suggested by Laakso and Taagepera (1979: 3–27):

$$N = 1/\sum_{i=1}^{n} p^2_i$$ where P_i is the proportion of seats of the *i*-th party.

Source: My calculations based on official data.

a clear difference between the first one or two elections, when hundreds of party lists are presented, and the subsequent electoral contests, when a process of natural selection has already begun, and a stable leadership, organization, identity, image, and programmatic commitments are also set up. The creation of new parties and movements becomes a more and more unusual event in all four countries.

Because of the low threshold and the high proportionality of Italian electoral law, the party system that first took shape in the second general election of 1948 was highly fragmented. A subsequent attempt was made by new parties to enter the electoral arena when in 1952–3 the Christian Democratic leadership tried to strengthen its position and win the majority of seats again, as in 1948, by changing the electoral law and imposing a majority premium (see above). But at the end of the decade the picture is stabilized and an extreme multipartism is established for decades.

The new party system of Portugal in the 1970s and early 1980s was characterized by limited multipartism, with a fairly strong, but gradually declining Communist Party. In the mid-1980s, however, a basic restructuring of the party system took place. As mentioned above, the change was actually initiated by an attempt to build a new party, the PRD, led by the former president, Ramalho Eanes. The failure of this attempt contributed to the triumph of the Social Democratic Party (PSD) in the 1987 elections: the absolute majority of parliamentary seats won by the PSD marked a shift to a predominant party system, which was maintained unchanged with the subsequent elections of 1991, when an absolute majority was again won, until 1995.

The party systems of Spain and Greece took shape quickly. In the Spanish case, however, the establishment of a dominant party (PSOE) since the 1982 election, until at least the 1993 election, left open a few features of the party system, such as the restructuring of the right after the breakdown of the centre party, the Unión de Centro Democrático, in 1981–2; and the uncertain role and establishment of regionalist parties and the internal divisions in the Communist Party, which split into three different parties during the 1980s (see below). That is, the stabilization of the system was not followed or anticipated by the stabilization of its components.

In Greece, the centre is the area that was eventually destroyed by the stabilization of a bipolar pattern of competition between Nea Dimokratia and the Socialist PASOK. But after the 1981 election, largely won by PASOK, a party system with a strong dominance of the incumbent party seems to be established for most of the decade up to the 1989 elections.

On the whole, the initial impact of the electoral threshold and the simple development of competition were to allow a few, definite parties to dominate the electoral and political arenas and to prevent the entrance of new forces for a few years or decades. The party systems achieved a definite structure of party competition, their own competitive logic, and some degree of stabilization. More serious problems remained at an intra-party level in each country, and above all in

Spain, while such a process can always be interrupted and reversed because of change of some basic aspect, such as partial crises and deliberate action by party leaders. In Portugal the rightist Democratic Social Centre (CDS) went through a reshaping and changed its name to the Popular Party between its 11th Conference in January 1993 and the 13th in February 1995. In Greece the dominance of PASOK had waned since the end of the 1980s, as reflected by the three elections in 1989–90, but there was also a split in Nea Dimokratia and the formation of Political Spring (POLAN) in 1993,[73] because of serious disagreements with the external and domestic policies of the Mitsotakis cabinet; another split in PASOK in 1995 with the formation of the Democratic Social Movement (DIKKI), which gained 4.4 per cent and 9 seats in the 1996 election; and an even division in the extreme left between Communists and Synaspismos with the mutual autonomization. As a result, PASOK was voted back into power after the election of October 1993, characterized by a high TEV score (17.7) (see Figure 2.1), but it also won the 1996 election despite the split that affected it and the formation of DIKKI. This also confirms the intra-party divisions and problems that were present in those years. However, after 1989 the alternation seems to become a key aspect of Greek democracy, which brings about innovation vis-à-vis the previous decade of PASOK rule.

In spite of name changes, reshaping, and splits, in the three countries a change of the party system from a dominant party system to a limited bipolar multipartism was not anticipated—or followed—by a change in the main parties: AP-PP and PSOE in Spain, Social Democrats and Socialists in Portugal, and PASOK and Nea Dimokratia in Greece are still the principal actors in the political arena at the end of the 1990s.

The opposite situation emerged in Italy in the early 1990s with the change in the electoral law (see above) and above all with the formation of important new parties and the splintering or disappearance of old ones. The two key phases of the change occurred in 1991 and 1994, but the apparent beginning of the change can be traced back to the end of the 1980s, when local lists flourished. The left was the first segment of the political continuum to undergo crisis[74] and profound transformation. In the case of the Italian Communist Party (PCI), this slow, gradual process came to a head with the fall of the Berlin Wall in November

---

[73] The new party Politike Anoixe (Political Spring) gained 4.9% and 10 seats in 1993.

[74] Of course, one of the main manifestations of the crisis is its declining electoral performance (to 26.6% in 1987 from 34.4 ten years earlier, in 1976).

1989.[75] A new party was created in February 1991 with a new name, the Democratic Party of the Left (PDS), and new logos (see Ignazi 1992, Weinberg 1995, Baccetti 1997). A segment of the old PCI with more orthodox communist views created a splinter party, Rifondazione Comunista (Communist Refoundation), with roughly one-third/one-fourth of the electoral size of the PDS: 5.6 to 16.1 in 1992; 6.1 to 20.4 in 1994; and 8.6 to 21.1 in 1996. At the same time the extreme left-wing party, Democrazia Proletaria (Proletarian Democracy), which under other names had been to the left of the old PCI for almost twenty years, disappeared.

The other main aspect in the first phase of change is the formation, growth, and success of the Lega Nord (Northern League), whose first party conference was held in February 1991. The party is the result of an association of various Leagues and other local lists, especially from Veneto, Lombardy, and Piedmont, which all together had won about 6 per cent in the regional and municipal elections of 1990, with a curvilinear trend: 8.7 in 1992, 19.4 in 1994, but 10.1 in 1996. This new party occupied the space left vacant by the crisis of Catholic culture following the well-known, widespread process of secularization in those regions; it is rooted in precise territorial identities, and has been a successful way of exploiting localist, anti-centralist, anti-party, anti-southerner positions and in supporting the taxpayers' protest.[76]

One of the most interesting effects of the new electoral system is in the so-called 'anticipated reactions'.[77] That is, even earlier than the March 1994 elections, but anticipating the anti-centre impact of those quasi-majoritarian mechanisms (see above), the DC, already internally

---

[75] But the process of democratic integration of the PCI had at least two previous key moments: in 1973, with the so-called strategy of the 'historical compromise', aiming at the formation of an alliance with Catholic forces and even with a Catholic party, Christian Democracy (DC); and in 1978–9, when the PCI supported Andreotti's cabinet during a difficult period of terrorist attacks. Later, democratic integration advanced and the party held important internal debates which gradually changed its identity. But the objective presence of the USSR on the international scene with its traditional links with the party was still seen by some as a possible anti-democratic point of reference for Communists and a cause for fear. The disintegration of the USSR and subsequent fall of the Berlin Wall heralded the final stage of this break-up. As a consequence, on the one hand, anti-communism no longer had good reason to exist; on the other hand, that break-up was also the definitive answer to the old internal debate on 'real Socialism': the Communist alternative had been made bankrupt. It may be recalled that a new artificial form of anti-communism was rebuilt by Forza Italia in the 1994 electoral campaign—and it also survived later on.

[76] Also the disappearance of the communist–anticommunist cleavage after 1989 contributed to opening up the expression of discontent among northern middle classes, which viewed the Northern League as the best interpreter of their attitudes (see Mannheimer 1991, Belotti 1992, Diamanti 1992, Mazzoleni 1992, Segatti 1992, and Diamanti 1995).

[77] This is the well-known notion by Carl Friedrich.

divided, split into different groups. In fact, following the replacement of its party secretary in 1993 and a long intra-party struggle, a new Partito Popolare Italiano, Italian Popular party (PPI), was born in January 1994. The DC's conversion was also preceded and accompanied by schisms both to the left and right: some leaders entered the right-wing Alleanza Nazionale (National Alliance, ex-MSI) (see below); others formed the Centro Cristiano Democratico (Christian Democratic Centre), and became part of the centre-right electoral coalition, the Polo delle Libertà (the Pole of Freedom) in the 1994 elections; others had already formed, in the summer of 1993, another group, led by a former DC politician, Mario Segni, who presented only a few candidacies in the 1996 election under a different name and symbol; still others formed a party and entered the leftist coalition with the name of Cristiano Sociali (Social Christians), with PDS and only a few candidacies in 1996; others left the party to become members of a tiny leftist group, la Rete (the Network), close to the PDS; and, finally, a few entered the new Forza Italia (Go Italy!).

As to the Socialist Party (PSI) a similar story may be told. That is, its crisis and breakdown resulted from the direct impact of the 'Mani Pulite' investigation on the leadership, first, and the electorate later on (see previous section). This was already evident in the electoral campaign of February and March 1992. In fact, the first party élites to be investigated for corruption were the Socialist ones. The second factor of crisis is the political immobility of its leaders—first of all, of Craxi, tied to the two main DC leaders of the time (Andreotti, as prime minister, and Forlani, as party secretary since 1989) by a pact. In this party the crisis is also manifested, first, in the struggle for a new secretary, actually elected in early 1993 (Benvenuto); later, in the exit from the party of a few leaders who entered either Alleanza Democratica, which was no longer present in 1996, or Forza Italia, when it was formed; and finally, in the split up of the party after the 1994 elections into different small pieces. Some lists making reference to the old Socialist tradition reappeared in 1996, but only the Laburisti were able to get some seats in 1996.

Similarly, the Liberals and Republicans have all suffered schisms and have almost disappeared. Segments of them survived with different names and symbols by joining either the PDS-led Alleanza Progressista (Progressive Alliance) or the centrist electoral coalition Patto per l'Italia (Pact for Italy), formed by the PPI and the Patto Segni (Segni Pact) or even the Polo delle Libertà. After changing their party secretary several times, the Social Democrats became such a small group that they were virtually eliminated by the majoritarian bias of the new electoral law.

As for the right, partly as a result of its strong performance in the local by-elections in 1993, the Movimento Sociale Italiano (Italian Social Movement, MSI), led by Gianfranco Fini, seized the political initiative by maintaining and even softening its rightist conservative positions. Except for some small extremist groups, the secretary was very careful in conveying a clearly defined democratic image. This was also helped by the recruitment of conservative democratic intellectuals. The two further decisive steps in the direction of democratic integration were the inclusion of MSI-AN in the Berlusconi cabinet after the 1994 elections, as the staunchest ally of Forza Italia in a heterogeneous coalition,[78] and the transformation of the party in a new Alleanza Nazionale, with its Christian-Democratic component, in early 1995. In this case, as in the case of the PDS and Rifondazione, the survival of a minoritarian MSI because of the action of nostalgic neo-fascists is an event that the leader of the AN and previous secretary of MSI had to evaluate positively, but that limited the success of AN in the 1996 election.

In the second phase of change (1992–4) the most important element was the foundation of a new party, Forza Italia. At the approach of the 1994 election it became evident that the delegitimation and crisis of both the DC and the PSI, as well as the other tiny, moderate centrist parties (PLI, PRI, PSDI) had created a vacuum within the vast moderate electorate.[79] In this very favourable context and after a period of incubation and secret debates, in January 1994 Forza Italia was founded under the leadership of the television magnate Silvio Berlusconi. Within only a few weeks of its birth, opinion polls indicated that it would become the largest party in the new parliament. The above-mentioned political vacuum in the centre and centre-right accounts for the startling surge of Forza Italia in public opinion surveys. But the massive use of television propaganda is the additional necessary condition by which to explain both its speedy formation and success: the ownership and control of three national television channels and the virtual control of several other local networks gave Berlusconi's party an enormous asset during the electoral campaign. In addition, he was able to exploit such an asset by taking advantage of some loopholes existing in the law governing electoral propaganda. A careful, conscious use of

[78] In fact, in the coalition there were Forza Italia, MSI-AN, and two smaller groups, the Centro Cristiano Democratico and the Unione di Centro, but also the Northern League.

[79] Let it be recalled here that the local by-elections in important towns in June and November–December 1993, held under the new majoritarian law approved in March 1993, had an immediate polarizing impact, and their results, which on the whole were favourable to the leftist coalition, also contributed to Berlusconi's decision to enter politics.

opinion polls also suggested to him how the existing political vacuum in the centre/centre-right could be filled by the issues that later on were to characterize his electoral propaganda. Thus, first of all, hopes of success were grounded on the combined effect of the supply of a 'new product' by an entrepreneur with great expertise in advertising, and a demand for 'new products' emerging from civil society (see also Diamanti 1994).

No established situation, however, was achieved even after that election. In a few months, at the end of 1994 and January–June 1995, there was a split in the Northern League with the creation of Federalists; a split of the Popular Party between those closer to centrist positions and the secretary Buttiglione and those closer to the centre/centre-left led by Bianco; an alliance of the CCD with the new Cristiano Democratici Uniti (Christian Democratic Union, CDU), on the one hand, and with a piece of the old social democrats (European Liberals), on the other; a reshuffling of tiny socialist groups, on the centre-left, with the formation of the 'Lay and Socialist Coordination' and of parliamentary groups with other socialists, republicans, and Democratic Alliance MPs, named 'Democrats'; and even a split in the extreme left of the Communist Refoundation and the consequent formation of the 'Communists for Unity'. In addition, a new movement was set up by a Catholic and old Christian Democratic leader, Prodi, the Movement for Prodi, which later on was able to build an electoral coalition, named the Olive, with PDS, Verdi, Laburisti, the Rinnovamento Italiano, led by the technical prime minister in the 1995–6 cabinet, Dini, and won the 1996 election against the Polo, formed by Forza Italia, AN, CCD, CDU and Pannella–Sgarbi list. On the whole, a real earthquake in terms of new parties and movements, splits, fusion, and electoral coalitions, which fully changed the Italian political arena.

Number, size of parties, and other systemic features

PF, ENP, and determining whether or not new parties or movements emerge must still be complemented by an additional qualitative analysis of the number and relative size of parties and other systemic characteristics.[80] In fact, in the previous analysis the implication for patterns of partisan competition may remain still unclear. Thus, by other qualitative rules for counting, more useful for an analysis of this aspect of the party system, Italy is distinctly different from the other countries. Throughout the 1950s, 1960s, and part of the 1970s, Italy had at least seven relevant parties: one (Christian Democracy) with a

[80] On the topic there is a large traditional literature: from Duverger (1958), Blondel (1968) to Sartori (1976).

plurality of votes and a pivotal position, but also at least six other relevant parties, some with coalition potential (Liberals, Republicans, and Social Democrats), or on the way to acquiring coalition potential (Socialists), or with blackmail potential (Neo-Fascists and Communists).[81] The changes of the 1990s bring about a much higher fragmentation, first of all, in the sense that there is no longer a party with a clear plurality of votes, but two large, non-homogeneous electoral coalitions with two parties of a similar strength (Forza Italia and PDS), three middle-size parties (AN, Lega, Popular Party), a few small parties with a strong coalition potential (CCD-CDU, Rinnovamento Italiano, Verdi, and above all Rifondazione Comunista). The break-up of the DC and the split in the left account for this result. That is, the point to stress is not that in 1996 there were about nine relevant parties, but that there is not a larger party, as the DC was, in condition to control the others.

In Spain, in contrast, for fourteen years (1982–96) there has been only one main incumbent party (PSOE), which faced only one significant electoral rival with no—though increasing—potential of coalition and low blackmail potential up to the middle 1990s (the Popular Party), less substantial opposition from the left (PCE-Izquierda Unida), a centrist rival that vanished altogether in 1993 (Centro Democrático y Social), and several regional parties (but mainly Convergència i Unió and Basque Nationalists) acquiring more and more coalition potential after 1993. Similarly, in Portugal, after 1987 up to 1995 there was only one main incumbent party (Social Democrats), supported by a single-party parliamentary majority, which faced smaller opponents on the right (Centro Democrático e Social-Popular Party) and left (Socialists and Communists). In Greece, the main incumbent party as of 1974–81 was Nea Dimokratia, with opposition from Socialists, Communists and, between 1977 and 1979, the fading centre (EDIK). Following the PASOK victory in the 1981 election, there was an alternation in power and the situation was reversed: Nea Dimokratia became the main opposition party, but PASOK maintained power until the end of the decade. Accordingly, during that decade the party system is closer to a predominant configuration, followed by crisis and the establishment of a bipolar situation (see Chapter 6).

In terms of sheer numbers, Greece has a three-party format; Portugal a four-party format; Spain four nationwide parties and several regional parties complicating the picture; while Italy had seven parties and, after 1994, nine parties. When the size of parties is also

---

[81] That is, the power of intimidation of opposition parties (see Sartori 1976: 123).

considered, a few points should be added. During the period 1982–96 in Spain and 1987–95 in Portugal there were predominant party systems with one main party—respectively Socialists and Social Democrats—at the centre of the political arena. But later on, the change to bipolar, limited multipartism is clear: the pattern of competition is changed. In fact, in Portugal and Spain respectively the 1995 and 1996 elections openly emphasized the end of the dominant party system and the consequent change of competitive patterns with the victory of the Portuguese Socialists and of the Spanish right of Partido Popular (PP). Greece was close to a limited and polarized multipartism in its first years of democracy (see Mavrogordatos 1984), but had a predominant party situation during the whole process of consolidation (PASOK) until the end of the 1980s and a tripolar structure during that phase with Communists as a third excluded pole.[82] Since then bipolarity and limited pluralism have become the characteristics of that system. In spite of being a multiparty system, Italy also had a predominant party (DC) during the most important phase of consolidation (1948–53), and much fluidity in the early 1990s with extreme pluralism and new polarizing issues (see Morlino 1996). The direction of competition was clearly centrifugal only in the Italian case until the early 1970s, and again centrifugal in the early to mid-1990s on different bases (see Morlino 1997, and below), while the other three-party systems exhibited centripetal patterns of competition, despite the presence of leftist or isolated regional forces and, in the Greek case, a high (although declining) degree of polarization.

If the level of competition is scrutinized, as measured by the difference between the strongest electoral party and the others, at the end of the 1980s it is Greece which stands apart from the rest. To it Italy may be added after 1994. The competition was very low in Italy until the early 1990s, and low in Spain until 1996 and Portugal until 1995. Thus, only in Greece was there a high level of competition and, therefore, a strong possibility of alternation, as shown by the return to government of Nea Dimokratia in 1990 and again of PASOK in 1993.[83] Once again, the prominent role of one party emerges in all four cases. Does the

---

[82] The definition of the Greek party system according to the typology by Sartori has been debated for a long time: polarized pluralism or not? (see e.g. Mavrogordatos 1984 and Seferiades 1986). The changes at the end of the 1980s brought the party system toward bipartism, even if still with some degree of polarization. Undoubtedly, however, the actual competition became centripetal, rather than centrifugal, and even Communists tried to compete with a non-radical PASOK in the second part of the 1980s.

[83] It may be remembered here that the defeat of the Socialists came only after two highly conflictive elections, held in the same years and in spite of the gravity of scandals involving the same Papandreu. This can be explained by the penetration of PASOK in Greek civil society. It will be discussed below in the text.

presence of a central, crucial party during consolidation have a special meaning in countries with non-democratic experiences? Is there a possible relationship between this and the way consolidation took place in the countries examined? I will come back to this question later in this book (see Chapter 6).

A different way of exploring the patterns of competition is to see if there has been a stabilization of cleavages. If the party system is divided in two camps in accord with the left–right cleavage, the most common and important division in all four countries, and then the I-BV is used (Table 2.12), there is clear evidence that stabilization has occurred in all four countries, and in two of them (Italy and Portugal) there is also a following destabilization: in Italy such a stabilization occurred after 1948; in Spain following the 1982 alignment and even after the Popular victory of 1996; in Portugal after the Social Democrats' victory in 1987; in Greece after the 1981 alternation in spite of the bipolarism established since 1990; but in Italy the destabilization is revealed by the 1992 election and in Portugal by the 1995 election. In each country, stabilization followed a critical election that involved higher electoral instability and change. Once stabilization occurred, high TEV could still take place, but I-BV was low.[84] At first glance, it might appear as if the party system was still fluid and changing; but the low I-BV characteristic of electoral behaviour indicates, instead, that voting has actually been structured by class, or at least left–right, cleavage. This further suggests that I-BV is a better indicator of party-system stabilization than is TEV. The marked stabilization of the Spanish party system following 1982 is clearly reflected in these I-BV figures: following the 7.4 score for 1982, I-BV has remained consistently very low (2.6 in 1986, 1.7 in 1989 and 1993, 0.9 in 1996)—lower even than such scores for Greece (23.51 in 1981, but 3.40 in 1985, 4.69 and 0.5 in 1989, 2.15 in 1990, and 4.3 in 1993; see Table 2.12).

In the case of Spain, an additional cleavage is highly significant— that between centre and periphery. Here, too, the evidence of stabilization following the 1982 election is evident. The share of the total vote received by regional parties nearly doubled between 1977 and 1979, increasing from 6.2 per cent to 11.1 per cent, only to fall to 7.4 per cent in 1982. Following that election, however, their share of the vote became more predictable. Regional parties received 9.5 per cent of the total vote in 1986, 10.8 per cent in 1989, 10.9 per cent in 1993, and 10.4 per cent in 1996.[85]

---

[84] Here it should be added that the cases suggest a fairly strong consistency between the two measures. However, the hypothesis is highly plausible and can really take place.

[85] On this topic see Montero (1992: 252). The Catalan regional party system is much more stable than that of the Basque region. The first may be defined as a predominant

In opposition to Spanish stability, there is Italian change. In fact, this same cleavage is becoming more and more meaningful since 1992: particularly in northern areas of the country, Lega and other localistic lists went from 1.28 in 1982, and 2.25 in 1987 to 10.5 in 1992, 9.6 in 1994, and 10.7 in 1996. Also the mobilization of this additional cleavage must be included in the analysis of the Italian crisis.

TABLE 2.14. *Stabilization of parliamentary élites*

	I	II	III	IV	V
New members					
Italy	—	55.6	37.0	36.0	34.7
Spain	—	49.5	66.5	47.7	
Portugal	—	52.0	25.2	46.2	40.0
Greece	—	38.3	41.0	12.6	
Senior members					
Italy	—	44.4	63.0	64.0	65.3
Spain	—	50.5	33.5	52.5	
Portugal	—	48.0	70.0	47.2	52.8
Greece	—	61.6	58.8	87.2	

Note: The percentages of new and old (re-elected) MPs are indicated. I, II, III, IV, and V indicate the legislatures. The beginning of each legislature coincides with the electoral year (see Table 2.10).

Sources: For Italy, Cotta (1979: 317); for Spain, Luz Moran (1989: 76); for Portugal, Braga da Cruz (1988: 113–15); and for Greece, Alivizatos (1990: 139).

Political Élites

Stabilization or destabilization of electoral behaviour and the emergence or change of patterns of party competition have so far focused on the mass level. The élite level is also highly relevant, especially with regard to the stabilization or destabilization of party leadership and, more generally, of the political class. This is the fourth dimension to analyse if the processes under scrutiny are to be better described.

In the Italian case, stabilization of the top party leadership was almost immediate, with minor changes in subsequent years. In the other three cases, however, some parties had very serious internal

party system with Convergència i Unió as the main force until 1995. The Basque system is a highly polarized pluralism with fragmentation, and instability (see also below). Besides, it is interesting to contrast the stability of the electoral cleavage at a country level with the transformations of actual relationships between centre and periphery (see the previous section on institutional aspects).

problems, with high levels of conflict, including splits and the formation of new parties (see above). These three cases also reflect differences: Greece, where party leadership is further reinforced by certain
provisions of the electoral law (see above), most closely resembling
Italy. Instability in party leadership was at times a serious problem in
Portugal, primarily among the centre and centre-right parties following the death of the PSD leader Francisco Sá Carneiro in an airplane
accident in 1980 (see Lopes 1988); it was sometimes very serious in
Spain, above all in the extreme left and right with changes of leadership, splits, and internal conflicts (see Gunther 1986*a*, 1987, and Chapter 4). Some differences among these countries with regard to
stabilization of the parliamentary political class can be seen in Table
2.14, which presents the percentage of newly elected members and of
the senior members in the first legislatures following the installation of
democracy in each country. Italy and Greece show the clearest decline
in newcomers and growth of seniority among members of parliament.
Although an anomaly distorts the results for Portugal, i.e. the 1980
election to the third legislature occurred only a short time after the
1979 election to the second parliament, the same trend is apparent.
The results for Spain, however, are inconclusive: the simple truth is
that in Spain there is no stabilization of parties, and consequently of
party élites until the end of the 1980s. The stabilization of the party
system, pointed out in the previous section, is grounded on the socialist stabilization and the instability of other parties. But in the PSOE a
fairly high turnover is maintained to better control party discipline.[86]

Overall, these data suggest that party-élite stabilization is greatest
in Italy and Greece. In the same vein, Italy shows an enormous
turnover of parliamentary élite in 1994, when there are also changes in
the party system. In fact, from 28.2 per cent of newcomers in 1987 there
is an increase to 42.2 in 1992 and to 71.3 in 1994 (see Verzichelli 1995).
That is, more than two-thirds of MPs were elected for the first time in
this election.[87] Portugal's political leaders appear to have achieved
some stabilization by the mid-1980s, while Spain lagged behind,
largely due to continued instability among party leaders on both the
left and the right flanks of PSOE, as well as within some regional parties. These patterns deviate somewhat from those observed in the
analysis of electoral data, where Spain exhibited signs of much greater
stabilization.

Table 2.15 again summarizes the results of the main indicators of
consolidation by taking into account electoral, party, and élite domains.
As for Tables 2.10 and 2.11, the year not only indicates when the phe-

---

[86] I shall come back to this relevant aspect in Ch. 5.
[87] For other important details on this see Ch. 6.

TABLE 2.15. *Consolidation: electoral, party, élite domains*

	Italy	Spain	Greece	Portugal
TEV: decline	1958	1986	1985	—[a]
Critical Elections	1948	1982	1981	1987
PF: stabilization	1953	1986	1981	1987
ENP: stabilization	1953	1986	1977	1987
Establishment of Competitive Patterns	1953	1982	1981	1987
Parliamentary Élites: declining turnover	1948	—[a]	1977	1976

Note: [a] As suggested in the text, the empirical data for the country are inconclusive for this indicator.

nomenon stably appears, but implicitly also that the indicator is relevant for that country. In this sense Italy has had a stabilization of the main aspects of elections, party system, and political élites since 1953 (or even earlier), but such a process became more evident during the 1950s. The same may be said for Spain: the indicators suggest 1982 as the symbolic year of consolidation, but it is not possible to forget that the existence of the processes behind the indicators must be confirmed in the following years, as actually happened. By the same token, 1981 and 1987 are the symbolic years important for, respectively, Greece and Portugal. The analysis unfolded up to now also suggests that some priority among the indicators should be taken into account. The qualitative indicators of the establishment of competitive patterns and the related years are the most salient indicators. It is also worth stressing that in the same country some indicators suggest an earlier consolidation than do others: this partially depends on the kind of examined phenomenon (e.g. in Spain the critical election was in 1982, but the stabilization of PF or ENP obviously became manifest only in the following election in 1986), and partially on the actual inconsistency of a complex multifaceted process (e.g. again in Spain the establishment of local powers came later than the other feature and had also an acceleration in 1993).

As in Table 2.10, the indicators of Table 2.15 stress the existence of the four processes of consolidation at the examined levels. Table 2.16 provides a different picture: the indicators of crisis in the different domains are apparent only for Italy in the same years suggested by Table 2.11. In Greece a more limited crisis emerged with the involvement of institutional, electoral, and party aspects, and also with the establishment of party bipolarization. In Portugal and Spain no serious crisis emerged if not in the type of party system and the related patterns of competition: there was a change from a predominant or

TABLE 2.16. *Crisis: electoral, party, élite domains*

	Italy	Spain	Greece	Portugal
Anticipated Elections	1992–6	no	1989–90	1979–80 (1983–7)
TEV: growth	1992–4	no	1993	—[a]
New Parties and Movements	1991–6	no	no	no
PF: growth	1992–6	no	no	no
ENP: growth	1992–6	no	no	no
Change of Competitive Patterns	1992	1996	1989	1995
Parliamentary Élites: higher turnover	1994	no	no	no

Note: [a] As suggested in the text, the empirical data of the country are inconclusive on this indicator.

quasi-predominant party system to bipolarism with a limited number of parties (see Chapter 6). Again it is necessary to stress that the indicators point to a period when the observed phenomena became manifest, but actually the crisis may exist earlier: for example, a closer analysis of the Italian case will emphasize that (see Chapter 6).

Units of Analysis and Questions to Answer

Up to this point a series of data on institutions, elections, parties, and élites has been examined. The main purpose has been to develop a more precise analysis of consolidation and crisis by beginning with a detailed empirical examination of the processes. One additional consideration is, however, necessary: while it is not possible to connect immediately and precisely the electoral and party domains with the other domains, the approach that is followed here (see Chapter 1) brings into focus features of parties and elections as key empirical indicators for consolidation and crisis and places the institutional indicators (see Tables 2.10 and 2.11) in a secondary position for the moment.[88]

Thus, the data suggest that there are four processes of consolidation in the four countries; they are multifaceted; and different years have to be picked as *terminus ad quem* in connection with the feature of interest. If the attention is on the whole process, then with some approximation and deliberate choice the span of time to explore is for Italy

[88] Which are the connections and the directions of causality among the factors underlying those indicators will be addressed in Ch. 6.

from 1948 to the end of the 1950s, when indicators of consolidation have been already present for a few years; for Spain from 1978 to the mid-1980s; for Greece from 1974 to the mid-1980s; and for Portugal from 1976 to 1986–7 (see again Tables 2.10 and 2.15).

With reference to the period after consolidation when the principal aspects of the democratic regime are established, Italy is the only country where there is an apparent phenomenon of crisis during the period 1992–6. As noted above, in the other three countries there is only an evident change of patterns in party competition. That is, the crisis and change are limited to some important aspect of the party system: it is a partial crisis of the party system. The span of time to explore is when the crisis became apparent, but also the preceding years must be considered in explaining those crises and changes. Consequently, for Italy, the period from the 1980s up to 1996 is the span of time to explore; for Spain from the early 1990s to the 1996 election; for Greece from the end of the 1980s to the early 1990s; and for Portugal from the early 1990s to the election of 1995. For all four cases my explanations will reconsider the consolidation period by attempting to establish a connection between the two phases.

In the following chapters the research will move from simple description to a more detailed analysis of aspects, dimensions, and explanations of the two processes in the four countries. The two processes will be examined separately. The key question of the third, fourth, and fifth chapters is: what are the roots or anchors of consolidation, or what is there behind the institutional and other indicators of consolidation concerning élites, parties, and elections? Although this question will involve other more specific problems, the theoretical approach presented in the first chapter should explain the reasons why the focus will be on the collective and élite actors, their attitudes of legitimacy, their organization, and their control of resources. Eventually, the purpose of this analysis is reconstructing the empirical models of the entire process of consolidation in the four countries (see Chapter 6).

The central questions of the sixth and seven chapters will concern not only the deep, apparent differences between the Italian crisis and what takes place in the other countries, but also the main dimension of the process evolving around the concrete issues each democracy must cope with, the reactions of people, and the possible changes in preceding anchors of consolidation. More precise empirical models of crisis and partial crisis will be suggested.

Before concluding this chapter one final consideration is needed. Despite all the indications provided in this chapter it is not possible to evaluate yet what are the basic characteristics of consolidated democracies or those that are involved in some kind of crisis. This will become apparent only at the end of the analysis of consolidation when the models of the process are suggested (Chapter 6).[89]

[89] The same will be true for the dominant party system and its variations, which emerged as the most important party system up to now.

PART II

Dimensions of Consolidation

3

Consensus and Legitimation

Mass and Élites

When the multifaceted problems of legitimation are addressed (see Chapter 1), the main point of departure is to investigate how large and diffuse consensus and passive obedience, and how widespread positive attitudes of legitimacy and support for democratic institutions are. This means examining both mass and élite levels in terms of consensus and legitimation. It also involves the problem of reasonable consistency between attitudes and behaviour, at least at the beginning:[1] if there is legitimacy, supportive actions are also expected; if there is consensus, acquiescence, obedience, or compliance are likewise expected. In this vein, above all, two directions seem more promising and relevant for consolidation: mass consensus and élite legitimation or legitimacy. The first aspect may be expressed by the existence and strengthening of general attitudes of democratic acceptance and the strictly related presence/absence since the beginning or the gradual fading away of other non-democratic institutional alternatives at the mass level. The second aspect is to consider party élites openly supporting or opposing the democratic regime in their declarations and behaviour in different political arenas (elections, parliament, cabinet).

Worker strikes do not seem the most revealing phenomena to explore in the process of consolidation. They are usually correlated with the dynamics of the labour market and the organizational strength of unions (see e.g. Cella 1979 and several others). Therefore, it is not possible to connect safely the decline of strikes to the growth of democratic consensus or legitimation. The decline in strikes may imply worker

---

[1] Such an assumption makes the empirical analysis much easier, but the consistency cannot always be taken for granted. In fact, on a few occasions some feature of the process under analysis is accounted for by a lack of consistency. As will be seen in Part III, the Italian crisis is characterized by a long phase of inconsistency. However, looking at attitudes and behaviours at mass and élite levels is a way of making an additional step in the 'interactive approach to transition' proposed by Tarrow (1995: 208 ff.). In this chapter an analysis of only a few resulting dimensions is performed on the grounds of empirical and theoretical reasons.

demobilization, weaker unions, and more effective police actions, rather than an increase in consensus. Strikes might be a mode of action by workers who fully accept democratic institutions and rules,[2] rather than an indication of lower consensus or legitimation. In this vein, the trend of strikes is rather more useful in understanding protest and pressures on political élites for change in a democratic direction or of democratic rules and policies. This is very likely the case of Spain where the high mobilization of the period 1976–80[3] is followed by a similar strong decline and demobilization of workers later on (see Espina 1990, Fishman 1990). The trend may be interpreted rather as a late side-effect of the social pacts stipulated among government, opposition, and unions since 1977, beginning with the so-called Moncloa Pacts (see Yruela and Giner 1988; Miguélez Lobo and Prieto 1991; and also Maravall 1981: 26–31). In Italy during the early 1950s, the decline of strikes actually did indicate worker demobilization, weakening and splitting of unions, and an active police and magistracy in the prosecution of violent actions due to worker protest (see Cella 1979, Feltrin 1991, Scarpari 1977). In Greece and Portugal the level of strike activity is low or very low until mid-1980 (see Chapter 7). On the whole, the strong decline of labour conflicts partially overlaps with the consolidation process in the early 1980s and in this sense is only indirectly related to consensus and legitimation.

By the same token, the disappearance of terrorism and of other episodes of violence is not the correct feature to investigate in controlling legitimation and even consensus. Three reasons support this point: (i) episodes of violence or terrorism are the actions of minorities, sometimes financed by foreign sources, and therefore either the decline or the growth of such episodes suggests very little for the present analysis; (ii) these episodes may even be radical reactions against an already existing, massive legitimacy and a strong achieved consolidation; (iii) they are often related to definite traditions of some groups in a specific country and, therefore, they are not recurring phenomena in most other countries. This said, the terrorist actions of the Basque ETA appeared in Spain during the last years of Franco's authoritarian regime and have been present for almost two decades in Spanish democratic politics, but no trend related to legitimation can be neatly determined. It can rightly be affirmed that growth of consensus and legitimation, complemented by the other aspects of consolidation, are found at the beginning of the decline of terrorist episodes after the peak years of 1978–80, and some stability is the trend between 1981 and

---

[2] On the meaning of strikes see Cella (1979) and others.

[3] Although there is some discrepancy among the different sources during these years (see Fishman 1990: 216), the trend is basically the same.

1985.[4] Therefore, there is some idiosyncratic connection between consolidation and terrorism in the sense that the first phenomenon is one of the reasons for the decline of the second.

Episodes of terrorism have been taking place in Greece for years, but again the same reasoning may be applied. In Italy and Portugal a few violent events happened during the years analysed here, and particularly in Italy they may be better related to the hatred and conflicts left open after the civil war in 1943–5; in Portugal, despite the fact that the new regime had been installed by a *coup d'état*, subsequent episodes of violence were unusually few (see also Chapter 7).

Two Different Pictures

In considering the general attitudes of democratic acceptance two pictures immediately emerge: Italy in the 1950s vs. the other three countries in the late 1970s and early 1980s. In Italy during the 1950s and even later, scholars found strong and widespread alienation, apathy, and dissatisfaction. In 1958, that is, just at the end of the considered period of consolidation, La Palombara and Waters found a general 'unconditioned' acceptance of democracy in only 40 per cent of the youth,[5] despite the fact that being between 18 and 25 years old they were born between 1933 and 1940 and, therefore, had either not been socialized or only partially socialized during fascism. According to those authors, 32.2 per cent of those interviewed showed a 'conditioned' acceptance of democracy by agreeing with the statement that 'the democratic system is the only system that will allow us to develop economically.' But, and most importantly, in reply to the same question almost 24 per cent thought that democracy was either 'not adaptable to Italy' (16.9 per cent) or a system that 'slows up development and progress in our country' (6.9 per cent) (La Palombara and Waters 1961: 49).[6] In 1959, in path-breaking research, Almond and Verba discovered in Italy a political culture characterized by 'unrelieved political alienation': 'Italians tend to look upon government and politics as

---

[4] With an additional decline later on, in the second part of the decade. For the data of the late 1980s and 1990s, see Ch. 7. Moreover, Reinares (see esp. 1989: 637–43) points out other factors, such as the more effective police actions and international agreements, before mentioning legitimation and higher partisan stability. On the large literature on terrorism in Spain see also Llera Ramo (1993) and again Reinares (1991).

[5] The question was on the agreement with the following statement: 'The democratic system may have many defects, but it is still the best system of government' (see La Palombara and Waters 1961: 49).

[6] The range of answers is completed by 4% 'no response' (La Palombara and Waters 1961: 49).

unpredictable and threatening forces, not as social institutions amenable to their influence' (1963: 308). Furthermore, 'Italy . . . presents us with the curious anomaly of a political system in which the formal democratic constitution is supported in large part by traditional-clerical elements who are not democratic at all. Opposed to the constitution is a left wing, which, at least in part and at the rank-and-file voter level rather than among party élite, manifests a form of open partisanship that is consistent with a democratic system' (ibid. 115–16). Thus, 'it is paradoxical that the majority of politically involved and informed Italians are opposed to the contemporary constitutional and democratic regime, and that the bulk of the support for this regime comes from Italians who are oriented as subjects or as parochials' (ibid. 309–10).

With reference to the same years, Scoppola (1977: 31 ff. and 67–8) also points out the persistence of traditional, non-democratic attitudes in the middle classes, which constitute the core of Christian Democratic voters, and the maintenance of views of politics learned during the fascist years. Through a few opinion surveys Luzzatto Fegiz (1956) showed how deeply critical and dissatisfied people were in the early and mid-1950s. Moreover, in his 'Italy: Fragmentation, Isolation, Alienation' (1965), again La Palombara recalls that the republican choice was refused by almost half of the electorate in the referendum on the monarchy, held in 1946 (see ibid. 284). According to an opinion survey at the beginning of 1950, 40 per cent were in favour of a monarchy against 31 per cent in favour of a republic, and 29 per cent were indifferent (Luzzatto Fegiz 1956: 431), and at the end of the 1950s (1958) still 61 per cent thought that the choice between monarchy and republic was a crucial problem (Luzzatto Fegiz 1966: 544).[7] La Palombara also confirms Almond and Verba's analysis, and eventually depicts a dark situation up to the point of affirming 'the fact that the republican government remains relatively intact means neither that d'Azeglio's Italians have materialized nor that the Republic can survive many more years on its culturally uncertain problematic foundations' (ibid. 297).

When a key related issue, such as the evaluation of the authoritarian past,[8] was explored, the results were even more obvious, and only apparently ambiguous and puzzling in the few surveys that broke the taboo on fascism. First of all, in the already quoted survey conducted in 1958 by La Palombara and Waters, 59.8 per cent of those interviewed

[7] Vis-à-vis 74% of the sample who affirmed this in 1946, at the moment of the referendum.

[8] Morlino and Montero (1995: 234) labelled the opinion of the past 'legitimacy by default'.

TABLE 3.1. *Attitudes towards fascism and democracy in Italy, 1958 (%)*

	Pro-democracy	Anti-democracy	n.a.
Anti-fascism	37.6	27.3	15.1
Pro-fascism	53.7	68.4	26.9
n.a.	8.7	4.3	58.0

Source: La Palombara and Waters (1961).

expressed positive attitudes toward the past considering fascism either 'an excellent thing for our country' (5.7 per cent) or 'an excellent thing for our country if it had stayed out of war' (27.5) or even 'a blessing for Italy if there had not been so many traitorous acts committed within and against it' (26.6 per cent). A negative evaluation of such a past is given by only 34.2 per cent of respondents. However, as suggested by Table 3.1, there is no consistency between the opinion on fascism and the pro-democratic attitudes. In fact, by combining the answers on democracy (see above) and those on fascism, 53.7 per cent appear pro-fascist and pro-democratic at the same time and 27.3 per cent anti-fascist and anti-democratic. Thus, positive evaluation of the past and related inconsistency have to be explained.

It is only obvious that with the elapsing of time the fascist experience appears more and more distant with a poorer salience and impact on contemporary politics. Thus, among the surveys carried out in the 1960s, one of the best, conducted in 1968 (see Barnes 1972), addressed the issue of the fascist legacy in terms of mass attitudes and political behaviour.[9] By adopting several indicators, and through an insightful analysis, Barnes (ibid. 17–18) concluded that 'our most important finding is that very little of contemporary Italian political attitudes and behavior can be linked to Fascism'. Finally, from the 1970s to the 1990s surveys usually ignored such a question. On the rare occasion when a question dealt with the fascist past, fascism appeared as a distant, but not despised experience for most of people. In 1972 another opinion survey showed that 21.5 per cent of the respondents retained positive or fairly positive attitudes towards Mussolini (Doxa 1972), that is, a much higher percentage than the share (8.7 per cent) of the extreme right-wing party, Movimento Sociale Italiano-Destra Nazionale (MSI-DN), in the elections of that year. In a 1985 survey, which included questions on fascism, only 6.5 per cent of Italians responded that the fascist experience was a good thing, but—interestingly enough—again

---

[9] But not explicitly in terms of opinions of the past.

inconsistent results appear when these responses are compared with others (see below and Morlino and Mattei 1992).

Thus, on the whole, in Italy during the 1950s there was a low or 'conditioned' acceptance of democracy, and in this sense a low mass consensus, few aspects of alienation, but widespread positive opinions about the past fascist experience, particularly among the youth. Building on La Palombara and Waters's survey, one may stress the existence of that decisive group of people who had a 'conditioned' vision of democracy, that is, the 30 per cent believing in democracy only as a system allowing economic development and staying in between the 40 per cent more openly pro-democracy and the 24 per cent against it (see above). But among this 30 per cent there are young people who are still sympathetic to fascism, despite the war, millions of deaths, and severe economic problems. The simplest explanation of this inconsistency in people who maintain pro-fascist attitudes and pro-democratic ones and belong to both groups (those conditionally democratic and those more strongly democratic) is that most Italians accepted (and some of them even praised) their non-democratic past, but at the same time, in a different historical moment and after a bloody war, also accepted the democratic reality, by itself or as a way to economic development in the contemporary international context, characterized by the Marshall Plan, the alliance with the USA, and the beginning of a European agreement, but with low enthusiasm and many doubts.[10]

The same data analysed above suggest that at a mass level there was room for political alternatives, but the interwoven distribution of ideological beliefs, the past experience, and present reality made these alternatives impossible to be actually implemented by some élite. In fact, at the same time, there were strong sympathies for fascism and the impossibility of making it an actual alternative because of the previous negative collective memories of the war and the modalities of democratic installation through an anti-fascist alliance among all democratic and non-democratic party leaders. That is, those sympathies could be expressed in an anonymous survey, but not translated into actual behaviour: fascism was an experience impossible to propose openly. As will be seen below in this chapter, the same party with a neo-fascist ideology was considered anti-regime and had no potential for cabinet coalition. There were weaker sympathies for a leftist alternative, also with an anti-democratic component (see Table 3.2), but again the support for such a communist alternative could be declared, but not actually translated into consistent behaviour: again the modalities of installation with the participation of some liberal, moderate

[10] On the authoritarian preference and positive opinions about the fascist past see also the section on 'No Other Game in Town'.

TABLE 3.2. *Attitudes towards democracy according to left–right self-placement in Italy, 1958 (%)*

	Left	Centre	Right
Pro-democracy	53.0	87.0	48.0
Anti-democracy	42.5	12.4	48.0
n.a.	4.5	0.6	4.0

Source: See Table 3.1.

forces and the whole left, in addition to the international context with Italy in the NATO alliance, are sufficient factors to explain such an impossibility of 'translation'.[11] Even in the centre there was an anti-democratic component (see again Table 3.2), with evidently no autonomous alternative proposal, but which additionally weakened the democratic one. Thus, to put it briefly, at a mass level three political alternatives received the sympathies of three consistent groups of people: the existing democratic arrangement, the fascist one, and the communist one. But the second was part of an intensely hated past, which was also impossible to implement, and the third one was weaker for international reasons. Moreover, the two alternatives blocked one another giving an indirect, strong boost to the relatively weak democratic choice. In this way the same anomaly pointed out by Almond and Verba is better explained.

The 1985 survey mentioned above with reference to Italy is the Four Nation Survey,[12] which is also important to get a good picture of the other three countries: it was conducted in a moment when Spain and Greece were at the end of the consolidation phase, and Portugal was in a key decisive period for the same process (see Chapter 2), whereas Italy was at the very beginning of a long critical period (see Part III). Moreover, not only was it carried out in the other three countries at the same time, but also included the two items on democratic acceptance

[11] But not to explain the process of consolidation. To do that other factors have to be considered (see the following chapters).

[12] This survey, directed by Julián Santamaria and Giacomo Sani, was conducted in the spring of 1985. 8,570 people were interviewed: 2,000 in Portugal, 2,488 in Spain, 2,074 in Italy, 1,998 in Greece. Norma for Portugal, Centro de Investigaciones Sociológicas for Spain, DOXA for Italy, and the National Centre of Social Research for Greece performed the fieldwork. The Portuguese research group was formed by Mário Bacalhau and Maria José Stock; the Spanish by Rosa Conde, Ubaldo Martínez, José R. Montero; the Italian by Giovanna Guidorossi, Renato Mannheimer, Leonardo Morlino, Giuliano Urbani, Maria Weber; the Greek group by George T. Mavrogordatos, Ilias Nicolacopoulos, Constantinos Tsoucalas.

Dimensions of Consolidation

and the opinion of the past in Southern Europe.[13] The first item asked the classic question: 'is democracy preferable to any other kind of regime?'[14] And it is fairly obvious that for all four countries the question is more meaningful and there are more self-conscious opinions of democracy as a type of regime than elsewhere, as the citizens of these countries have also experienced other types of regimes (authoritarian or totalitarian), either personally or through the collective memory embedded in the culture of the society.[15] The second question refers to the evaluation of the non-democratic past, and again this is also meaningful for all four countries, with the caveat on Italy already suggested above.[16]

TABLE 3.3. *Attitudes towards democracy in Southern Europe, 1985 (%)*

	Italy	Spain	Portugal	Greece
Democracy preferable	70	70	61	87
Authoritarianism preferable	13	10	9	5
All the same	10	9	7	6
D.k., n.a.	7	11	23	2
Opinions on the past				
Bad	37	28	30	59
Part good, part bad	43	44	42	31
Good	6	17	13	6
D.k., n.a.	14	11	15	4

Source: Four Nation Survey.

[13] The two questions in the survey were phrased in the following way: 'With which of the following statements do you agree? (1) Democracy is preferable to any other regime; (2) in some cases an authoritarian regime, a dictatorship, is preferable; or (3) for people like me it is all the same.' For the opinions about the past, 'On the basis of what you remember about Salazarism [or Francoism, Fascism, dictatorship], do you think that: (1) it was in part good and in part bad; (2) it was only bad; or (3) all considered, it was good.'

[14] In Morlino and Montero (1995, 233) general attitudes of this kind were defined 'diffuse legitimacy'. Here they are more precisely labelled 'democratic acceptance', as the main indicator of a general mass consensus. The main reason for the different label, which seems analytically and empirically useful, is in the fact that, as suggested in Ch. 1, legitimacy involves a stronger commitment to democracy.

[15] In Italy, by the time of the 1985 Four Nation Survey, people who would have had personal experience with the previous authoritarian regime as an adult or potentially politically active teenager would have been 58 or older; in Greece and Portugal, all of those over age 27 in 1985 would have had personal experience with authoritarianism; and in Spain, all of those 24 years of age or older would have had direct personal experience with an authoritarian regime. On this problem see Weil (1989).

[16] As will be suggested by the quotations, the following part of this section and the next three sections will draw heavily on Morlino and Montero (1995).

Table 3.3 presents the distributions of attitudes in the four countries, with the addition of Italy in a moment that is far away from the consolidation years, but meaningful for the possible comparison with the 1950s. High levels of democratic acceptance are shown in all four countries: specifically, two out of three people expressed a preference for democracy, whereas one out of ten would have preferred an authoritarian regime in some cases; two-thirds of all respondents believed that democracy works; and only a very small minority evaluated the past authoritarian experience positively.[17] More interestingly, some differences emerge among the four cases. In Italy, if the response on the preferability of democracy is compared with the 1958 results and, as in the 1985 question there is no difference between full and conditioned acceptance of democracy, the total number of people accepting a democratic regime is almost the same: 70 per cent in 1985 and 72.2 per cent in 1958. This suggests that the key, crucial difference is rather in the authoritarian preference and the opinions of the past, above all the evaluation of the fascist past, which in 1985 was much different and more negative than in 1958.

On the whole, as for Italy in 1958, Table 3.3 should be read in terms of positive attitudes toward democracy and in this sense as democratic acceptance and consensus rather than a stronger commitment as suggested by legitimacy. An attempt in this second direction, that is, to view the legitimacy at a mass level has been made by Heimer, Vala-Salvador, and Leite Viegas (1990), when in a 1988 survey in Portugal they make a distinction among different general attitudes toward democracy, and explicitly mention the 'active support' for democracy, manifested by 38.9 per cent of respondents vis-à-vis 51.3 per cent who expressed a passive acceptance. Although the first question of Table 3.3 cannot be compared to the question addressed by Heimer and his colleagues, their result shows that behind the manifestation of democratic preference there can be more than consensus. But how much more it is not possible to measure with the available data, and it may even be unnecessary to do it if there is élite support (see also below).

With regard to the opinions of the past, Greeks were consistently more critical in their evaluations than were Portuguese, Spanish, and Italian respondents, who expressed some degree of ambiguity or ambivalence. Added to these mixed opinions there are higher percentages of positive evaluations of the past in Portugal and Spain (13 per

---

[17] Among those surveyed who expressed an opinion (i.e. 'don't know' and no answer are left out), acceptance of democracy was even stronger: 79% in Portugal, 78% in Spain, 75% in Italy, and 89% in Greece. Later on, in a Spanish survey of 1989 the preference of democracy is basically the same: 68% democratic preference, 10% pro-authoritarianism, 10% indifferents.

cent and 17 per cent, respectively). These higher percentages, however, come as no surprise if we consider the duration of Salazarism (almost half a century) and Francoism (about forty years) and the inevitable attachment to a regime of such duration, particularly among the older generations.

A comparison of pro-authoritarian responses to the first two questions reveals an interesting pattern. In Italy—it may be recalled—the 6.5 per cent who evaluated the authoritarian past as positive may be matched with the 13 per cent who stated that 'an authoritarian regime, a dictatorship, is preferable' in some cases. That is, during the almost thirty years between 1958 and 1985 most positive opinion on fascism disappeared, but limited new authoritarian attitudes have emerged. The reverse appears to have been true of Spain and Portugal, where fewer respondents found an authoritarian regime preferable in the abstract (9 per cent and 10 per cent, respectively) than favourably evaluated the previous authoritarian regimes (13 per cent and 17 per cent). This would suggest that some nostalgic supporters of the past in Spain and Portugal converted to pro-democratic commitments (on this see below, and Morlino and Mattei 1992: 142–3). These findings accord with those of other studies, showing that most of those who had positive attitudes towards Franco and were ideologically identified with Francoism also accepted the new regime: only 4 per cent of respondents interviewed by DATA in 1981 totally identified with Francoism and maintained clearly anti-democratic positions (see Linz *et al.* 1981: 614). In this sense the explanation is the same as was given for Italy in 1958: not a refusal of the past, but an adaptation to the new democratic situation.

It is, however, worth recalling other data on the positive perceptions of the past. As for Spain, Linz stresses that in 1978 39.6 per cent of the Spaniards considered positively or fairly positively Franco's regime (Linz *et al.* 1981: 589). That percentage becomes even higher, very close to 50 per cent, in a survey conducted the following year, 1979, that is, in a phase of crisis of legitimation in Spanish democracy (see Gunther, Sani, and Shabad 1986). Finally, in Portugal in 1978 35 per cent still considered that Salazar's and Caetano's were the regimes or governments which had governed the country best (Bruneau 1984: 113; and Bruneau and MacLeod 1986: 93). In Portugal in 1984, that is, one year earlier than the Four Nation Survey, 35 per cent is still the percentage of those praising Salazar and Caetano's governments (Bruneau and MacLeod 1986, 94). In Greece, because of the short duration (seven years) and the low acceptance and legitimacy of the military regime led by Papadopoulos (see above), the positive attitudes towards the authoritarian past are almost absent.

Other additional data point out that, unlike Italy in 1958, in the Southern Europe of 1985 there are no alternatives to the democratic arrangements: not only is the historical past definitely over, but there are also no longer any serious challenges to the democratic regime from authoritarians.[18] In this aspect Southern Europe has become similar to other European countries. The data to recall concern again the preference for democracy over authoritarianism among citizens of European Community countries in 1992, that is, even when Italy is in a critical situation and the other countries have concluded the phase of consolidation (see part III). Despite the economic crises that have beset all of the Southern European countries at some point during the 1980s or early 1990s, support for democracy has strengthened in all four countries. Between 1985 and 1992, the percentage of those polled in EC countries who stated that they preferred democracy increased from 70 to 73 in Italy, from 87 to 90 in Greece, from 70 to 78 in Spain, and from 61 to 83 in Portugal. At the same time the preference for authoritarianism remained basically stable: in Italy it grew from 13 to 14 per cent; in Spain went from 10 to 9 per cent; in Portugal it stayed at 9 per cent; and in Greece went from 5 to 4 per cent. Preference for democracy or for authoritarianism in 1992 were close to the average for the European Community (78 per cent and 9 per cent, respectively) in three of the four Southern European countries, and Italy's score of 73 per cent was not below or above the European average by a very wide margin (see Morlino and Montero 1995: 238).

A better understanding of the 'constrained' presence of an institutional alternative for Italy and the absence—with ambiguities—for the other three countries can be gained by looking at the links between the presence of the collective memory of the past among people and the contemporary problems. In the first perspective, the point is what is actually left of the past political experience and what has gone forever. Such a question was also shown to be still particularly relevant in Germany during the 1980s, while it seems to have been more latent in the four countries. As in Germany, Southern Europe had dramatic and long experiences with authoritarianism, which were often inextricably related to several other aspects. Fascist Italy ended in an international war and a civil war, yet fascism was widely accepted and supported in early 1940 up to the first defeats and the bombing of Italian towns and the civil war affected the North and not the South. Francoism lasted for forty years and in spite of everything was still in power when Spain had its economic growth in the 1960s. Portugal had been an authoritarian

---

[18] This conclusion is strengthened by an examination of the age of those holding authoritarian attitudes. See below and Morlino and Mattei (1992); Montero and Torcal (1990: 116–40); and Heimer, Vala-Salvador, and Leite Viegas (1990).

regime for forty-eight years: for most people there was no other known political reality; a long colonial war, however, laid the bases for the *coup d'état* of 25 April 1974. The military regime in Greece broke down when it began, and lost, a confrontation with Turkey over Cyprus. Furthermore, the coalition at the grassroots of the new Italian democracy was, first of all, an anti-fascist coalition; the new democratic regime in Portugal profoundly changed the previous political élite, the rules and, on the whole, in this country there is a limited sense of continuity with the past; the Greek democracy totally wiped out the military experience; only in Spain were most of the personnel and rules of Francoism transmitted to the new democracy.

Moreover, for at least two countries (Spain and Greece) the salient past is also the political situation that immediately preceded the authoritarian regime. Conversely, the pre-authoritarian years are virtually irrelevant for Portugal because of temporal distance from the Republic, the length of authoritarianism, and—very important—the lack of strong determining episodes of civil war or bloody conflicts and deaths. They were also not especially relevant in the case of Italy at the mass level: the position of the Catholic Church is very different in the 1940s from what it was in the 1920s and Catholic hierarchy decided to support wholeheartedly the new democracy, but the installation of fascism happened in a context of semi-legality and no strong negative memories are attached to it. This is not so for the other three countries. The large widespread consensus, the same acceptance of the past and of democracy at the same time, the moderation of workers that Pérez Díaz (1987), Fishman (1990), and others found in their research, can only be explained by the profound presence of the memory of the radicalization of the Second Republic and the subsequent civil war in Spain (see also Maravall 1981). The remembrance of civil war and of the 'limited democracy' of the 1950s and 1960s with the Communists outlawed, but actually in the parliament under a different label, is also part of the Greek collective memory, as is the lack of consensus and legitimacy from the right to the military regime. These two countries seem to be in a classic situation where the learning process worked efficaciously at a collective level.

When the other aspect is considered, that is, present problems, the differences between Italy and the other three countries are particularly evident. Whatever would have been the country under scrutiny, all transformations that had intervened during the thirty years between the 1950s and 1980s easily account for that difference. It included at least the fact that by those years democracy had won the challenge of economic development and, in addition, in the late 1970s the pressures and appeal of the democratic European Community created strong expectations of additional development. To this a few idiosyncratic considerations should be added (see also below). In Greece, despite several attempts, Papadopoulos's regime never achieved consolidation;[19] eventually neither the monarchy nor any of the conservative groups, which were against Papandreu[20] in the late 1960s, supported the military Junta; and the failed attempt of solving Cyprus's dispute with Turkey delegitimized the military regime even more. In Spain, and more partially in Portugal, although the previous authoritarianisms had maintained a favourable opinion, there was a widespread consciousness that they belonged to the past even among the main élites who had supported them: the death of Franco and the intervention of the captains were the turning points in the beginning of a change that most people were waiting for.[21]

The considerations suggested above explain the lack of rightist alternatives better than of leftist alternatives. Again the 1985 survey gives the opportunity of confirming more neatly something that also began appearing in the 1958 survey on Italy, where the left appeared more democratic than the right: 53.0 per cent against 42.5 per cent and 48.0 per cent against 48.0 per cent (see Table 3.2). That is, the left had more positive attitudes towards democracy than the right, and this emerges from Figure 3.1 very well. The speculation is related to what has been affirmed above: the left had learned the positive features of democracy through the experience of harsh suppression by rightist, authoritarian regimes. It may be added that by 1985 a Socialist, moderate left either were or had been in office in all four countries. Spain may be also noted because rightists still had open, non-democratic leanings (see Figure 3.1). This is indirectly confirmed by Italian data in 1985: because of the elapsing of time in Italy the line of strong preference for democracy is more horizontal indicating a weaker difference between left and right than the other three countries, and the line of no preference goes up only in the extreme right.

The data presented up to this point indicate that by the mid-1980s the existing democratic regimes were accepted by all sectors of society, and there was no significant support for non-democratic alternatives.

[19] An interesting theoretical problem in the case of Greece is how the very authoritarian installation was possible with a limited amount of resources and support. The simple answer is that actors with resources of influence, such as the monarchy, refrained from intervening, leaving room for the success of the *coup d'état* on 21 April 1967. On this see Diamandouros (1986).

[20] The father of the socialist leader after 1975.

[21] The analysis of democratic installation is important for the explanation of developments in the consolidation process. See Morlino (1986a and 1986b) for a theoretical perspective, and O'Donnell, Schmitter, and Whitehead (1986), esp. the contributions by Diamandouros, Maravall and Santamaria, and Maxwell for the theoretical and empirical analysis of those installations.

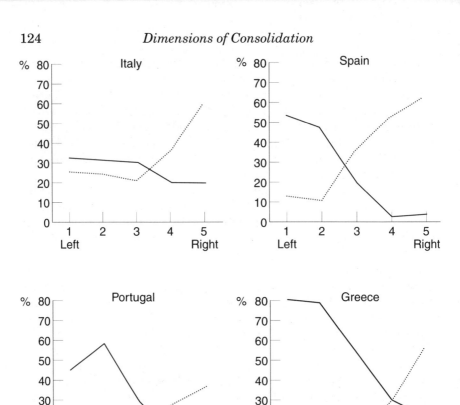

FIG. 3.1. *Preference for democracy by left–right self-placement (%)*
Note: The dotted line refers to 'no preference for democracy'; the continuous line to 'strong preference'.
Source: See Table 3.3.

However, as for Italy in 1958, the resulting picture has to be comple-mented by some mention of general orientations towards politics. Table 3.4 provides a country-by-country comparison. The most positive atti-tudes towards politics (interest, commitment, enthusiasm, and pas-sion) were held by Greeks. Portuguese respondents, once again, had the highest percentage of non-response, along with a large number of responses reflecting non-involvement with politics. Spanish respon-dents also expressed high levels of indifference towards politics, but their attitudes were, on balance, somewhat more positive than those of the Portuguese. Italy, which in 1985 is very far away from the period of

TABLE 3.4. *Feelings towards politics (%)*

	Italy	Spain	Portugal	Greece
Positive: interest, commitment enthusiasm, passion	25	29	20	65
Indifference, diffidence, boredom	47	54	52	26
Negative: irritation, disgust	27	10	16	8
D.k., n.a.	1	7	12	1

Source: See Table 3.3.

consolidation, stands out as having both high levels of negative attitudes towards politics and low levels of involvement with politics. Nearly three out of every four Italians were either not involved in politics or had negative feelings about politics. When left–right self-placement as a control variable is introduced, the same basic pattern discussed above could be observed: respondents on the left were more positive in their feelings about politics while those on the right were more negative, and centrist and centre-right respondents were less involved with politics.

The data presented here suggest some specificities in Southern European political culture, that are consistent with Malefakis's analysis (1995) on political and socio-economic 'contours' of Southern European history. Two-thirds or more of the Italians, Portuguese, and Spaniards interviewed in the Four Nation Survey expressed negative feelings towards, or non-involvement with, politics. Eventually, these findings distinguish citizens of these three countries from their Northern European counterparts. To what extent are these largely affective evaluations accompanied by parallel cognitive orientations? Are these attitudes related to perceptions of personal efficacy, that is, to respondents' assessments of their own capabilities for influencing politics? To address these issues an 'index of political alienation', combining responses to three questionnaire items dealing with 'internal' and 'external' efficacy, was constructed.[22] The resulting data reveal the

[22] The three statements that served as the basis for the index were: (1) 'Politicians do not worry about people like me'; (2) 'Politics is so complicated that people like me don't know what is going on'; and (3) 'Those in power always follow their personal interests' (see Morlino and Montero 1995: 250–3). For a good analysis of these items see Mattei (1987: 105–33). The definition of political alienation basically follows Finifter's notion of it, particularly with reference to the dimension of political powerlessness (see Finifter 1970: 389–410; and 1972). This focus on inefficacy is clearly distinct from several related concepts, including the more negative concept of Gamson (1968: 56–7), according to

extent of alienation from and negative attitudes towards politics and political élites in this population: in Italy 57 per cent of people felt alienated, in Spain 43 per cent, in Portugal 57 per cent, and in Greece, again a notable consistent exception, 32 per cent; no alienation concerned 4 per cent of respondents in Italy, 8 per cent in Spain, 3 per cent in Portugal and of course 15 per cent in Greece (see Morlino and Montero 1995: 252).

The findings on the attitudes towards politics and the related index of alienation are also consistent with those of several other studies. As noted above, thirty years ago Almond and Verba described an alienated political culture as characteristic of Italy in the late 1950s. Two decades later (in a somewhat different historical context), Sani (1981) described that political culture as 'reticent'. Maravall (1981) and, more recently, Botella (1992: 121–36) similarly have described Spain's political culture as one characterized by a lack of popular interest, perceptions of inefficacy, a critical scepticism, and a lack of confidence in political élites. Maravall referred to this combination of attitudes as 'democratic cynicism', while Botella described them as 'cynical democratism'. Maravall further argues that a cynical view of politics has long been a central trait of Southern European political culture and this trait could even be a rational judgement based on long experience of politics as the abuse of power. Both authors stressed the apparent contradiction between negative attitudes towards politics and basic acceptance of the regime.[23] These data also clearly reflect the apparent contradiction between strong acceptance of the regime and several negative attitudes.

Thus, democratic acceptance in Southern Europe may be high, but the political climate in which it exists is characterized by largely negative affective and cognitive attitudes, again with the exception of Greece. This combination of conditions would suggest once more that the level of democratic consensus has its origins not so much in a cluster of positive attitudes but rather in the rejection of the authoritarian past or the distancing from it[24]—a hypothesis consistent with the exceptional status of Greece among the four countries. It may be recalled that the Greek military regime existed for the shortest period

which authorities are regarded as 'incompetent and stupid'; various scholars' conceptualizations of 'social' alienation; or Schwartz's concept of 'estrangement'—the 'perception that one does not identify oneself with the political system' (1973: 7). See also Citrin, McClosky, *et al.* (1975: 1–31); and Wright (1976).

[23] See also Almond and Verba (1963), Sani (1980: 273–324), Maravall (1995, ch. 1); and for a discussions of political cynicism Fraser (1971: 347–64), and Agger, Goldstein, and Pearl (1961: 477–506).

[24] O'Donnell (1992: 31–7) sets forth this same hypothesis in his survey of democratization experiences in Latin America.

of time and was never consolidated; the violent and repressive phase of establishing that regime was more recent (hence, more vivid in the historical memories of Greeks), and accordingly, as the data revealed, its repudiation by the general public was more widespread and extreme than was true in the other three Southern European cases.

Consensus and Perceived Efficacy

Another way of viewing consensus, and particularly the acceptance of democracy, has been suggested by Lipset and slightly modified by Linz and others working on the Spanish case: they leave aside the dimension concerning the past (and the existence of perceived alternatives) and consider only two main dimensions: democratic acceptance, in my wording here, and perceived efficacy (see Lipset 1959; Linz *et al.* 1981; Vila and Gómez Reino 1980). In fact, it is reasonable to assume that the satisfaction of basic demands through specific governmental actions can induce people to form, maintain, or strengthen positive attitudes towards the democratic regime. Popular perceptions of the capability of political institutions to solve problems may be particularly important to the success of new democracies where mass consensus may be low and not deeply rooted in society. Thus, the perceived efficacy of a regime is among those attitudes which are fundamentally related to the positive perception of its political institutions as the most appropriate means of government.[25]

Other scholars, however, have also raised doubts about the possibility of distinguishing between legitimacy and efficacy in empirical analysis (see Muller and Jukam 1977: 1561–95). The high correlations that often result suggest an undetermined causal structure linking the two concepts (see Loewenberg 1971: 170–95). In this vein, opinions about the legitimacy of a regime are linked to judgements of the merits of incumbent authorities, perceptions of governmental performance, and/or the gap between respondents' ideals and political reality (see, for instance, Weil 1989: 698). In Southern Europe it is possible to distinguish analytically between positive attitudes towards democracy or legitimacy, in the wording of Lipset and Linz, and efficacy. The first and most important reason is the same that brings Southern Europeans to reply consciously to the question on the preference for democracy or for authoritarianism. That is, such a possibility is based on the

---

[25] Dahl (1971) emphasizes the importance of perceived efficacy. It should be pointed out that the efficacy we are discussing here is that of the democratic regime, not the perception of personal political efficacy, which will be considered in the next section of this chapter.

non-democratic experiences of Southern Europeans, even though these occurred at different times and with different duration and intensities: Greeks, Portuguese, Spaniards, and Italians have clear frames of reference when asked about political alternatives to democracy, the desirability of democracy in the abstract, and regime performance. The personal experiences or collective memories culturally and attitudinally equipped Southern Europeans to separate the legitimacy (i.e. the acceptance, in my words) of a regime from perceptions of its efficacy, although the ability to make these distinctions may gradually decline as the passage of time makes the authoritarian experience more and more irrelevant to the collective memory. In contrast, when respondents in well-established democracies lacking a non-democratic past are polled, their lack of any similar experience makes questions about political alternatives to democracy highly abstract and unrealistic to them. Lacking a meaningful conception of political alternatives, they are likely to recall efficacy or performance when asked to evaluate legitimacy (i.e. democratic acceptance) (see McDonough, Barnes, and López Pina 1992).

Using these two dimensions and the questions on the preference for democracy and how democracy works, a typology emerges consisting of 'full democrats', who both acknowledge the unconditional acceptance of democracy and regard their democratic regime as efficacious; 'critics', who prefer democracy over authoritarianism but regard their own regime as non-efficacious; 'satisfied', who regard their democracy as efficacious, but would prefer an authoritarian regime under some circumstances; and 'anti-democrats', who are the opposite of full democrats.[26] The data from the 1985 survey, presented in Table 3.5, reveal even more clearly how few Southern Europeans hold negative attitudes towards their present democratic regimes. Anti-democrats, who are negative with regard to both democratic acceptance and perceived efficacy, represent a tiny minority in all four countries, but let it not be forgotten that Italy is very distant in time from the consolidation period. At the opposite extreme, three out of four Portuguese, Spaniards, and Greeks, and two out of three Italians can be categorized as full democrats. All four democratic regimes enjoy a high level of acceptance of democracy.

Previously, levels of satisfaction and perceived efficacy were much lower, especially given that these political contexts were characterized by rising expectations and economic crisis. Accordingly, frustration, disillusionment, and disenchantment were widespread during those

---

[26] This terminology is based upon a four-part categorization first developed by Lipset (1959), and subsequently applied to the study of the Spanish electorate by Linz *et al.* (1981).

TABLE 3.5. *Democratic acceptance and perceived efficacy in Southern Europe (%)*

		Acceptance	Efficacy
		+	−
		Full democrats	Critics
+	Italy	65	19
	Spain	75	12
	Portugal	77	9
	Greece	84	11
		Satisfied	Anti-democrats
−	Italy	7	9
	Spain	7	6
	Portugal	10	5
	Greece	3	2

Source: See Table 3.3.

first years (see Maravall 1995: 13 ff.). Nonetheless, negative perceptions of democratic efficacy did not affect the level of legitimacy to the same extent. This phenomenon is consistent with Linz's argument concerning the relative autonomy of democratic legitimacy from perceived efficacy. Although such autonomy was lower during the first phases of regime change, it helped the new Southern European democracies to cope with problems arising from the gap between social expectations and the attempted solution of serious economic and social problems (see Linz 1990; Linz and Stepan 1989: 41–61). As the data presented in Table 3.6 clearly reveal, the correlations between preferences for democracy over authoritarianism, on the one hand, and satisfaction with the working of democracy (perceived efficacy), on the other, are rather low. In no case do the correlations (Pearson's) reach 0.30. Thus, according to one crude statistical indicator, the conclusion is that efficacy 'explains' less than 10 percent of the variance in the democratic acceptance. The questions involving regime preference and satisfaction appear to be tapping different dimensions, although theoretically related ones. As noted above, Southern Europeans were able to distinguish between legitimacy and efficacy, such that dissatisfaction with the working of their democracies was not mirrored by a decrease in the general preference for a democratic regime.[27]

[27] Such a distinction had a behavioural manifestation in voting. A preliminary analysis of attitudes on diffuse legitimacy and perceived efficacy reveals that democratic legitimacy is quite widespread, while voters diverge significantly in their perceptions of the efficacy of their democratic governments. These diverging evaluations of efficacy are strongly related to voters' support for or opposition to government in each country. It goes

TABLE 3.6. *Correlations (Pearson's* r) *among democratic acceptance, opinions on the past, and perceived efficacy*

	Democracy works well	Opinions about the past
Democracy preferable		
Italy	0.24	0.26
Spain	0.29	0.33
Portugal	0.16	0.25
Greece	0.21	0.34
Democracy works well		
Italy	—	0.00
Spain	—	0.19
Portugal	—	0.09
Greece	—	0.26

Source: See Table 3.3.

A more detailed examination of the Spanish case lends more persuasive support to this conclusion. The four surveys conducted by Barnes, McDonough, and López Pina—in 1978, 1980, 1984, and 1990—included similar items measuring legitimacy or democratic acceptance, according to the term adopted here, and efficacy. Their data confirm both of the conclusions stated above. First, they indicate that the autonomy of legitimacy from efficacy increased with time, as the new regime became consolidated: Pearson's correlations between indicators of positive orientation towards democratic government and satisfaction with 'the way democracy is working in Spain' were 0.81 in 1978, 0.68 in 1980, 0.57 in 1984, and 0.59 in 1990 (see McDonough, Barnes, and López Pina 1986: 751). Second, despite an accumulation of unsolved problems during the 1980–1 period (including an upsurge of Basque terrorism, a divisive debate over regional autonomy, the deep crisis of the incumbent party Unión de Centro Democrático, UCD, and even an attempted *coup d'état* in February 1981), the new Spanish democracy remained largely accepted. The number of critics (loyal democrats dissatisfied with the performance of the government) increased almost threefold (11 per cent in 1978, but 32 per cent in 1980), and these negative evaluations only improved after the PSOE came to power in 1982, with 12 per cent in 1985 and 11 per cent in 1989. The number of respondents expressing anti-democratic sentiments remained acceptably low: 12 per cent in 1978, 18 per cent in 1980, and down to 6 per cent in 1985 and 7 per cent in 1989. In short, Spaniards were able to distinguish between governmental performance and the democratic regime, and

without saying that the differences are consistent with the dividing line separating incumbent parties from opposition parties in each country.

they did not blame democracy for their problems. While the increase in the number of critics eventually contributed to a profound electoral realignment, this was not accompanied by a meaningful increase in support for anti-democratic solutions (see Linz 1989; Montero and Torcal 1990; Maravall and Santamaria 1986: 71–108; and Di Palma 1984: 172–87). It should be noted that this finding also holds with regard to Italy, with its low levels of perceived efficacy.[28] Thus, all four Southern European countries clearly display a lack of linear and transitive relationships between democratic acceptance and (perceived) efficacy.[29]

This analysis suggests that the relationship between regime acceptance or consensus and perceptions of government efficacy is rather loose. This finding holds up despite considerable cross-national variance regarding perceived efficacy: perceptions of efficacy were low in the early 1980s in Spain and Portugal but have increased substantially since, but the trends are quite different in Italy (where levels of satisfaction remained consistently low) and Greece (where perceived efficacy declined somewhat in 1990). In neither of these latter two cases, however, has there been a decline in the level of acceptance.[30] When a different process, such as crisis, is considered, then efficacy or inefficacy may acquire an autonomous higher salience for the democratic regime. This hypothesis will be developed in Part III of this book.

Some Explanations to Emphasize

What is most striking about the extent of acceptance of these regimes is that, with some interesting exceptions, such sentiments are evenly distributed throughout all sectors of these societies.[31] An extensive analysis of possible relationships between preference for democracy, opinions about the past, and perceived efficacy, on the one hand, and on the other the most commonly analysed socio-economic variables (such as income, occupational status, social class, education, age, and

---

[28] On this see also Part III.

[29] For a similar conclusion see also Maravall (1995: 276–7).

[30] For data on Spain, see Montero (1992); for Portugal, see Bruneau (1983: 21–42); for Italy see Morlino and Tarchi (1996).

[31] An interesting partial exception is the negative correlation (Pearson's $r = -0.30$) between religious practice and democratic legitimacy we find in Spain. These correlations are much weaker in the other countries: -0.16 in Greece, -0.10 in Portugal, and 0.07 in Italy. The political salience of this cleavage has been documented in many studies: see, for example, Gunther, Sani, and Shabad (1986); Linz *et al.* (1981); Montero (1986*b*: 131–59) and Pérez Díaz (1987: 411–66). Another significant exception is the Basque region of Spain, which is not separately examined in this chapter. For surveys of the extent of legitimacy accorded to the Spanish constitutional monarchy in the Basque region, see Llera Ramo (1992).

religious practice), produced low or very low correlations. In other words, there is no specific social group or demographic group which is differentiated from the rest of society by higher or lower levels of preference for democracy.[32]

In contrast, correlations with an important political variable, self-placement on the left–right continuum, are much more substantial. Earlier in this chapter this variable was significantly related to other variables on democracy. To take this analysis one step further, an index of positive attitudes towards democracy was constructed by combining respondents' answers to the questions on democratic preference, opinions about the past, and the way democracy works. This produced three categories of respondents: those who gave the most positive answers to the preference for democracy and perceived efficacy questions and the most negative assessment of the authoritarian past; those who gave negative or indifferent responses to the preference for democracy and perceived efficacy questions and positive or mixed evaluations of the authoritarian past; and respondents who set forth mixed evaluations or selected intermediate response categories.[33] There are significant cross-national differences concerning the link between this index and the left–right continuum. The relationship is strongest in Spain and Greece, with correlations of 0.45 and 0.47, respectively. With regard to the other two countries, the correlations are much lower: 0.16 for Italy and 0.23 for Portugal.

Figure 3.1 depicts the cross-tabulation of left–right self-placement and this index of positive attitudes towards democracy (for the sake of clarity, the intermediate weak support category is not presented). The strength of the relationship between left–right self-placement and this cluster of attitudes in each country can be seen clearly. This graphic depiction, moreover, corrects one error of interpretation that might have been made on the basis of correlation coefficients alone: the correlation in Portugal between the left–right variable and this index of acceptance is depressed somewhat by a curvilinear relationship linking the two.

Separate correlations between left–right self-placement and the individual components of this index reveal patterns that might help to interpret these findings. The relationship between evaluation of the

[32] McDonough, Barnes, and López Pina (1986) arrive at a similar conclusion for Spain, using panel survey data from 1978 to 1984.

[33] 'Don't know' responses and non-responses were excluded from the calculations. Marginal distributions among these categories indicate that positive attitudes were most prevalent in Greece, where 56% of respondents fell into the 'strong preference' category (as compared with 32% in Portugal, 28% in Spain, and 27% in Italy). The 'non-preference' category produces a mirror-images distribution: it included 26% of Spanish and Italian respondents, 19% of Portuguese, and 13% of Greeks.

authoritarian past and left–right self-placement shows that there is more left–right polarization of such opinions in Spain (Pearson's r is 0.53) than in Greece (0.46), Portugal (0.33), and Italy (0.31). Perceptions of governmental efficacy are also less strongly associated with left–right self-placement in Italy (Pearson's r −0.11) and Portugal (0.05) than they are in Spain (0.22) and Greece (0.26).

To interpret these findings the point of departure is the literature on the left–right dimension that sees both an ideological and a partisan component included in this variable. This would suggest that some of these findings are affected by partisan orientations.[34] Accordingly, the performance of parties in government (clearly relevant to the perceived efficacy dimension) and the positions taken by parties and their leaders on the issue of diffuse legitimacy greatly affect the attitudes of partisan respondents. This interpretation of variance in democratic acceptance acquires some credibility when the partisan preferences of respondents are introduced as a control (see Morlino and Montero 1995: 249). Partisanship has a strong effect on perceptions of efficacy. This influence is not particularly surprising, since, in essence, respondents are being asked to evaluate the efficacy of a democratic government that is under the control of a particular party or coalition. Consequently, PSOE voters more favourably assessed the performance of democracy under the PSOE government in 1985 than did supporters of other parties; PASOK voters gave even higher marks to Greek democracy under PASOK leadership; and supporters of parties in the 1985 Italian coalition government (the PSI, PSDI, PRI, PLI, and DC) more favourably evaluated their government's democratic performance than did supporters of parties occupying the opposition benches. The only significant exceptions to this pattern were Portuguese Socialist voters, whose party was involved in the collapsing government coalition in that period and was on the verge of a long period as part of the opposition.

If the partisan preferences are controlled with the opinion on the past and the perceived efficacy, other aspects can be pointed out. First, in all countries, voters for parties of the right gave the least positive responses to democratic acceptance and perceived efficacy questions and most favourably evaluated the authoritarian past. Second, despite the opposition status of the Portuguese, Spanish, and Greek communists, their supporters expressed more strongly the acceptance of

[34] This is, for instance, one of the main conclusions of the research by Inglehart and Klingemann (1976: 243–76); and by Arian and Shamir (1983: 139–58). Also see, for example, Laponce (1981); Sani (1974: 193–208); Sani and Montero (1986); Klingemann (1979: 215–54); and Mavrogordatos (1987: 333–42). Evans (1996) shows the salience of the left–right continuum by emphasizing also the connections between this dimension and the ideological content of left and right.

democracy than did socialists, whose party was either the only or the dominant party in the government. In general, as seen with the self-placement, respondents of the leftist parties were significantly and consistently more positive about democracy than those of the rightist parties. This is particularly apparent when incumbency is controlled (such as by combining the 'full democrats' and 'critics' presented in Table 3.5). Moreover, in the case of Spain (where time-series data are readily available), it is noteworthy that respondents on the left were even more supportive of democracy than those on the right in 1978, when the centre-right Unión de Centro Democrático was in government. To these observations it may be added that in Italy and, to a lesser extent, in Greece parties are more important and visible in society than in the other countries. This issue will be analysed in the next chapter. Here, if only party identification is considered,[35] fewer Spaniards and Portuguese (43 per cent and 48 per cent, respectively) identify with a party than do Italians (57 per cent) and Greeks (72 per cent).[36] While Italy ranks high in terms of the portion of its population identifying with political parties, it should be recalled that the correlation between left–right self-placement and democratic acceptance was significantly lower than in the other Southern European countries. Conversely, Spain had the fewest party identifiers and the highest correlation between democratic acceptance and the left–right continuum. This would suggest that the ideological component of the left–right continuum becomes more relevant if partisan attachments are not particularly widespread, intense, or salient. Furthermore, both the ideological and partisan components are relevant if there is a strong, widespread presence of parties in society. In 1985 this latter condition

[35] Among the measures suggested in the literature, here Mannheimer and Sani (1987), who utilize two indicators of partisanship, will be followed. They are: the classical item ('Tell me whether you feel very close, close, neither close nor distant, distant, or very distant . . . for each of the parties shown in this list') and a second version which includes an affective-reactive dimension ('When someone criticizes the party you have voted for in the last election, how do you normally react?: (1) it bothers me as if they were criticizing me; (2) it does not bother me, but I do not like it; (3) it makes no difference to me'). Party identification is graded accordingly. Uncommitted respondents represent 57% of those interviewed in Spain, 52% in Portugal, 43% in Italy, and 27% in Greece. A similar rank-ordering is produced if only responses to the classical partisanship question are examined: those who regarded themselves as very close to a party were 48% of respondents Spain, 49% in Portugal, 52% in Italy, and 70% in Greece.

[36] Additional recent data, from a Eurobarometer survey conducted in 1989 (see Schmitt 1990: 169–81), show even lower levels of identification in Spain, where 30% declare themselves to be very close to, fairly close to, or merely sympathizers with a party, while in Greece 57% do so. In Portugal the identifying percentage is roughly the same, 49; in Italy those identifying with a party are, surprisingly, a larger percentage, 63. For additional contributions on this topic, see Schmitt (1989: 122–39), Mannheimer and Sani (1987), Mannheimer (1989a), Richardson (1990), and Gunther and Montero (1994: 467–548). On this see also the next chapter.

appears to apply to Italy and Greece, while the former most clearly applies to Spain; Portugal is near the middle on this continuum.

Left–right self-placement, therefore, consistently and significantly affected the propensity of citizens to acknowledge regime acceptance and to perceive a higher efficacy. The two components of this factor are relevant in different ways in the four countries. In Greece, the two aspects appear to mutually strengthen each other. While there is a stronger ideological component and greater polarization in Portugal, more frequent turnover of parties in government is reflected in a low correlation between left–right self-placement and democratic acceptance. In Italy, parties have been dominant for a long time, and polarization largely decreased during the early 1980s. Spain seems to be the case in which the left–right component is strongest. In all of these countries, the left–right dimension appears to function as an orientation device, a compass to simplify the political universe and make it more understandable. In general, then, left–right self-placement has an autonomous meaning and political attitudinal content, including orientations regarding regime acceptance. These attitudes may be associated with, but are certainly not equivalent to, specific partisan loyalties (see Sani and Montero 1986: 155 and 185).[37]

'No Other Game in Town': Two More Questions

At this point it should be clear how the data presented here support the comparative proposition formulated by Linz and Stepan (1989: 46), according to which 'political perception of desired alternatives has a greater impact on the survival of democratic regime than economic and social problems per se'; but with the additional aspect suggested by the Italian case where the alternatives are perceived, but are impossible to implement: as discussed above, there are different alternatives and they are in contrast with one another; because of either the memory of the past or international reasons they are frozen or non-manifested.

On the whole, the presence or absence of institutional alternatives to the just installed democratic regime depends very much on the perception of the authoritarian or non-democratic past in all four countries.

---

[37] There is no doubt, however, that the relationship between left–right orientation and other values and attitudes deserves to be explored more closely. Its ambiguities have already been underlined by other authors such as Mavrogordatos (1987), and Van der Eijk and Niemoller (1983). Sani and Montero (1986) did that for Spain; Sani (1981: 235–79) for Italy and Spain; Bacalhau (1978) for Portugal; Mavrogordatos (1983) for Greece; and Condomines and Durão Barroso (1984: 405–28) for Portugal, Spain, and Greece.

On the basis of research conducted in Italy during the 1950s and of the Four Nation Survey regarding all four countries in 1985, a few data and comments were already suggested in previous sections of this chapter.[38] Here, the characteristics of the non-democratic opinions are more closely analysed to understand how extreme rightist or leftist parties will keep alive in the four countries, and if the authoritarian residual attitudes may become the bases for action and protest against the present democracies in moments of economic crisis and tough political conflicts.[39]

The percentages, given in Table 3.3, on the authoritarian preferences have two components: they are in part formed by new authoritarian opinions, but unavoidably also by the persistence of the old opinions of those who had supported the previous non-democratic regimes. As already seen, authoritarian solutions are the least preferred in Greece, that is, in a country where the authoritarian military experiment was never able to consolidate itself. With reference to the other three countries, authoritarianism appears to be more preferable to the Italians than to the Spaniards or the Portuguese. In Italy (1985) the relative higher incidence of pro-authoritarian answers could be due to the mutually reinforcing result of the time elapsed from the Second World War—that is, the most negative aspects of the regime are forgotten— and of the dissatisfaction displayed by the Italians about the way democracy works;[40] in Spain and Portugal, the lower percentages could be ascribed to the long duration of the authoritarian regimes as well as the short time elapsed from the inauguration of democracy. Therefore, a very first review of the presence of authoritarian or democratic attitudes in these countries shows that a deeper analysis of them has also to consider their previous political experience. That is, as also seen in a previous section of this chapter, the key problem still is how South-

---

[38] This section is largely indebted to Morlino and Mattei (1992).

[39] Let it be remembered that the complex phenomenon of the disappearance or persistence of authoritarianism in those countries can be explored at three different levels. The first one, typically *institutional*, concerns the crisis of the authoritarian regime or institutions. It was just mentioned above and is the most evident. The second one is *social*, and concerns the persistence of authoritarian patterns of behaviour in the different sectors of society, such as the family or the labour relationships, and so on (on this point see Bobbio 1984). The debate on the connections between the two levels is open. Only some attempt was made to systematically connect the two levels (see Eckstein and Gurr 1975). However, let us stress that to date the inconsistency between a politically democratic regime and an authoritarian society seems the rule rather than the exception. A third level of analysis, an *attitudinal* one, is a way of connecting society and politics, although with a more limited scope. Its main dimension concerns opinions of acceptance, consensus, or support to political institutions from the society. Here, this third level is considered.

[40] It may be added that 28% of Italians say that 'democracy does not work', while this answer is provided by 11% in Portugal, 20% in Spain, and 14% in Greece.

ern European societies have dealt with their historical past in terms of their collective memory.

Table 3.1 for Italy and Table 3.3 for the other three countries also gives data on the opinions about the past. If the answers to the two questions on authoritarianism and the opinion about the past are considered, the differences between these percentages stress that, at first glance, room exists for a new authoritarianism at least in Italy and Portugal. In fact, in Italy authoritarianism is preferable for 7 per cent more people; in Portugal such a difference is 4 per cent; but in Greece there is virtually no difference and a likely overlapping; and in Spain a very interesting aspect emerges: at least a part of the population which retains a positive evaluation of the past does not prefer authoritarianism for their present situation.

If the answers to both questions, on the preference for the regime and on the evaluation of the past, are cross-tabulated, a typology can be formulated. Thus, new authoritarian attitudes can be identified while at the same time assessing respondents' consistency in the evaluation of past and present regimes. Two categories, pure democrats and authoritarians, emerge where the political attitudes remain consistent and two other categories, neo-democrats or neo-authoritarians, where there is inconsistency.[41] The result is shown in Table 3.7.

TABLE 3.7. *Preferences for democracy and authoritarianism: a typology*

	Italy	Spain	Portugal	Greece
Democrats	36.7	31.1	31.9	60.3
Neo-democrats	39.1	46.9	45.8	28.8
Indifferents	8.7	5.4	6.5	4.5
Neo-authoritarians	11.7	7.3	10.2	3.8
Authoritarians	3.8	9.1	5.6	2.6
(N)	(1,710)	(2,002)	(1,484)	(1,896)

Source: See Table 3.3.

[41] The typology was devised by putting together the question about democratic preference and the opinion of the past. Thus, *pure democrats* are those who answered 'democracy is preferable' to the first question and 'the past was bad' to the second one; *neo-democrats* are those for whom 'democracy is preferable', but the 'past was good' or 'in part good, in part bad'; *indifferents* are those for whom 'it is all the same' and 'the past is bad' or 'in part good, in part bad'; *neo-authoritarians* believe that today 'authoritarianism is preferable', but 'the past was bad' or 'in part good, in part bad'; *old authoritarians* think that 'authoritarianism is preferable' and 'the past was good'; *nostalgic authoritarians* think that 'it is all the same' and at the same time 'the past was good'. In the tables old and nostalgic authoritarians have been collapsed in one category that has been simply labelled *authoritarians*.

The typology emphasizes the impact of the past on people's opinions and the actual size of authoritarian leanings in the four societies. In our perspective, attitudes' inconsistencies are the most relevant feature, as they display the change and disappearance of authoritarianism and the appearance of new non-democratic leanings. Therefore, the two most interesting categories are the neo-democrats and the neo-authoritarians. They are also very meaningful in size: the sum of both categories is over 50 per cent in all countries except Greece (see Table 3.7). In addition, the first one of the two categories presents high percentages: 28.8 in Greece, 39.1 in Italy, 45.8 in Portugal, and 46.9 in Spain. Again in three out of the four cases—Greece is still the exception—this category is the largest one. Also the percentages of neo-authoritarians are higher than those of authoritarians, with the Spanish exception. And, however, the whole non-democratic opinion (neo-authoritarians and authoritarians together) is fairly meaningful in size: 16.4 per cent in Spain, 15.8 per cent in Portugal, 15.5 per cent in Italy, and 6.4 per cent for Greece.

To better clarify these categories, *neo-democrats* may be defined as people who do not deny their authoritarian past: their allegiance to democracy is more recent, and it might be less strong than that of pure democrats. They are people who accepted the authoritarian rule in the past and now accept the democratic regime. They can be divided into two subgroups: those who simply accept the existing authority, the 'obedients'; and those who changed their minds, the 'converted', whose reasoning is: we were right in supporting authoritarianism in a given period and we support democracy nowadays, in a different historical moment, when the threats of revolution or radical policies as well as the threats of reactionary policies or the *de facto* suppression of civil and political rights have disappeared. The 'converted' could also be individuals who were satisfied with the previous authoritarianism, because of the good economic performance, but later became satisfied or ready to accept also the way democracy performs economically. The 'obedients' are rather part or manifestation of a subject or even parochial political culture. The 'converted' should be an expression of a more active, if not participant political culture (see Almond and Verba 1963), which may be very much influenced by economic results.

The *neo-authoritarians*, who consistently form a larger group than the old authoritarians, point to negative reactions towards the regime. Some of them supported democracy in the past, when authoritarianism was triumphant, and that kind of opinion was also very difficult to maintain, but later when democratic institutions were established they were disillusioned and came to support an authoritarian solution. For them the desencanto had very negative consequences. Of course, an authoritarian reaction may be stronger in a country where the non-democratic experience is very far back in time and was not directly experienced by most people. In fact, those reactions are particularly strong in the Italian case, where the highest level of dissatisfaction with democracy is also found (see Table 3.7).

On the whole, if the trend towards new democrats is stronger than the opposite one towards new authoritarians, the picture is more fragmented than it appeared to be at the beginning, and democratic attitudes deserve to be better qualified as we tried to do with the 'obedients' and the 'converted' (see also Morlino and Montero 1995). When, however, one tries to understand, if not to explain exhaustively, who are the authoritarians (and the neo-democrats), age is the first explanatory factor to consider if the hypothesis on the new wave of authoritarianism as a reaction to democracy, because of the dissatisfaction with the way democracy works and the complementary hypothesis on the persistence or remnants of an old authoritarian political culture are correct. Table 3.8 supports this point. Age is a salient variable in all the cases. And it is even more salient in the Greek case, where authoritarian attitudes are the weakest.

As largely expected (see the last line for each country in Table 3.8), the percentages of authoritarians is much lower among young people (i.e. those under 30) than those over 45 and this difference is very strong in all countries except Portugal. Thus, the authoritarians are the people who approached politics for the first time and formed their political values during the authoritarian period. At the time of the survey they belonged to the two highest echelons of our age groups. Italy confirms this point. In fact, because of the time distance from fascism we should expect that in Italy the age factor is less relevant. In fact, the last line of the section on Italy in Table 3.8 displays a relatively lower sensitivity to the age factor. Of particular interest is the Greek case, as well. Here, in a context of low authoritarianism, more accentuated attitudes in favour of authoritarianism (48.9 per cent, i.e. almost half of the whole group) are shown by people between the age of 46 and 60 in 1985, that is between the ages of 26–33 and 40–7 in 1965–73, when Greece witnessed the phases of democratic crisis, installation of the military regime, and its breakdown.

The salience of neo-authoritarianism indicates that this is really a new group of people who are probably unsatisfied with the democratic regime, and these people are the youngest ones. Such a hypothesis is suggested mainly by the Italian case, in spite of the long democratic persistence in that country, and by the Portuguese one: neo-authoritarians belong mainly to the first two age groups. It is not supported, however, by the two other cases: in both Greece and Spain the highest percentage of neo-authoritarians are in the 46–60 category. This means that in the two countries there is a sort of curious nostalgic attitude: people would prefer authoritarianism today, in spite of the refusal of the authoritarian experience in their past.

A complementary element to take into consideration is that, on the one hand, there are evident age-related differences in attitudes, here analysed, between the youngest people and the oldest ones; on the other hand, the middle groups sometimes contribute to form a trend (i.e. the percentages decrease as age increases or vice versa among the authoritarians and the other categories. Thus, on the whole, there is 'sensitivity' of age toward democracy and past experiences, but other more refined and precise hypotheses are not adequately supported by the data.

Among the other socio-economic variables, some interesting points arise in relation to education and religion. With regard to education, neo-authoritarians are as much educated as neo-democrats (only in Spain is there a greater difference), less educated than democrats (except in Portugal), and much more educated than indifferents. The neo-democrats are the most educated group in Italy and, by and large, close to democrats. The only case where there is a clear relationship between education and those attitudes is Spain. The general low level of education makes Portugal less meaningful on this variable. But in the other three countries there are clearly two clusters: on the one hand, democrats, neo-democrats, and neo-authoritarians and, on the other hand, indifferents and authoritarians. Thus, on the whole, a hypothesis suggesting 'the authoritarians (and indifferents) are people with elementary education' works fairly well in all countries, and particularly well in Spain. Different attitudes, including the neo-authoritarian one, require some political analysis and the latter entails some extent of education. This is particularly so in Italy where the authoritarian past no longer belongs to the direct experience of most people.[42] Religion is relevant only in the Spanish case. This finding has already been pointed out in other research (see, e.g. Gunther, Sani, and Shabad 1986; Montero 1986b). Here it may be added that religion is salient in Spanish politics, and it is also salient in the authoritarian choice.[43] In addition, Catholic beliefs are stronger among authoritarians rather than among neo-authoritarians (and very weak among democrats). In Greece and Portugal, but not in Italy, neo-authoritarians are less religious than authoritarians; democratic opinions seem less strongly religious in Portugal and Greece, while in Italy a real impact cannot be appreciated; the indifferents are the smallest group

[42] For more data on this see Morlino and Mattei (1992).
[43] On the positions of the Catholic Church see the last section of this chapter.

TABLE 3.8. *Democrats and authoritarians by age*

Age	18–30	31–45	46–60	61–over	(N)
Italy					
Democrats	24.7	30.7	25.3	19.3	(628)
Neo-democrats	26.6	29.4	23.8	20.2	(669)
Indifferents	30.4	29.7	24.3	15.5	(148)
Neo-authoritarians	29.5	29.5	26.5	14.5	(200)
Authoritarians	15.4	29.2	26.2	29.2	(65)
Spain					
Democrats	38.7	32.1	18.1	11.1	(630)
Neo-democrats	26.8	29.7	26.7	16.8	(945)
Indifferents	23.6	19.1	25.5	31.8	(110)
Neo-authoritarians	21.8	27.9	34.7	15.6	(147)
Authoritarians	14.2	23.0	31.7	31.1	(183)
Portugal					
Democrats	28.4	23.9	27.3	20.4	(469)
Neo-democrats	25.3	21.6	28.7	24.4	(665)
Indifferents	29.2	18.8	27.9	25.1	(96)
Neo-authoritarians	30.2	30.9	21.5	17.4	(149)
Authoritarians	26.5	7.2	27.7	38.6	(83)
Greece					
Democrats	31.3	26.6	27.1	15.0	(1143)
Neo-democrats	23.5	25.9	33.9	16.7	(545)
Indifferents	18.8	28.2	32.9	20.0	(85)
Neo-authoritarians	26.8	25.3	32.4	15.5	(71)
Authoritarians	4.1	18.4	48.9	28.6	(49)

Source: See Table 3.3.

in Italy, but the largest one in Greece. On the whole, the only general conclusion to draw is that today religious beliefs are not strongly related to democratic or authoritarian attitudes.

The two main political variables, left–right self-placement and party affiliation, are very sensitive to the authoritarian choice. It may be recalled here that the left–right self-placement also has an ideological or issue component, not only a partisan one (see Laponce 1970 and 1981; but also other authors). Thus, the two variables overlap only partially. With regard to the left–right variable (Table 3.9), two key aspects immediately come out. First, all authoritarians locate themselves more to the right than the other groups. This confirms that authoritarianism affects the left much less: it belongs more to the right and to previous historical experiences. Greece is the country where authoritarian opinion is more clearly identified with the right (8.55 vis-à-vis between 6 and 7 in the other countries in a scale from 1 to 10). The more central Portuguese self-placement, however, is rather the result of a compensation between the two wings.

Secondly, authoritarians are more extremist than neo-authoritarians. This feature shows the true meaning of the two different positions very clearly. An opinion against the democratic regime implies a self-location on the extreme right side of the ideological spectrum for authoritarians, whereas for neo-authoritarians it may mean being on either the left or the right sides. In this perspective, Greece appears to be the country where neo-authoritarians also have a rightist component.

TABLE 3.9. *Democrats and authoritarians by left–right self-placement*

	Italy	Spain	Portugal	Greece
Democrats	3.90	3.65	4.43	4.07
Neo-democrats	5.05	5.11	5.70	6.03
Indifferents	4.26	5.16	5.50	7.01
Neo-authoritarians	4.87	4.89	5.44	6.34
Authoritarians	6.58	6.91	6.03	8.55

Source: See Table 3.3.

An additional relevant consideration is that the opinions of neo-authoritarians are fairly balanced either because they are simply more centrist or because of a compensation between rightist and leftist leanings. However, this group places itself in a position very similar to the one chosen by neo-democrats, again because of the same two reasons mentioned above. Finally, the democrats show centre-left ideological leanings.

The overlap between party affiliation and left-right self-placement confirms what has just been said. Thus, first of all, the more central self-placement of neo-authoritarians may be seen as the result of a leftist component of this group. In other words, it is a result of a compensation between a more rightist component and a leftist one. In fact, neo-authoritarians are among the Greek Socialists, the Italian Communists (and also Christian Democrats), the Spanish Socialists, and even among the Portuguese Communists who are likely to be the most leftist among all Southern European voters. This suggests the hypothesis of a critical, dissatisfied component in the leftist end of the spectrum as the most relevant element in the neo-authoritarian choice, although neo-authoritarians are also present in the centre or centre-right.

With regard to the other group, the authoritarians, the connection between them and rightist parties is an obvious one. Such a connection is an exclusive one in three out of four countries. But, in addition, there is the noteworthy presence of these attitudes in all the main Portuguese parties except for the Communists.[44] Thus, Portugal is the only country where old authoritarian attitudes are widespread in almost every party.

Interestingly enough, there is a meaningful neo-democratic opinion in the rightist parties of all countries, except for Italy where basically the time elapsed from fascism makes more difficult the existence of that category among the MSI affiliated, who, however, go on belonging to the authoritarian camp. Still with reference to Italy, the presence of neo-democrats among Christian Democrats appears particularly meaningful.[45]

An additional feature and difference between authoritarians and neo-authoritarians emerges when, again with reference to parties, the preference of those two groups in supporting no party or a one-party system is controlled (Table 3.10). As expected, about 40 per cent of authoritarians in Portugal and Spain are in favour of these institutional arrangements. It may be recalled here that recurring features of governmental propaganda in these two authoritarian regimes were the delegitimation of parties and the support for a one-party system, which was never actually carried out with mobilizational, totalitarian characteristics.

In the Italian case, the elapsed time and habituation with parties account for the lower percentage, whose actual meaning should be rather related to no support for any party because of their negative, conflictive, divisive impact on politics. Moreover, this sort of opinion is another recurring tenet of authoritarian opinions which was largely widespread during the authoritarian phases in Spain and Portugal.

In Greece the strong identification of authoritarians with the rightist Nea Dimokratia, the highest identification among all authoritarian opinions (see Morlino and Mattei 1992), helps to explain the relatively low percentage of not identified people or supporters of a one-party solution. It may be recalled that the authoritarian experience in Greece can be traced back to the Metaxas period during the second half of the 1930s;[46] that experience was much shorter than the Italian one (twenty years), and even shorter than the other two experiences (forty-eight years in Portugal and thirty-nine in Spain). Thus, the quasi-fascist Greek experience is the shortest and the most distant in time.

[44] And the PRD, newly formed by President Eanes, at the time of the survey (1985).
[45] Again, for more data on this see Morlino and Mattei (1992).
[46] The *coup d'état* that gave power to General Metaxas took place in early August 1934.

TABLE 3.10. *Preference for no parties or only one party*

	Italy	Spain	Portugal	Greece
Democrats	4.3	8.3	7.6	8.3
Neo-democrats	3.9	9.7	17.1	9.9
Indifferents	15.8	25.0	28.1	19.0
Neo-authoritarians	10.0	21.8	16.5	12.5
Authoritarians	29.2	39.0	35.7	14.0

Source: See Table 3.3.

Furthermore, parties have always been present in Greek politics except during the military period (1967–73).

The positions of neo-authoritarians are very different on this aspect. The competitive aspects of party politics appear to be more clearly acknowledged by this group in all four countries. This said, the relatively higher percentages of this group in Portugal and Spain seem to be the result of a sort of 'pulling' effect, due to the highest figures in the other category, the authoritarians. Also in this case the non-competitive view of politics may come from critical attitudes towards democracy as well as from the meaninglessness of parties and competition in the political arena. In this sense, those attitudes appear to be more related to criticisms against democracy than to authentic support for an authoritarian institutional alternative.

Supposedly, the democratic and neo-democratic opinions give almost no support to anti-party beliefs. But the Portuguese exception is fairly surprising: in that country neo-democrats consider the possibility of democracy without parties or with only one party. *Ex post facto*, this appears to be a clear indicator of the negative perception of highly conflictive multipartism and the need for political stability. In retrospect, these attitudes may very well account for the electoral result in 1987 which gave a dominant position to the Social Democratic Party. Only residually does the lack of a liberal-democratic party tradition before Salazarism help to account for those opinions.

To sum up, although they are not large groups in Southern European societies, authoritarians and neo-authoritarians present different, salient characteristics. In addition, there is a large group of neo-democrats with other relevant features. Thus, from a socio-economic point of view, age and education are the two most crucial factors. Age has minor relevance for neo-democrats, but it is the main factor which differentiates neo-authoritarians from authoritarians. As for education, it is low among authoritarians and higher among neo-democrats and neo-authoritarians, which in this respect are very close. This suggests how the processes of political socialization are salient in the four countries.

Second, the rightist self-placement of authoritarians is complemented by a rightist and a leftist self-location of the other groups. Also, interestingly, neo-authoritarians and neo-democrats display similar average scores on this variable because of a compensation effect between rightist and leftist components in both groups, as well as a third moderate centre component in both groups. Thirdly, there are neo-authoritarians in the Communist and Socialist parties of our countries and at the same time neo-democrats in the rightist parties. Fourth, while neo-authoritarians partially acknowledge parties as the key institutions in democratic politics, authoritarians are much more tied to old tenets and opinions which have much in common with rightist opinion some time ago, during the last phase of those non-democratic regimes. In addition, there is a neo-democratic sector in Portugal which has hardly accepted the connection between democracy and multipartism and loaded multipartism with negative perceptions, such as considering the parties as being at the roots of higher conflict and instability.

If these four elements are drawn together, a fairly clear picture emerges: neo-authoritarians are more educated people with critical attitudes toward the regime because of dissatisfaction with and alienation from the new democratic experience; authoritarians are much more linked to the authoritarian historical past and their support for that experience endures; but neo-democrats make up a group, quantitatively larger, which does not deny the past and plainly accepts the new reality.

This general picture, however, needs to be amended when the question of 'how democracy works' is analysed.[47] Actually, except in the case of Italy (see also Part III), in the other three countries authoritarians and neo-authoritarians are very much dissatisfied and critical (see above, esp. Table 3.5). The extent of dissatisfaction is much higher in the first group, whereas if the hypothesis suggested above were completely correct profound critical attitudes should also be found in the second group, as in the Italian case.[48] Basically, the neo-authoritarian opinion seems plainly to be a more moderate one than that of the first group: 'democracy works in spite of many defects' is the predominant answer in that group, while the

---

[47] The question was: 'With which of the following statements do you agree? 1. Our democracy works well; 2. Our democracy has many defects but it works; 3. Our democracy is getting worse and soon it will not work at all. . . .'

[48] The widespread highly critical attitudes of Italian political culture have been widely discussed. For an overview see Guidorossi (1984); more recently see Morlino and Tarchi (1996), and Part III.

more critical evaluation is predominant in the other group. In fact, the high percentage for the last answer, that is, the belief that democracy has no future and the situation can only 'get worse' and that there is no reform possibility, is the most characterizing aspect of authoritarians when compared with all other groups, neo-authoritarians included.

A higher extent of moderate dissatisfaction is openly displayed by democrats and neo-democrats in comparison with neo-authoritarians. The attitude is that democracy may have 'many defects, but it works'. With regard to neo-democrats, this may suggest that the larger sub-group among them is formed by the 'converted' (see above), who were hypothetically considered particularly sensitive to democratic perfor-mance. If this is so, it should be additionally confirmed by controlling with other variables (see below). On the whole, however, the interme-diate, more moderate response polarizes the reaction of all groups, except the authoritarians, the most critical ones.

Strong discontent and political alienation are higher among the authoritarians, while the neo-authoritarians are in a more ambiguous space: they are relatively critical, but not alienated as much as the other two groups which accept the existing democratic regime. In this sense, only in Italy are the neo-authoritarians (and the indifferents) very dis-satisfied, and therefore the third answer received the highest percent-age of responses from this group: 'democracy is getting worse.' In the other three countries, the distinctive attitude of neo-authoritarians is that they always show a larger component of highly critical and alien-ated responses than the other two groups of democrats.

If the picture drawn above is taken for granted, the next most salient question is whether non-democratic groups would be open to becoming active and involved against the existing institutions. If this sector is ready to become active, they could create serious problems for our coun-tries, for example in a moment of economic crisis. To provide an answer to this question the first variable to consider is the interest of people in politics.

Paralleling what is suggested above (see e.g. Table 3.4), none of the groups considered here shows a particularly strong interest in politics. Democrats are relatively more interested than authoritarians in all four countries. In Greece and Spain, neo-authoritarians are as interested as neo-democrats. Similarly, in Portugal this same group, which voted for every party of the political spectrum and is highly dissatisfied, is also as active as the group of democrats. In Italy, the opposite takes place: the neo-democrats are again very close to democrats in their more active attitudes, which are higher than those of neo-authoritarians.[49]

---

[49] For a more detailed analysis of these data see again Morlino and Mattei (1992).

TABLE 3.11. *Average support for strikes, demonstrations, and occupation*

	Italy	Spain	Portugal	Greece
Democrats	57.8	70.8	50.6	67.1
Neo-democrats	44.7	43.4	27.0	56.8
Indifferents	46.5	40.0	18.5	44.7
Neo-authoritarians	44.0	40.2	40.4	56.2
Authoritarians	33.0	28.9	26.7	35.8

Source: See Table 3.3.

Is a high interest in politics complemented by a willingness to become active? Here again the difference between the two authoritarian groups is revealed. The authoritarians are not seriously open to involvement in different forms of protest, such as demonstrations or occupations (see Table 3.11). The neo-authoritarians are a little more ready to protest. Curiously enough, on the whole, the support for protest is higher than the interest in politics, but it is also related to it. It is very plausible that the partially higher interest in politics of neo-authoritarians—but not in Italy—and their willingness to support or even engage in unconventional forms of participation may be accounted for the age factor: younger people are usually more open to such forms of protest. However, the main point is that none of the two groups shows particularly active attitudes, and in almost all cases they are more or much more passive than the democrats.[50]

The analysis of the two variables just mentioned may also be useful in exploring the subgroups that were indicated speculatively among the neo-democrats (obedients and converted). A control with the variable on 'how democracy works' (see above, and Morlino and Mattei 1992) suggested that if the distinctions between the two subgroups are accepted, the 'converted' are dominant because of the more critical attitudes of the whole group towards the regime. But are these attitudes also active? That is, are interest in politics and potential for activation higher among the neo-democrats than among the indifferents or the authoritarians? Or are they much closer to the indifferents, thus demonstrating the dominance of passive attitudes? No single answer is good for all four countries. In Greece and Spain the neo-democrats appear to be more active. Thus, the 'converted' should be dominant, consistently with the other variable on the working of democracy. In Portugal the neo-democrats are lower than the neo-authoritarians and

[50] In a different sense, such a potential for participation is stressed by Inglehart (1990) in an analysis using data from most of the democratic countries.

closer to the indifferents on both variables. This seems to suggest some dominance of the 'obedients' among the neo-democrats. In Italy the picture is more ambiguous: the neo-democrats show a higher interest in politics than the neo-authoritarians, but a similar potential for participation (Table 3.11). Thus, for this country no conclusion can be drawn. This is perfectly consistent with the fact that after so many years the two subgroups ('obedients' and 'converted') are merged and it is virtually impossible to diffentiate them.

This analysis confirms that the historical past is basically over in 1985: the old authoritarians make up a tiny group, while at the same time the high percentages of democrats and neo-democrats display that there are no conceivable alternatives to the present democratic arrangements. The authoritarians do not seem to provide a challenge in any sense. In addition, when the 'potential for activation' is considered, it is very low, and in any case lower than that of democrats.

Neo-authoritarians are younger people with no nostalgic memory of the past, and with a discontent which is more limited in intensity and widespread among people with different political leanings. On the whole, their positions are more ambiguous, in a sense, and more moderate, in another, than those of authoritarians. This group is more consistent and also more open and willing to participate in political action. But it will not be possible to overcome their discontent or to win them over to democracy because they are partially tied to the historical past and partially to a more recent dissatisfaction.

A much larger and salient group is formed by neo-democrats. They are more educated people who do not deny or forget their past political experience: the epoch of dictators, the military in politics, and the one-party system. However, they consider critically the present democratic performance and, as neo-authoritarians, may be ready for mobilization and participation in difficult or emergency situations. In fact, at least in Greece and Spain the 'converted' seem to prevail over the 'obedients'. As with neo-authoritarians, they are not a challenge to democracy. But because of their critical attitudes and readiness to participation, these large sectors of society form an influential body of public opinion that may well be either the basis for new rightist protest movements and parties or the ground for stimulating sound actions by political élites.

Élite Support

As seen in this chapter, the problem of mass consensus has been mainly analysed in terms of democratic acceptance and the existence of regime alternatives. This was a way of partially overcoming the well-known problems of inconsistency between attitudinal aspects and behaviours as well as the acknowledged superficiality and volatility of those attitudes. Moreover, this analysis brings to the fore a few other issues. First of all, in the presence of a more or less large consensus, the thrust for the legitimation (or delegitimation) process comes from the action of political élites or social élites that act in the political arena (see also Linz 1990: 143–64; and Morlino 1986*a*). In this sense it is necessary to consider the roles of party élites as translators of popular sentiments into overt actions for or against the existing democratic institutions. The expression of fundamental attitudes by parties, movements, or other political groups, in programmes, ideologies, and their behaviour in parliament and other democratic arenas have a significant impact on democratic consolidation. Not only do system-supportive attitudes and behaviours, and the absence of anti-system parties, show that there are no alternatives to the existing regime, but they also demonstrate the breadth of support for democratic institutions. Indicators of such supportive positions include the stands taken by parties on specific issues and in ideological or programmatic declarations, the behavioural conformity with the democratic rules of the game, the eschewing of violence as a political tool, and the availability of the party for inclusion within a government coalition with other parties that accept it. Indicators of negative, delegitimizing positions of a party are likewise seen in its ideologies, programmes, and stands on specific issues, but also in the recognized non-capacity of participating in cabinet coalitions (coalitional incapability).[51]

More precisely, ideologies, declarations, programmes, and also decisions and policies pursued by party élites indicate the 'subjective' dimension of pro-regime, semi-proregime, and anti-regime qualities of a party. That is, support or more or less radical opposition to the democratic institutions can be detected. The coalitional capability in all its different forms (from one-sided parliamentary abstention, to bargained abstention, external, i.e. without its own ministers, support of cabinet on specific issues, external support for the governmental programme, support of cabinet with its own ministers in secondary or key positions) is the main indicator of 'objective' pro-regime or anti-regime qualities of a party, where the key aspect is if and how other parties accept or refuse the anti-regime party, sometimes only for strategic calculus. The 'objective' integration of a party is also seen at a mass level by checking if a party is considered by the public and voters as a democratic party, a party that the average voter would vote for or, however, would

---

[51] A number of these indicators are proposed by Linz (1978); and also by Morlino (1985). The importance of anti-regime parties in the consolidation process is also stressed by Higley and Gunther (1992).

not be openly discarded by most of the citizens. Of course, these dimensions can only be indicated through a mass survey. As with the coalitional capability, the integration of an anti-regime party or its possible transformation into such a party does not happen all of a sudden, but it usually goes through different steps that may even take a long time to unfold, and leaders' choices, decisions, and strategies are crucial in this sub-process. Moreover, although analytically the 'subjective' integration precedes the 'objective' one, the reality is often different: the steps in one dimension cross the steps in the other or the 'objective' integration even comes first. As we will see below, such a crossing, with a surprising coalitional capability gained by Greek Communists, took place in Greece at the end of 1989 with the crisis of PASOK.[52]

A detailed empirical analysis of the relevant data is not necessary here. However, a few points on how parties are linked to the democratic institutions illustrate the extent to which legitimation has taken place in Southern Europe. First, extreme right-wing parties have virtually disappeared from three of these four party systems. In Spain, the high-water mark for parties of the far right was 1979, when they received 3 per cent of the total vote and elected one deputy; they subsequently vanished, receiving less than 0.05 per cent of the vote in 1993. In Greece and Portugal, right-wing political groups did not achieve a parliamentary presence of any sort, except for Greece in the election of 1977. That year a group of ultraconservatives who had splintered from Nea Dimokratia received 6.8 per cent of the vote, but they then disappeared in the 1981 elections. In Portugal, the extreme radical right never overcame 1.1 per cent of the vote, achieved in 1979, and an average of 0.6 per cent for the period 1976–91 (see also Costa Pinto 1991). In Greece and Portugal, the authoritarian alternative, which had ruled for seven and forty-eight years respectively, was fully delegitimated and therefore became politically extinct (see Herz 1982, Diamandouros 1986, and Maxwell 1986*b*). While not fully delegitimated, the Spanish authoritarian right was also less viable: anti-Franco sen-

---

[52] Building on a distinction drawn by Tarrow (1982), Zariski (1986) suggests another distinction, that between 'endogenous legitimacy', concerning an opposition party that maintains the allegiance of its activists, members, and followers despite changes in political positions, and 'exogenous legitimacy', that is, the legitimacy gained by an opposition party recognized as fit to rule. This is an intelligent way of analysing more in depth the transition from anti-regime positions to pro-regimes ones. It should be clarified, however, that the target of legitimation is the party (either by its own members or by other parties and the public). In contrast, the 'subjective'/'objective' distinction concerns the attitudes and behaviours of anti-regime parties toward the democratic institutions, and the endogenous legitimacy is one of the facets of the 'sujective' integration, while the exogenous legitimacy concerns the 'objective' dimensions. In other words, the legitimacies of Zariski only partially overlap with the anti-regime status and the process of integration discussed in the text.

timents were not terribly strong or widespread, but in a modernized and more European society parties with an authoritarian appeal had no chance of success (see previous sections). In addition, none of these former authoritarian regimes has maintained a mass-mobilization capacity or socialized their respective populations in a manner that would have perpetuated the authoritarian option.

From this perspective, the Italian case is quite different: an extreme right-wing neo-fascist party (MSI) consistently received 5 per cent of the vote throughout the 1950s and has remained viable until the recent past (see Ignazi 1989, and Tarchi 1997). The mobilizational characteristics of fascism—the rejuvenated mobilization of fascist 'black shirts' during the Repubblica Sociale Italiana (RSI), 1943–5, helped by a highly proportional electoral law, largely accounted for the birth of this anti-system party, which has maintained an ambiguous relationship with violent terrorist groups (see Ferraresi 1984, and Minna 1984).

A more interesting trend is found among parties of the non-extremist right. Nea Dimokratia (ND) played a key role in the founding of Greek democracy, but both the Portuguese Centro Democrático Social (CDS) and the Spanish Alianza Popular (AP) began by adopting relatively ambiguous positions towards the authoritarian past and in the new democratic regime subsequently integrated themselves fully into the framework of democratic competition. In Portugal, the right—some of whose leaders were survivors from the Caetano period—had political and organizational difficulties at the very beginning, in part because of the leftist leanings of the *coup d'état* which inaugurated the new regime (see Nogueira Pinto 1989: 196; and Bruneau and Macleod 1986, 77). Despite their organizational weakness, rightist groups made clear their reservations about the new regime: in 1976, the CDS was the only party to vote against the constitution. Within a few years, however, thanks to the gradual, but profound change in the nature of the regime itself, the trend towards legitimation was complete: the CDS participated in coalition cabinets (see Chapter 2) and played a role in supporting the new democratic system.

In Spain, Alianza Popular underwent a similar transformation. The AP had leaders whose origins were rooted in the Franco regime, and many of its voters maintained favourable attitudes towards Franco (see Montero 1986a: 370). But in the aftermath of a schism, triggered by parliamentary ratification of the constitution in 1978, the party adopted an unequivocally pro-system stance. Party leader Manuel Fraga's unwavering support for the constitution that he had helped to write, as well as the party's opposition to the attempted coup of February 1981, underscored its shift from initial ambiguity to a declared loyalty to the democratic regime. In addition the party consciously sought to moderate its ideology and adopt a more centrist stance (see Gunther, Sani, and Shabad 1986: 194; and López Nieto 1988). But it was at the end of the 1980s that the party also broke all personal links with the Francoist past thanks to a high internal élite turnover and to its adaptation of his values and programmes to the other European Popular Parties to which PP joined in the European Parliament (see also Gangas Peiró 1995: 226).

The other important development was the general moderation in the initial stands of Southern European socialist parties, their full acceptance of the respective democratic regimes, and their successful attainment of government posts in all four countries. In the Italian case, the Socialists' embrace of the existing democracy was slow to occur and can be dated mainly to after the Soviet invasion of Hungary in 1956. Socialists moved from a semi-loyal stand to one of full loyalty following their detachment from the Communists. In the early 1960s, they joined the DC in the governing coalition (see Chapter 2). The Spanish PSOE was, from the very beginning, a democratic party. The party's transformation therefore involved moderation of the economic proposals and programmes of the party. This change closely paralleled the programmatic reforms adopted by the German Social Democratic Party at its 1958 Bad Godesberg conference. At its extraordinary Congress in September 1979, the PSOE, under the leadership of Felipe González, abandoned all Marxist elements in its ideology. As in the case of the German SPD, this was an important turning point for the party and paved the way for its transformation from an opposition party to a governmental one (see Puhle 1986: 332; Román Marugán 1987: 509; Share 1989, ch. 3; and Gunther 1986b).

The Greek Socialist Party, PASOK, followed a parallel road. In 1974, PASOK emerged as a pro-democratic, but radical, anti-capitalist, and fiercely confrontational party with a Marxist vocabulary. During the second half of the decade, however, the party became increasingly moderate and centrist. Specifically, a dogmatic and sectarian conception of socialism was gradually watered down, becoming a more generic commitment to change, characterized as much by greater moderation and pragmatism as by a fervent nationalism. At this point a 'viable legitimate governmental alternative identified with the non-communist left' had been built (see Diamandouros 1991; also see Clogg 1987, Appendix and 217; Featherstone 1987: 119; Spourdalakis 1988: 180; and Mavrogordatos 1983).

The same process of moderation can be seen in the evolution of the Portuguese Socialist and Social Democratic parties, although with some variations on this theme. The basic difference distinguishes between parties whose first experiences under the new democracy were ones of opposition to conservative governments and those socialist parties which were at the core of the democratic process from the very beginning. The PSOE and PASOK are good examples of the first pattern: in order to enhance their electoral acceptability and come to power they were motivated to adopt more moderate, centrist programmatic stands and to accept a market, capitalist economic structure. The Portuguese Socialists were characteristic of the second group of parties. They had first adopted Marxist positions, but then quickly and completely embraced democratic pluralism emerging as the staunchest defenders of pluralist representative democracy. They were at the core of the Portuguese consolidation process beginning in the 'hot summer' of 1975 and continued to moderate their stands until the formation of the central block in 1983 (see Stock 1985; and Robinson 1991–2).

With the exception of the Portuguese Communist Party, the same phenomenon can be observed farther towards the leftist end of the political continuum. The manner in which the Italian Communist Party (PCI) changed its stand between the installation of the new regime and consolidation of democracy is most outstanding. The PCI had been very active and important in the Resistance, in drafting the constitution, and, more generally, in the very founding of the new democracy. It voted in favour of the whole text of the constitution (December 1947) and even in March 1947 in favour of its much debated Article 7, which acknowledged the treaty (*Concordato*) between the Catholic Church and the Italian state, signed by Mussolini in February 1929. After 1947–8, however, when the economic and ideological choices of the Christian Democrats and other moderate, centrist parties in favour of private enterprise and market became clear, and when the outbreak of the Cold War contributed to the strong bipolarization of the party system, the Communists became an anti-regime force. During the following decade, no process of legitimation occurred. On the contrary, the Communists where frozen out of power at the national level from May 1947 on. This fact was only partly offset by their presence in local governments of central Italy and in the parliamentary arena, where they were very active, particularly in the legislative committees.

With the elapsing of time, out of the main phase of consolidation, the Communists gradually underwent a process of negative integration into the system. Communist legitimation advanced very slowly, through a series of landmark events: in 1963, the Socialists formed a new cabinet with the Christian Democrats, and the Communists remained more isolated and excluded by the existing democratic forces; ten years later, after the mobilization of 1968 and above all, the Chilean military coup against the socialist experiment of Allende, in

1973–5, the Communist leader, Enrico Berlinguer proposed the so-called 'historical compromise' with the Catholic forces and later launched the idea of Eurocommunism, that is, of a Communism very different and distant from Moscow, living and growing in the Western democratic institutions; in 1976, Berlinguer even accepted the Italian military alliance in NATO; still in 1976, after the spectacular electoral growth of that year (+7.2 per cent), to cope with the critical moments of Italian democracy the party decided on parliamentary abstention to let most of the bills be approved by the floor or in the Committees; in 1978–9, the Communists entered a parliamentary majority, which supported a cabinet led by Giulio Andreotti (see Table 2.10); and in 1989–91 the party developed and made the crucial decision to change its name to the Democratic Party of the Left (PDS) (see Di Loreto 1991; Flores and Gallerano 1992; and Ignazi 1992); in 1993, they entered the parliamentary majority with three ministers, who, however, resigned after twenty-four hours; in 1996 they became a key component of Prodi's cabinet.

The Spanish Communist Party, partly as a reaction to the dramatic experience of the Spanish Civil War and partly in exchange for its legalization in April 1977 (shortly before the first democratic election), became a loyal force from the very beginning of democratic inauguration (see González Hernández 1989; Gunther, Sani, and Shabad 1986; Gunther 1986a; and Mujal-León 1983). The very decision regarding the Communist legalization, made by the prime minister, Suarez,[53] removed any possible exclusion of the left from the initial democratic transition, overcoming a difficult, profound historical division, even at the cost of provoking negative reactions in the army and laying the basis of the future problems that emerged with some degree of army politicization (see Chapter 2). Accordingly, the party played an active role in the politics of support for democratic installation: it accepted the monarchy and the Spanish flag (1977), participated in the framing and approval of the constitution (1977–8), gave up the traditional ideological tenets such as Leninism (1978), and promoted a strategy of large coalitions by negotiating and helping to implement the Pactos de la Moncloa (1977). PCE leaders openly declared that the consolidation of Spanish democracy was one of the main objectives of the party (see Gunther, Sani, and Shabad 1986: 166). Since the PCE was a pro-regime party from the very beginning, there was no process of legitimation at all. In this respect, the evolution of the Communist Party in Spain was very different from that of the Communist Party in Italy, and also in Portugal and Greece.

---

[53] See the detailed reconstruction of this event in Varela-Guinot (1990).

In Greece, the KKE, that is, the larger of the two communist parties which emerged from the split during the military regime, shifted from a non-loyal stance and exclusion in 1974 to a position of full loyalty towards the democratic regime only in 1988–9. At the moment of democratic inauguration, the KKE was an orthodox communist party, close to the Soviet Union and maintaining the traditional conceptions of dictatorship of the proletariat and democratic centralism (see Clogg 1987: 171). It attracted 10 per cent of the vote in the first election, mainly concentrated in urban constituencies. Since it won nearly four times as many voters as its Eurocommunist rival, the KKE-Es, its position of superiority was established very early on orthodox, traditional positions. This is basically so until the mid-1980s, as may be seen also at a mass level. In fact, in 1985 the image of the party is still that of an extremist formation within the electorate: in a survey conducted in the greater Athens area 30 per cent of the sample declared the possibility of voting for the KKE against 46 per cent and 41 per cent who made the same declarations for, respectively, PASOK and Nea Dimokratia (Dimitras 1987: 81);[54] still in 1985 25 per cent of Greeks, interviewed in the Four Nation Survey, judged KKE an authoritarian party (see Guidorossi and Weber 1988: 225).

After 1985, when the competition from PASOK led to an erosion of its electoral support and the prospective of decline (Kapetanyannis 1987), the party began forming, in December 1988, the Synaspismos (Coalition of the Forces of the Left and Progress) in alliance with the old KKE-Es, which in turn has become the Greek Left (Elleniki Aristera, E.AR.). This alliance had been possible thanks to the jettisoning of traditional, orthodox tenets, and the open acceptance of democratic institutions and of Greek membership in the European Community. At the end of the 1980s, two key events, one international and one domestic, pushed the party definitely towards integration: the profound changes and disintegration of the Soviet Union meant that the party had completely lost its international reference point; and a domestic crisis caused by scandals and by the bad economic performance of the PASOK government opened the way to a new and unprecedented role for the party in government. The culmination of this process was its participation in a coalition government with Nea Dimokratia in 1989–90 (see Part III). The party's subsequent behaviour reaffirms its complete integration within the regime, its leaders' wild Marxist rhetoric and verbal nostalgia for the past notwithstanding, despite its breaking the alliance of the left in 1991 and the transformation of Synaspismos into an autonomous party in June 1992.

[54] Of course, it was possible to indicate more that one party and the question was intended to check the degree of radicalization within the party system.

The evolution of the Portuguese Communist Party bears a striking resemblance to that of Italy's. In both cases, Communists participated in the founding of the new regime and at the beginning held government posts, even at the local level. But when the regime subsequently became more and more similar to the other European liberal, pluralist democracies, the Communist Party turned into an anti-regime force ostracized by the other pro-regime parties (Bruneau and Macleod 1986: 49). In a third phase, which in the case of the PCP began in the mid-1980s, the party tried to break its isolation by supporting the election of the Socialist Mário Soares as president of the Republic (in the second round of balloting), by unfolding a strategy of alliance with the PRD to compel the Socialists toward a new governmental coalition, or by developing a parliamentary behaviour where the Socialists may need their votes on specific issues. The ideological positions of the party, however, were adjusted only marginally in the 12th Congress of Oporto (December 1988), where for the first time the party openly committed itself to pluralist democracy. Even before the dramatically altered international situation in 1989–90, the term 'advanced democracy' gradually replaced 'revolution' in the new party programme. The party stated its opposition to the process of democratization in Eastern Europe, was critical of Gorbachev, and favoured the authoritarian Chinese leadership. This resistance to change, coupled with the outbreak of intra-party conflicts, contributed to the party's electoral decline: in 1991, the PCP received only 9 per cent of the vote—less than half the level of electoral support it had enjoyed in the late 1970s and early 1980s; and later in 1995 it was able to maintain the same strength (8.6 per cent). As in the case of the French Communist Party, substantial changes are most unlikely as long as Alvaro Cunhal remains in control of the party (see Bruneau and Macleod 1986; Pacheco Pereira 1988; and Gaspar 1990). This is fully consistent with: (i) 26 per cent of people who considered the PCP as an authoritarian party, with the rightist CDS at 16 per cent (see Stock 1988: 156); and (ii) the highest percentage of people (36 per cent) vis-à-vis the other three main parties, who declared the PCP as very distant from them. In December 1992, the new elected secretary, Carvalhas, maintained a basic continuity in party lines. In any case when the Social Democrats won the majority in 1987 the PCP had become a force excluded by the political arena, though the Socialist victory of October 1995 might change this situation by overcoming the exclusion.[55]

This picture would be incomplete without a brief overview of regional nationalist parties, particularly in Spain. The legitimation processes

[55] On the democratic integration of Southern European Communist parties described above see also Bosco (1997).

involving these parties had a broad array of implications—not only for the democratic regime, but for the stability of the state and civil society itself since they directly pertained to the acceptance and acknowledgement of the unity of the country, with all its administrative, judicial, and military aspects. Here, too, a process of legitimation took place. The Basque PNV did not vote for the constitution in 1978; however, in spite of ambiguities still present in the mid-1980s, by those years it can be considered a party that had accepted both the Spanish state and its democratic regime. By the end of the decade, moreover, the PNV had become an incumbent party at the regional level, in coalition with the PSOE. In fact, the coalition agreement signed by the PNV and PSOE included commitments at the national level, as well as those pertaining to the formation of a Basque regional government.[56]

Catalan groups and parties have always been more moderate than Basque parties and have been unequivocally committed to democratic values. Centre–periphery conflicts have become much less tense, moreover, since enactment of regional autonomy statutes and rejection by the Constitutional Court of the most potentially explosive elements of the 1983 Ley Orgánica para la Armonización del Proceso Autonómico, and also as a result of habituation to and acceptance of the status quo.[57] Finally, the more radical, anti-system separatist party, Herri Batasuna, which has long been considered the legal façade of the Basque terrorist organization, ETA, was not able to win more than 1 per cent of the national vote throughout the 1980s, while the somewhat less radical Euskadiko Ezkerra (Basque Left) abruptly adopted a pro-system stance after 1981 and became increasingly moderate, eventually merging with the PSOE in advance of the 1993 election. As mentioned at the beginning of this chapter, terrorist violence itself, after peaking in 1980, declined sharply (see Llera Ramo 1993; and Reinares 1989).

Thus, the political parties of all four Southern European countries have been transformed through the processes of legitimation, although at different speeds and with somewhat different features. The process was very slow in Italy; it began in the late 1940s, and by the end of the 1950s the regime enjoyed only a limited legitimacy, with anti-system forces on both the right (the neo-fascist MSI) and the left (the PCI) that regularly won a combined total of about 30 per cent of the vote. By the

---

[56] On the dynamics of a polarized and fragmented regional party system in the Basque country, see Linz and Montero 1986; Llera Ramo 1989; and again Linz 1986; and Llera Ramo 1993.

[57] Survey research in the early 1990s revealed high levels of satisfaction within these regions with 'how autonomy works': 48% of Catalans expressed their satisfaction, as did 44% of Basques. See Montero and Torcal 1990: 69; and also Chapter 2.

early 1960s, the previously semi-proregime forces, such as the Socialists (PSI) (with 13–14 per cent of the vote), had been integrated. This
meant that during the first fifteen years after 1948 the pro-regime
forces were basically limited to those participating in the unstable government coalitions formed by Christian Democrats (DC), Liberals
(PLI), Republicans (PRI), and Social Democrats (PSDI). These were the
parties that by supporting the cabinet and in its legislative activity
actually supported the democratic regime. In other words, there was an
internal party system, formed by DC, PLI, PRI, PSDI and later on by
PSI, that excluded the parties at both ends of the political spectrum.
The broader party system, with its more radical patterns of competition, has been characterized by Sartori (1976) as polarized pluralism.

The Spanish case is very different from the Italian one. By the time
of the 1982 election, the extreme right had virtually disappeared from
the party system, as had several tiny parties of the extreme left;
Alianza Popular had shifted to an unequivocally pro-regime party and
had basically integrated itself, in spite of continuing links until the end
of the 1980s with a party élite that had been mayors and governors in
the previous regime; the Communist Party, its own internal crises and
schisms notwithstanding, had played a crucial moderating role at key
stages of the transition and consolidation processes: since the beginning of the democratic inauguration Carrillo and the other leaders
accepted the new democratic institutions and promoted a strategy of
alliances; and the Socialist PSOE had transformed itself into a stable,
centrist political force. Only in the case of the Basque regional party
system was the legitimation process slower in developing.

In Greece and Portugal, regime legitimation exhibited important differences, but they are both closer to Spain than to Italy. In Greece, the
right was very supportive of the installed regime, which, after all, had
been created by Karamanlis and Nea Dimokratia. Even PASOK, which
initially had adopted a rather semi-loyal stance towards the regime,
moderated both its rhetoric and its behaviour and adopted a fully loyal
stance by the early 1980s. The Greek Communists have also been integrated into the regime. Their integration stemmed from the weakness
of the two communist parties, which were subordinated following the
electoral success of PASOK in 1981. While the KKE's rhetoric is consistently hard-line and Marxist in tone, the party's participation in a
coalition government with Nea Dimokratia in 1989–90 marks the end
of the process of legitimation. If 1985 is taken as the *terminus ad quem*
of consolidation, then the KKE is still in a basically anti-regime position, excluded from any possibility of governmental alliance.

The Portuguese right also came to support the regime, but only after
several years and two significant revisions of the constitution (see

Chapter 2). The Portuguese Communist Party, meanwhile, remained under the control of an orthodox Communist leadership and maintained a semi-loyal stance towards the democratic regime—thereby consigning itself to a process of electoral decline. It may be noticed that later, at the beginning of 1990, a more thorough integration is undertaken (see Bosco 1997).

When these four systems are arrayed on a continuum measuring the legitimacy achieved by the democratic regime in the year that is considered the *terminus ad quem* of consolidation, Italy is located closer to the low sector of the scale: it is a case of partial, limited, and exclusive legitimacy. Portuguese democracy is also somewhat limited in the achieved extent of legitimation, given the continuing semi-loyalty and orthodox Communism of the PCP. Greece is at the opposite end, especially in light of the dramatic entry of formerly mortal enemies, the Communists and the conservatives of Nea Dimokratia, into a coalition government in 1989. But that democracy is much closer to Portugal if the year to consider is 1985. A largely inclusive legitimacy was achieved by Spain, where, by the end of the 1980s, regional anti-regime forces such as Herri Batasuna were becoming increasingly irrelevant. Also, the right of Alianza Popular is integrated in the regime, despite the lack of 'objective' complete integration according to the sectors of the moderate voters. If the legitimacy of parties is regarded as the sole criterion for consolidation, the Italian case in the late 1950s is one of limited consolidation, Spain and Greece in the 1980s is an example of large, widespread consolidation, and Portugal is a case of relatively more limited consolidation.

It is important to note that in three out of four of the countries the legitimation process has not been linear. In Italy, it was basically frozen during the most intense years of the Cold War, between 1948 and 1956. In Spain, a period of difficulty followed substantial initial progress: between 1979 and 1981 this was manifested at the mass level in the so-called *desencanto* (disillusionment) and at the élite level in the breakdown of the Unión de Centro Democrático, which had governed Spain throughout the installation of the new democracy. These were also the peak years of Basque terrorism, accompanied by increases in electoral support for separatist parties. In Portugal, until the first important constitutional revision in 1982, there was a long phase during which it was even unclear what kind of democracy should be installed and considered legitimate, a radical socialist regime or a pluralist democracy, closer to European models. Only in Greece was the process basically linear: in fact, the legitimation process was really only relevant to the Communists until the end of the 1980s, and there were no significant periods of backsliding.

In the processes of legitimation described above there are important variations among the four countries in how the processes unfolded, as well as the configuration of partisan forces in the new democracy. Several of the factors that led to important variations have been explored, also when the mass consensus has been analysed. Here, with regard to differences between Italy and the other three cases, one specific variable still has to be stressed. The presence of an extremist, non-democratic right with the positions toward democracy, the style, the ideology and programme of MSI, AP, or CDS, appears to be a function of the type of authoritarian regime that existed in each country prior to the transition to democracy. Italy, which has had a significant extreme, anti-democratic right-wing party for decades, had a regime of mobilization with a key role performed by the totalitarian party and its mass organizations, while the authoritarian regime of the other three countries did not have such party structures or even had policies of demobilization. The presence of a non-democratic right was also facilitated by such developments during its protracted post-Mussolini transition as the establishment of the fascist Italian Social Republic (RSI) and the civil war. In Spain, some ambiguity towards democracy among those on the right resulted from the long duration of Francoism and the economic growth that occurred in the final phase of authoritarian regime, while in Portugal this was partly a residual reaction against the radical leftist aspects of the 'Revolution of the Carnations'.

Cross-national differences of the far left are also largely explained by historical events that occurred at the time of democratic transition. In Italy the re-establishment of party politics in the mid-1940s was affected by the fascination of Socialists and Communists with a leftist alternative to the existing order, strengthened by the experience of the Resistance, and supported by the USSR. The transitions of the mid-1970s, however, occurred after Eurocommunism had already developed as an alternative perspective and ideological stance. The Communist alternative subsequently entered into a period of decline until, in 1989, the collapse of Communism in Eastern Europe and the Soviet Union closed off an important historical era.

Forms and Paths of Legitimation

In this concluding section the lines of the entire analysis on consensus and legitimation will be summarized. First, among the possible different dimensions of analysis (mass and élites, attitudes and behaviour, and its mutual interweaving), mass consensus and élite legitimation were emphasized. The main reason for this choice, supported by common sense and empirical data, is that the democratic élites—not only, but mainly party élites—may begin and unfold a process of legitimation that needs the kind of supporting actions those élites perform with continuity. But such actions may be successful if at the mass level there is some mass consensus. And this may even be so in the Italian case, where there were alternatives, but the rightist one was non-viable because of the collective memory of war and last years of fascism, and the leftist one was also non-viable because it was blocked by the rightist preference and by a realist élite attitude on the left toward the present international context of the Cold War.[58]

On the whole the two dimensions—mass consensus and élite support—interact with one another and different levels of the first or the second combine to achieve the same result in terms of the entire process of legitimation. Thus, some level of mass consensus is crucial for the whole process of legitimation. Mass consensus is explored through the analysis of the general democratic acceptance and the related lack of alternatives. Moreover, on the one hand, in all four countries a realistic political culture emerged, where support for democracy is high, where there are no viable alternatives to democracy, and where the authoritarian past is regarded with nostalgia only by small minorities. At the same time, on the other hand, pervasive feelings of political alienation and cynicism, an intense distrust of élites, and particularly party élites, in spite of the acknowledgement of their role in politics, were found.

In the mid-1980s, the level of mass consensus is fairly high and on the whole very close to that of other European countries with a long experience of democratic institutions. This implies that the same possibility of detecting a trend, for example by matching the data of 1985 with those of 1992 (see above) is very limited.[59] However, there is some growth, especially in the Portuguese case that began at the lowest level (see Table 3.3). Moreover, looking at the Italian data of the 1950s, another aspect strongly emerges: La Palombara and Waters's data suggest that the whole preference for democracy, the conditional and unconditional ones, are very close to the 1985 data. This implies that it is most important to look at the authoritarian preferences and opinions about the past. Empirically, and with some extent of approximation, the mass consensus in Italy in the 1950s is fairly low, not too far from the pole of a continuum where institutional alternatives exist vis-à-vis another pole where alternatives are absent and no authoritarian

---

[58] But as will be seen better in the next two chapters this is not enough to explain the Italian consolidation.

[59] It may be recalled that in 1992 the main phase of consolidation was already over.

preferences are present. In this sense, Greece has the highest consensus; Spain and Portugal are relatively lower.

The élite legitimating, or delegitimating, actions are seen in the continuous support they provide for the democratic institutions. And according to this reasoning the party élites are the most important to analyse. However, in these supporting actions a salient role must also be acknowledged to other institutional and non-institutional élites, such as the army, the top bureaucracy, and the judiciary, but also the entrepreneurial and economic élites or the union leaders and the church hierarchies.

Regarding the military, the point is particularly important for Portugal, and also for Spain and Greece, and it has been mentioned in Chapter 2: their integration in the existing regime is part of consolidation and is basically explained by the role the political élites are able to perform. With the relevant, but partial exception of Greece, entrepreneurial élites were linked to previous authoritarian regimes. Their democratization is a long process of habituation that may have been completed in Italy in the 1980s, that is, after thirty-five or forty years of democracy. Actually, the common, recurring attitudes of those élites are of 'institutional indifference', complemented at the beginning by the consciousness of the economic strength of their role. Italy is the clearest case among the four (see Morlino 1991*a*).

The weaker or stronger legitimation of union élites is a more interesting point that also emphasizes the role of partisan élites and the interrelationships between these élites and followers at the mass level, particularly in terms of consensus of the latter and support of the former. In addition, despite what some authors think and affirm, the impact of time emerges. This point is well illustrated by Spain. Union élites made an open, clear democratic choice in accepting the Moncloa Pacts in 1977; the pacts were implemented and renewed for a decade thanks to the moderation of workers; a habit of élite participation and partnership in shaping the governmental economic policies unfolded; and at the same time, this meant stronger legitimation of democratic institutions.[60]

In the other three countries there is not such an experience. In Portugal, where a body for the coordination of economic policies, the Permanent Council for Social Coordination, was created in 1984 (see the next chapter), there were not the same consequences as in Spain: at the very least, a higher radicalization was an obstacle to parallel developments. As in Italy and Greece, in Portugal the ideological lines suggested by partisan leaders are predominant. Consequently, the process

[60] It is not necessary to develop this point in detail. A few authors have already done this. See Pérez Díaz (1987).

of legitimation is influenced by that condition: mixed career patterns among party élites and union leaders, the management of resources which are useful for the unions, the participation of union leaders (and middle-level or grassroots élites, as well) in electoral campaigns, the same contribution to the definition of party platform and programmes are the key features that explain why there are very close relationships between parties and unions according to ideological lines (see the next chapter). The process of legitimation is consistent with this situation, and consequently there is almost no difference in how that process unfolded within party élites and union élites. It is not necessary to repeat the same considerations developed above for parties.

Regarding the church hierarchies, the important cases are Italy and Portugal. In fact, the first one is the only case where Catholics learned very clearly the lesson of fascism and made a conscious decision to support a party such as Christian Democracy, led by a strong personality very close to the Vatican, De Gasperi. This is a case where there was an interventionist choice, further specified by the support of only one party (see Poggi 1975). The choice is not repeated in Spain and Portugal: the Vatican II Council and the previous commitment in favour of Franco and Salazar, but also the different historical moment, accounts for the differences with Italy. Between Spain and Portugal there are other relevant differences. Since the beginning of the democratic transition in Spain there was a 'wait and see' position: non-supportive of Francoism during his last years of crisis, the Catholic Church accepted the new regime, openly intervening only when a basic issue, such as divorce or abortion, was at stake.[61] In Portugal a much different situation emerged and consequently the Church had to take a different stand by immediately turning its neutral, conscious, waiting position into a more active, conflictive position. First of all, during the period 1975–6 the Episcopal Conference and hierarchies could not accept the radical leftist ideologies of cabinets with Communist participation. Later on, and particularly since 1979, when a document on the topic was published, all archbishops and bishops made very clear their support for democratic institutions and denounced the popular *desencanto* against democracy (Mattoso 1994: 260–71). Consequently, since 1979, the positions of the Church became much closer to that of the Italian or Spanish hierarchies, perhaps with a few differences in terms of more traditional positions and more recurring interventions and tensions on classic topics, such as private teaching, family, abortion, and Christian values, but also unemployment and social inequalities,

---

[61] See the large excursus by Pérez Díaz (1993: 145 ff.), but also González Blasco and González-Anleo (1992).

which included making propaganda for civil disobedience in 1984, when the Socialist bill on abortion was passed.[62]

The extent of legitimation in the four countries has been described in the previous section. In this dimension the existence of a trend, and even moments of stop and go (see above), is much clearer and evident: in Italy the growth of legitimacy primarily concerns the integration of Socialists; in Spain, partly the Socialists and Communists; in Portugal, up to 1987 the integration of Communists is still far from complete and at the beginning and until the early 1980s for sectors of élites, the rightist party included, the project of liberal democracy was still unclear; in Greece, the integration partly regards Socialists, and later also Communists. Figure 3.2 plots together the two dimensions and roughly draws the trends in the process of legitimation. This is shorter and more incomplete in Italy; it is longer and more difficult in Portugal and in Greece, if in this second country 1985 is the symbolic year to consider for the basic end of consolidation; it appears more successful in Spain where in the mid-1980s the existence of an anti-system regional élite and population may be recalled. Thus, on the whole, as approximately suggested by Figure 3.2, at the considered end of the legitimation, which is mostly relevant for consolidation, the Italian legitimation is exclusive; on the contrary, the Greek one is quasi-inclusive in 1985, as the inclusion of the extreme left only came at the end of that decade with the governmental experience of KKE; Portugal also is in a position of quasi-inclusiveness in 1987: the difference with Greece is the much larger Greek refusal of the past and the higher mass consensus; only the Spanish legitimation is more inclusive than the other two. Let it not be forgotten that the process of legitimation also goes on and back, stops and continues again in the following years, out of the main consolidation phase, as clearly shown by the Greek case.[63]

In the concluding remarks of this chapter, another fundamental set of questions involving the legitimation process may be addressed: what are the possible requisites for successful legitimation on the basis of the Southern European experience? While all four Southern European democracies have been legitimated, it is clear that not all contemporary or historical examples of the transition to democracy have been so fortunate. What kinds of factors were conducive to legitimation in Southern Europe? If the passage of time is important in helping new democratic systems to put down strong roots, what initial factors help to explain how these processes are initially set in motion and main-

[62] Of course, the traditional support for the government by the Orthodox Church does not allow one to raise similar issues in Greece.

[63] Let it be pointed out that in this section I use 'legitimation' to indicate the whole subprocess, so that both mass consensus and élite legitimation are included.

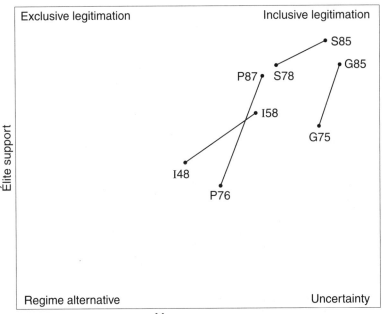

Fɪɢ. 3.2. *Space and paths to legitimation*
Note: The symbolic years of beginning and end of the core consolidation process have been considered. Thus I48 means Italy in 1948, I58 Italy in 1958, and so on.

tained? One clue emerges from research on the roles of party élites in this process. Some studies have focused on processes of élite convergence or élite settlement as the specific mechanisms involved in establishing regime legitimacy (Higley and Gunther 1992). Despite some definitional differences, these processes are highly compatible with my conceptualization of consensus and legitimation, although the latter is broader than these élite studies insofar as it pays much greater attention to both mass and élite dimensions of the phenomenon.[64] Let me recapitulate each of the Southern European cases in search of factors conducive to legitimation.

---

[64] From an élitist perspective, a long phase of legitimation may be characterized as convergence rather than settlement. However, settlements can also play key roles in initiating the legitimation process. See Gunther (1992) on Spain, and Higley and Gunther (1992) on other empirical cases. For a presentation of this élitist theoretical framework also see Higley and Burton (1989: 17–32); and Field, Higley, and Burton (1990: 149–82).

In the Italian case, such key factors include the negative memory of the earlier fascist experience and of the war, the appearance of a democratic Catholic option, and the alliance of the Christian Democrats with other smaller centrist parties (Republicans, Liberals, and Social Democrats). All of these factors, together with certain policies introduced by De Gasperi, helped to initiate the consensus and legitimation processes.

In Spain, whose transition unfolded in a different historical period and within a developed and complex society, factors conducive to the triggering and continued progress of legitimation included the moderating effect of the collective memory of civil war, the political and economic appeal of other European countries, widespread (but vague and amorphous) mass preferences for democracy, and the deliberate decisions of élites (see Maravall 1981; Pérez Díaz 1990; and Gunther 1992). Recurring social pacts linking the government, unions, and business associations, as well as the pacts for autonomy concluded by government and local élites, also contributed to the legitimation process (see Pérez Díaz 1987). A general effect of these pacts was unavoidably to confer legitimacy on the existing regime and to integrate the social groups and their representatives into that democracy.

In Portugal as well, the appeal of the European model of a pluralist democracy and the refusal to consider the radical left alternative proposed by the 'revolution' and by those political groups who persistently tried to implement it, were at the heart of support for the kind of regime which eventually was consolidated by Socialists, Social Democrats, and even the rightist CDS. Indeed, this large core of support for a pluralist democracy was a vital prerequisite to make a basic decision for the consolidation (if not the establishment) of a democratic regime—the 1982 constitutional reforms, which politically neutralized the military and eliminated its odd (and undemocratic) 'protection' of the new regime.

In Greece, the previous negative experience of the military regime, widespread democratic attitudes, the shift of the Socialists towards more moderate positions, and the democratic initiative of Karamanlis and Nea Dimokratia explain the beginning and the development of legitimation.

Moving beyond these country-specific factors, several broader considerations stand out. First of all, as suggested in the introduction, the international factor is only indirectly relevant as it is 'translated' by domestic élites. In fact, in addition to their past experiences and élite learning of them, the Cold War for Italy in one direction and the appeal of Europe and other European parties in a different direction contributed to the radical positions of Italian Communists in the 1950s and to the moderation of Socialists twenty years later. Particularly, in the 1970s and 1980s European democracies became successful models to imitate, and also thanks to the received support, party élites were much more convinced to follow the moderate Western European route (see Pridham 1991 and Whitehead 1991).

Second, at the beginning of the legitimation process, the key decisions are made by founding élites during the installation of the new democratic regime. Subsequently, however, these decisions must be supported and electorally strengthened by the people. Legitimation, thus, involves two sets of decisions, the first at the élite level and the second at the mass level, the latter being manifested in the electoral success of democratic parties, a mass-level choice that is, of course, highly conditioned by the representational biases inherent in the electoral law and by the ability of democratic parties to direct, if not to control, civil society. The electoral success of the party or parties that governed during the democratic installation phase is often very important. For this reason, the breakdown of the UCD in Spain created the most difficult moment of the entire consolidation process, to the point of contributing to an attempted coup in 1981; the ability of the Socialists to replace the UCD with a stable democratic alternative was crucial for the success of democratic legitimation, and later the consolidation process. Initially, then, a democratic system is largely created by a few actors or even by only one party. Later on, during the process of legitimation, other actors must be involved, even if to a limited extent. Thus, the virtuous circle of legitimation is initiated. Italy and Portugal are the clearest examples of this, with the entry into government of increasing numbers of parties spanning broader segments of the political continuum (see Morlino 1986b: 439–59).

The collected data and other research mentioned above show that the connection between legitimation and efficacy, that is, at least the decisional efficacy perceived at the mass level, is weak or very weak. The obvious consequence is that efficacy can be relevant for the growth or decline of the existing consensus or legitimacy in a specific democracy, but it is barely salient for the legitimation of democratic institutions that are much more related to all aspects mentioned up to now.[65]

Finally, it is worth noting that in three out of the four cases the party systems that have been stabilized are the predominant or quasi-predominant party variety. This has been already mentioned in Chapter 2 and will be discussed again in the next chapter. Here one explanatory hypothesis is worthy of mention: it is likely that predominant or quasi-predominant party systems emerged in Italy (under the

---

[65] On this see Part III.

Christian Democrats), Spain (the Socialists), and Portugal (the Social Democrats) as a result of the delegitimation and self-exclusion of the right (due to its involvement with past authoritarian regimes) and of the extreme left. Greece is not an exception to this pattern, in part because its right was never delegitimated through close association with a military-dominated authoritarian regime (indeed, it was a prominent leader of the right, Karamanlis, who played the central role in establishing the new democracy) and in part because of the bias towards bipolarity inherent in its electoral law.[66] But before coming back to discuss these aspects in Chapter 6, the 'anchors of consolidation' will be explored in the next two chapters.

[66] For other cases of predominant party systems see Pempel (1990).

4

Parties and Party Organization

The Membership

Chapter 3 traced the bottom-up direction of consolidation. Here and in the next chapter the opposite path will be followed by exploring the important anchors of consolidation connected with party organization and relationships between parties and interests. The development of party organizations and of relationships among parties, interest groups, and individual citizens are the two most significant modalities for influencing and also controlling civil society, even if these links are actually imposed by systemic aspects or institutional rules.[1] At the same time, they are important bases for the stabilization of the party systems themselves, that in their turn have acquired their own internal logic (see also Chapter 1).

TABLE 4.1. *Identification with political party (%)*

	1958	1985	1989
Italy	76.0	52.0	63
Spain		47.5	30
Portugal		48.9	49
Greece		69.6	57

Sources: For Italy in 1958, Doxa Survey (1958); for the four countries in 1985, The Four Nation Survey, and in 1989, Schmitt (1989: 183–4).

In considering party organization in this section the development of widespread party identification among the electorate will be included. The classic starting point is that the main purpose of organizational structuring is to set limits to competition, to maintain and expand a stable electorate that shares the ideology, values, and programmes of parties, but also to develop collective identities. In this sense looking at

---

[1] On this see the following chapter.

party identification may be a way of exploring the existence and development of party organization. The data presented in Table 4.1 reveal that party identification was widespread in Italy by the late 1950s: 76 per cent of Italians interviewed by Doxa identified with a party. These data are consistent with a regional survey conducted in Emilia and Romagna shortly thereafter (1958), indicating that 75.5 per cent identified with a party (Spreafico 1963: 691). They are also close to levels of party identification at about that same time in Germany (76.5 per cent in 1961) and the United States (72.5 per cent in 1956), but higher than levels of identification found in France (53.0 per cent in 1958, when the Fourth Republic collapsed) and even Norway (66.0 per cent in 1957).[2] It is interesting to note that much lower levels of party identification were found in later surveys of Italy: by 1985 they had fallen to 52 per cent; they had recovered somewhat, to 63 per cent, by 1989. As the data in Table 4.1 show, only Greece has levels of party identification similar to those found in Italy. In 1985 the already quoted Four Nation Survey found that party identification in Portugal and Spain was at the same level, but many other surveys have shown that Spain is definitely the country with the lowest party identification in Western Europe (see Schmitt and Mannheimer 1991: 31–54). The main explanation of levels of identification is commonly considered the extent of ideological conflict, but the mutually reinforcing action of organization should not be discarded; on the contrary, here it is stressed.

On the basis of these data a more developed party organization is expected in Italy and in Greece than in Portugal and Spain. It may be added that the relatively lower level of identification in Greece might point to a lower level of party organization than in Italy, even a much lower one if one notes that the smaller number of parties in Greece facilitates higher identification. Further analysis will confirm if this is so. The extent to which parties are capable of establishing supportive organizational structures is an important factor related to the stabilization of party systems and in this sense has been here defined as an 'anchor of consolidation'. As clarified long ago by Duverger (1958), its main thrust comes from the logic of party competition, which induces parties to create organizational resources to win over and retain a larger share of the voters in the electorate.[3]

Regarding the different 'faces' of party organization (see Katz and Mair 1994), the attention to the *party on the ground* or the membership organization suggests a common measure of organizational develop-

[2] The sources of these data are: for Germany, Zohlnhofer (1969: 154); for the United States, Campbell *et al.* (1966: 251); and for France and Norway, Converse and Pierce (1986: 77).

[3] A more detailed discussion of this aspect is provided in Chapter 1.

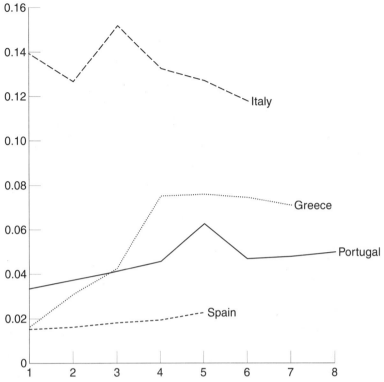

F$_{\text{IG}}$. 4.1. *Total estimated rate of party membership: Southern Europe*
Note: The total estimated rate of party membership at the country level is the estimated number of party members as a percentage of the electorate in each election. The
numbers on the horizontal axis correspond to the first to the eighth elections following
the democratic installation. For the precise years see Table 2.12.
Sources: Official electoral data and various sources for party membership (see Tables
4.2–4.5).

ment, the total estimated rate of membership (TERM) at a country
level—that is, the ratio between the total estimated membership of all
parties in the electoral year and the electorate in that election.[4] Overall, TERM may be regarded as measuring the extent of party penetration into society or, from a possible opposite perspective, the extent of
the 'partisan associability' of society. As can be seen in Figure 4.1,
Greece and especially Italy are the two countries with the highest

---

[4] The measure of specific membership rate, that is, the ratio of members and votes cast
for the same party, was suggested by Duverger in his path-breaking volume on political
parties (1958). See this index, applied to our countries in Tables 4.2–4.5. For the Socialist and Social Democratic parties, Bartolini (1983: 189) proposed an additional measure,
the membership ratio index of a given party as a percentage of the total electorate. Here,
as explained in the text, a third kind of measure is advanced, the total estimated rate of
membership (TERM).

membership rates, while Spain lags very far behind, and Portugal is in between Greece and Spain.

On the whole, Figure 4.1 confirms the Bartolini and Mair (1990: 235 ff.) findings on the negative correlation between the index of organizational density and the aggregate electoral instability: the two countries with higher stabilization are also those with higher membership rates, and vice versa. Moreover, while Bartolini and Mair only consider leftist parties, here all parties are taken into account and consequently the findings are even more noteworthy. In other respects, however, these data do not fit well with the analysis of party systems in terms of stabilization (see Chapter 2): the Spanish party system and (more recently) that of Portugal have become stabilized, and yet their party-membership rates remained quite low. Another hint of the relatively weaker relationship between membership rate and stabilization in our cases can be seen in changes over time regarding Italy. Italian membership rates were clearly declining at the same time that the Italian party system was becoming more stable, both electorally and in terms of party leadership.

These data suggest that this face of party organizations, as measured by total membership rates, is only a minor part of an overall explanation of stabilization. Besides, in some respects these data may be misleading. In the Italian case, the democratic period after installation was one of demobilization following the Resistance and the turmoil near the end of the war. The aggregate figures presented in Figure 4.1 conceal the fact that individual parties were undergoing distinctly different processes of change: specifically, the Christian Democrats were developing an impressive organizational structure and penetration into Italian society, while at the same time the Communist PCI was experiencing a long-term process of membership decline. These mixed patterns can be seen better in Figure 4.2, which breaks down total membership levels by party, by indicating the specific membership rate.[5] The decline of the Communist Party was perhaps inevitable, given that the PCI emerged from the Resistance as by far the largest party and was bound to decline in membership as mass mobilization subsided in the 1950s and early 1960s.

The data on party membership levels in Italy stand in stark contrast to similar data from Spain, as can be seen by comparing Figure 4.2 with Figure 4.3. The installation of democratic regimes in these two countries differed markedly in one key element: the degree of mass mobilization which characterized the two transition and consolidation processes. The transition and consolidation periods in Italy were

---

[5] As in Tables 4.3, 4.4, and 4.5.

Parties and Party Organization 173

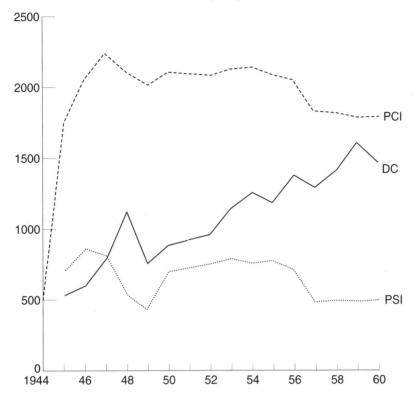

FIG. 4.2. *Membership of main parties: Italy (thousands)*
Sources: For the Communist Party, Ghini (1982: 237); for Christian Democracy, Rossi
(1979: 27); for the Socialists, Spini and Mattana (1981: 56).

accompanied by extremely high levels of mass mobilization, as also
suggested by high levels of party membership. Spain stands at the
opposite end of the continuum. During the first years following the
death of Francisco Franco, all parties except the Communist PCE had
extraordinarily low levels of membership compared with Italy. Even
the Communist Party should be regarded as poorly developed organizationally, insofar as its peak membership in the first years of the
democratic era was only one-tenth that of the PCI during a comparable
period. Following the collapse of the PCE after about 1980, the party
had only a minimal organizational presence in Spanish society. It is
interesting to note that the low level of party membership in Spain also
parallels the relatively low levels of voter turnout characteristic of most
Spanish elections (see Montero 1990: 3). Clearly, these data are indicative of the much lower levels of ideological mobilization and polarization that characterized the Spanish transition to democracy. This

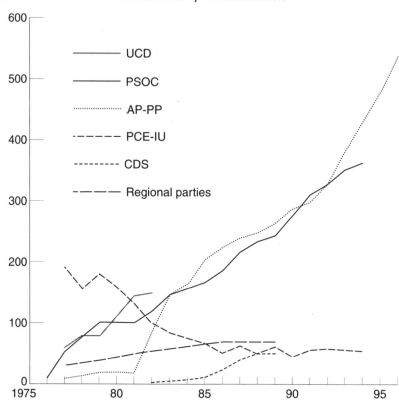

Fɪɢ. 4.3. *Membership of main parties: Spain (thousands)*
Sources: Various party and journalistic sources.

sharply distinguishes the Spanish case from that of Italy. Even after a decade and a half of organizational development, the two largest parties in Spain were able to attract only about one-eighth as many members as did their Italian counterparts. And, as Tables 4.2 and 4.3 reveal, membership rates in Italy have consistently remained vastly higher than those in Spain. A first, simple conclusion, provided by these data, is that in Italy and Spain two different party organizations developed in terms of party on the ground: the mass party, which was more common in Italy, is virtually absent in Spain. This point, however, has to be confirmed by controlling other dimensions of party organization.

The intermediate position of Portugal and Greece also emerges when the data on party membership rates are calculated. In Greece the total membership rate is 7.5 in 1983 and 7.0 in 1990, when all parties are

TABLE 4.2. *Rate of membership in main mass parties: Italy*[a]

	1946	1948	1953	1958	1963	1968
DC	7.5	8.8	10.5	11.3	13.7	13.7
PSI	18.1	—[b]	22.7	11.5	11.5	—[b]
PCI	47.5	—[b]	34.9	27.1	20.8	17.6

Notes: [a] The membership rate is the number of party members as a percentage of the total number of votes cast for that party. [b] Data not available for these years: in 1948 the PSI and the PCI had joint lists; in 1968, the PSI had joint lists with PSDI.

Sources: My calculations based on official electoral data and membership data provided by Ghini (1982: 237) for the Communists; Rossi (1979: 27) for the Christian Democrats; Spini and Mattana (1981: 56) for the Socialists.

TABLE 4.3. *Rate of membership in main mass parties: Spain*[a]

	1977	1979	1982	1986	1989
AP-PP	—[b]	2.0	3.0	4.2	5.0
PSOE	1.0	1.8	1.1	1.9	2.7
PCE-IU	11.8	8.0	10.0	7.8	3.4

Notes: [a] See Table 4.2. [b] Data not available for this year.

Sources: My calculations based on official electoral data and membership data from various party sources.

TABLE 4.4. *Rate of membership in main mass parties: Portugal*[a]

	1976	1979	1983	1985	1987	1991
CDS	—[b]	—[b]	5.6	3.6	10.2	10.5
PSD	1.9	—[b]	5.5	3.9	3.6	4.8
PS	4.8	5.9	5.8	3.9	3.7	4.2
PCP	14.6	14.6	19.5	22.3	28.9	32.4

Notes: [a] See Table 4.2. [b] Data not available for these years: for 1976 there are no membership data for CDS; in 1979 CDS and PPD (then PSD) had joint lists.

Sources: My calculations based on official electoral data and membership data from various party sources.

TABLE 4.5. *Rate of membership in main mass parties: Greece*[a]

	1977	1981	1985	1990	1993
ND	0.9	7.4	8.5	12.9	—[b]
PASOK	2.1	4.0	7.5	6.3	4.9
KKE	20.8	—[b]	15.9	3.7	—[b]

Notes: [a] See Table 4.2.   [b] Data not available for these years.

Sources: My calculations based on official electoral data and membership data (for party data, see Figure 4.5).

considered; in Portugal, 6.0 in 1983 and 4.5 in 1990 (see Gunther and Montero 1994: 504). The specific membership rate confirms and augments this result. In fact, the Portuguese data (Table 4.4) show a growing membership rate for the PCP and a high rate for the CDS, but in both cases the high figures are accounted for by the electoral decline of those parties rather than by a real change of both formations (see the next section). More interesting is the parallel trend of the PS and PSD: two competing parties that tried to enlarge their membership with the latter being the dominant party (PSD) and the former becoming the main opposition party. The higher development of membership is confirmed for the ND and PASOK (Table 4.5). Also in this case the parallelism of ND and PASOK development suggests a high competition between the two parties. But again more qualitative data are needed.

These data further suggest that there is a connection between incumbency and the growth of membership. In Italy, the Christian Democrats were the incumbent party from the very beginning of the transition to democracy in 1944–6. The DC's problems in establishing an adequate organizational network became particularly acute following the party's electoral victory in 1948. Indeed, that triumph was largely the result of extensive efforts by the various organizations of the Catholic Church. Clearly, from the standpoint of party building, it would have been necessary for the DC to build its own autonomous structures, particularly in order to counteract the extensive Communist organization. Under these circumstances, incumbency significantly facilitated the party's organizational growth,[6] but alone it does not explain the growth. The DC became an incumbent party as early as 1944, but the most acute problem of organizational development came

[6] Interestingly enough, the opposite happened in Greece, where incumbency created inertia in the organizational development of both Nea Dimokratia and PASOK, while being in the opposition brought about a developing party organization (see below, next section).

during the later phase of consolidation and competition with the PCI. In contrast with the partially successful efforts of the DC, the Socialist Party experienced no growth in party membership—neither in the short term nor over the long term. Instead, it largely accepted a position secondary to the Communists, until the Hungarian uprising of 1956.

Incumbency was also relevant to party membership growth in Spain. Indeed, it appears that membership growth tends to follow rather than precede electoral success. The Unión de Centro Democrático (UCD) had virtually no organizational structure when it came to power in 1977. Its position of incumbency, however, greatly facilitated the construction of a significant mass-membership base over the following five years. Similarly, the most substantial period of membership growth by the PSOE occurred after, not before, its electoral triumph in 1982.

While it is clear that electoral success greatly facilitates the growth of mass affiliation to parties, to what extent does a large base of party members improve prospects for electoral success? The Spanish data are indicative of a relationship, where other aspects are relevant, and often much more so. The governing UCD and the PCE were the two parties with the largest membership base in the period preceding the 1982 election, but both were devastated in that contest. Conversely, Alianza Popular (AP), renamed Partido Popular in 1989, had virtually no mass-membership base prior to 1982, but in the election of that year it surged from 9 seats in the Congress of Deputies to 106. This basically happened for systemic reasons, that is, the space made available in the centre and centre-right by the breakdown of the UCD. In any case its spectacular increase in party membership followed, rather than preceded, the 1982 election: by 1985, its membership base had quintupled.

Data concerning the organizational development of Portuguese parties (see Figure 4.4) also undermine the notion that a mass-membership base is a key element for electoral success during the consolidation phase, some reservations concerning the reliability of these membership data notwithstanding. This is most clear with regard to the Portuguese Communist Party (PCP). Not only had the PCP experienced substantial membership growth between the first elections and the mid-1980s, but throughout this period it was the largest party, sometimes by a very wide margin over its rivals. Nonetheless, the PCP experienced a substantial electoral decline throughout the 1980s: its share of total votes cast fell from 18.9 per cent in 1983, to 16 per cent in 1985, 12.5 per cent in 1987, 9 per cent in 1991, and 8.6 per cent in 1995. Data regarding the Socialists (PS) and the centrist Social Democrats (PSD) suggest a correlation between mass membership and electoral success, but doubts concerning the proper direction of causality

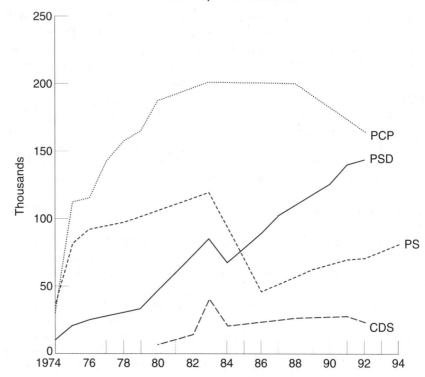

FIG. 4.4. *Membership of main parties: Portugal (thousands)*
Sources: Various party and journalistic sources.

again call into question the value of a mass-membership base as a significant electoral asset. To be sure, the PS suffered a substantial
decrease in affiliation (most likely due to a leadership crisis and a reaction by militants to the austerity policies of 1983–5)[7] preceding its 1987
electoral defeat, but it is clear that the greatest growth in membership
experienced by the PSD occurred after its unprecedented electoral
triumph in that year and coincided with its status as the sole party of
government.

Similar conclusions can be drawn from an examination of Greek data
on membership in PASOK (see Figure 4.5). Party membership experienced its most rapid rate of growth following PASOK's 1981 election
victory. Between 1977 and 1981, a period of Nea Dimokratia government, PASOK had between 50,000 and 100,000 members. In the two

---

[7] After a slight but appreciable growth of membership (16–17%) during the years of
incumbency (1977–82). See Stock (1988: 169).

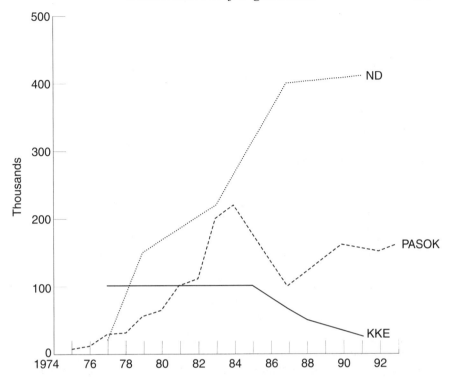

Fɪɢ. 4.5. *Membership of main parties: Greece (thousands)*
Sources: For Nea Dimokratia, Pappas (1995: 311) and party sources (the members of
youth organization, ONNED, are included); for PASOK, Spourdalakis (1992: 182) and
party official sources; for the Communists Kapetanyannis (1987: 166) and Vasileiou
(1991: 22).

years following the party's 1981 election victory, however, affiliation
with PASOK nearly doubled, from 110,000 to 200,000. Following several scandals, poor economic performance under the PASOK government, public reaction against an excessive personalism in public
affairs, and the party's electoral defeat in 1989, it was, however, incap-
able of maintaining this level of affiliation, which fell to 100,000 by
1990. Mass-membership patterns relating to other Greek parties
depart somewhat from those observed above. Nea Dimokratia (see Figure 4.5) started from a very low membership base during its initial
period of predominance (20,000 in 1977 and 150,000 in 1979), but experienced substantial growth in the late 1980s: ND membership
increased from 220,000 to 400,000 between 1983 and 1991.[8] This time
electoral success and incumbency cannot explain such a doubling of

[8] The author is grateful to Takis Pappas for providing membership data for Nea
Dimokratia.

members. Reorganizational efforts of the ND and a strong bipolarization seem better candidate hypotheses to explain those results. Again,
however, a more definite answer has to wait for the analysis of the
other organizational dimensions. With regard to the communist KKE,
the most noteworthy aspect of mass membership is its relatively low
level. Consistent with most other West European communist parties,
which relied heavily on the development of a large membership base,
the KKE was remarkably successful in the early years of democracy
with an estimated 100,000 members, including 30,000 members
belonging to the youth organization (Kapetanyannis 1987: 155 ff.). Ten
years later the decline is evident: the membership rate in 1985 is lower
than earlier (see also Table 4.5) and in 1989 with 7.6 is still lower.
Thus, KKE is still a mass integration party, but its progressive decay
is clearly apparent.

When Southern European parties are put together in terms of their
levels of affiliation, Italy stands at one end of the continuum—with parties whose levels of mass membership reflect substantial organizational development—Spain is at the opposite extreme, and Greece and
Portugal are somewhere in the middle, with Greece closer to Italy, as
was already suggested by party identification figures. A more precise
idea of the order of magnitude of these differences may be gained by
comparing membership rates of the largest party on the left of centre
in each system about a decade after the first democratic election of the
new regime. The range is quite extreme: the Italian PCI had a membership rate of 27.1 in 1958, PASOK had a score of 8.9 and the
Portuguese PS 8.6 in the mid-1980s, while Spain's PSOE had a membership rate of just 1.9 in 1986. Again, the same rank order along this
organizational dimension is confirmed. A relevant additional hypothesis, however, suggested by membership data and its timing is that the
growth of membership follows electoral success, rather than precedes
it, above all when the success is later reinforced by the assumption of a
governmental position. On the whole, the analysis of the other dimensions will confirm this: electoral success comes first and organizational
growth later, even if it is additional growth.[9] To be sure, such growth
is important for the institutionalization of the party, the stabilization
of the party system, and, of course, more or less partially, for the consequent consolidation.[10]

[9] On this see also the research at the local level conducted by Craig (1992) in Spain.
[10] On these considerations see also below, this chapter, and the following one. Here it
may be added that every analysis of membership data needs a note of caution because of
the reliability of those data, which basically depends on the type of party. As Duverger
(1958) pointed out, the members are very important for some parties and they keep more
scrupulous records of them; other parties do not take care of members and their records.
Moreover, there is the well-known problem of inflating the figures for image and

The Coexistence of Different Models: Italy

To this point, very little has been said about the other two organizational dimensions (the internal structures of the party and the party in parliament) (see Katz and Mair 1994), and the resulting types of parties that performed central roles in the consolidation processes in these countries. Let us turn our attention to this qualitative examination of party organizations during the relevant periods of democratic transition—that is, since the 1940s in Italy and the 1970s in the other three countries.[11]

In Italy during the late 1940s and 1950s, the three main mass parties developed in accord with at least two different models. The Christian Democrats emerged as a confessional or denominational party, already very close to the catch-all party model (see Kirchheimer 1966). The Communist PCI, in contrast, was the classic party of mass integration, and the Socialists attempted to imitate the Communist model, albeit with limited success. A similar mass party model was adopted in the formation of the neo-fascist Movimento Sociale Italiano (MSI), which had abandoned the more traditional pattern of a hierarchically organized party with militias (see Ignazi 1989, ch. 2). The Liberals and Republicans, meanwhile, could be regarded as opinion parties and, at the same time, élite parties. In spite of their recurring references to the socialist model, the Social Democrats, led by their founder, Giuseppe Saragat, occupied an intermediate position between the mass party and the party of notables (see Vallauri 1981). Finally, the small traditional parties, which participated in cabinets as junior partners of the Christian Democrats, had very limited organizational structures.

A closer look at the DC reveals that, despite the structures provided for by party statutes, most of the Christian Democrat organization remained on paper.[12] To be sure, there was a steady growth in membership after 1948, but basically the electoral strength of the party was

propaganda reasons or also because of factional conflicts or impending party congresses. Of course, a simpler problem of sources also exists: in a few cases there were different records for the same years. The apparently most reliable source has been taken into account.

[11] The best way of analysing the qualitative features of party organizations, and also the relationships between parties and interests, seems a country-by-country approach. This is so because of the systemic elements implied in this analysis and its salience. In this sense, this is the kind of analysis where a case-oriented approach is preferred to a variable-oriented approach (see Ragin 1987).

[12] Accordingly, the attempt by Amintore Fanfani (the party's secretary between 1954 and 1959) to create a modern mass party with a large membership, a central organization, and, above all, a diffuse peripheral structure should be evaluated as a partial failure. For a detailed analysis of the organization during those years, see Poggi (1968).

derived from the support of Catholic organizations. Thus, the DC was dependent on external organizations and its own organization was fairly weak. Indeed, throughout the first decade of Italian post-war democracy, the party was defined by its closeness to various religious organizations, the Italian church hierarchy and the Vatican. Accordingly, the core areas of DC electoral strength were located in those areas of Northern Italy where the Catholic subculture was strongest. An additional aspect of the DC during these years was the development of organized fractions. The six fractions that emerged initially had their own *de facto* structures, including their own press agencies or supportive media (see, above all, Zuckerman 1979). Closely associated with this organized factionalism was an extensive network of notables.

The organizational characteristics of the Communist Party were profoundly different.[13] Its dominant feature was the classic Leninist-Gramscian 'democratic centralism', in which decisions were made by leaders following the cultivation of loyal support rather than consensus; recruitment was through co-optation from above; and autonomous factions were strictly forbidden. Party activists—ideologically motivated militants—played a much more important role than in the DC: they were a key asset, working for the party, running its electoral campaigns at a local level, and disseminating propaganda without monetary compensation (see Galli 1966: 166; and Alberoni 1967). Unlike the DC, which counted very much on Catholic parishes, the Communists had a capillary organizational network at a local level, based on cells and sections, which were organized according to functional and territorial principles, respectively. Over time, workplace cells gave way to territorial units and sections (Poggi 1968: 132). In essence, a Leninist party organization designed for revolutionary and extra-parliamentary action (e.g. strikes, demonstrations, riots) was organizationally transformed to fit better with the requisites of peaceful democratic competition, such as in electoral campaigns or in representing the interest of peasants and workers in the parliamentary arena. The party thus abandoned its most characteristic Leninist aspects.

During the 1950s, the Socialists, a party theoretically very close to the Communists, actually became profoundly different. The party's *nuclei aziendali socialisti* (NAS), which corresponded to Communist cells, never really developed during the 1950s. Instead, the principal organizational units were the provincial federation. Given the low level of grassroots participation, these federations became bases for creating and maintaining the power of local notables. Thus, what was ostensibly

[13] On the extensive literature on the topic, see Poggi (1968), Ilardi and Accornero (1982), and Tarrow (1967).

structured as a mass party was also a party of notables, within which factions flourished and, after 1957, became autonomously organized, each with its own structure. The Socialist PSI had a small, but stable membership following a sharp decline between 1955 and 1957, as well as a stable membership rate. Its organization was much weaker than those of the DC and PCI, and its members were much less active: while the Communist Party had a ratio between militants and members of 1 : 18, and the DC's ratio was 1 : 23, the ratio between militants and members of the PSI was 1 : 50 (see Cazzola 1970: 41–2).

Among the smaller parties, the neo-fascist Movimento Sociale Italiano was unique. Not only did it not participate in cabinets with the Christian Democrats (as did the Liberals, Republicans, and Social Democrats throughout the 1950s), but its organizational characteristics were also different. Indeed, if we ignore the association of sectors of the party with violent fascist extremist groups, its organizational model would be similar to that of mass-based socialist parties: the section was the primary local unit; provincial federations and the central committee were important; but the secretariat and the national executive had the greatest political power.

Finally, the Liberals, Republicans, and Social Democrats—all of which received less than 10 per cent of the vote throughout the 1950s—may be regarded as élite or opinion parties, with a middle-class electoral appeal. Compared with the other Italian parties, they had few members and no real intermediate organizations or diffuse mass presence.[14] Instead, they were best characterized by the strong, prominent leadership of a few politicians and continuous governmental incumbency for almost the whole decade.

If three other important features of party organization are taken into account, a strong consistency with the previous aspects come out very neatly. In other words, within the models of mass party, here represented by the DC, PCI, and PSI, the more developed the central and peripheral organization and the higher the number of members, the more numerous the party staff, the larger the financing of party activities and the weaker and more dependent the role of the parliamentary component of the party.

However, with regard to staff and party financing no precise figure is available for the 1950s and 1960s. Galli (1966: 167–8) suggests that during these years the staffs of the PCI and the DC formally consisted of a few thousand people vis-à-vis about one thousand people working for all other parties. But this figure does not give an adequate idea of the staff of the three main parties. In fact, mainly at a local level in

[14] For example, the PLI had only 170,000 members in 1957, the PSDI had between 123,000 and 150,000 in 1958–9, and the PRI had fewer than 50,000 members in 1963.

communist areas, in Catholic regions, and in the South of Italy a large number of public civil servants had been working for their own party. Thus, their activity substantially integrated the work of the party formal staff, by profiting from the governmental positions which the DC and the PCI, and also the PSI, had been maintaining at a local level in the Comuni and Provinces, and also profiting from a mutual tolerance in the local branches of the central administration, e.g. in the Postal Service, often staffed with abundant personnel clientelistically hired.

In the absence of any law on state subvention[15] and of any rule on campaign financing,[16] the amount of money employed for party activities is not possible to determine; and even the rule of law would have left much room for additional financial support such as to make barely meaningful the public figures of the formal budget. However, again some elements were well known at the time and have been recently confirmed by documents and witnesses. For the DC the main sources of party financing became the so-called 'black funds' of public economic agencies. They went to party branches, but also to some internal faction of the party. The second main sources were the private contributions of industrial entrepreneurs, mainly from the oil sector and building firms. For Communists the large financial support coming directly and indirectly, mainly through import/export business from the USSR, was massive and it accounts for the enormous organizational apparatus set up by the party, and even for their hegemony in the ancillary organizations where also the Socialists were present, such as Partisan Associations, leisure time associations, and several others. In addition, from the end of the 1940s and until 1956–7, Communists generously financed the PSI, which was even more bound to defend and maintain unitarian positions in this way. When in the party the internal equilibrium among the various fractions began changing during the party conference of Venice (1957), and the Autonomists led by Nenni clearly prevailed in the conference of Naples (1959), the party had a serious economic crisis (see Landolfi 1968: esp. 119). With the entrance of the centre-leftist cabinets in the 1960s some sources of financial support began becoming similar to those of the Christian Democrats, that is, mainly from the industrial public sectors.

With reference to the parliamentary component of the party, the so-called parliamentary party, vis-à-vis the central organization and the party leadership, analysis of statutes and of several indicators of parliamentary careers and recruitment patterns allows us to reach conclusions which are again very consistent with the organizational articulation, sketched above. In the early 1960s, the formal conceptions

---

[15] The first bill was passed in 1974. See below.
[16] Some minimal rule was approved in 1985.

of the party, suggested by the statutes, show that for the Communists the parliamentary party was non-existent, for the Socialists there was its quasi-non-existence, and for the Christian Democrats the acknowledgement of it was complemented by the granting of some autonomy within the clear statement of its dependency on the non-parliamentary party.

In fact, the MPs or the parliamentary groups are not at all mentioned in the Communist 1957 statute at all; their presidents are allowed to participate in the meeting of the Socialist Comitato Centrale, but without the right to vote. Conversely, with regard to Christian Democracy, MPs are ex-officio participants of national party conferences; a number of them (30 deputies and 30 senators), elected by the national conference, the presidents of the two parliamentary groups, representatives (6 deputies and 6 senators) of them, with all components of the cabinet, who are usually MPs, are members of the Consiglio Nazionale; in addition, the presidents of parliamentary groups are members of the Direzione (and the ministers can be invited to its meetings). However, the dependency on the party becomes clear when the DC statute suggests that the regulations of parliamentary groups, issued by them, have to be approved by the Consiglio Nazionale.

In this case the reality is basically consistent with the statutes. First of all, if the patterns of recruitment are analysed, then of course a very clear party-parliament pattern can be seen in all cases, that is, the necessity of a period of activity in the party before being elected to the parliament for that party. But in terms of both membership and assumption of offices in the party, the longest period of socialization before becoming an MP is in the Communists; it is a relatively shorter period in the case of the DC, where there were also deputies or senators—about 13–15 per cent—who were in parliament without having held any party office before their election (until the early 1960s); and an intermediate period for Socialists, oscillating between percentages closer to the PCI and then the DC (Cotta 1979: 176–8).[17]

Second, in spite of the growing presence of MPs in the Socialist Conferences and party executives (see Cazzola 1970: 120), the highest overlap between party leadership and parliamentary members is in the DC; the lowest one in the PCI; with Socialists in an intermediate position (Cotta 1979: 102–3). An indicator such as the extent of this overlap measures the parliamentarization of the party and in this sense it suggests what is the role and presence of the parliamentary party in the party as a whole.

[17] With regard to a more comprehensive analysis of Italian patterns of recruitment for the three major parties, see again Cotta (1979: 196 ff.).

If as a third indicator the parliamentary leadership is considered, then, in the case of the PCI, (a) the leaders of the parliamentary groups have their bases in the party; (b) they are actually appointed by party decisional bodies (secretariat and direction) without any open competition or participation of the interested parliamentary group; (c) the parliamentary leadership is not relevant in achieving greater power in the party. In the case of the Christian Democrats, if the first aspect is similar, with regard to the second one there is competition and influence of parliamentary groups in the election of their leadership. The third aspect is also completely different from that among the Communists: given the kind of multi-leader party already at the end of Fanfani's secretary, the parliamentary leadership can became a point of strength for the intraparty competition with the party main offices. The PSI is very close to the Christian Democrat model (see Cotta 1979: 352–4). Overall, as seen, Italy was the Southern European country with the most highly developed party organization during the most decisive stage of democratic consolidation. The reasons and consequences of that will be seen later in this chapter.

The Socialist Stabilization: Spain

In comparison, party organization is rather poorly developed in Spain, although the growth of party membership during the 1980s was indicative of a certain institutionalization of parties. These parties were not, however, organized along the lines of the traditional integration or mass organizations typical of Italy in the 1950s, but were catch-all parties, in which leaders played extremely important roles while the significance of members and organizations is relatively slight. The low level of party organizational development in Spain has been attributed to the country's multifaceted modern social structure, and its 'de-ideologized' political culture following many years of anti-party Francoist propaganda.

The PSOE, the dominant force in the party system after 1982 up until 1993, is a very good example of the weakness of party organizational development, complemented by an excellent electoral performance over more than a decade.[18] On paper, the party's organizational model is similar to that of other European Socialist parties, with a great prominence given to membership, to the section as the main basic organizational unit, and to the different organizational levels. In actual

[18] As expected, on this party there is much research, although it is not usually focused on the organizational features. See Share (1989), which also deals with PSOE organization.

practice, however, the PSOE underwent a considerable transformation, from a radical, divided leftist party to a unified, centrist electoral organization dominated by strong leadership.[19] The party has a federal structure. The *agrupación local* is the primary local unit and is integrated, in turn, into provincial, regional, and national organizational structures.[20] But the first, actual organizational pillar is a small top-level body, the Federal Executive Commission, with wide powers in all aspects of party life. During the 1980s the consequent strong centralism was partially tempered by the growing role of regional federations as far as the state decentralization was implemented with large transference of resources to Autonomous Communities. The second key mechanism is the majority system adopted in the internal party elections. The actual working of this mechanism brought about the underrepresentation of internal minorities (and reinforced the oligarchical trend) (Maravall 1992: 15). The third feature is the forbidding of organized 'tendencies', but since 1983 not of 'currents of opinion', and every effort was made to maintain the control of the party by Alfonso Guerra, the deputy leader of the party in charge of the organization.

In the case of the PSOE building a unified party was a vital necessity as well as a possibly crucial asset. In fact, its internal dynamics were further complicated between 1977 and 1979 by mergers with several Socialist formations, which sometimes contributed to internal conflicts. The response to the considerable internal instability that erupted in 1979 (largely triggered by Felipe González's ultimately successful attempt to moderate the party's ideology by dropping the Marxist reference) was to enforce greater internal discipline, perceived as lacking in the party (see Puhle 1986: 336–7). Also, at the September 1979 extraordinary congress, at which the party's ideology was formally modified and moderated (a development of great relevance for subsequent democratic legitimation), rule changes were enacted to inhibit the growth of factionalism and reinforce party discipline.[21] This substantially contributed to the PSOE's largely successful effort to become a cohesive party. After the party came to power in 1982, party congresses were increasingly dominated by elected or appointed public officials, as were the intermediate structures of the party: 61 per cent of delegates in the 1984 30th Congress and 67 per cent in the 1990 32nd

[19] The internal stabilization of the party may have played an important role in its electoral success in 1982, and its subsequent incumbency contributed to its further stabilization (see Gunther 1986b: 22–3).

[20] For a detailed analysis of party formal organization prior to 1982 see Román Marugán (1987); for the 1980s see Gangas Peiró (1995).

[21] In 1983, there was some relaxation of these constraints: currents of opinion were again acknowledged within the party, and provisions were enacted to provide for increased participation of minorities in party organs (Tezanos 1989: 469).

Congress were elected or appointed public officials (see Maravall 1992: 15; also Tezanos 1983). Accompanying this conversion of the PSOE into a body whose overriding function was to win elections and form governments, party officials in charge of information, propaganda, party image, and relations with the press increased in importance.

For this kind of party it was essential to establish and maintain full control of elected parliamentarians. This was successfully done through: (1) the mechanism of electoral list formation that put all decisions in the hands of the Federal Commission; (2) the formal subjection of the Socialist Parliamentary Group to the directives of the party's top body, as ruled by art. 49 of federal party by-laws (see Satrústegui 1992: 40); (3) other ways of maintaining vote discipline in the Cortes or more general party discipline, such as a fairly high rate of renewals (see Morán 1996: 19; Gangas Peiró 1995, 155). To be sure, another useful mechanism to maintain party discipline and the unity of the party was the established incompatibility between elected representative offices and party positions. Of course, the 1983 Statute also allowed a few exceptions for the higher levels, which made even more powerful the leading group of the party. The financial support for the PSOE and all other parties comes from public funds, in addition to the members' fees and limited donations. It is ruled by several laws. Several scandals and prosecutions in the late 1980s and 1990s, concerning mainly—but not exclusively—Socialists apparently suggest the importance of other sources of financing.[22]

On the whole, the party is an electoral-professional party, very close to the model sketched by Panebianco (1982), that has been run by a small cohesive leading group up to the late 1980s, where the catch-all strategy is partially made up for by an expansion of the budget in the social policies with the growth of beneficiaries (see also Ferrera 1996) and relatively high and persisting worker support: in his 'worker-representation index', grounded on survey data, Merkel (1992: 28) calculated for the PSOE a 1.26 in 1975 and a 1.25 in 1990. Consequent low participation, oligarchical trends, and emerging internal divisions are some of the recurring dangers that this kind of party ran and actually suffered in late 1980 and later.[23]

Paradoxically, the stabilization of the Spanish party system with a predominant PSOE was facilitated by the weakness and instability of several of the other parties: during the 1980s most parties, except the PSOE, changed leaders and split. That is, there was the stabilization

[22] On the perception of the problem of financial support for parties in a comparative perspective see Del Castillo (1985).

[23] On this see the next chapter. In fact, the factors mentioned in the text are part of the explanation of crisis and change.

of the party system mainly because of the strong stabilization of a party and its élite, but not of all parties. Here the theoretically relevant aspect is the apparent, empirical possibility of distinguishing between the stabilization of parties and of a party system, and the fact that the two processes can even proceed in the opposite direction in the medium term.[24]

By far the most dramatic example of this instability was the disintegration and collapse of the governing Unión de Centro Democrático, an electoral coalition of fourteen groups, whose leaders were never able to transform it into a reasonably unified party despite the glue provided by governmental incumbency. Personal conflicts and strong internal disagreements on different policy issues accounted for that. In 1982, this breakdown paved the way for the PSOE's accession to power as the predominant party. Indeed, the highly visible struggles among UCD leaders throughout the two years preceding that election (which contrasted starkly with the new-found cohesion within the PSOE) was the principal cause of the PSOE's smashing victory.[25]

Following the disappearance of the UCD, the right-wing Alianza Popular became the principal challenger to the right of the PSOE.[26] From the time of its founding until the immediate aftermath of the 1989 elections, the AP was also beset with problems of élite-level instability. Born in 1976 as a coalition of seven small groups headed by former high-ranking officials of the previous regime, Alianza Popular initially established a centralized organization under the charismatic Manuel Fraga Iribarne. In successive elections, the AP entered into a series of unstable alliances. It formed the Coalición Democrática with two other parties in 1979 and the Coalición Popular with other political groups in 1982. While it later (1988) abandoned this practice of forming unstable alliances with small clusters of conservative élites and transformed itself into the unified Partido Popular (1989), over the course of the first six national elections the party presented itself to the voters under four different names. These earlier alliances with other small conservative groups and the successive incorporations (especially numerous following the collapse of the UCD in 1982) of new conservative élites into the party also gave rise to a series of destabilizing and highly public conflicts, culminating most dramatically in the resignation of Fraga in December 1986. This was followed by an unstable

---

[24] On this distinction see also Mair (1989). For an explanation of such a phenomenon see below in the text.

[25] For obvious reasons the collapse of a large governmental party has attracted the attention of several scholars. See especially Gunther (1985: 7–41; 1986c), Huneeus (1985), and Caciagli (1989).

[26] No relevant party was to the right of the AP-PP. On the misfortunes of the extreme right in Spain see Heywood (1995c).

period of unsuccessful party leadership under António Hernández Mancha, and eventually to the return of Fraga following the 1989 election. It was only after Fraga's retirement from the presidency and the orderly transfer of party leadership to José María Aznar (1990) that élite relations within the party were stabilized, a change that contributed to the party's significant advance in the 1993 election and the victory of the 1996 election over the Socialists, to the detachment from the Francoist heritage through a turnover of those involved in the previous regime, as mayors or governors, who had been the middle-level élite—so close to Fraga—of the party for years and almost disappeared with the candidacies for 1993 elections.

In an organizational sense, after the first period when the presence of basic territorial units was overcome by the province as the principal level of party organization for such matters as elections to party congresses, the party went through several adaptations with six different statutes up to 1993, and the key moments of reorganization after—not before—an electoral success. This is so after 1982 and 1989. A basic persisting feature is the prominent role given to the president of the party in the whole management of the party and in sketching its political lines. Another recurring aspect is given by the financial difficulty this party had and, above all, at the beginning by its small central staff. The main adaptive changes concern the shifting of some important decisions—e.g. on the candidacies at the local level—from the central level to that of Autonomous Communities, the development of coordination bodies among the different regions and organizational levels, the efforts of overcoming internal divisions, also by imitation, to cope with the Socialist competition.[27] In this sense, the PP achieved a degree of stabilization much later than the PSOE, and with Aznar it is a catch-all party that presents and establishes a liberal-conservative image with a great deal of attention to the Catholic Church, to youth, and also to the skilful management of media, even gaining by the late 1980s the highest membership among the Spanish parties (see Montero 1989: 517).[28]

Another challenger to the PSOE was the tiny Centro Democràtico y Social (CDS), founded by Adolfo Suárez in 1982 following his withdrawal from the party that he had created, the UCD. The CDS was initially dominated by its strong president, Suárez. Unlike the UCD, the party had a small homogeneous élite and a strongly personalized lead-

[27] For example, the 1993 statute absorbs the rule on incompatibilities among elective and party offices, already adopted by the PSOE.
[28] The organization of the AP until 1982 is closely examined by López Nieto (1988); for the following decade see Gangas Peiró (1995); especially on the internal divisions see López Nieto (1995).

ership. After achieving some moderate success in the 1986 and 1989 elections, however, the CDS was totally destroyed in 1993, failing to elect a single deputy in that contest.

Fragmentation and crisis in both organization and leadership are the most distinctive facets of the lack of institutionalization in the PCE, which in 1986 attempted a rebirth by forming the electoral coalition Izquierda Unida (United Left) with a few other leftist groups. This strategy obviously raises one crucial question: what happens when a typical, very organized communist party decides to renounce its traditional identity? This transformation had its origins in the period immediately preceding the transition to democracy in Spain. Under the leadership of Santiago Carrillo, for example, the party in 1976 shifted its basic unit of party organization from the functionally defined cell to the more open, territorial *agrupación local*. Accompanying this formal organizational shift was a broader attempt to transform a Leninist party into a more open mass mobilizational and more moderate party with a Eurocommunist ideology, also formally dropping the Leninist tenets (1978). While this may have fit better with the dynamics of competitive politics in the new democracy, the uneven transformation of the party, coupled with internal divisions and the complete lack of consensus over the future role of 'democratic centralism' or over the political strategies to follow, and the emergence of a centre-periphery conflict (especially regarding the status of the Communist Party in Euskadi), contributed to substantial and ultimately debilitating conflict within its ranks. Such a conflict culminated in a series of schisms, massive defections of party militants, and a devastating electoral defeat in 1982 (see Gunther, Sani, and Shabad 1986; Gunther 1986*a*; and González Hernández 1989). By the mid-1980s, the PCE was splintered: fragments of the once unified party could be found within the Basque Euskadiko Ezkerra, the Catalan PCC, and two other tiny 'parties' founded in the mid-1980s, one of them by none other than Santiago Carrillo himself. The United Left coalition strategy was part of an effort to overcome this fragmentation, but fluidity and instability persisted in that segment of the political continuum to the left of the PSOE. Even in the 1993 election, held at a time when registered unemployment exceeded 21 per cent of the labour force and the governing PSOE was racked by a variety of scandals, Izquierda Unida failed to make any significant electoral advance at the Socialists' expense. But at the end of the 1980s, from an organizational perspective the new coalition had been able to fully transform itself into a decentralized party with autonomous regional, provincial, and local levels, but with the central control of financial resources, resolution of discipline conflicts, formation of electoral lists for general and European elections, and the shaping of strategic lines of the party. In other aspects the competition and imitation with the PSOE was also apparent, such as the approval of that incompatibility passed also by the Popular Party. More originally, there was the attempt of the IU to define itself as a political movement, actually to relate the coalition with all existing movements, from intellectuals to women, to *vecinales* movements,[29] and also more closely with the existing unions. Despite internal problems, difficult relationships among the component of the coalition, lack of institutionalization, the experience of the IU points to a different party model not made by media and communications professionals or of organization and management, and in this sense indicates another possible path to follow—to be sure, with uncertain results.[30]

An overview of the Spanish party system would be incomplete without reference to several important regional or regional-nationalist parties. The plain fact is that a system of 'non-state' wide parties overlap and condition the country-wide parties, described above.[31] The most important of these are the Catalan Convergència i Unió (CiU), the Basque Partido Nacionalista Vasco (PNV), Euskadiko Ezkerra (EE), and Herri Batasuna (HB). The CiU is actually an electoral alliance of two distinct formations (Convergència Democràtica de Catalunya, CDC, and Unió Democràtica de Catalunya, UDC),[32] which joined in 1978. The CDC was a moderate, centre-right Catalan nationalist party with a fairly developed organization but catch-all characteristics and dominance by its prominent leaders. The UDC was a much smaller party, whose programmatic stance and organizational characteristics were typical of Christian Democratic parties: it had a longer tradition than the CDC and ancillary organizations for women and young people, as well as an allied trade union; by way of comparison, the CDC had only a youth organization. This electoral alliance worked very well, making CiU the third largest parliamentary group in the Cortes in 1982, 1989, 1993, and 1996. It has also become the dominant party in Catalan regional politics.[33]

In the Basque region, the situation is very different. The Basque regional party system is characterized by extreme instability and increasing fragmentation. Prior to 1978, there were only two signifi-

---

[29] That is, movements formed by people living in the same area of a town with issues and problems related to that area.

[30] A more detailed analysis of organizational dimensions is in Gangas Peiró (1995); but see also the overview and the considerations developed by Heywood (1994).

[31] A good overview of all these parties is in Montabes (1994); on the Catalan party system see Colomé (1993).

[32] On the UDC, see also Culla (1992).

[33] On Catalan elections see the excellent overview by Pallarés and Font (1994).

cant Basque nationalist parties: the historic PNV and the left-wing Euskadiko Ezkerra. During the constitution-writing phase of the Spanish democratic transition, however, the EE split, and a more radical organization, Herri Batasuna, emerged to more clearly articulate demands for revolutionary change and Basque independence from Spain. HB is not even a party; it is an anti-system coalition of political groups and movements and is close to the terrorist organization ETA. The EE, meanwhile, absorbed much of the Eurocommunist élite that was defecting from the PCE within the Basque country. In 1992, it was itself absorbed within the regional federation of the PSOE. The PNV split as well, and from it emerged, in 1985, a new party, Eusko Alkartasuma (EA), under the leadership of the former PNV Basque regional government president, Carlos Garaikoetxea. The PNV remained a conservative, Catholic party, with deep roots in the region (except in the province of Guipúzcoa), a decentralized structure, and a strong preference for provincial—and municipal—level autonomy within the Basque regional government. The EA staked out a more social-democratic stance, favouring a strong regional government vis-à-vis local levels of government, and a more dogmatic defence of Basque national interests than was being articulated by the PNV (which, in the late 1980s, had begun to cooperate with the PSOE at both the regional and the national level). Thus, the Basque regional party system stands in sharp contrast with that of Catalonia: unlike the Catalan party system, characterized by stabilization and the emergence of a regionally predominant party, the party system in Euskadi has exhibited instability, fragmentation, and polarization (see esp. Linz 1986; and Llera Ramo 1993 and 1994).

An important characteristic of Spanish parties, in general, is the increasing role played by both media and party leaders and the personalization of political life. Electoral success is highly dependent on the ability to establish intra-party stability and cohesion, under a strong leader, as was typified by the PSOE beginning in the late 1970s. A key explanatory factor which differentiated the party politics of Spain from that of Italy was the low ideologization of political conflict and the correspondingly low polarization of partisan politics at the national level. In contrast with Italy, where the mass party with a strong organizational network was the prevailing type (be it a denominational party or a mass integration party with roots in the class structure), in Spain the predominantly electoral party of professional politicians has become the most common reality. Relatively little development of organizational networks has taken place. The Spanish way in the stabilization of the party system is grounded, instead, on the relative dominance and cohesion of the party that has strong leadership,

PSOE, and at the same time on the weakness, division, and instability of other parties. Significant change would occur if the second of these two elèments were to change, as announced by the marked electoral advance of the Partido Popular in the 1993 elections, following its internal stabilization and organizational growth, as actually happened in 1996 with the electoral victory of this party (see the next chapter).[34]

From Fractions to Unification: Portugal

Among Portuguese parties, the Portuguese Communist Party (PCP) was the most organizationally developed from the very beginning of the transition. It was the only party that in 1974 was able to grow immediately from about 2,000 members, who were underground at the moment of the coup, to 15,000 in July and to 30,000 in October who at that moment were seriously committed and ideologized militants. With a classical organizational structure (largely rooted in its tradition of underground opposition) for this kind of party, the PCP had a strong leader, a persisting base of militants, and tight party discipline, characterized by the well-known 'democratic centralism'. This structure seemed well suited to coping with the demands of the 'revolutionary' situation that followed the collapse of the Salazar-Caetano regime. At the end of the revolutionary phase of the Portuguese transition, however, and particularly during the 1980s, the party experienced a slow electoral decline and an organizational decay (see, among others, Alves da Costa e Sousa 1983: 497–543; Pacheco Pereira 1988: Gaspar 1990: 45–63; Gaspar and Rato 1992; Patricio and Stoleroff 1994: 90–116). As a consequence of obvious reasons, which include the political isolation of the party and the clear evidence that the possibilities of revolution are over, in the late 1970s and early 1980s there were serious problems of recruitment, a crisis of militancy, and the functioning of the middle-level organization with untrained cadres (see Bruneau and Macleod 1986).[35] However, it was precisely that organization that made the electoral (and even organizational) decline slower, and for an additional reason. The potentialities of the organization to persist and to maintain many militants and voters for as long a time as possible, despite at least the isolation of the party and the rigidities of its strategic lines, are grounded on a simple fact: since the beginning (1974) voters and militants are concentrated in the same 'red areas'. Likewise as

---

[34] A careful review of the literature on Spanish parties is in Padró-Solanet (1996).

[35] It may be recalled (see above in the text and Table 4.4) that the growth of the membership rate does not falsify this point: such growth is the result of electoral decline, not an increase in militancy.

in the Italian case with the Communist dominance in Emilia and Romagna, Tuscany, and Umbria, here a Communist subculture has its deep roots in some areas of Lisbon, in Setúbal, and in Southern Alentejo (Évora, Beja, and Southern parts of Santarém).[36] Slowing down the decay is only an obvious consequence.

In terms of both ideology and organizational characteristics, the party that stands at the opposite end of the continuum is the conservative, rightist Centro Democrático e Social. Since the beginning, the CDS was a loosely structured coalition of independent politicians and local notables, founded in mid-1974 by officials of the previous authoritarian regime (see Bruneau and Macleod 1986; Stock 1986). Although its ideal references concern traditional Catholic values, in many ways it resembles the small, élitist, and lay Italian opinion parties, except for one important difference: the CDS was not continuously in government, as those parties were. That is, the party has no grassroots organizations and strong centralization. The data on membership (see Figure 4.4) are basically unreliable, whereas the oligarchical tenet is a much more real characteristic in the functioning of the party. On the whole, the organizational centralization, the oligarchical principle, the low internal participation are, however, complemented by a rather cohesive party. Accordingly, the parliamentary groups are clearly dependent on the party leadership, but there is a strong overlap between party leaders and MPs, that on average has been close to 40–50 per cent. The party has a *classe gardée*: they are the propertied social groups that since the beginning saw in this party the defender of their interests, threatened by the radical, leftist programmes and policies of the first years after the coup. During the years, the CDS has not successfully undergone a process of organizational structuring. The efforts of leadership in this direction, however, brought to the new Partido Popular in 1995 that went on maintaining the same basic positions and support of CDS (see Chapters 2 and 5).

The two most important parties in Portuguese democracy to date are the Socialists, the PS, and the Social Democrats, the PSD. On paper both would appear to be mass parties with a highly organized structure with traditional local units, such as sections and 'nuclei'; in actual practice, however, they suffered internal divisions for years and consistently have much more developed vertical relationships, rather than horizontal ones, among the different organizational levels with consequent oligarchical features (see Stock 1988: 163–4). In both the PS and the PSD the internal divisions brought to internal conflicts and instability with internally organized fractions in the PS and an inner circle

[36] The basic electoral data that display the geographical distribution of votes is in Aguiar (1994).

of 'barons' in the PSD; both have suffered schisms on a few occasions; and both have experienced a turnover in leadership, although for different reasons (the Social Democrat Francisco Sá Carneiro died in a plane accident in December 1980, while the Socialist Mário Soares was elected president of the Republic in 1986). The two competing parties slowly followed a similar path of institutionalization by gaining a higher internal cohesion during the years or at least a much lower degree of fractionalization and a stronger leadership (see Magone 1995 and next section). The parliamentary groups of both parties are controlled by party leaders, also thanks to the electoral system that put the formation of lists in the hands of parties. Neither party has an over-representation of specific social groups. Their main social bases and élites belong to the middle classes and their leaders consciously pursue a catch-all strategy. The two parties differ, however, in a few important features.

The PSD had a developed, integrated organizational structure that included grassroots organizations with local strongholds, regional leaders, and notables; a formal organizational structure at a country level, based upon the eighteen electoral districts; the usual national committees; and a few ancillary organizations, such as youth and women's branches. As already stressed, for years the party has been riven by factions and internal divisions, up to the point of being labelled as an association of 'barons'. Such fractionalization was especially disruptive in the immediate aftermath of Sá Carneiro's death. The situation changed substantially after 1985, under the strong leadership of Aníbal Cavaco Silva. His electoral successes and extended period in government greatly reduced the internal divisions and contributed to the stabilization of internal organizational structures (see Bruneau and Macleod 1986, ch. 4; and Stock 1986).

To better understand this party a characteristic organizational aspect has to be mentioned here. This is the role of the president, directly elected by the party Congress, that has been for years the dominant organ of the party and had to be held fairly frequently, i.e. every two years. This organizational role could give the best opportunity to control the Congress and the 'barons', and to formulate the best strategic lines of the party without any internal constraint. Actually, however, this possibility was only exploited by Sá Carneiro. Later none was in condition to lead the party. The position was eliminated in 1983, and in the following year the leader formally became the president of the National Political Commission with a strong Congress. When in October 1985 Cavaco Silva was elected the new president of the party, a strong leader was again in office, and he was able to exploit the organizational opportunity by controlling a decentralized body with all its 'barons'. In this sense Santana Lopes (1988) rightly summarizes in the formula 'dependency on charisma' the necessity of a strong leadership for that kind of party. It may be additionally stressed that in this party the role of the president is actually made by a previous strong leader, and not the opposite, that is, in this case a strong role cannot strengthen a weak leader who is not in any condition to control an articulated party with local notables.

The Socialists had a much older organizational tradition. But following the re-establishment of the parties in 1974, the PS was only able to build weaker local and intermediate organizational structures with difficulty in maintaining active sections between one election and another, and with serious problems of recruitment at the middle level for a long time. It also had a different type of organization, closer to the classical workers' parties: its organizational features included both territorially based sections and professional or interest-group units, provincial or district federations, a national committee, a secretariat at the centre of several internal problems and disputes, later (1981) abolished, a political commission elected by the national commission, and a secretary-general who is the party leader, helped in his duties by a permanent commission very close to him. The organization was complemented by a youth association, but no women's organization.

For years, even under the leadership of Mário Soares, internal factions continued to flourish: Soares was actually able to maintain his leadership only through skilful management of internal conflicts where he took the function of arbiter. The party's leader was really only able to consolidate his position in 1983, after the electoral success of that year (see Gallagher 1989; and Robinson 1991–2: 6–26). At this point institutionalization had been on the way only thanks to strong personalization within the party. Accordingly, with the election of Soares as head of state in 1986, the party lost its founding father and again suffered a long internal crisis. None of the other party leaders was subsequently able to secure and consolidate a strong leadership position (see again Stock 1986; and Bruneau and Macleod 1986), despite a somewhat higher party cohesion achieved after the party congress of 1988. A new real leadership was established much later and consolidated when Guterres won the 1995 election.

With reference to party financial aspects, since the beginning Portuguese laws ruled on the public support through the parliament and in connection with the gained votes. As in most of the other European countries the additional sources are the fees of party members and with some constraints other private contributions. Also in 1993 the Portuguese Assembly came back to regulate this aspect (see Meirim 1994). In mentioning the financial support it may be interesting to emphasize the open regular, and enormous, financial help that for years the German Friedrich Ebert Foundation, linked to the PS, the Friedrich Neumann Foundation, close to the PSD, and the Konrad Adenauer Foundation and Hanns Seidel Foundation, both close to the CDS, gave to those parties.[37] The reasons for this support are evident, and consequently it has almost disappeared in recent years.

To conclude on Portuguese parties: only the PSD has successfully institutionalized itself. It became the dominant party in the country after 1987, while for several years and because of different reasons the other three parties have continued to undergo changes and have continued to suffer from instability and organizational deficiencies at least until changes in the popular attitudes and a rebuilding of the Socialists paved the way to their victory in 1995.[38]

Between Charisma and Personalization: Greece

A profound transformation of the Greek party system also occurred following its re-emergence in the mid-1970s.[39] Moreover, since 1974 the system still evolved from the predominant power of Nea Dimokratia (ND) to an attempt at a new predominant party configuration with the Panhellenic Socialist Movement (PASOK), and after the critical 1989–90 period to a polarized two-party system. This involved two alternations in power between the two major parties, ND and PASOK, the decline and virtual marginalization of the communist parties—the KKE (which until the end of the 1980s was close to the Soviet Union) and the Eurocommunist KKE-Interior (see Kapetanyannis 1987; and Chapter 3)—and the disappearance or the marginalization of smaller political groups, such as the EDIK or other splinter formations from ND and PASOK (see Calligas 1987).[40] Given the very limited number of parties and a long trend toward bipolarization, a few organizational transformations of the two main parties reveal very well and clarify the

[37] While the probable external financial support received by the PCP was not open and clear.

[38] On the first years of the Portuguese party system until 1982, see Aguiar (1983); on the later years until the Socialist victory see the next chapter.

[39] Spourdalakis (1996: 172–6) discusses the main differences (and similarities) with the previous party system of the 1960s, but he especially points out the profound innovation in terms of party organization: 'one can truly talk of mass parties in Greece only after the demise of Junta' (ibid. 174).

[40] Actually, later the party system became more fractionalized with splits in Nea Dimokratia before the 1993 elections and in PASOK before the 1996 election (see also Ch. 2).

changes within the party system. They may be divided in two clearly distinct phases (1974–81 and 1981–9) according to the party that was in office.

Nea Dimokratia was created in September 1974 and in the subsequent months a few obstacles to its organizational development became evident. The first problem may be defined as a 'personal contradiction' for the party: on the one hand, Karamanlis was the charismatic founder of ND and he was deeply convinced of the importance of building a party organization for the same democratic consolidation; on the other hand, his very presence and crucial role in both the foundation of Greek democracy and of the party did not leave room for party cadres to develop the organization he wanted. The second, even more salient obstacle was the extent of continuity in terms of personnel: as pointed out by Pappas (1995: ch. 3), in 1974 one-third of parliamentarians (78 out of 216) were aged politicians with previous experience in the pre-Junta centre party (ERE). More generally, in the building of ND a key role was performed and maintained by local notables, even if 'new men' without previous political experience. Of course, this middle-level élite was opposed to organizational development: a strong party apparatus could have controlled and limited the power of local notables, who became even more important in the party during the late 1970s (see below).

These two factors were strengthened by other aspects in maintaining a weak organization until the early 1980s. The fact of being the incumbent party with a very large or large majority after the 1974 and 1977 elections does not create the necessity of developing an organization: the state resources may appear a much more effective way of maintaining loyal support, above all in the rural areas of the country. This is what Pappas (1995) defines as 'organizational inertia'. The same author also stresses the ideological weakness of the party: defending the national interests and commitment to economic growth are too weak programmatic lines to be capable of mobilizing people and maintaining support, as, on the contrary, PASOK was doing during the same period with a much higher effectiveness (see below).[41] The third aspect refers to party internal tensions. On the one hand, there is the division between the traditionalist élite, more open to maintain the old patronage system and worried by the extreme rightist opinion,[42] and the reformists who are more prone to switch toward the centre, also profiting from the dissolution of EDIK. On the other hand, another deep division concerns the parliamentary élite with the local linkages and the party cadres that try to bypass such an élite.

[41] On the ideology of ND see also Katsoudas (1987: 96–8).
[42] On the extreme right see Kapetanyannis (1995: 129–44).

The consequent organizational weakness means that the organization on paper had a limited translation in practice, but a side-effect shaped a peculiar organization with a stronger role for the parliamentary group. Furthermore, among the three tiers of organization (central, regional, and local), the central four organs (general assembly, administrative committee, executive committee, and president) were mirrored by similar bodies at the regional level (except the party leader), but the local level remained undetermined even on paper, in both the 1977 and 1979 statutes. The lack of a strong extra-parliamentary party apparatus left room for the parliamentary party that became even stronger in the late 1970s. In fact, in the congress of 1979 where the parliamentarians were over-represented it was decided that the leader of the party would have been elected by the simple majority of parliamentary group; the group of those elected in the Voulí became as central an organ as the others; parliamentarians were appointed in the main governing body of the party, that is, the administrative committee; and at the same time the power of the party congress was limited.[43] On the whole, during the 1970s ND was a conservative party of notables, essentially relying on its charismatic leader, Constantine Karamanlis, and on 'MPs and their clientelistic networks for communicating with the electorate and rallying mass support' (Lyrintzis 1984: 106).

PASOK tells a different story. Between September 1974, when it was founded, and its resounding electoral victory in 1981, that is, in seven years PASOK was able to establish a fairly developed grassroots organization without any comparison in the previous Greek political experience. Its main distinguishing features included a populist programme, a charismatic leader, and an authoritarian style of leadership (see Diamandouros 1991). In addition to the common and usually meaningless appeal to social justice and equality, populism meant a strong anti-rightist position, a programme of profound but largely undetermined change, a vague Third World ideology of dependency with Marxist elements, a strong nationalism, a radical appeal to the under-privileged, a thrust for population mobilization, but also no specific *classe gardée*.[44] It is very difficult to speak of a catch-all strategy in a proper way, that is, as a development from a mass integration party, but the indiscriminate

[43] All organizational indications come from Pappas (1995).

[44] The definition of Greek populism is given from a partisan and organizational perspective. Such a definition largely coincides with that provided by Collier Berins and Collier (1991: 788), with some adaptation to Greece: 'A political movement characterized by mass support from the urban working class and/or peasantry; an element of mobilization from above; a central role of leadership from the middle sector or élite, typically of a personalistic and/or charismatic character; an anti-status quo nationalist ideology and program.' For other analyses on Greek populism, see Sotiropoulos (1991), Pappas (1995), and the various articles in Clogg (1993). PASOK's ideology is also well analysed by Featherstone (1987: 112–34) and by Achimastos (1996: 351 ff.).

and successful appeal to all strata of Greek society is very clear.[45] An analysis of either voters, especially in 1981 (Spourdalakis 1988: 212), or members confirms this. Also the worker representation index, suggested by Merkel (1992: 28), shows figures very close to a neutral result and consequently to a lack of *classe gardée*: from 1.10 in 1975 to 1.03 in 1990, with a European average of 1.28.[46] To this there can be added a relative homogeneity in the geographical distribution of the vote among the different regions. Actually, since 1977 and even earlier electoral success became the key absorbing goal for the entire party, and accordingly all features were subordinated to such a goal.

The populist dimension is perfectly consistent with the established party organization. At a national level, its main decision-making bodies were the powerful president, which was Andreas Papandreu from the foundation up to his death in 1996, the eight-member executive bureau, the central committee, and the party congress, but the very first congress is in 1984 and the second in 1990, that is, two congresses in sixteen years with rules and procedures that were largely bypassed when not ignored (on this see Spourdalakis 1988: 254 ff.). At the intermediate level, there were prefectural or regional assemblies and committees, but this level never actually worked. Indeed, party cadres drew legitimacy from the party's leader rather than from party members and sympathizers (see Sotiropoulos 1991, esp. ch. 3). At the local level, clubs on a territorial basis, professional units, and organizational cells show a rich organizational articulation, but behind it there was above all a mobilizational activity, again with electoral purposes. Additionally, the presence and activity of two ancillary organizations, the Student Front (PASP) and the Socialist Movement of Workers, must be considered.

At the beginning (1974–5) the party's militants and élites were divided in different groups. They formed five different ideologically defined factions: social democrats, Marxists, a Third World group, self-management socialists, and a non-ideological group (see Sotiropoulos 1991).[47] Their origins were in the threefold heritage of the party: the old wartime resistance movement with a wide popular base, the left-wing pre-Junta centre party (EK), the group acting against the colonels (Clogg 1987: 123). Divisions and conflicts among the different factions with different origins were organizationally solved only through the

[45] See the careful, prudent distinctions by Spourdalakis (1992: 110–16) on the various dimensions of 'catch-allism'.

[46] Recall similar data for the Portuguese Socialist Party.

[47] Other authors (e.g. Spourdalakis 1992: 163) make reference to other factions, such as the Conformists, formed by the old politicians of the pre-Junta Centre Union party, the left, composed by the war generation and the anti-Junta resistance group, and the technocratic group.

strong role performed by Papandreu, the leader *maximo* that almost everyone in the party was open to accept. Expulsions and resigning from the party were an important additional part in this process through which the party became a unified body under the strong charismatic rule of Papandreu. And again the aim of achieving electoral success justified every action.

Overall, PASOK did not resemble other European Socialist parties. The strongly dominant role of only one person, the weak middle-level élite (see Spourdalakis 1988), the ideological mobilization around vague catch-words, the organization of members from above, the lack of a tradition of militancy and activism do not allow a serious parallel with the European Socialist tradition. Only more marginal aspects place the party closer to those other parties with the same label, such as the dependency of the parliamentary group on the party apparatus (and again mainly on Papandreu); a strong overlapping between MPs and the party élite sitting in the central committee; or the recurring various sources of financial support, including state subsidies, fundraising campaigns, donations and, as revealed in the late 1980s, also bribes.

The elections of 1981 inaugurated the second phase in the institutionalization of PASOK and ND (see below). The alternation in power had a great impact on the organizations of both major parties. The main reasons for the political mobilization of PASOK were over; on the contrary, there were reasons for demobilization since the activists, local leaders, and local groups could and actually did create problems for the government; in fact it was almost impossible to keep the electoral promises Papandreu had made. The factions were always on the verge of reviving in a more conflictual way. The most obvious ways out were: on the one hand, at the local and intermediate levels to push the party and to create a consensus around the government fighting popular disenchantment and exploiting the incumbency to bring back the old tradition of patronage, which had been labelled 'bureaucratic clientelism' (Lyrintzis 1984);[48] on the other hand, at the party élite level, to co-opt into the state apparatus members of the different factions, and maintain some equilibrium among them (see Sotiropoulos 1991, ch. 3). The many obvious consequences, which actually took place during the middle and late 1980s, were the demobilization and undermining of grassroots organizations, the additional weakening of the autonomy of local party units, the emptying out of the party élite from inside, and the exit or dismissal from the party of other more rebellious militants.

[48] This alone can explain very well the enormous growth of membership after the electoral success of 1981, despite the weakening of the local party organization (see the previous section and also below).

A key aspect that remained unchanged was the central charismatic position of the party leader, Papandreu. And this may bring us to speak of a *charismatic party*. Another key aspect that, on the contrary, deeply changed was the party penetration into the state apparatus.[49]

A second, different phase of PASOK is almost perfectly mirrored by the second, transformative period of ND. In 1980 this party lost its founding charismatic leader and in 1981 lost a strong electoral confrontation with PASOK. If one thinks that, in contrast to PASOK where Papandreu had to conquer his key role, Karamanlis had been the undisputed leader and founder of ND,[50] and the incumbency was a strongly characterizing aspect of the same party since its foundation, the party was expected to be and remain in disarray for years. Actually, the fading away of most of the obstacles to organizational development and the bipolarization of the party system resulted in a miracle: the phoenix resurrected from its ashes. Thus, first of all, in the early 1980s the party was put into a corner in the parliament and in the streets, while PASOK tried to build its dominance. Now there was no more justification for inertia. The founding leader was gone, and even the old symbol with his picture had been changed (since 1979). The older and more traditionalist notables were disappearing. Moreover, even a strong traditionalist leader, such as Averoff, elected president of the party after Rallis,[51] perfectly understood the reasons of organizational development. The bipolar competition made up for the ideological weaknesses of the party, which, however, also switched to a clearer neo-liberal position,[52] and completed the miracle. In fact, the well-known organizational effect of competition, described by Duverger (1958) and others to explain the organizational development of conservative parties in Europe in response to the Socialist challenge, can be applied here.[53]

Thus, Nea Dimokratia gradually changed its organization. Rallis and Averoff were the leaders of the party during this internal transitional period and they began making great efforts to change and strengthen the organization. Even more successful was Mitsotakis since 1984.[54] His strategy of reorganizing the party at a local level to

[49] On the changes in PASOK organization, see Spourdalakis (1988), Clogg (1987), Lyrintzis (1989: 44), and above all Sotiropoulos (1991); on party penetration of state and the consequent patronage see Sotiropoulos (1991) and below.

[50] On this see Pappas (1995).

[51] Who in his turn had been elected after Karamanlis.

[52] This was particularly true with the leadership of Mitsotakis, since the electoral campaign of 1985.

[53] The most classic example being the British Conservative Party. See Panebianco (1988).

[54] On the internal party clashes for the leadership see Clogg (1987: 164 ff.).

achieve a more rational, consistent mechanism in a condition of gloss-ing over local notables has a key moment in 1986 with the new statutes. On the basis of the new rules, (i) the parliamentary group lost the power of electing the president of the party, since then entrusted to a special body formed by party representatives at the district level; (ii) in the formation of electoral lists, the proposals were formulated again at the district level, a first screening was done by the executive com-mittee, and the final decision was made by the president; (iii) a central administrative apparatus was created to supervise party organization all over the country.

Despite some costs of this operation with a split and the creation of a new Party of Democratic Renewal (DIANA), which disappeared later in 1994, the success of these efforts can be seen in the increase in ND membership from 97,000 in 1979, to 200,000 in 1986, and to 400,000 in 1991; in the new activism of the youth organization (ONNED) and in the women's sector of the party; in the internal renewal of the middle-level élite, very evident in the 1989 election, with political personnel close to the leader;[55] and as a consequence of all that the emergence of a new strong leader with Mitsotakis.[56] The overall transformation of ND into a party similar to PASOK in terms of the social distribution of voters was an additional consequence: they began coming from a broader array of groups and social strata in all parts of the country, and there was no longer a rural, provincial higher representation. But, the most visible indicator of this success is likely to be in the crisis devel-oped at the end of the decade thanks to the vocal opposition of ND up to the winning election of June 1989.[57]

A cursory analysis of the main communist party is enough to com-plete the Greek picture. The KKE has been an orthodox, classic com-munist party in all its different features: the relatively high militancy and mobilization at the beginning of the democratic period; the classic organization characterized by the secretary-general, the political bureau, the central committee, the congress, the intermediate prefec-tural federation, the territorial units and the traditional cells, the ancillary youth organization (KNE) and, above all, more substantively by democratic centralism and strong internal discipline; the highest electoral presence in urban areas, especially Athens and its outskirts, Piraeus and some islands (e.g. Lesbos, Samos, Lefkos, and Kefallonia), from 1977 to the 1980s. Of course, the electoral decline of the party and

[55] Drettakis, quoted by Pappas (1994: 18), gives a figure close to half of elected par-liamentarians in June 1989, 46.9%.

[56] The information on the 1986 statutes and data on membership were kindly pro-vided by Pappas (1995 and personal communication).

[57] On this see Chs. 5 and 6. On the ND in the 1980s see Alexakis (1993).

its organizational decay since the late 1980s to the 1990s does not change the type of party.

Institutionalization and Stabilization

In the previous sections the multifaceted processes concerning the institutionalization[58] of the different parties in the four countries have been described. In that account, at least three questions still deserve a closer analysis and a more definite reply: (i) in the institutionalization of those parties are there specific, recurring features to stress for all cases; (ii) what are the explanations for the kinds of institutionalization that eventually occurred; (iii) is it possible to be more precise on the connection between stabilization of the party system and the institutionalization of parties, that is, what makes the organizational development an 'anchor of consolidation'?

With reference to the first problem, in all considered parties institutionalization comes through the development of an extra-parliamentary structure, the achievement of the control of a parliamentary party, and the settlement of public financial support. These are the most obvious features that develop. The example of ND, which went from a strong parliamentary role to its weakening and a new position of leadership and apparatus, which meanwhile was massively developed, is evidence of this recurring institutionalizing path. But other more important elements stand out. The first one concerns the possible, but not necessary, development of a relatively large membership. The additional qualitative analysis confirms that this dimension may develop later when the party takes a governmental position. This is the case of Christian Democracy in Italy and the Socialists in Spain, but in the first case the Catholic ancillary organizations gave enormous support and in the second there was the extraordinary event of the breakdown of the UCD that left an open space for a party that was ready to attract the moderate voter. In this sense, clearer examples are the Greek PASOK and the Portuguese PSD. In both cases the electoral success was the result

---

[58] On the general definition of this notion see Ch. 1. Here, 'party institutionalization' is the emergence and the stabilization, to some extent, of a consistent organization in its different dimensions that altogether configurate a specific model of party. This definition adapts to empirical needs suggested by Panebianco (1988) and grounded on autonomy and system interdependence. Mainwaring and Scully (1995) also adopt this term with reference to the party system. Here stabilization seems more suitable for the party system: adopting different terms for different phenomena is always better; in addition institutionalization is a 'stronger' term, while party system is not really an institution (but a set of related institutions). In the empirical sense there is not much difference between the two authors and here.

of the previous development of internal organization, and later with the electoral success and the gained incumbency there was an additional success in terms of membership. In other words, discarding the relevance of membership organization and the related penetration of society, in terms of both getting electoral success and maintaining it, may be suggested by the simple analysis of the membership figures, but it is denied by a further scrutiny of other features. The subsequent organizational decay of incumbent parties that rely on other 'anchors' and may end up by losing the government is consistent with this more complex picture (see next chapter). Again, the Greek PASOK and the Portuguese Social Democrats confirm that.

The second aspect is perhaps even more relevant: a crucial component of institutionalization is the achievement of a unified party or, at a lower level, at least overcoming a strong factionalism. As suggested above, in Spain the breakdown of the UCD is accounted for by this impossibility. Again, in Spain, the success of PSOE lay in the shaping of a unified, disciplined party. Such success may be more uncertain and volatile than that gained with a massive super-developed organization, but if the incumbency is added then other 'anchors' may be set in motion to maintain their institutionalization and success. The overcoming of centrifugal effects and of the competitive handicaps settled by a network of local notables and related factions is a key moment in the institutionalization of the Greek ND and the Portuguese Socialists and Social Democrats, as it had been at the very beginning of their democracy with the Spanish Socialists. Within the Italian Christian Democracy the presence of factions is made up for by another very strong glue, the religious affiliation and the connected anti-communist ideology. However, as suggested by Panebianco (1988), here it may be confirmed that a stronger internal factionalization shows a lower party institutionalization, as also happened to Italian Socialists.

An additional consideration is that institutionalization also developed through the achievement of some consistency among its various related dimensions: although they may develop at different moments, those dimensions, in relations among them, adjust one another, gaining a higher effectiveness that should result in every activity of the party: at the grassroots level and at the electoral level, in the parliament or, in some cases, in the cabinet, in formulation and implementation of policies. As evident in the Italian case, there is full consistency between a developed mass membership, a strong central apparatus, a unified party, and a weak parliamentary party. In Spain the membership facet is underdeveloped, but this is made up for by strong leadership and incumbency in addition to a unified party, a central professional apparatus, and a weak parliamentary party. And, however, eventually the penetration of party organization in that society is lower in that country. In Portugal and Greece the achievement of such consistency may be seen in some parties, such as the PSD, ND, or PASOK, or also in the communist parties.

A consequent reflection should be added. The achievement of consistency points to at least two basically different forms of institutionalization: that achieved with mass parties and high membership and that achieved with a 'lighter' professional electoral party (see Panebianco 1988), as with the Spanish PSOE. Also the second mode may be effective, although it is difficult not to conclude on its higher uncertainty (see above). Intermediate solutions are also possible, if some extent of effective consistency is gained, such as a fairly developed grassroots organization and a strong leader who controls the local notables, as in the Portuguese PSD. The simple fact is, however, that the second more relative institutionalization is sometimes the only way out, because the first type of institutionalization with mass parties or also a more attenuated version of it are impossible because of the lack of related conditions. This brings us to the second question: how do we explain the different kinds and levels of institutionalization that occurred?

A considerable amount of research on Italian parties indicates that key explanatory factors of the overdeveloped party organization include the fascist legacy, a wide network of Catholic structures, a large public sector, and, last but not least, ideological[59] and party polarization (see, among others, Barnes 1967; Tarrow 1967; Alberoni 1967). As seen above, a complex system with several different models of parties, a number of related ancillary organizations, and a thick network of links with civil society resulted from the interaction of these factors.

However, a peculiar stress requires the analysis of political traditions. The fact is that when fascism breaks down, the middle classes— also the Catholics—are more inclined to accept the appeal of the new democratic parties. Particularly, some democratic leaders were keenly aware of the empty space left by the disappearance of the regime and the Fascist Party in those middle classes. De Gasperi is one of these leaders, and he explicitly raised the problem of winning the consensus—and the support—of groups educated into politics during fascism. In 1943 the regime broke down, and the desire to cancel and forget the broad-based and resolute consensus toward fascism which had provoked the war and all the consequent disasters became very marked. In such a situation, the void in the political arena left by the sudden

[59] Barnes (1966) emphasized that organizational development is best achieved when the ideological dimension is a relevant feature of political conflict in the country.

disappearance of the PNF gave the democratic parties the best condition to attain and to maintain the widespread support of the Italian population. Thus, the void was easily filled. As Scoppola points out, some cautious, moderate, and conservative choices of the Christian Democrats during the 1940s as well as a few conflicts between the pre-fascist generation of Popolari and the new Catholic generation, educated during fascism, are accounted for only if one considers the persistence of traditional, non-democratic attitudes in the middle classes and the maintenance of visions of politics learned during the fascist years, which were very difficult to forget for the youth (Scoppola 1977: 31 ff. and 67–8).

Germani (1975) and Zangrandi (1962) have pointed out how the juvenile socialization into political participation during the famous meetings of the Littoriali or on other controlled occasions could in itself create the opportunities for the actual participation and the opposition which could later become very difficult to control. In other words, a key point in the fascist legacy is the habit of political participation even—but not always and sometimes with potentially opposite results—of a formal and very passive type which is then bequeathed to the new democracy. This sort of habit is fertile ground for democratic parties to cultivate.

In this vein, fascism may be considered responsible for the creation of new collective political identities, and for the habit of party identification in non-private daily life, above all for the middle classes which entered politics mainly through the first middle-class mass party formed in Italy, i.e. the PNF (see also Petersen 1975). In other words, there are three strongly related aspects that eventually led civil society towards the same goals and results: first, the habit of political identification; second, the disappearance of the object of previous identification; and third, the necessity of cancelling the experience of the war and the regime that provoked it. For the democratic parties this was the best ground on which to build. When the impact of ideology and polarization are added, the institutionalization of parties with its strong continuity for decades is more completely explained.

For a better understanding of this point let us consider a completely different hypothesis, that of a fascist regime which does not promote political participation, albeit of a passive and controlled type, and where the party and its ancillary organizations do not play a relevant role. That is a situation where there is no mass participation and the role of the party as the organizer of consensus is not crucial. This is the hypothesis of fascism as a *demobilizational regime*, such as in Spain during Franco in the 1950s and 1960s. Had this been the case, the mobilization in the period 1943–6 would still have been massive, but would not have been strengthened by those habits of collective identification already mentioned, and it would probably have been more difficult to institutionalize them. In contrast with the North, which already had experiences of (democratic) mass politics before fascism, the South would not have experienced mass politics. Consequently, the conditions of development of the new democratic parties, even of the DC, would have been much more difficult to establish than actually was the case.

The political traditions that are strengthened by the existing conditions at the moment of democratic installation are also very important to explain the other three cases. A parallel or a contrast with Italian experience can be helpful. Thus, in Spain the demobilizational traditions, the recurring anti-party propaganda, and the strong memory of civil war (see Maravall 1981) in a more modern, non-ideologized society may explain very well why the party institutionalization basically concerns only the PSOE that was also the most developed mass party during the 1930s and before Francoism. But traditions and existing conditions also explain the difficulties for a rightist party with roots in the old delegitimized authoritarian regime as well as the problems of a Communist left that cannot flourish in a society with moderate middle and working classes and low ideologization.

The lack of party traditions and, more generally, democratic traditions are a central aspect in explaining the Portuguese uncertainties, and their strong presence is an obstacle for Greek parties. In Portugal, the lack of any party presence in the past and, on the contrary, a strong corporatist tradition, that is, of a completely different criterion of representation, are beginning difficulties. The fact that until 1982 the dominant problems of the regime were related to the role of the army and to a few crucial characteristics of democracy (see Chapter 2) explains the slow pace in the institutionalization of the PSD and the PS. It eventually occurred to a different extent: the PSD much more than the PS, but for a rightist party, such as the CDS, it was impossible to reach some institutionalization for years. In Greece, party traditions were an obstacle for the institutionalization of Nea Dimokratia and conditioned the development of PASOK: on the one hand, local notables and habits of clientelism and, on the other hand, civil war remembrance and resistance to the military Junta, were decisive. Only ideology and polarization, caused by electoral laws and strong leaders, were able to overcome those obstacles and achieve institutionalization in both PASOK and ND, but those traditions contributed to shape the institutionalization.

Despite the greater attention paid to the traditions of the country, the comparative explanation of party institutionalization may be explored through a 'decremental approach' that points out the various factors to be taken into account. More precisely, Italy is the case where all the main parties were able to achieve high institutionalization. As noted above, this is the result of several causes. In Greece, there is also high, but less stable, institutionalization for all relevant parties: the fascist traditions and the highest polarization brought about by the Cold War were absent, but not the other reasons, largely—not totally though—overlapping with the Italian ones. In Portugal a more partial institutionalization, which actually regards only one party (PSD) and a subsequent similar phenomenon in another party (PS), can be explained by the lack of mobilizational political traditions—be they either authoritarian or democratic—and by the low bipolarization. In Spain the even more partial institutionalization is accounted for by the low ideology and radicalization that are still present in the previous cases.

Concerning the forms and explanations of institutionalization, let it be stressed that there is the empirical possibility of a partial institutionalization, that is, one concerning only one party and not all the main parties. This happened in Spain and Portugal. Under such a hypothesis, the explanation is that the assimilating side-effects of competition were slower to come out, because of the existence of contrasting obstacles. They mainly include long internal conflicts, as in the Portuguese PS and the Spanish AP-PP; and a fading away but existing exclusion of a party related to the delegitimated past, as for the AP-PP.

The third problem to explore here is singling out the more precise connection between party institutionalization and the stabilization of the party system. In Chapter 2 a few indicators and measures of stabilization of the party system were analysed as indicators and measures of consolidation. Here, first of all, it is relevant to control the different extents of systemic stabilization among the four countries. For this purpose a simple cumulative index has been constructed by picking up the total volatility (TEV), the inter-block volatility (I-BV), the party fractionalization (PF), and the effective number of parties (ENP). The I-BV also gives the possibility of evaluating the left–right cleavage, which is very important in our countries (see also below), and the ENP allows one to take into account the stabilizing impact of electoral law, as PF is calculated on the votes cast for each party.[60] The index (see

[60] As the index is cumulative, its logic is very simple. It may be pointed out that while with regards to TEV and I-BV, the closer to zero the values are the higher the stabilization, for PF and ENP the lower the difference between one value and the following one, the higher the stabilization. Accordingly, for TEV and I-BV mean values were considered; for PF and ENP the means of the differences between each value and the following one has been taken into account. These values were standardized according to the usual rules suggested by the SPSS package. The resulting values have been put in a scale with

TABLE 4.6. *Index of party system stabilization*

Italy	Spain	Portugal	Greece
0.52	0.0	0.21	0.27

Note: See n. 60.

Sources: Official electoral data.

Table 4.6) confirms the stabilization of all party systems, but at the same time it shows the much higher Italian stabilization, followed by the Greek, with Portugal and Spain in a decreasing trend and Spain fairly away from the other countries. Of course, the figures also suggest the salience of other elements, such as the longer period of stabilization in Portugal or the salience of other 'anchors' in the very strong Greek stability.

When the consistency between stabilization and institutionalization is controlled, the result is the expected one, but it is meaningful: the lowest stabilization is in the country (Spain) with the lowest relative party institutionalization; the highest in the country (Italy) with the most developed penetration in terms of membership organization. Fairly close to Spain, Portugal is the country where there is the institutionalization of one main party—similar to Spain—and some degree of institutionalization of the other main party (PS), and Communists, as well. With the institutionalization of both main parties in the same decade, but also as suggested by ENP's measure with a strong impact of electoral law, Greece is very stabilized.[61] Its problems emerged later on, at the end of the 1980s. Thus, on the whole the index stresses a high consistency between party-system stabilization and party institutionalization. Accordingly, the simplest explanation is confirmed, that is, the organizational development is in a position to create more stable links with the same voters and in this way contribute to the stabilization of the party system. Of course, the institutionalization of one or more parties may later come to stabilize a possible electoral success, achieved thanks to a contingent cause, such as the death of the leader of the main competing party or the disruption of a competing party by internal conflicts, and so on.

the lowest value (that for Spain) equal to zero, and the other ones follow. The examined span of time has been the same for the four measures, but a longer one than indicated in this and the previous chapters to better check the extent of stabilization. Consequently, for Italy it goes from 1948 to 1963; for Spain from 1979 to 1989; for Portugal 1976 to 1991; and for Greece 1977 to 1989. Of course, the higher the index, the higher the stabilization.

[61] The effect of the electoral law and other rules will be considered in Ch. 6.

Two more observations before concluding this chapter. The ideological polarization among parties has been mentioned as an explanation of party institutionalization, and also with reference to the stabilization of the party system. Indeed, in this respect it must be regarded as a double-edged sword. On the one hand, it can help to promote the organizational development of parties, as well as widespread party identification among their supporters. From this perspective, it can contribute to the stabilization of parties and electoral behaviour. On the other hand, partisan polarization can intensify conflict within new democracies, which in turn may bring about a further radicalization over time and a greater likelihood that parties, their leaders, and their supporters might be moved to break some of the fundamental rules of peaceful democratic competition. This can obviously be detrimental to the prospects for regime consolidation. Conversely, responsible, moderate behaviour by political parties may contribute decisively to consolidation of the new democracy, but such moderation can also undermine the solidarity among élites and supporters of political parties, thereby impeding party-system stabilization.

This analysis also suggests that party institutionalization does not appear to be a necessary prerequisite for successful democratic consolidation. There are the other 'anchors of consolidation' that may be added or alternatives to party institutionalization. The case of Spain is revealing in this regard: virtually all observers agree that Spanish democracy was consolidated by the mid-1980s, and yet at that moment there are political parties weakly organized in Spain; in addition, in the early 1980s the most decisive phase of the consolidation process coincided with a period of considerable party-system instability. The Greek case is also revealing in another direction: the analysis of party organization (and its explanation) is compelled to mention the problem of incumbency, public resources, and clientelist networks. One may still argue, however, that the organizational characteristics of parties may be of some importance in determining what particular pattern the consolidation process will follow as well as what specific kind of democratic regime becomes consolidated. It is with this set of questions in mind that attention is devoted to an analysis of the relationships between state, parties, and civil society in the next chapter.

....

5

....

State and Civil Society

Interests and the State

As also suggested in this chapter, the classical view of political parties is one in which stable linkages with different sectors of civil society are secured through the organizational development of parties themselves and their respective ancillary organizations. In this view, the key variables include an organizational network with central, intermediate, and local structures, activists and militants who give life to these institutions, and, at least, a well-articulated set of partisan values. Furthermore, linkages between parties and specific sectors of society can be strengthened through the logic of partisan competition itself.

The cases, however, suggest that this is not the only way to follow. A second anchor by which parties establish stable relationships with civil society and especially with more or less organized interest groups or sectors of society is in the making of public policies and the related allocation of state resources. In this process the linkages are not grounded on ideology and party organization, but on economic interests and the manner in which they are affected by the activities of the public sector.

This is still a typical modality of representative function, where parties serve as institutions which channel interests into decisional arenas. In performing this function, parties should be in some way independent of interest groups. From a normative point of view, this should enable them to combine the specific interests of groups with general interests of civil society, and thus be better able to attain the kind of efficacy that is also necessary to secure a higher degree of legitimacy and support. In his classic discussion of institutionalization, Huntington (1968: 20) unfolds this reasoning and emphasizes the need for parties to maintain their autonomy from a particular group and the desirability of aggregating the interest of several groups.

In Chapter 1 I suggested that one way of looking at relationships between parties, on the one hand, and interest group or individuals, on the other, is to see whether parties and the party system, as a whole,

are able to perform a gatekeeping role for the groups, or whether interests depend on parties for their satisfaction.[1] As already stressed, gatekeeping may play an important role in democratic consolidation, since
it induces the most relevant sectors of civil society to accept the key,
crucial role of parties, at least as intermediate institutions to aggregate
demands, settle priorities, and possibly solve problems that directly or
indirectly affect the everyday life of citizens.

In Chapter 1, I also mentioned five main possibilities for party–group
relationships: from party *dominance* or, in a stronger form, *occupation*,
to *symbiosis*, *neutrality*, and *direct access*. This set of relations between
parties and interests can be explored in three specific domains: (i) the
relationship between parties and entrepreneurs or organizations of
propertied interests, also in agriculture; (ii) relationships between parties and unions; and (iii) particularistic relationships and policies
towards individuals, but also towards social groups regarding the distribution of public sector resources, that is, party patronage.[2] To this
can be added the opportunity of looking for corporatist arrangements
that also contribute to the anchoring. Spain and Italy again emerge
from this analysis as very different from each other; Greece and Portugal are seen to more closely resemble Italy than they do Spain, but
some additional diversities also become apparent.

Dominance and Control: Italy

In Italy, the 1950s were a period of party dominance vis-à-vis civil society. In the words of Farneti (1973: 31–40), this was a 'decade of political society', that is, of parties. During the immediate post-war period,
in the agricultural sector the association of landowners, the Confagricoltura, was constrained by the need to defend the interest of its members in the new democratic context and seek the support of the parties
and their leaders, and consequently opted for neutrality and a multiparty appeal. In the 1950s, however, this association changed its strategy and established a privileged relationship with the governing DC
and other rightist parties (especially the Liberal PLI and, in the south,
the MSI and Monarchists).

A distinctly different kind of linkage was established between the DC
and the association of small landowners, the Coldiretti. Its exclusive
political relationship with the DC was that between a party and the

---

[1] For the definition of 'gatekeeping role' see Ch. 1.

[2] On this notion, see e.g, Kristinsson (1996: 435): 'Political patronage . . . means the
selective distribution of material benefits to individuals or small groups in exchange for
political support.'

trade union generated by it. In this way one can speak of symbiosis, characterized by a coincidence of values, two different spheres of action, a relationship of equal standing with the delivery of electoral support in exchange for favourable decisions. This was, however, only partly true. First of all, the DC with its various currents was very different from a worker party that has a truly symbiotic—and exclusive—relationship with its own trade union. In short, a relationship in which the party is dependent on the trade union for its electoral support. In this case, the support of civil society or of the social groups involved was derived to a considerable degree from the basic support of the Church and its lay organizations (see e.g. Poggi 1963, La Palombara 1964, Manoukian 1968), at least until the DC built itself a proper organizational structure in the 1950s and the Coldiretti formed its own power base in the above-mentioned public arenas.[3]

Thus, if one finds some aspects of symbiosis in the relationship between the party and the Coldiretti, such as the absence of the executive of the second organization in the first, or the *de facto* delegation of the management of governmental agricultural policy by the DC to the Coldiretti, the relationship between the party and the organizations of the small farmers is better defined in terms of the domination by the former of the latter. Indeed, the presence of the exponents of the Coldiretti in the Ministry of Agriculture, even at the level of Under-Secretary, in parliament with numerous elected representatives, or in the parliamentary Commissions of the sector, is paralleled—and this is more important—by the presence of numerous party exponents in the executive at the provincial and local levels, starting from the early 1950s; the clear political exploitation of land allocation during the implementation of the agrarian reform;[4] and the formulation of crucial sectoral programmes and decisions in the party arenas, with subsequent decision-making in the governmental and parliamentary arenas.

To really understand what happened in this sector the reference to a peculiar pact is compulsory. This is the agreement which developed progressively between the Coldiretti and the Confagricoltura, centred on a public agency, the Federconsorzi, in which both groups were accommodated, and succeeded in protecting their interests since the early 1950s. In this context, the DC again played a central role in linking itself to the two interest groups, and in bringing about the complete

---

[3] Lanza (1991) notes that in 1951 following an internal reform, the figure of the 'ecclesiatical councillor' appeared in the organization. The truth being that during this period the Church paid great attention to the rural classes.

[4] Indeed, the party was present in the agrarian reform agencies with its own leaders. The delegation of the direction of agrarian policy came about instead in the Federconsorzi and in the public insurance agencies, as noted above.

marginalization of all the forces, unions included, of the left, from the Federbraccianti to the Alleanza Contadini.

In the industrial sector the situation was not substantially different. In this sector, too, there was the dominance of the DC through a penetration of public agencies, and the marginalization and isolation of the organized groups of the left. Party control over access to the decision-making arena was not challenged either by the industrial entre-preneurs' association, Confindustria, or by the trade unions. DC dominance over the industrialists evolved in the course of three different periods. The first coincided with the democratic transition and installation of a new regime (1943–7) and was characterized by great hostility between the government and business élites: until the exit of the left from the governing majority in May 1947, the influence of Confindustria was very limited and mainly channelled through the PLI. The second phase began after May 1947 and featured a situation of *duopolio*: the DC was strong politically, but needed an industrial sector committed to economic reconstruction. It was thus forced to concede to Confindustria (which had maintained its privileged relationships with the bureaucracy from the outset) decision-making influence in the management of public policy—particularly, concerning the implementation of the Marshall Plan—and in the attempt to solve the most pressing sectoral problems (see also La Palombara 1964). In the policy-making process, however, the influence of Confindustria was not direct, but was primarly channelled through the ministers of economics, led by the Liberals. In fact, throughout this period the peak business association established a particularly symbiotic relationship with the PLI: in addition to non-overlapping leadership, there was a coincidence of political values and policy proposals between Liberals and industrialists. The third phase of party dominance came after the break-up of the *duopolio*, when, as of 1953, Confindustria suffered a decline in both membership and political initiative. At this point the DC was weaker in terms of parliamentary seats, but fairly stronger in terms of party organization and of its role in the expansion of the public sector and credit facilities managed by the public banks.

The relationship between parties and trade unions also changed over time. In the first period of transition and installation, party dominance was clear-cut: ideological divisions affected all aspects of activity, and there was extensive electoral mobilization of the trade unions. But these relationships were complicated by a previous decision (1944) to create a unitary trade union. With the split in the trade unions in 1949–50, a second phase began. Parties became even more dominant, partly because of the fragmentation, demobilization, and membership decline experienced by trade unions. A further confirmation of party dominance over labour is given by the fact that during this period trade unions never adopted a clearly autonomous position in the area of industrial relations. Only in the early 1960s did a clearer differentiation of their respective roles appear; thereafter, trade unions often took their own initiatives, separately from parties, and assumed a somewhat greater degree of autonomy.

There was also some penetration of the DC by the Catholic trade union, the CISL, in parliament. Representatives of the CISL organized their own faction within the party, although the DC maintained its autonomy and refused to passively submit to the policy proposal of the CISL. The influence of the parties of the left in the Italian General Confederation of Workers (CGIL), or of the Republicans in the Italian Union of Workers (UIL), hardly requires explanation: there was a common understanding of party–trade union relations in which the party played the dominant role in the formulation of political options. Within the context of the 'negative integration' of the left (see Linz 1974*b* and Chapter 3), trade unions sought to retain respective clienteles by maintaining high visibility in parliamentary activity. For this, they needed the support and collaboration of parties. Thus, trade unions largely accepted this dominance, since their relations with parties gave them a role in drawing up electoral lists and access to the parliamentary arena in general. Given the more developed ideologies of parties of the left, there was a greater coincidence of values which reinforced party dependence. Finally, one should recall that participation in trade union activity was one of the main channels of leftist party activism.

On the whole, in the industrial sector, there were two main features which characterized the relations between interest groups and politics: fragmentation and demobilization. With regard to the first, in addition to the Confindustria, there were two main artisan associations, split along political-ideological lines since 1946. Located close to the DC were the smaller entrepreneurs (and artisans proper) in the Confederazione Generale dell'Artigianato, and on the left, the Confederazione Nazionale dell'Artigianato. In addition, there were the association of small entrepreneurs, the Confapi,[5] created in 1947, and, above all, the association which covered public industry, the Intersind, created in 1956. On the trade union side there were three main organizations from 1949 to 1950 (CGIL, CISL, UIL) to which one can add CISNAL, on the extreme right, and the so-called autonomous trade unions. Thus, one finds fragmentation accentuated on both sides by class conflict. The

[5] The presence of small businesses in the Confindustria with its characteristics, differences, and problems is discussed by Mattina (1991). However, the Confindustria always had considerable difficulty penetrating the small business sector.

main consequence of such fragmentation was the simultaneous and objective weakening of the Confindustria and the trade unions, and the space left open to the parties of government as a result.

Demobilization affected entrepreneurs and workers alike. Both the Confindustria and the trade unions experienced a clear drop in membership which reached its lowest point around the mid-1950s.[6] In addition to the quantitative facts—primarily, the non-renewal of membership by the small businesses—the phenomena of demobilization was particularly evident for the Confindustria, in the diminished importance of the association itself. One can indeed maintain that from the mid-1950s onwards, when it had become clear that the existence of the central institutions of a capitalist system had become an uncontested political reality and, at the same time, the weakened position of the trade unions was very evident, the Italian business community withdrew from the political arena. Where necessary it sought direct contact with government and party leaders, thus bypassing its own association. It no longer needed the strong impact that the latter could bring to bear on governments and consequently relegated their association to second place. In this sense, the weakening of the association was the clearest indicator of the perceived strength and legitimacy of the social group, represented by the association.

As far as the trade unions were concerned, there were other factors that support the hypothesis of a phase of stabilization of industrial relationships characterized by demobilization: they are the reduction in the size and length of strikes; the problems connected with the renewal of the national contracts; and the relative stagnation of wages. Nevertheless, a further clarification at the trade union level is essential: demobilization—highlighted primarily in the drop of trade union membership—mainly affected the new CGIL in the 1950s (Feltrin 1991). Consequently, there was a demobilization of the working-class forces of the left. Indeed, it took place primarily at the level of the active working population and ran roughly parallel to the marked decline in PCI membership during the period. CISL membership, on the other hand, oscillated throughout the 1950s, but was never in clear decline and indeed in some years even experienced an increase in membership. Here too, trade union membership ran parallel to DC membership (see Feltrin 1991, Tables 1–2).[7]

---

[6] One should note that the decline in the membership mainly regards small businesses (see Mattina 1991). In general, the decline of the influence of the Confindustria is highlighted by various authors. See La Palombara (1964: 331), and the following paragraph.

[7] It may be recalled (see Ch. 3) that Coldiretti and Confagricoltura also carried out an integrative democratic function. The Coldiretti managed, by means of a solid parliamentary representation, to integrate the peasant farmer class, by demonstrating also a strong mobilizing capacity. The Confagricoltura, in turn, managed to render the new

The expansion of the public sector played an important role in these party–interest group relationships. In the agricultural sector, the Federconsorzi, agrarian reform agencies, public pension agencies, and the Cassa per il Mezzogiorno conditioned all relations between the main incumbent party, the DC, and interest group associations (see above). The same was true of the industrial sector. The role played by the Institute of Industrial Reconstruction (IRI) in economic reconstruction, the creation of the National Agency for Oil (ENI) in 1953 and the Ministry for State Investments in 1956, the laws on hydrocarbons (1957), the activity of the Cassa per il Mezzogiorno in the industrial sector, the presence of the public banks, and the creation of a series of public agencies—all controlled by the parties in government—profoundly affected the relationships between government parties, on the one hand, and enterpreneurs and trade unions, on the other.[8] For ideological reasons, the left supported the expansion of the public sector, not understanding until it was too late that such public intervention would have important political side-effects. Thus, in the 1950s, the enlargement of the public sector, the creation of the Cassa per il Mezzogiorno, and other parliamentary initiatives culminated in the establishment of a clientelistic system which would function as the core of particularistic ties between civil society and parties such as DC, PLI, and PSDI in some parts of the South.[9]

Patronage is the other feature that characterizes the relationships between Christian Democracy and individuals as well as non-organized groups, above all in Southern Italy. This means that there is a widespread party patronage and some Christian Democrat middle-level élites are real 'brokers' of local and individual interests, being able to transfer central resources to the periphery in different ways, but

reality acceptable even to those groups damaged by government measures taken at the time. As for the Confindustria, there was no marked problem of acceptance of the new democratic regime, given the immediate acceptance of the thesis of 'fascism as an interlude', proposed by Croce and immediately taken up by Einaudi and other PLI leaders. Yet, the playing down of the role of Italian industrialists in the success of the fascist movement, and the acceptance of the new liberal structures was not sufficient in the renewed political context. It seemed above all to have been a problem of their recognition of their own union interlocuter, and it was precisely the weakness of the trade union movement that made it possible to dispense with the recognition of this actor. One must remember, finally, the existence of maximalizing elements in the trade unions that refused to recognize the legitimacy of either profit or the market, and also democracy as such. In this sense, the industrial sector achieved its own consolidation again thanks to the weakness of the trade unions (see Morlino 1991*a*).

[8] Maraffi (1991, esp. chs. 7 and 8) stresses the role of Fanfani in the construction of the public sector.

[9] A much more detailed analysis of the relationship between interest groups and parties in Italy during the 1940s and 1950s is in Morlino (1991*a*). On the development of clientelism in Italy, see Graziano (1980); and also Pasquino (1980).

always through state agencies or bureaucracy.[10] The attention—not mediated by organized associations—to the potential needs of civil society demonstrated *ad abundantiam* the role of party gatekeeping and, in particular, that of the DC in the various sectors, e.g. agriculture, industry, or trade. It was precisely the sheer volume of microsectional legislative initiatives promoted by the party system that stressed that role of gatekeeping, and also the search for legitimation by means of clientelistic practices (Morisi 1991, Tables 13–20).[11]

To conclude, the party–group relationships were characterized by the domination of the former over the latter, when interest associations were mass organizations, such as the unions, where numbers count. Such relationships were instead characterized by neutrality and control, that is, from the point of view of groups, a multiparty appeal, an alliance with the DC, the accommodation within the regime and dependence on that party when interest associations were élite organizations (Confindustria and Confagricoltura), where resources count. The relationships of domination/control were further characterized and strengthened, and in part caused, by the DC control of key public institutions in agriculture and industry.

This outcome is explainable if one focuses on the development of the process. The establishment of relationships began after the turning point of the period May 1947–April 1948, and was expressed in two clearly distinguishable phases. The first began with the DC electoral victory in 1948, thanks to the support of the Catholic community and the Southern *notabilato* (oligarchy). It was moreover characterized by the political-ideological choices that reassured landowners and industrialists alike, by the consequent government and parliamentary decisions, and by the concessions and negotiations at the level of invisible politics, with both opposition and the main organized groups, above all the entrepreneurs. In other words, there was the immediate acquisition of a position of party gatekeeping and of domination/control of the organized and non-organized groups alike,[12] thanks primarily to the dominant position of the DC after the 1948 elections and to a strong, unitary, and authoritative leadership. Because of this initial position of dominance (and because of a fear of the 'subversive' left), all groups referred to the DC. The DC in turn was strengthened in its control of political access by this fact alone.

[10] On this topic, which concerns not only Southern Italy, there is a large literature. See, for example, Allum (1975), Caciagli *et al.* (1977), Graziano (1980).

[11] In the Italian case local government has had an integrative effect, albeit less relevant than the parliamentary one, for the left, which compensated for its exclusion: the left has remained in local government in the so-called 'red' areas from the outset, earning stable positions of power and solidly acquired interests.

[12] As one can deduce from an examination of parliamentary activity (cf. Morisi 1991).

In the second phase, after the electoral defeat of the DC in 1953, the position of the party was furthermore strengthened thanks to the penetration and creation of public agencies by the government. This outcome was concretely due to the existence of institutions created by fascism (e.g. IRI), or promoted by it (the Federconsorzi). Such public agencies facilitated the DC in controlling organized and non-organized interests alike, and characterized democratic consolidation in Italy.

When domination and control over groups and sectors of civil society were established and at the same time the propertied associations no longer felt a serious danger from the left, they became less relevant. In fact, they subsequently demobilized, left the political arena as collective actors, adapted themselves in the institutions of actual government in the sectors of agriculture and industry, and established preferential relationships with the relative ministerial committees, competent ministers, and local governments.

Control and Autonomy: Spain

The Spanish picture is the very opposite of the Italian one. An authoritarian tradition, society, and economy developed along different lines at the time of regime change and an altered international situation largely explain the differences between the two cases. The several associations established in the agricultural sector mirror the diversities in Spanish agriculture: four are of national size, but there are a few others of some importance.[13] None of these associations either achieved high political salience or established links with a specific party (see Pérez Díaz 1987, ch. 13). The problem of legitimation, which existed in Italy during the 1940s, was not present there during the late 1970s when most of the associations were created. Thus, there was no sense that a rightist, perhaps ambiguously democratic, political force would become the monopolist representative of an agricultural group. Since 1982 the relationships of these associations with the socialist government and particularly the Ministry of Agriculture are limited to informative and consultative meetings.[14] The pluralism of the sector, the political neutrality of these associations, and the differentiation in voting behaviour of their members contrast sharply with the Italian

[13] The four national associations are: the National Confederation of Farmers and Breeders (Ganaderos) (CNAG), which is the only member of CEOE among the agricultural associations (see below); the Coordination of Farmers' and Breeders' Organizations (COAG); the National 'Central' of Young Farmers (CNJA); and the Union of Agrarian Federations of Spain (UFADE). See De La Fuente Blanco (1991).

[14] For a good overview of agricultural organizations see De La Fuente Blanco (1991).

situation and at the same time are its characterizing facets in the established political relations. From the perspective of consolidation the political salience of all these organizations is close to zero.

The associational structure in the Spanish industrial sector is also different from the Italian one. There is a monopolistic association, the Spanish Confederation of Entrepreneurial Organizations (CEOE), created in 1977 as a peak association, where different sectoral federations and groups of entrepreneurs converged.[15] The 133 affiliated associations cover 1,300,000 firms (see Schmitter 1995: 299). Unlike its counterpart in Italy, an association of public firms was never created. Moreover, in 1980 the CEOE was able to integrate the association of medium and small entrepreneurs (CEPYME), which, however, maintained some autonomy within the CEOE. This was possible because of the flexible model of organizational decentralization, maintained by the CEOE, that also allowed the integration of other sectoral organizations and the creation of new ones (see Jerez Mir 1992).[16] In fact, during these years, the CEOE was undergoing an impressive process of growth and organizational development.

With regard to relationships with parties, Spanish industrial associations are autonomous. Indeed, the CEOE has maintained a manifest position of neutrality vis-à-vis parties and the party system as a whole. This position was complemented by an open pro-democratic endorsement of the necessity of breaking with the previous regime (see Martínez 1993). Although there is a clear distinction between the period before and after 1982, a well-defined distance was always maintained between the interest group and the party leaders (see Pérez Díaz 1987: 164). Before 1982, unlike the Italian case, the business association established no ties with the governing party, the centrist UCD. On the contrary, the relationship was characterized by tension: in the 1977–8 period, entrepreneurs protested against the Moncloa Pacts and governmental economic policy in general; and in 1981, an attempt was made to create an allied party out of parts of the UCD (which was then in the process of breaking up) and the Alianza Popular (see López Nieto 1988; and Pérez Díaz 1987: 163). In this moment CEOE tried to establish indirect access to the decisional arena by creating its own party.[17] To this it may be added that when only business people—and not the

---

[15] Other associations, such as the Circle of Entrepreneurs or the Association for Entrepreneurial Progress, are of much more limited importance.

[16] For the basic characteristics of the Spanish industrial world, see Bueno Campos *et al.* (1989).

[17] It is worth noting that despite the tensions that were mentioned in the text, from 1976 to 1981 there were at least 58 cabinet members who had occupied positions in the industrial and banking sectors (see Jerez Mir 1992: 41). This suggests the existence of thick informal networks that overcome the official relations with CEOE.

official position of the association—are considered, until 1979 they were very much in favour of the UCD, and also voted for this party. Later on, in 1980 and 1981, the distancing from the UCD and the movement towards the AP also concerns them, and not only the association (see Martínez 1993).

Paradoxically, the election of a Socialist government in 1982 was followed by better relations with the governmental party: given the moderate, pragmatic policies of the PSOE cabinet, which objectively was pro-business, a stance of sympathetic neutrality was then adopted. Despite the non-homogeneity of the business group and inside the organization, the growing confidence toward González and PSOE was also the result of acknowledging the more assertive, efficient economic policy of the Socialist government (see Martínez 1993).[18] Moreover, and very important, the quasi-corporatist economic agreements up to the mid-1980s further contributed to the independent identity of employers and their political autonomy, but also to building a rich, integrative relationship with ministries and the bureaucracy, which gave them possibilities for participation and actual lobbying. The business associations and groups at the regional level, particularly in regions such as Catalonia and the Basque Country, had parallel experiences (see Molins 1994).[19]

During the emergence of Spain's new democratic regime and up to the mid-1980s, a sort of bipartisan union system became established at the national level. The two dominant trade unions were the Comisiones Obreras (CCOO) and the General Union of Workers (UGT). There were also minor independent unions, such as the Syndical Worker Union (USO), which was close to Catholic positions, and regional bodies, like ELA-STV in the Basque Country or INTG, later CIG, in Galicia, which became important in those regions (see esp. Köhler 1995).[20] This immediately suggests that the development of trade union associations evolved in a manner quite different from those in Italy.

First of all, there was a low density of membership. All unions claimed to have a high number of members: in early 1980 the Comisiones declared about 2,000,000 members, UGT was close to 1,500,000, and the others an additional 800,000 members (see e.g. Schmitter 1995: 300).[21]

---

[18] The sympathetic neutrality is fully consistent with the hypothesis of Pérez Díaz (1985) about a mutual 'exploiting' of the entrepreneurial class and the political class to achieve their different interests.

[19] For additional studies on entrepreneurs and the attitudes of the business élite, see Martínez and Pardo Avellaneda (1985); Rijnen (1985); and Jerez Mir (1992).

[20] No relevant regional unions developed in Catalonia. Only a higher concentration of National Confederation of Workers' (CNT) members can be noticed.

[21] These figures are inflated. There are a few other sources that suggested lower affiliation, but some figures that could be closer to reality are virtually impossible to know.

Despite this, the density was much lower than that of all other Southern European countries. Again with differences among the sources, during the 1980s the percentage was around 10–15 per cent.[22] In this picture at least four phenomena deserve attention. As is evident from the union elections of the same decade, the extent of union representation remained high: approximately 80 per cent of workers participated in the various elections. The existing unions became stronger and stronger: elected representatives of other lists declined from 20.4 in 1978 to 8–9 per cent ten years later (see Martínez Alier and Roca Jusmet 1988: 40). The level of union fragmentation declined: the two main unions achieved about 80 per cent of elected candidates. Perhaps because of the expectations raised by the Socialist government, at least in 1990 the more moderate UGT grew at the expense of the CCOO by winning 40.2 per cent of elected representatives vis-à-vis 34.3 per cent of CCOO's representatives in 1986 (see Martínez Alier and Roca Jusmet 1988: 40), and 43.1 per cent versus 34.4 per cent in 1990 (see Fernández-Castro 1993: 53–4). Moreover, with a high depoliticization of strikes a curious situation of established institutions that were distant from workers seemed to emerge. This may be strengthened by the status of public institutions that the unions acquired by getting state buildings and public financial funds, in addition to a more obvious acknowledgement of rights of union representatives (see Del Campo García 1995: 206–7) and to a less obvious right of collective bargaining for the unions with at least 10 per cent of votes in syndical elections (see Grassi 1992: 14; and Fernández-Castro 1993).

It is consistent with this picture that, since at least 1980, unions and union leaders behaved as moderate collective-bargaining organizations which rejected the notion that they were 'transmission belts' for political parties (see Pérez Díaz 1987, ch. 8; and Fishman 1990, esp. 163–80). Accordingly the relations with parties were not those of dependency. The Comisiones were close to the Communist Party and already well organized in several economic sectors with overlapping membership, but gained greater and greater autonomy with the declining electoral success of the PCE and its internal divisions. Moreover, unlike in Italy, the entire left was not excluded from the political arena. Consequently, CCOO did not depend upon the party for representation. The UGT was at the beginning very close to the Socialists, and formally all PSOE members were required to join the union. But again a trend toward more and more autonomy emerged as the competition of Comisiones

---

[22] The data that other authors provided are different. For example, Mella Márquez (1992: 336) suggested a 7.5 density of membership in the mid-1980s, the OECD-Spain (1991) gave 16 per cent in 1995, and Miguélez Lobo (1991: 219) 11 per cent.

pushed them to defend the interests of workers even against supposedly close governments, and the same goverment had to decide and
implement austerity programmes. By 1988 the increasingly centrist (if
not centre-right) economic policies of the PSOE government led to a
complete breakdown of relations between the Socialist Party and trade
unions, culminating in the UGT's participation in the anti-government
and, consequently, anti-socialist strike of December 1988. Finally, the
very economic agreements of late 1970 up to 1986 with government and
entrepreneurs developed union identity and greater autonomy.[23] Thus,
a relationship of symbiosis that characterized both main unions went
through a process of distancing vis-à-vis the parties, and later on in a
confrontation with them (see Chapter 5).[24]

Spain also differs from Italy with regard to the evolution of its public sector. On the one hand, there is a growth of bureaucratic personnel: during the 1980s (1982–91) the civil servants working for the
Autonomous Communities increased enormously and numbered about
560,000, but this was only partially the result of transference from the
central government.[25] During the same years, the expenses for public
administration, as a percentage of GNP, also slightly increased from
16.4 to 17.8 (see López López and Utrilla de la Hoz 1994: 87); and,
above all, up to 1982 the higher public expenses were largely explained
by welfare payments (see e.g. Pérez Díaz 1987: 115). On the other hand,
and in contrast to Italy, whose public economic sector expanded considerably during the 1950s, the economic public sector was substantially reduced in size, as the product of the Socialist Party's 'industrial
reconversion' policies of the 1980s. The main major state holding company, the National Institute of Industry (INI), employed 254,000 workers in 1980, but 198,000 in 1985, and even fewer, 146,600, in 1990 (see
Martín Aceña and Comín 1991: 595). Indeed, the Organization for Economic Cooperation and Development reported in 1989 that on the
whole 30 per cent of workers who were employed by public economic
enterprises were dismissed over the course of that reform programme.[26]

However, state institutions are relevant in another sense. For about a
decade there were quasi-corporatist arrangements with the mentioned
monopoly of CEOE, the public role of the two main unions, and a series
of agreements that were bargained at the central level and perhaps more
importantly in several regional arenas, where local associations,

---

[23] On this topic, see Pérez Yruela and Giner (1988); and Miguélez and Prieto (1991).

[24] On the relationships between unions and parties see also Köhler (1995).

[25] For these and other data on public bureaucracy see Chislett (1994).

[26] For details on this topic see Papeles de Economía Española (1989) and Martín
Aceña and Comín (1991).

regional governments, and parties are involved.[27] Some authors (see Pérez Díaz 1987, chs. 2 and 3, and 1990) defined 'meso-government' and 'meso-corporatism' as this kind of situation, where despite the low affiliation rate, and consequently an expected lack of union control of workers, there was a basic implementation of bargained pacts, at both the central and regional levels. This is explained not only by the union influence, suggested above by the participation in elections, but also by the serious economic crisis, the mentioned worker moderation, and the open support of party élites (see Pérez Díaz 1987: 78 and 108 ff.). Of course, in a modern or modernizing society there are other unions, associations, and interests that overcome such arrangements. Moreover, in the Spanish case at the central level, conflict replaced agreement in the late 1980s, and since 1983 CCOO participated in the meetings but did not sign any agreement on income policies. Besides, some of the most important decisions were made by the government and voted on in parliament without union support.[28] However, the integration provided by institutions, fora, state agencies, and the bargaining process of Spanish quasi-corporatism contributed to an anchoring of the democratic regime.[29] The consideration still to add is that this anchoring is characterized by the low participation of civil society (see above) and, as shown by subsequent events, high instability.

Finally, Spain and Italy are alike insofar as party patronage was widespread in both systems. The spoils system or *sottogoverno* led to the partisan appointment of thousands of officials to posts in public enterprises, as well as national and local government.[30] Pérez Díaz (1987: 70) furthermore points out that a substantial enlargement of the political class resulted from the establishment of seventeen autonomous regional governments, complete with parliaments, cabinets, and administrative structures. This same phenomenon occurred in Italy, when the process of regionalization led to the establishment of fifteen new governmental systems. It differs from Spain insofar as this development occurred between ten and fifteen years after the main

---

[27] Details on social pacts are in Zaragoza (1988). An analysis of open, flexible, and government-induced Spanish corporatism is in Pérez Yruela and Giner (1988: 125–50), and Fernández-Castro (1993). Interestingly, Foweraker (1987: 57–72) emphasizes the differences between the corporatism under and after Franco and defines the second one, much less institutionalized than the first one, as 'charismatic corporatism' to indicate practices made by leaders 'outside of any normative legal framework'.

[28] The union participation index, formulated by Compston (1995: 99 ff.), would score very highly in Spain, but also would overlook these crucial aspects, as it is based on the degree of consultation and the wideness of agreements.

[29] An analysis that fully denies the existence of Spanish corporatism is developed by Köhler (1995: esp. 191).

[30] Gillespie (1990: 132) reports that 25,000 such appointments were made between 1984 and 1987. On this see also see Pérez Díaz (1987: 71); Cotarelo (1989: 307); and Cazorla (1992 and 1994).

phase of consolidation, but parallels it as the implementation of regions developed a new large political class at a middle level and several vested interests around these institutions. The obvious side-effect is a contribution to the consolidation of the existing institutional arrangement.

The nature of the relationships between party and civil society in Spain closely approximates the gatekeeping model, but in a different way from that of the other three countries. The development was facilitated by several factors. These factors are not the party control or dominance of parties over interest groups. They include control of the decision-making agenda, especially in parliament, by the incumbent party, the predominant status of the strong and unified Socialist Party in the party system at the national level (in turn facilitated by the electoral law and various parliamentary regulations), the mediation of relationships between individuals and the state by thousands of professionals in the administration and the public sector, and a strong vested interest in maintaining the existing democracy by a large stratum of society. Under these circumstances, there was no real need to build a large party organization. Indeed, the environment for the consolidation process, which had facilitated the development of strong parties in Italy (especially ideological polarization and the Cold War), differed greatly in the case of Spain. In the aggregate, as seen above, this led parties to maintain a more neutral stance vis-à-vis organized social groups, and vice versa. At the same time, some clientelist, partisan penetration of the state complemented the predominant party in controlling a few sectors of society.

Dominance and the Public Sector: Portugal

Portugal and Greece are much closer to the Italian model than to the Spanish one. The point of departure for Portugal is the attempt to install a radical, socialist regime following the coup which toppled the Salazar-Caetano regime. The constitution of 1976 and legislation enacted in 1977 created a very large public sector: between March 1975 and July 1976, 244 firms were nationalized, and this brought under state control several other firms. Consequently, a state monopoly in banking, insurance, oil refining, petrochemical industries, cement and fertilizer, and virtually all the basic and infrastructural industries was established. The mass communications media were also placed largely under public ownership, and in the agricultural sector, agrarian reforms brought about the creation of large numbers of cooperatives (see Bruneau and Macleod 1986: 182–5; Barreto 1989; Ávila de Lima

1991: 209–39; and De Lucena and Gaspar 1992: 135–87). Although legislation enacted in 1983 partially loosened the state's monopolistic control of these economic sectors,[31] it was only with the constitutional revision of August 1989 that this situation was largely reversed.[32]

In the agricultural sector, first of all, pluralist arrangements and societal corporatism, as a re-emergence of old authoritarian tradition, became established at the same time. In fact, agrarian reform brought about a large mobilization of the agricultural world and a subsequent bipolarization, which was later institutionalized. Despite the presence of other smaller or sectoral associations (see Moyano Estrada 1988), the two main associations that monopolize the representation of the agricultural world are the Confederation of Portuguese Farmers (CAP), founded in January 1976, and the National Confederation of Agriculture (CNA), created in 1978. Being a confederation, the first one had no individual membership, but 77 other smaller associations.[33] Its main goal was defending the interests of small and middle farmers and also larger landowners, who felt threatened by the agrarian reform, the taking over of the land, and the radical leftist programme of 'Revolution of the Carnation'. The CNA is an umbrella association, formed by 253 smaller different associations and cooperatives,[34] representing the interests of small and middle farmers and aiming at the defence of the 'Revolution' with class revindicative purposes and even an additional anti-governmental radicalization after 1981. The mobilization of the agrarian world complemented by bipolarization account for the high affiliation to both associations, while no precise relative difference in size can be evaluated. At the same time, moreover, part of the old 'gremios' became cooperatives, the traditional cooperatives remained and consequently the Conferation of Agricultural Cooperatives of Portugal (CONFAGRI), created in 1985, received part of the property of the old gremios[35] and acquired higher economic relevance, so that it began performing a representative role, but without basically challenging the political and syndical positions of CAP or CNA.

The relations of the two associations with parties are of great interest. Since the beginning CAP enjoyed its autonomy, but it was looking for political allies. The high ideological mobilization and the conflictual purposes of maintaining or changing the reform, at governmental

[31] For example, in cement and fertilizer as well as banks and insurance (see Bruneau and Macleod 1986: 188).

[32] But on this, see the next chapter.

[33] According to an EC Report (1985) 72 associations in the mid-1980s.

[34] In 1985 the number of different affiliated associations was 492 (see EC Report 1985).

[35] Other properties of old corporatist institutions became part of the public sector. See De Lucena and Gaspar (1992).

and parliamentary levels, had compelled those associations to look for partisan alliances and consequently they had already established the gatekeeping role of parties. Thus, CAP supported Eanes in the electoral campaign for his first term. Later on, it became very close to the rightist CDS and the centrist PSD in a relationship of shared values and overlapping political goals, that can be defined as party tutelage or quasi-symbiosis. CNA was strictly linked to the Communist Party: it was not the well-known 'transmission belt' for the Communist Party, but again a strong tutelage was established and in this sense a symbiosis can be envisaged in this case, too. The parallelism between the two peak associations, however, was hiding a different role played in the agricultural world. Because of its closeness to the incumbent party, in the mid-1980s CAP was present in the Permanent Council of Concertation (see below), in the Economic and Social Committee of the European Community, and in several other committees that were part of the Portuguese corporatist mechanisms to shape agricultural policies. On the contrary, the CNA had been basically isolated for years: an 'institutional isolation' according to Ávila de Lima (1991: 236), due to its radical pro-communist positions. In this picture, the CONFAGRI is obviously much closer to CAP, and they are both in the CES (see below n. 41), while the CNA did not even accept its representative legitimacy.

The Portuguese business élite had been delegitimated by their previous support for the Salazar regime, and their organization remained poorly developed. But above all, the discontinuity with the previous corporatism is set up at the very beginning (1975) with the nationalizations and the consequent destruction of the most important industrial groups. Consequently, it was not possible for them to establish a strong, influential autonomous role (see De Lucena and Gaspar 1991: 847–903). This did not imply absence or passivity. On the contrary, there are three main associations that basically monopolize the representation of the business world and trade.[36] They are: the Confederation of Portuguese Industry (CIP), created in 1975 and with 74 sectoral and regional associations representing about 40,000 firms and 20 directly affiliated public or private enterprises ten years later; the competing and smaller Portuguese Industrial Associations (AIP), founded in 1860, but revitalized in 1978 to limit the influence of CIP, with about 1,400 firms in the private sector, 4 sectoral associations, and 40 public enterprises in 1985, and with regional diffusion; and the Confederation of Portuguese Trade (CCP), created in 1976 with whole-

---

[36] For a more exhaustive analysis of these associations, also from an organizational point of view, see Gaspar (1988).

sale and retail trade federations, which represents 126 sectoral and regional associations of commercial firms.[37]

The CIP is the association that is most influential. In fact the AIP has been closer to the government and the CCP is more moderate, but at the end they both had to follow the initiatives and positions of the CIP. Basically, two phases characterized its relations with governmental parties. The first one ends in mid-1985: this is a decade of contrasts and conflicts, despite an intermezzo at the end of the 1970s or the attenuation of them in other specific moments. Obviously, the confrontation was between a side, the CIP, that emphasized serious Portuguese economic problems and pointed to their solution through a much greater role given or acknowledged to private entrepreneurship; and the government with Communist participation or Socialist dominance, that followed the line of nationalization and public intervention in the economy. In this first phase, however, the three associations are involved in consultative bodies, are allied in the Permanent Council of Concertation (see below), and formed a National Council of Industrial Associations (CNAE) where they worked together to defend private enterprise interests, and also a National Council of Employers (CNEP). The CIP especially tried to directly represent these interests, as a sort of party by itself, even criticizing the rightist CDS on some occasions and through other public declarations and activities. Political instability and a highly ideological climate accounted for this. On the whole, during this decade conflictual neutrality is a more precise definition of its relations with the parties.

The second phase began with the electoral growth and success of the Social Democratic Party and at the same time with the very important accession of Portugal to the European Community in 1986: there was autonomy and neutrality, but no more conflict, and open alliances took place on several occasions with deeper involvement in the existing consultative mechanisms, primarily the Permanent Council. The key point to remember, however, is that in both phases the government led the game: as noted above, there was some autonomy and neutrality of these groups and their acceptation of democratic institutions was important, but their political and economic salience was fairly limited.

It is worth noting that in a similar unstable and highly ideologized context during the end of the 1970s up to the mid-1980s the agricultural associations had been looking for party support and consequently established the gatekeeping role of those structures (see above). At the same time, an opposite outcome, such as autonomy and neutrality, and

---

[37] These data are provided by the EC Report on Portugal (1985). On the development of relations among these associations and other smaller ones see the well-informed research by Gaspar (1988).

attempts at direct access, emerged with the CIP. The explanation lies mainly in the characteristics of the different associations: the mass level of political mobilization in agriculture gave room for party élites and militants; while this space is precluded with an élite association and social group. In other words, to express their 'voice' the peasants needed political structures which performed that role—their associations were not enough; on the contrary, the entrepreneurial élite was able to articulate its 'voice' by itself: they did not need even the rightist party support.[38]

Contrary to entrepreneurial associations, trade unions quickly established and maintained close links with political parties. The density of membership is close to that of Greece: between 29 and 30 per cent according to different sources.[39] The main unions are two in number. The first one is the General Confederation of Portuguese Workers—National Trade Union Liaison Committee (CGTP-IN), created in 1974 and with a membership of about 1,300,000 workers in the more mobilized, ideological, and difficult years (1983) and of 550,000 at the end of that decade in the more stable years (1989) (see Schmitter 1995: 300 and 294), together with 153 trade unions, 18 federations, and 44 trade unions associations in the mid-1980s (see EC Report 1985). The second one is the Portuguese General Workers' Union (UGT-P), founded some years later, in 1978, with a membership of about 981,000 workers in 1983 and 350,000 at the end of the decade (see Schmitter 1995: 300 and 294), and with 49 trade unions.

The powerful CGTP-IN was closely allied with the Communists. Indeed, for many years this union federation came closer than most contemporary Western European unions to being an authentic 'transmission belt' for the Communist Party. Only after the collapse of communism in Eastern Europe in 1989 did this relationship begin to change (Taborda Barreto 1991: 459). The second largest union, the UGT, was in strong competition with the first one and connected to the PS and PSD with the presence of Socialists and Social Democrats in the union bodies, thanks to an agreement between them, but also vice versa with the election of a few union leaders to parliament and leading organs of the two parties.[40] These links, however, were so strong as to induce the unions to adopt strategies in accord with partisan goals,

[38] As Hirschman (1970) suggests, 'voice' means protest, and this is the meaning here. Differences in levels of education or income are not relevant, as in the CAP, for example, there are also larger landowners.

[39] See Schmitter (1995: 294), who reports data of 1989, and an OECD-Portugal (1990–1) that refers to 1988. The density that is officially declared by unions is much higher, e.g. 80 per cent in 1986 (see Taborda Barreto 1991: 587).

[40] According to Taborda Barreto (1991: 607) they were ten in the 1985 and 1987 elections (4 to PS and 6 to PSD and later vice versa). See also De Lucena and Gaspar (1991) on the topic.

thereby politicizing labour relations. This situation began to change only in the late 1980s (see Stoleroff 1988: 147–64; and 1990: 45–55; Taborda Barreto 1991; and De Lucena and Gaspar 1991).

On the whole, the Portuguese party system assumed its gatekeeping role through a non-linear process, with several moments of crisis and considerable governmental instability (see Chapter 2) up to the mid-1980s, and with the key role played by the public sector. That is, governmental dominance emerged because of the resources provided by a large public sector. In fact, party appointments of managers and boards of directors of firms became the rule in the public sector. Moreover, as in the cases of Italy and Spain, there was also a significant number of patronage appointments to the administration, contributing to an enormous expansion of the bureaucracy: from 196,755 in 1968 to 372,086 in 1979 (see De Sousa Santos 1986: 178), and to 435,795 in 1983 in the various sectors, but with greater growth in the central administration (see de Vasconcelos 1990, Table 5). Indeed, in the case of Portugal, state resources were proportionately larger (and the private sector, consequently, was less significant) than in Italy: in 1989 expenses of the public sector were almost 40 per cent of GDP (Balabanian, Bouet, *et al.* 1991: 114). This brought Bruneau and Macleod (1986: 195) to note that, 'the state's role in the Portuguese economy is predominant.'

Another aspect, however, deserves specific attention. As late as the second half of the 1980s, the Tripartite Council,[41] created in 1983 and formed by representatives of business, labour, landowners, and the government, was entirely dominated by the government and the incumbent party. Portugal is the country in Southern Europe that built on its corporative tradition and its extensive regulation of industrial relations (see e.g. De Sousa Santos 1986: 185 ff. and Pinto 1989), mostly translated in formal institutions. In fact, behind the agreements of 1987 or 1988 on several aspects concerning modernization of the economy, the economic and social tripartite agreement of 1990 between government, entrepreneurs, and unions, the 1991 agreement on professional education, the 1992 social agreement signed by UGT and entrepreneurs, and the 1993 social pact there were formal institutions (CPCS, first, and CES later), even inserted into the Constitutional Charter with the revision of 1992.[42] It may be additionally

---

[41] This is the Permanent Council of Social Concertation (CPCS). Later, in 1992, there was a constitutional revision and the creation of the Economic and Social Council (CES) (see art. 95). This Council is organized through three Committees: the previous CPCS, which has been maintained, the Committee on Regional Development and Territory Management (CDROT), and the Committee on Economic and Social Policy (CPES).

[42] See above, the previous note.

specified that for most of the 1980s and even later on, with only some minor exceptions, the Communist union did not sign those pacts, despite being present with the UGT on several consultative sectoral, and non-sectoral, committees.

Thus, on the whole, the dominant party role was achieved through the politicization of a very large public sector in a relatively less developed country. To be sure, this factor was conducive to party dominance through the most classic patronage and the control of one of the main unions, the UGT. It was only partially offset, however, by the relatively weaker development of party organizations (see above). At the same time, the modes of establishing such positions were also characterized by the integration of organized interests in several consultative committees and especially the national ones (see above). In the most important of them, the dominant position achieved by the PSD after 1987 allowed that party and its leaders to establish crucial control over the interests already mentioned above.

At this point it is possible to stress a basic difference between Portugal and the other two countries. In Spain the predominant position in the party system was achieved because of the breakdown of the UCD and a large electoral success, partially explained by that breakdown; the gatekeeping role came afterwards. Likewise, in Italy the prominent position—although not as strong as in Spain—is also the result of an electoral success thanks to Catholic support and anti-communist feelings; the gatekeeping role became clear after the elections of 1948 and later. On the contrary, in Portugal the gatekeeping role was gradually achieved thanks to the resources of the public sector, which paved the way for the victory of the PSD in the 1987 election and the consequent transformation of the party system from four-party pluralism to a predominant-party system.[43] It should be recalled that between 1983 and 1985 the 'central block' was also formed by the Socialists. The discontent against them, coalesced and expressed by the new party created by President Eanes, and then the loss of their leader (Soares), when he was elected to the presidency, left an open space for the Social Democrats, and they were able to take advantage of it. With some caution due to the partial unreliability of the data, this interpretation is also supported by a sharp decline in Socialist membership after 1983–4.

Occupation and Penetration: Greece

The complex, articulated relationships between interests, on the one hand, and mainly Nea Dimokratia, PASOK, and the Communists, on

[43] On the dominant position of parties in the four countries see the next chapter.

the other hand, are defined by party control and even occupation of interests. During the 1980s, this process reached the point of a very weak possibility of defending its interests by the same associations, as they were basically transformed in arenas of party competition. In the attempt at stopping the growing power of the Socialists, who being in the government were profiting from the large state resources in a very centralized administrative arrangement, and implementing a capillary policy of patronage, both ND and the Communists began a radical competition that would have resulted in a deep party penetration of every association. In this way the stabilization of party control is firmly achieved, but it remained open which was the party that was able to gain such a control between PASOK and ND. As will be seen in the next chapter, at the end of the decade the Socialist domination of society is stopped and partially reversed.

In the agricultural sector,[44] the small cooperatives (PASEGES) are complemented by other associations, such as GESASE and SYDASE. Most farmers are organized through the cooperatives, 147 unions according to a European Community report (1981). The membership of PASEGES was growing and reached close to one million in the mid-1980s. Two different moments of this organization are very obvious: the first one during the ND government with the leading group close to the incumbent party; and the second one when PASOK won the 1981 elections and tried to gain control over this important organization in different ways, such as an organizational reform in 1982, acceptance of 130,000 new members between 1981 and 1982, and a new reform law in 1985 with two subsequent revisions. Despite those efforts and the traditional dependency of PASEGES on state subsidies, however, during the 1980s both ND and PASOK went on keeping almost equally divided control of this organization, with KKE in a minoritarian position. Furthermore, those efforts brought about a negative backlash for the Socialists, even from among supporters belonging to the cooperatives, and in 1987 PASOK lost the majority in the leading body.[45]

The role of parties within PASEGES is better understood when complemented by the party presence in the other agricultural associations. The GESASE, set up again in 1977 by PASOK and KKE, and at that moment excluded by cooperative organization, never had great success. It was not even mentioned by the EC report of 1981, but according to Mavrogordatos's data (1988), it had a membership of 100,000 in 1983,

---

[44] In the analysis of agricultural and other sectors, the research by Mavrogordatos (1988) is still the leading source of information and reflection on the whole phenomenon of party–society relations during the 1980s. See an abridged version of this research in Mavrogordatos (1993).

[45] The electoral data were given by Mavrogordatos (1988).

despite the repeal of the legal monopoly of representation by PASEGES in that same year and the granting to GESASE of certification power. This association became controlled by Socialists and Communists together, with strong tensions and conflicts among them. In the mid-1980s the foundation of SYDASE by ND was a competitive reaction in this sector. Without state subventions the new organization was able to achieve a slightly lower membership than GESASE. Thus, in agriculture there are three main organizations, but the cooperatives are still the dominant ones, and consequently they remained the main arena of confrontation among the three parties.

Since the beginning of the democratic regime, showing a consistent continuity with the past, the business world was not only fragmented along traditional sectors, such as shipping, industry, and commerce, or along the size of firms with the division between small entrepreneurs and the large ones, but also along territorial lines and inside the main sectors.[46] The main associations were: the EEE, which gathered the shipowners; the SEV, which was the dominant association of entrepreneurs; the small business association (GSEVE) with tradesmen and craftsmen; and several commercial associations, such as the SSESE (EESE since 1987), as the most important one, and other regional and powerful federations in the main urban areas.[47]

As in Portugal, at the beginning of democratization the Greek business élite and its representative associations, but especially EEE and SEV had been delegitimated because of their close relationship with the military regime.[48] This contributed to their weak organizational development, but also to the initial tensions and problems with Nea Dimokratia: not even that conservative party, and its leader, were open to forgive the closeness of those groups to authoritarian colonels, whether strong or weak. The confrontation and open protest of those organizations became much stronger when the radical PASOK won the election and entered the cabinet. Between 1983 and 1985, however, the previously conflictual relationships with the Socialists changed, and a second neatly different phase began. Above all, after 1985, once the Socialists understood the necessity of private investments and accordingly also abandoned the previous radicalism by adopting more

[46] The Greek interest groups are carefully indicated by the report of the General Secretariat of the Economic and Social Committee of the EC (1981).

[47] In his fine analysis of Greek interest associations Mavrogordatos (1988) also mentions the aborted attempt at building an association that should have overcome the fragmentation of those sectors by representing at the same time industry, commerce, small tradesmen and artisans, and other activities in the private sector.

[48] The pro-military attitudes of the two associations are partially different. EEE was much closer to the colonels than SEV, which was worried about the EC freezing Greek accession. However, as Mavrogordatos points out, the SEV and industrialists were also suspiciously regarded when the new democracy was inaugurated.

moderate and orthodox economic policies, this cooperation was no longer surprising, and a mutual alliance with the governmental recognition of SEV's prominence among industrialists was established (see Fakiolas 1987: 183 and 188). A third phase will be inaugurated in the late 1980s and especially the early 1990s, when the industrialists' organization showed an increasingly activist face, keeping its distance from both of the main parties, PASOK and ND and concluding agreements with unions (see also next chapter).

For commercial associations and small business the situation is partially different. In fact, among the various commercial groups, the compulsory Chambers of Commerce included,[49] Nea Dimokratia was very much present or even majoritarian, and never were the Socialists in a condition to obtaining a prominent position. In the small business sector, shopkeepers and craftsmen included, GSEVE represented about 20 per cent of the social groups of reference and suffered because of serious organizational problems, such as the over-representation of provinces and consequent 'ghost' local associations, and a leading group who had accepted the authoritarian regime (see Mavrogordatos 1988: 91; and Kritsantonis 1992: 608–10). After 1984, the situation was reversed and the Communists monopolized that association with ironic consequences, such as in 1986 the offer of pay increases by GSEVE, led by KKE, and the refusal of the main unions, hegemonized by loyal Socialists. This episode emphasized how the representation of interests was totally subordinated to party logic rather than to the very interests that should have been defended.[50] Thus, while for commerce the Socialist presence is only partial, but the penetration by all parties is actually total, for small businesses the Communists' domination is very large, but again the party penetration is total.

Trade unions in Greece mean, above all, the large confederation of labour, the GSEE, with more than 500,000 members and according to some authors a membership rate close to 25 per cent or slightly higher.[51] Behind the apparent unity of the confederation, however, there is high fragmentation, which is also accentuated by a few organizational characteristics: an enormous number of autonomous primary unions, very easy to create and control; two different inter-

---

[49] They are present in all four countries.

[50] Mavragordatos (1988) refers to this and other similar episodes that all illustrate the same point.

[51] Here, the source is provided by the data from Mavrogordatos (1988, Table 7) and OECD-Greece (1990–1). If also the civil servant's union (ADEDY) is considered the total membership density goes up to about 35.0 (see Schmitter 1995: 294). Katsanevas (1984: quoted by Kritsantonis 1992: 615), however, gives different figures: according to him, the total density is between 27 and 33 per cent. Sotiropoulos (1994: 19) gives similar figures: between 27 and 32 per cent.

mediate organizations, the 'labour centres' and several main national federations,[52] with two different kinds of membership in the GSEE; the federations with the responsibility of collective bargaining; and the factory unions. Other factors of fragmentation were the attenuated division between white and blue collar workers; and the division between workers and employees in the private and public sectors, which besides, and according to the law, cannot merge with the ADEDY, the association of civil servants.

Given this high fragmentation, the state dependency on financial support, and the introduction of proportional rule in the union elections in 1982, the party penetration into the unions was an obvious outcome. In fact, as Mavrogordatos (1988) has argued, during the 1980s solid links of party dependency were established. From the party perspective, the control of unions is too important a stake from an electoral, organizational, and policy point of view not to receive the highest attention. In fact, PASOK built its union branch (PASKE) and so did KKE (ESAK), KKEes (AEM), and ND in 1985 (DAKE). The only questions are how large is the presence of a party vis-à-vis the other one or whether there is a dominant party, and when.

Here, two expected phases neatly emerged: the first one with the ND dominance until 1981 and competition between PASOK and KKE later on, with a continuing minoritarian presence of ND. However, in the mid-1980s the competition within the left turned into a harsh confrontation when the Socialist government tried to impose its austerity programme. The Socialist-Communist agreement within GSEE broke; a few Socialist union leaders reacted negatively to those policies and were expelled from the party; in the subsequent tough conflict the president and the treasurer were replaced, PASKE loyalists resigned from the executive committee; and a subsequent intervention of a court gave the entire control of the GSEE to the Socialists; but in the new 1986 elections PASKE only gained a plurality position with a divided opposition, Communists on one side and Conservatives of ND in the opposite side. The conflict went on up to 1989 with an administrative board where no party was dominant.[53]

To better understand the party control of unions some mention should be made of the state subventions and the introduction of proportional rule in 1982. Regarding the power of the Ministry of Labour

[52] Apparently, there are sixteen major national, sectoral federations, but the total number of them seems much higher, close to 40 in the early 1980s, according to EC Report (1981), and to 60 at the end of the decade (see Kritsantonis 1992: 616).

[53] This intricate conflict is described in different ways by Mavrogordatos (1988: 64) and Kritsantonis (1992: 617–18). But the basic meaning is the same: PASOK was striving for the control of the union. And this was particularly important at that moment because of the unpopular policies Papandreou was implementing.

to allocate state subventions to unions, there were different projects of reform by the Socialists, a law was passed, but during the 1980s no actual change came about. The change was only set in motion with the new legislation in 1990, which abolished the state subsidy and at the same time precipitated the unions into a desperate financial condition.[54] The implementation of proportional rule not only implied a partisan penetration of unions, but with the harsh confrontation and radicalization of competition it also had a side-effect, perhaps an unintended one, that is the 'squeezing' and the lack of real representation of worker interests. When there was court intervention in appointing union officials, or unions refused the wage increases offered by a small business association, when furthermore compulsory arbitration was more frequent than bargained agreements, and Socialist members reacted against the policy of their own party and were expelled, there is obviously a problem of effective representation. In Italy, too, there was party control of unions, but the interests were much more present in the government and parliament. In other words, the party control did not gloss over worker interests. To achieve that outcome, in addition to the policy position of the incumbent party (or coalition of parties), some additional factors have to be present. In the Greek case they are the side-effect of the radical, tough competition among the parties, and the institutional characteristics that do not allow much space for interests in parliament.[55]

On the whole, as in Portugal, in Greece the weak positions of the business élites, dependent unions, and other penetrated associations were also compounded by a large public sector. During the first PASOK government, this sector was further expanded: numerous industrial enterprises, banks, and insurance companies were added to the public sector. The end product is that almost 90 per cent of financial institutions were state-controlled, subsequent government efforts to privatize notwithstanding.[56] In the 1980s the State Business Reconstruction Organization, which took over firms in economic difficulties, paralleling the Italian and Spanish experiences during their respective authoritarian regimes, was created by PASOK. Also in the early 1990s, 67 out of 200 main firms were state controlled and the whole public sector employed 40 per cent of the wage-labour force.[57] A large public sector and a capillary bureaucratic structure imply that a large number of new administrative jobs were also created, up to the point that some authors speak of a welfare function performed by the state as 'dispenser of jobs': a 12

---

[54] See the next chapter and Kritsantonis (1992: 614–15).
[55] On this, see Ch. 2 and the first section of the next chapter.
[56] About these developments see the next chapter.
[57] On these data see Kritsantonis (1992: 605–6 and 622).

per cent increase in civil service personnel between 1981 and 1988 corresponds to a much lower 2 per cent increase in the labour force (Sotiropoulos 1991: 187–8 and 400). Government expenditure as a percentage of GDP reached 51 per cent in 1988 (Sotiropoulos 1994: 12). The obvious conclusion is that the state is 'the main employer' and 'the main agency for distribution of resources' (Koukiadis 1983: 232).

To complete the picture, however, other elements of continuity and newness must be added. As for the tradition, what has been said above with reference to the groups shows a very pervasive legislation. To legislation that ruled on even the details of associational or union activities by configuring a strong state tutelage, a few more telling aspects may be added: in the case of internal conflicts, the courts could intervene to appoint, although temporarily, the top leaders of a union, and on several occasions did so always in favour of the incumbent party;[58] there were compulsory arbitrations in collective bargaining, and they were much more recurring than the agreements concluded by union federations (see Mavrogordatos 1988: 68);[59] the unions or associations could perform, and performed, public functions; and despite reforms the important part of financial support came from the state.

PASOK leadership brought such legislative pervasiveness to its most extreme consequences. To implement its programme of populist *allaghe* (change), but also to win the competition with the other parties, it decided and enacted an impressive volume of legislation regarding the associations as well as the public administrative structures. Eventually, both associations and the state bureaucracy were almost totally subordinated to parties. In a specific sense, this holds true even with reference to business. In fact, during the first phase of more tense relationships with the associations of shipowners (EEE) or of industrialists (SEV), those social groups acknowledged the prominent role of the state (and of the incumbent party) in labour relations, and even beyond. Consequently, they acknowledged the prominent positions of the incumbent party.

Moreover, party occupation of secondary associations and the state appeared to be so widespread and penetrating that some Socialist supporters expressed concern about the weakening of the party's own organization (see Sotiropoulos 1991; and Spourdalakis 1988: esp. 242). Indeed, party appointments to the public sector were so numerous after 1981 that PASOK's organization was largely depleted of activists.[60] To

[58] On this see Katsanevas 1984, quoted by Featherstone (1990: 193–4).

[59] The law was changed in 1990 and a new voluntary system of conciliation and arbitration was established. See the next chapter.

[60] Sotiropoulos (1994: 13) recalls a political component of bureaucracy through the creation of ministerial committees, councils of advisers, and whole new ministries. This phenomenon finds a parallel in the Italian case during the 1950s, and even later on.

be sure, the Socialists tried to acquire a dominant position in the society and they were partially successful. The result of this attempt and of the reactions of the other parties was that the same civil society became more thoroughly controlled by the parties, even if not necessarily by PASOK only. This is, however, the key to understanding party–society relations during the socialist decade in office.

This analysis pushes in two related directions. First of all, it helps understand why a few Greek, and non-Greek scholars speak of state corporatism:[61] the state control of associations in a weak civil society is really pervasive; the group dependency or lack of autonomy is very large; some pluralist independence emerge in agriculture only because of the exacerbated competition among parties; as in Italy, the same business groups accept, and in some sectors look for, party-state dominance; the Greek tradition of a pervasive state gives a basic contribution to such an outcome. Of course when attention is turned from economic interests toward cultural, religious, or other non-material interests, pluralism becomes the rule.[62]

At the same time, this analysis stresses how powerful and capillary the party patronage was during the ND period, the Socialist decade in the 1980s,[63] and even later. However, according to Mavrogordatos (1997) during the PASOK decade there was an evident growth of clientelist practices in two complementary ways: on the one hand, there was the cessation of competitive examinations for entering public positions; on the other hand, when looking at specific sectors and organization massive manifestations of partisan appointments were evident, such as the temporary appointments of teachers in the public secondary schools, and of employees in the Telecommunication Company (OTE), in the National Bank, and even in a company, such as the Piraiki-Patraiki Cotton Manufacturing Company, that went bankrupt and became public in 1984. The most interesting point of this analysis is not the transition from a more traditional clientelism to a party clientelism, but that the socialist union, PASKE, was the main

---

[61] In addition to Mavrogordatos (1988: 115), Schmitter (1995: 313) speaks of a 'still . . . older, predemocratic system(s) of state corporatism'; Spourdalakis (1988: 229) of 'markedly corporatist labour relations system'; Sotiropoulos (1994: 18) of 'licensed corporatism'. And according to Koukiadis (1983: 232), the state maintained (and maintains) its 'tutelage' on the social groups.

[62] On this see Sotiropoulos (1994: 4), who writes about: 'the emergence of pluralism in the representation of interests other than purely economic ones, such as the interests of ecological, feminist, cultural, consumers and health and social provision movements.'

[63] More specifically, Sotiropoulos (1991: 86) defines the Greek experience as 'populist patronage'. Above, in this chapter the expression 'bureaucratic clientelism' (see Lyrintzis 1984 and 1993) was recalled. Papadopoulos (1989: 64–5) defines PASOK as a 'collective patron' by stressing how that party 'achieved an unprecedented degree of control over the state bureaucracy'.

beneficiary of it. This union, in fact, became 'the primary party machine through which the new kind of clientelism operated' (Mavrogordatos 1997: 21): even in the clientelist practices the strong links between the incumbent party and 'his' union was and remained very evident.

Again as with Italy, Greece is the country were the individual relationships between political bosses and people in search of jobs and protection are more developed in a way that characterizes the party–society relations and establishes strong links of loyalty with party leaders.[64] However, different from the Italian case, these clientelistic links did not become the basis of power for a group of ND or Socialist political 'brokers'. As in every populist context, further strengthened by a strong administrative centralization,[65] the prominence of the charismatic leader, be it Karamanlis or Papandreu, remained very strong and cumbersome. This consideration, finally, allows a better understanding of the Greek case vis-à-vis Portugal, where the role of the state is also dominant, but there are different traditions and a fully different process of regime transition and installation.

Gatekeeping, Patronage, and Corporatism

It is now possible to draw the lines of the analysis on the multifaceted, also overlapping relationships among interest associations, individuals, and parties. Despite some problem because of lack of precise data, the analysis focused on: (*a*) the gatekeeping role that the party system (and parties) performed, and the extent of it; (*b*) the patronage networks that were developed; and (*c*) the sectoral or wider corporatist arrangements that emerged. As a way of summarizing the analysis a few questions may be addressed. First of all, to what extent did interest associations establish more or less strong linkages with their reference social groups and, more generally, civil society? If even an approximate reply is not given, then the gatekeeping relationships with parties or the corporatist pacts have little relevance. When the fragmentation of associations, affiliation and membership density, and the participation in possible union elections has been checked, that is, the capacity of 'class governance' by interest associations (Schmitter 1995: 311), the situation in the four countries was the following.

[64] Pappas (1996: 38) also compares Greek party patronage with the Italian version.

[65] In the mid-1980s the regions were created in Greece to become the recipient of the funds of the EC Integrated Mediterranean Programme (IMP), but some degree of decentralization never did take place and, despite several declarations, until 1994 no direct elections for prefecture councils were held. See Verney (1994).

In the agricultural sector, Italy (Confagricoltura and Coldiretti), Portugal (CAP and CNA), and Greece (PASEGES, GESASE, and SYDASE) had associations with low fragmentation, high density of membership, and in this sense a strong linkage with respective social groups. Particularly in Italy and Portugal, the ideological divide strengthened such linkages by approaching a situation of dependency. In Italy the exclusion of leftist organizations limited the width of the corporatist arrangement, which is also partly present in Greece. No coordination may be seen in Portugal. Very differently from the other three countries, the Spanish agricultural associations have high fragmentation, low membership, pluralist arrangement, and no dependency, but only relative influence, on their social groups.

In the industrial sector, the monopolist asset of CEOE, its high influence on the entrepreneurs, and the agreement existing for a decade in Spain are not matched by any actor in the other countries. Again, on the contrary, fragmentation to a higher extent (Italy and Greece) or lower extent (Portugal) are the recurring patterns. Such fragmentation concerns the different associations (Confindustria, Confapi, Intersind, Confcommercio, and Confartigianato in Italy; EEE, SEV, GSEVE, and EESE in Greece; and CIP, AIP, and CCP in Portugal), but is also present inside the same association (see, especially, SEV in Greece). Given, however, its élite characteristics, even if without relatively high membership, all entrepreneur associations are influential or very influential vis-à-vis their social groups. Among unions, Portugal and Spain have two main dominant mass organizations, but the membership of the Spanish ones is much lower than that of the Portuguese unions. Despite this, the unions of both countries are influential or very influential with regard to their social groups. In Italy and Greece there is higher fragmentation, which is apparent in the first country, with at least three different unions which were aligned along distant ideological lines, and substantial in the second one because there is one union, the GSEE, but it is internally deeply divided. Corporatist coordination in Spain and Portugal is partial, and limited to some, but not all, unions and entrepreneur associations.

On the whole, except for the Spanish agricultural sector and despite the rich repertoire of differences, in a decade or a bit longer, the main interest associations were able to build linkages with their reference groups and establish either an influence on or even control over them. Consequently, no analysis of the consolidation process in these countries is possible without taking into account the mentioned interest associations. This brings me to the second question: how and to what extent were parties able to set definite linkages and even control organized interest groups?

There is some degree of autonomy in the positions of entrepreneurial associations; but even in this case the autonomy is complemented
by alliance and an objective convergence of interests: such alliance is
stronger in the Italian case; it exists in the case of Portugal and
Greece; and it is weaker in Spain. Despite the establishment of basic
gatekeeping, in the relationships between parties and unions there
are also evident differences: above all, in Spain the linkages between
the PCE and PSOE, on the one hand, and CCOO and UGT, on the
other hand, became politically weaker and weaker. In Italy, union
dependency and party penetration remained very strong; in Greece
the problem concerned which was the dominant party in GSEE, but
not whether parties were dominant; in Portugal the partnership of PS
and PSD in the UGT did not attenuate party penetration, but only
qualified it. Finally, gatekeeping is well established in the agricultural sector except for the Spanish associations, which are not linked
to specific parties. It may be recalled how heavily this sector is dependent on European financial support and how these aids are managed
by the Ministry of Agriculture and the regional authorities. Consequently, there are also links in this sector, but they are of a more
individual than institutional kind.

On a more general level, the main consideration that is suggested by
the analysis of party gatekeeping is that to establish such a role the
most important aspect is the extent of the fragmentation of parties and
groups: the lower the number of parties and the higher the number of
organized groups, which have some representative monopoly of the
social group, the higher the possibility of getting a gatekeeping position. This implies that a predominant party system is the most
favourable arrangement for that purpose. With the help of centralized
decision-making (see next chapter), a dominant or quasi-dominant
party that is the main party in the cabinet simply becomes a necessary
interlocutor for all interest groups. In addition, Southern European
cases suggest that at least two other factors are crucial. They are a disciplined, unified party, as the PSOE has been for years, and a few governing rules that allow the incumbent party to better manage
parliamentary decision-making, such as all rules that facilitate the
cabinet in passing its bill (see Chapter 2). Party organization may
make up for higher party fragmentation, and group representative
weakness in a passive society may do the same. That is, at the end the
picture is much more complex and a few different constellations of factors may be envisaged, and all of them give a similar outcome.[66]

A different, but also important, dimension emerges when the

---

[66] However, these considerations will be better developed in the next chapter.

relationships between parties and individual micro-interests are explored. The extent of party patronage can be difficult to evaluate precisely. However, within these limits the analysis above has emphasized developed clientelistic practices in Italy, especially in the southern regions, and in Greece. Spain and Portugal also present forms of patronage at a local level. And as is well known, cultural values characterized by deferent attitudes and statist beliefs, so embedded in Southern European culture, also account for the myriad micro-links that are established in this way in all four countries.

The corporatist arrangements are the third way of creating links among parties, associations, and civil society mainly through the integration of interests and parties together in the same network of consultative or bargaining state agencies. As noted above, Spain in a temporary and partial way and Portugal with a corporatist arrangement, where parties are dominant, are the only two countries where this dimension may be added. In Italy and Greece, the presence of corporative and pluralist elements at the same time can be seen in the agricultural sector.

At this point it may be worth pointing out that in some of the analysed countries there is a lower stabilization of interest groups. As for Greece, in the mid-1980s some fluidity of interest associations may be detected whilst party penetration and in this sense the links between parties and groups are well established. On the contrary, in Italy the stabilization of this sector is much stronger. From this perspective there is no necessary consistency between the stabilization of a party system and that of the interest association system.

The 'Top-down' Direction of Consolidation

The lines of the last two chapters may be easily drawn. The anchoring among parties, interest associations, and civil society has been described, also with reference to party organization in Chapter 4. Here, it was not relevant to analyse all connections between parties and people or describe the whole articulation of interest representation and how it is present in the decisional process. But it was rather more important to detect the main anchoring mechanisms that actually work in a democracy by contributing to its consolidation—and, in the perspective here pursued, to the crisis as well (see Chapter 1). With some simplification, which sacrifices the corporatist aspects by squeezing them into the relations between interest associations and parties, three dimensions characterize the process of consolidation by creating the anchoring described above. Figure 5.1 shows these dimensions by

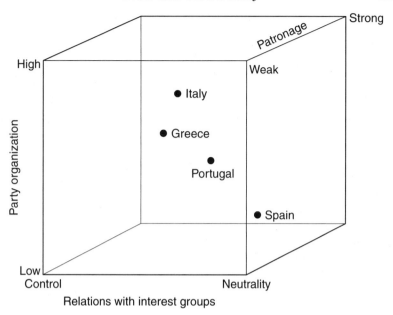

Fɪɢ. 5.1. *The top-down direction of consolidation: the main dimensions*

including party organization as discussed in Chapter 4.[67] The four countries are placed in the resulting space with the relations between interests and parties still simplified in a continuum where the poles are the full control of associations and a high neutrality of the same, and by taking into account all the aspects described in the chapter.

Again with an effort at simplification it is possible to indicate what characterizes these processes of anchoring. For Italy the previous discussion stressed the role of party organizations whereas all other actors and aspects are in an ancillary position; a similar reasoning may be done for Greece, but the personal connotations in the way parties are organized and established would point to the charismatic element, and again all other actors and aspects are in a secondary position; in Spain in the weaker party domain, interest associations, their relationships, and the peculiar form of corporatism, the role of élites seems a very prominent one; finally, for Portugal most of the aspects relevant in the other three cases are also important, but the distinctiveness is rather in the encompassing role that the state plays because of the nationalization and monopolies in the main sectors.

[67] For a different but interesting way of analysing party systems and interest groups together, see Golden (1986).

This reconstruction of anchoring processes leaves the working of the entire process of consolidation unexplained. In fact, the top-down dimension must be complemented by the bottom-up, as described in Chapter 3. In addition, the role of other factors, such as a few precise institutional rules and the kind of established party system, also have to be brought into the picture. This will be done in the next chapter, where the phenomenon of partial or deeper crisis will be explored in connection with consolidation.

PART III

Facets of Crisis

6

Beyond Consolidation

The Whole Process

At the end of Chapter 2, the time span of the four processes of consolidation were indicated. Consequently, the end of the 1950s for Italy and the mid-1980s for the other three countries were the *terminus ad quem* of those processes. Following the analysis of both main dimensions of consolidation (see Chapters 3, 4, and 5), it is now possible to reconstruct the whole process and the existing connections between the two main dimensions. Two general and simple hypotheses were confirmed by those analyses. First, all important aspects that were involved in the two sub-processes went through the actors, either collective or élite, and either institutional or non-institutional. The key actors in those processes were the parties, and, as seen in the previous chapters, the most relevant aspects concern the interweaving between party élites and a number of cultural, traditional, and interest-related aspects. All of those processes may be defined *as consolidations through parties*. Consequently, the point becomes: what are the more specific processes that developed within this *genus*?

Second, eventually the whole process of consolidation constitutes a partially different mix of factors in each country.[1] A few consequences emerge from this. On the one hand, a different mix produced similar results in terms of consolidation by confirming the 'multiple and conjunctural causation' that is advocated by Ragin (1987) as a key, recurring element of comparison. On the other hand, within a (partially) different constellation of factors a similar result is achieved since the weaker presence of a factor is made up for the stronger presence of another. It is therefore possible to label each process by pointing out

---

[1] In this sense the propositions put forward by Huntington (1991: 38) may be adapted to consolidation and confirmed: (1) No single factor is sufficient to explain consolidation in all countries or in a single country. (2) Consolidation in each country is the result of a combination of causes. (3) The combination of causes varies from country to country. (4) The causes responsible for democratic installation are not the same as those responsible for consolidation.

the factor that is relatively more present than the others. At the same time, at the end of the process different degrees of consolidation could be supposed, although not precisely measured, because of the absence of safe quantitative measures for the whole process. All this means, for example, that a lower stabilization of the party system does not necessarily entail a lower extent of consolidation, if there is higher legitimation.

Moreover, some paradoxes of democracy that were analysed by other authors, such as Diamond (1993), are confirmed. Above all, the strong presence of a factor may have a negative impact, whereas a weaker presence of the same factor performs a positive role in the resulting consolidation or in features of it. For example, party bipolarization may facilitate the stabilization of the party system, but excessive polarization may imply a high radicalization of the polity and widespread anti-democratic attitudes, thereby undermining the prospects for the consolidation of democracy.[2] Similarly, as seen in Chapter 4, party stabilization can benefit from the organizational development of political parties; but whereas under certain circumstances this may contribute to democratic consolidation, under other circumstances it might become antithetical to consolidation. As a matter of fact, a party that is opposed to democratic institutions and develops a strong capillary organization may use those organizational resources to mount a protracted struggle against the regime, with possibly disruptive consequences. These speculative remarks also suggest that the stabilization of parties may be neither necessary nor sufficient for the consolidation of a democratic regime. This is consistent with the cases of Spain and Italy: the democratic regime in Spain succeeded in becoming comparatively more consolidated than that of Italy, even though its parties were less structured than the Italian ones.

This reasoning brings us to reconsider in a different perspective the sub-processes scrutinized in the previous two chapters, by connecting the 'top-down' and 'bottom-up' institutional dimensions, which build consensus and legitimacy for the democratic regime. In essence, the consolidation involves an interweaving of consensus and legitimation, on the one hand, and different modes of control over civil society, on the other hand. A democratic regime may be consolidated under either circumstance, but with a distinctly different mix of characteristics and through different modes. As seen in Chapters 4 and 5, there can be a more or less accentuated control over civil society, which is achieved

---

[2] Thus, bipolarization has a double edge. On the one hand, it can help to stabilize parties and electoral behaviour by promoting party organization and identification. On the other hand, it may intensify political conflict and increase its potential for radicalization. See also Ch. 4 and conclusions.

through party organization, party gatekeeping, clientelism, and aspects of corporatism; or, on the opposite side of the same continuum, a more active, autonomous civil society, with a lower development of party organizations and an attenuated presence or the absence of the other aspects. The first situation is one of party dominance; the second, of neutrality. More precisely, this first simplified dimension implies that: (i) institutions acquire firm control over civil society up to the point of dominating it through parties, their organizations, patronage, state institutions, or the other modes described in Chapter 4 (*dominance*); or (ii) a more active, autonomous civil society and/or a situation of lower development of party organization gives civil society more autonomy vis-à-vis state institutions and parties (*neutrality*).

The other dimension involves the bottom-up relationship linking individuals with institutions through the fostering of regime consensus and legitimacy (i.e. growing acceptance of and support for existing democratic institutions). To simplify, two different outcomes are possible in this dimension: an incomplete, limited legitimation or a full legitimation of institutions, largely through the activities of parties and party élites. In Chapter 3, these alternatives were labelled as *exclusive legitimation* and *inclusive legitimation*, respectively.

Four different polar processes result from the combination of the two dimensions, creating a typology of consolidations (see Figure 6.1). The right-hand column reflects situations in which there is either a widespread democratic legitimacy from the beginning or a successful subprocess of consensus and legitimation develops, to the extent that

		legitimation		
		exclusive		inclusive
		---	---	---
	dominance	party consolidation		state consolidation
		ITALY	GREECE	PORTUGAL
control				
				SPAIN
	neutrality	maintenance		élites consolidation

FIG. 6.1. *Models and cases of democratic consolidation*

anti-regime and disloyal groups or parties are or become a tiny, unimportant minority—that is, situations where inclusive legitimation has been achieved. Under these conditions, some extent of democratic consolidation may occur even in the absence of dominant or even well-structured parties. The presence or absence of well-structured parties, however, may have an important impact on the particular process of consolidation, as well as on certain features of the consolidated democracy that emerges. A process that immediately follows the installation of a new democratic regime and is characterized by inclusive legitimation in combination with control of civil society through clientelism, a large public sector, and parties with substantial penetration into civil society can be regarded as a process of state-based consolidation or, more simply, *state consolidation*.

In the second possible outcome in this column, inclusive legitimation has been achieved but well-structured parties with the ability to control civil society are lacking. As I have argued, even under these circumstances party élites may play an essential role in fostering the legitimacy of the new democratic institutions and in supporting the process of democratic consolidation. Accordingly, this is an élite-based consolidation or, briefly, an *élite consolidation*.

What of those situations in which acknowledgement of the legitimacy of democratic institutions and practices is not widespread? Under conditions of limited or exclusive legitimation, dominant partisan control of society may be the only route to consolidation. In other words, in the absence of an inclusive legitimation of the new regime, party organization, party control of organized groups, and forms of party patronage may be necessary if the system is to become sufficiently consolidated. Under these circumstances, party structures organize and, at the same time, encapsulate internal divisions in society. They constrain the behaviour of individuals and groups in civil society, channelling that behaviour into democratic institutionalized arenas with the capacity to contain conflict. Over an extended period of time, habitual conformity with democratic rules of the game can lead to widespread internalization of key democratic behavioural norms. Control of civil society by governing parties can also prevent sectors of society from defecting to anti-regime extremist alternatives, insofar as they can provide incentives to groups to work within the system and deny rewards to those who overtly challenge its legitimacy. Over time, moreover, anti-regime parties and movements may tire of their exclusion from power and may seek to adapt to the prevailing democratic norms and institutions in order to gain access to the benefits of governmental incumbency. Several years under this kind of party control can culminate in a party-based consolidation or *party consolidation* of democracy.

In the absence of both widespread legitimacy in the immediate aftermath of a democratic installation and strong party control of civil society, consolidation is unlikely to occur. Both attitudinal and behavioural support for the new regime is weak or absent altogether; there is also exclusive and weak legitimacy, no party dominance, a fairly developed party system, but without strong links with sectors of the civil society. Under these circumstances, the regime is potentially unstable and is likely to survive only in an international context highly favourable to democracy. That is, in this fourth hypothesis the international aspects, which have deliberately been kept out of the picture, may become crucial to the resulting pattern (and the existence of the regime). I refer to this as *maintenance*.[3] No consolidation is possible, and a crisis is always a likely way out of the whole process.

The analysis in Chapters 3, 4, and 5 allows us to fit the four cases into the typology. Regarding the first dimension, about fifteen years following the inauguration of a new democratic regime Italy could be characterized as having secured an exclusive legitimacy—its democratic institutions and practices were regarded as legitimate or accepted only in a partial and limited way. In contrast, quasi-inclusive legitimacy was achieved in Greece, with the presence of a still anti-regime KKE in the mid-1980s,[4] and also in Spain, the diminishing challenges to the regime from regional nationalist groups notwithstanding. In 1987 Portugal is also characterized by a quasi-inclusive legitimacy, due to the continuing commitment to Communist orthodoxy on the part of the PCP leadership. Declining electoral support for the party, however, is also making this limitation of legitimation or legitimacy increasingly irrelevant. In these three cases, the legitimation process was largely sufficient to have consolidated the democratic regime by the mid-1980s, or a little later with regard to Portugal. In Italy, on the contrary, legitimation alone was insufficient to have consolidated the regime.[5]

Consequently, the 'top-down' component of democratic consolidation appears especially salient in the Italian case: otherwise, how could democracy be consolidated over the long term with a level of legitimacy which was initially so limited? The analysis now comes full circle: the party organization, party gatekeeping role, patronage and forms of corporatism, not necessarily all together, but in some specific

[3] Burton, Gunther, and Higley (1992: 5) refer to this as an 'unconsolidated democracy'. It may be immediately noted that no Southern European case will fill this fourth cell.

[4] But not later with the crisis at the end of the decade when a new cabinet was formed with the previously inconceivable alliance of the Communists and Nea Dimokratia. See Ch. 2.

[5] Over the following decade and a half, however, the legitimacy of Italian democracy spread such that a nearly inclusive legitimation of democracy (i.e. one that excluded only the neo-fascist MSI) was achieved by the end of the 1970s.

combination, can play an important role in the consolidation of every definite democracy. More specifically, if the legitimation process has not gone far enough to consolidate a regime, stabilization of the party system and some of the other factors may be indispensable for a successful consolidation process. This is what unfolded in Italy, where the legitimation process had succeeded in producing only a limited or exclusive legitimacy, but where party dominance was characteristic of the relationship with interest groups. Thus, the Italian process is one of party consolidation.

In their efforts to achieve and perpetuate themselves in power, parties attempt to attract and maintain support from sectors of civil society, at least in part through development of their organizations, interest group relations, and control of state resources. In order to acquire and maintain power (especially control of public sector resources), parties also must succeed in the game of democratic competition. Once they seriously enter into this game, however, they find themselves caught within a logic that, from the standpoint of consolidation, represents a self-perpetuating virtuous circle. Partisan competition entails an adjustment of parties (as intermediary representative structures) to civil society. Insofar as civil society has encapsulated the procedural aspects of competition within a framework of democratic norms and values, this adaptation will require substantial modification in the stands and behavioural styles of initially anti-regime parties and groups; failure to adapt will mean failure in partisan competition and, therefore, in the party's efforts to achieve and maintain itself in power. Similarly, stability, responsibility, and organizational development may enhance efficacy and effectiveness with regard to governmental policy-making and implementation, but it may also appeal to voters and strengthen the party's electoral position and relationships with interest groups. This self-reinforcing virtuous circle can contribute to consolidation, as a side-effect to the pursuit of purely partisan objectives.[6]

In Spain the process unfolded in a very different way. In contrast with the Italian case, the parties were relatively neutral in their gatekeeping regarding interest groups, and in general were weaker than parties in Italy: they were weakly structured, and an intermediate level of stabilization was achieved, the lowest one among the four countries (see Chapter 4). Within a short time following the installation of the new regime, however, widespread legitimacy was achieved (some small and declining regional pockets of anti-regime sentiment notwithstanding). Given the importance of the roles played by party leaders in

---

[6] This process is similar in many ways to what Burton, Gunther, and Higley (1992) have referred to as élite convergence.

the achievement of inclusive legitimacy, Spain may be regarded as an example of élite consolidation. The prominent role of élites is powerfully confirmed when some specific aspect of relationships among parties, civil society, and state is considered: not only with reference to neutrality, but also to patronage and corporatist pacts negotiated by party, union, and entrepreneurial élites.

In Portugal, the democratic consolidation process is indicative of a third pattern. The control dimension includes the stabilization of the party system with a prominent party (PSD), relatively more developed party organizations than Spain, party dominance of civil society, and a strong role played by the public sector until the end of the 1980s, when a reform of the constitution (1989) paved the way for private enterprise (see below). The legitimation process culminated in a quasi-legitimacy, without the complete integration of the Communist Party within the game of democratic competition. Overall, the importance in the consolidation process played by the resources of the public sector and the central corporatist bodies (see Chapter 4), that recalled the previous authoritarian tradition, leads to the categorization of Portugal as a case of state consolidation.

In Greece there was a strong stabilization of the party system and party organization, characterized also by continuity in voting behaviour. At the same time, the occupation of civil society by the incumbent party, a prominent role played by the public sector, further strengthening the incumbent party, and a developed party patronage also makes the Greek process similar to the Italian one. Unlike Italy, however, there is a weaker and declining, rather than stronger and growing, communist party and a democratic right rather than a neo-fascist party. That is, a quasi-inclusive legitimacy rather than an exclusive one, and in this way Greece is closer to Portugal and may also fit into the category of state consolidation. An additional aspect that should perhaps be emphasized in this case is the higher salient role performed by a leader, such as Papandreu: it may be regarded as being much more salient than either that of Social Democrat Cavaco Silva in Portugal or the Christian Democrat De Gasperi in Italy (see also Chapter 4). This aspect leads us to categorize Greece as having undergone a more specific process of charismatic consolidation, as a subcategory of state-based consolidation: at least in the Greek case, but even in other cases, no strong leader would have exploited the possibility of consolidation without the key contribution of the other elements that are characterizing state-based consolidation.

The differing consolidations were summarized in Figure 6.1. The basic thrust of the argument underpinning this typology is that a limited level of legitimacy, secured by democratic institutions and practices in the early stages of the consolidation process, can be compensated for by strong and stable parties playing a dominant role. While strong, stable parties may not be required for democratic consolidation in regimes that have achieved considerable legitimacy (as typified by the case of Spain); parties and their command of state resources may powerfully influence the character of the consolidation process and the kind of democratic regime which emerges. Therefore, in the end the more specific hypotheses suggested by the four cases seem to be the following:

1. If there is limited legitimacy and the democratic parties are entrenched in a sort of 'internal system', only formed by fully integrated and mutually legitimated parties, then the other processes of partisan control of society, in any of the forms mentioned above, become decisive for the resulting consolidation. In other words, when legitimacy is restricted, if some form of party organization and/or control of organized and non-organized groups is not clearly achieved, then even a weak consolidation is not possible, and another process will sooner or later take place, namely, the crisis.

2. If, on the contrary, there is widespread democratic legitimacy from the beginning, or a successful sub-process of legitimation develops to the point that anti-regime and disloyal groups or parties are or become a tiny, unimportant minority, then the other aspects are hardly relevant, or not relevant at all, in order to achieve consolidation. In other words, the greater the existing legitimacy (or legitimation), the less the party control of civil society is necessary to achieve consolidation.

3. If in addition to widespread legitimacy, there is a partisan control of civil society, the second phenomenon is not decisive for the consolidation (see above), but it is still important in characterizing both the process of consolidation and the pattern of consolidated democracy. To fail to analyse this aspect would hinder a deeper understanding of the whole topic.

The typology that emerged out of the four cases may be speculatively expanded to encompass other processes and empirical cases. The main directions to follow regard, on the one hand, the decline of legitimation and the stronger or weaker fading away of the various mentioned forms of controlling civil society (party organization, gatekeeping, patronage, corporatism). If there is a decline of legitimation, growth of discontent, protest, and at the same time the transformation of gatekeeping with parties that can be outbidded, no bounded conflictuality is seriously maintained, and/or other forms of controlling the civil society decline, then some form of crisis, be it a partial one or a larger and deeper one, is expected.

If on the contrary the extent of élite legitimation and mass consensus become much higher and inclusive, an active or more active civil society emerges, a thicker or looser network of institutions that allow for democratic integration and both the representation of interests and its participation in the decision-making process develops (outside and in addition to political parties), a clear open bipolarization with alternation and role of opposition become established, perhaps also with an intermediate important regional or federal level, then the fading away of mechanisms of controlling civil society is possible and a *societal consolidation* may emerge and become established. Accordingly, if there is a large private sector, an association may articulate its interests without party gatekeeping, patronage is a very minor aspect, while corporatist policies may be confirmed or decided. Figure 6.2 sketches out this wider, more speculative typology.

		legitimation	
		exclusive	inclusive
	dominance	party consolidation	state consolidation
control			
	neutrality	maintenance	élites consolidation
autonomy			
	direct access	crisis	societal consolidation

Fɪɢ. 6.2. *Models of democratic consolidation and crisis*

Before concluding this section two additional questions may be addressed about the key explanations of the empirical models suggested above. First, the analysis was not conducted in terms of cleavages, but the components of them were present in it.[7] In fact, the electoral aspects were considered at the level of empirical indicators of the process (see Chapter 2); the beliefs and values emerged in the analysis of consensus and support (see Chapter 3); and the organizational element of the actors and the 'top-down' dimension of the process

---

[7] See the definition suggested by Bartolini and Mair (1990: 215) with three elements: an empirical one, a normative one, and an organizational/behavioural one. See also the excellent essay by Gunther and Montero (1994) grounded on an electoral and attitudinal analysis of cleavages in Southern Europe.

were explored (see Chapters 4 and 5). Accordingly, in the perspective here developed a cleavage analysis would have confused what had to be divided and distinguished. This was the basic reason why this approach was discarded since the beginning, but at the same time its components were analysed.

Second, explaining the empirical models is a way to recall and summarize factors that were suggested in the previous chapters. In all cases the key explanations of the processes regard a set of factors belonging to the traditions of the country and factors that additionally appeared during the installation or even consolidation. Thus, for the Italian party consolidation, the two decades of quasi-totalitarian mass mobilization, the additional anti-fascist mobilization during the democratic installation, the strength of ideology, the strong presence of organized Catholic groups, and authentic ancillary associations for Christian Democracy, some degree of party bipolarization, reinforced by the Cold War, are the key explanations of that model. Here, the role of parties is strictly linked to mobilization and ideology. In Spain, the demobilizing tradition of Francoism with forty years of anti-party propaganda, the immediate decline of political participation during the early phase of installation, complemented by the waning of ideologies and the modernization of a complex society in some regions, the role of mass media in a modern or quasi-modern society, the *desencanto* at the mass level and the élite moderation, also as a reaction to the remembrances of the Civil War, and the appeal of democratic European models are at the roots of that élite consolidation. In Portugal the state consolidation followed the adaptive path imposed by the conflict between the radical, ideologically abstract project set forth by the 'Revolution of the Carnation' and its actors, with a consequent very wide public sector, and the appeal of the European democratic model, supported by other actors. In Greece the clientelist and statist tradition is complemented by the large public sector, a manipulative electoral law with a strongly reductive impact, and the presence of personalist, charismatic leaders, such as Karamanlis earlier, and Papandreu later.[8]

Which Types of Democracy?

In this section attention will be shifted from the processes to the outcomes, that is, to which specific democratic regimes became established

---

[8] It may also be recalled that a predominant party system is an outcome that regards all four countries, although in different ways. A closer analysis of it will be developed in the third section, when the resulting features of consolidation processes will be discussed.

at the end of the 1950s in Italy and in the mid-1980s in the other three countries. Such a shifting provides an opportunity for evaluating how those processes affected the outcome, and also illustrates the influence of the rules on the other aspects during consolidation, and vice versa. For this purpose, the three main democratic dimensions and the resulting combinations of them should be recalled from Chapter 1. They are: (1) the institutional arrangements concerning executive and legislative powers and the electoral system; (2) the number and relative size of parties, some specific organizational aspects, the extent of party internal cohesion, the role of the leader/s within them, and the composition and homogeneity or heterogeneity of the party coalition supporting the cabinet; (3) the autonomy or control in the relationships among parties, state, and civil society. Each dimension gave a simplified typology and then different democratic models that should also be recalled (see Tables 1.1 and 1.2).

Before proceeding any further, the established arrangements on each dimension need to be checked. Portugal, Spain, and Greece have become semi-parliamentarian regimes or 'chancellor' democracies, that is, parliamentary regimes where the role of the prime minister and cabinet prevails vis-à-vis the assembly. In this sense, all three regimes are either partially or largely majoritarian. As seen in Chapter 2, the process of adaptation was particularly relevant in Greece and Portugal. In Greece, with the passing of time, but especially after 1985, the role of the prime minister has become more important than that of the head of state, elected by parliament. The ambiguities of the constitution in defining the roles of the prime minister and the head of state are bypassed by the one-party cabinets, also by means of a reinforced PR. In Portugal, particularly after the constitutional revision of 1982, the neutralization of the army after 1986 and, above all, the establishment of a predominant party system after 1987, the adaptation opened the way to a chancellor democracy that is not modified by the direct election of the head of state and a relatively proportional electoral system.

In Italy, the electoral system was highly proportional and consequently 'neutral' vis-à-vis the parties: it simply mirrored the cleavages and conflicts existing in civil society and granted a parliamentary representation to every relevant political force. At the moment of consolidation, during the late 1940s and early 1950s, a different choice would have implied the further radicalization and the probable crisis and disruption of the regime. The same appropriateness characterizes the process of decision-making at the centre, which also aimed at being 'neutral', in the same way as the electoral laws. Namely, both the rules of decision-making and the established routines gave parliament the possibility of strongly influencing the cabinet.[9] In addition, there was the special role of several standing committees in the real working of parliament, and the existence of two chambers which were almost perfectly symmetrical and congruent.[10] Thus, in Italy a highly parliamentary regime is established and consolidated, but it is interesting to stress that the prominent role of Christian Democracy means that this regime worked as a semi-parliamentarian one or as a chancellor democracy at least up to 1953, but not later when it turned into a parliamentarism with proportional representation.

As seen in Chapter 2, decentralization is a salient aspect for Spain only. The other three countries are unitary states, and a minor decentralization was implemented in Italy since 1970. On the whole, Spanish 'autonomous communities' basically weaken the extent of majoritarian rule suggested by the combination of semi-parliamentarism and the electoral system.

Thus, both Portugal and Italy show how the party factor can manufacture the actual working of the constitutional rules. At the same time, the existing institutional differences maintain consequent differences on the full consistency of semi-parliamentarism. Accordingly, in Portugal the president remains a counterbalancing power vis-à-vis the prime minister, and he could again become a powerful actor in a transformed party system, while in Greece and Spain, for different reasons, this possibility is either non-existent or very low. The reductive impact of the electoral system has been higher in Greece than in the three other countries, and again the difference should be stressed (see Chapter 2). The Italian PR is not relevant in the first legislative assembly when the Christian Democrats were dominant, but later it allowed a growth of fragmentation that is maintained during the following decades.

When the party system is analysed, its adaptation and adjustment to civil society during the consolidation is clearly visible. As seen in Chapters 2 and 4, first of all, the stabilization of the party system, in terms of electoral behaviour and patterns of competition, is evident in Italy and Greece; Portugal being a 'latecomer' in this; while Spain is a case in which, after 1982, there was a stabilization of the party system, but not of the parties themselves. One element vividly emerges: the party system which was stabilized was the predominant party system in Spain from 1982 to 1996; a quasi-predominant system in Portugal, but only from 1987 to 1995; whereas in Greece there was a

---

[9] Such a possibility became a reality when the dominant role of Christian Democracy lost some of its strength in the late 1950s.

[10] See Lijphart (1984) for the notion of symmetry in terms of equal legislative powers of the two Chambers and congruence with reference to a similar representative basis.

dominance of PASOK from 1981 to 1989; and in Italy there was a dominant party (Christian Democracy) in an initial phase (1948–53) and later, after 1953, a heterogeneous multipartism with a main party.[11] Below in this chapter these party systems will more closely be analysed. As seen in Chapters 2 and 4, the Spanish PSOE is also a cohesive, disciplined party that supported one-party cabinets up to 1993; the Portuguese PSD is a divided party that is unified by the emergence of a strong leader, such as Cavaco Silva, since 1985; the Greek PASOK was also a cohesive party in the parliamentary support for the one-party cabinet, but above all it was dominated by a strong charismatic leader; after the death of De Gasperi, the Italian Christian Democracy was internally divided, although the Catholic values, the Catholic organizations, and the very incumbency performed a unifying role. Therefore, the party system and the related aspects refer to the first hypothesis (b1) of Table 1.1 (cohesive, predominant party system and one-party cabinet) with regard to Spain, to a similar hypothesis with the additional presence of a strong leader in Portugal and Greece, to a heterogeneous party system and a coalition cabinet, with a main party though, in Italy.

Finally, in the third dimension (autonomy vs. control), Chapter 5 illustrated how dominant the political society was, and the parties particularly, vis-à-vis civil society in Italy, Greece, and Portugal, while semi-autonomy seems the label that best defines the Spanish relationship in the same domain. If the three macro-dimensions are connected, Italy is very close to the conflictual democracy sketched in Table 1.2, where the parties are the key institutions of that regime; Spain and Portugal belong to weak majoritarianism whereas in the first case the counterbalancing effect of decentralization and in the second the counterbalance performed by the head of state should be stressed; and Greece seems to be close to a strongly majoritarian democracy because of the role performed by the government vis-à-vis the parliament, the electoral law with a high threshold, the role of parties, and the control over civil society.

The conclusions respecting the democratic models applied to the four cases appear consistent with the processes of consolidation, in spite of the fact that such a consistency between processes and outcomes is not necessarily requested. Spain and Portugal had different consolidations, which gave way to similar typological results: élite and state consolidations necessarily point to some extent of majoritarianism, if not for other reasons because in those consolidations, and relative results, the attention to efficacy is well present. Besides, the softening of

---

[11] On this notion see below.

majoritarianism is basically achieved through institutional means: in Spain, the regionalization that is ever growing (see below); and in Portugal, the role of the head of state, who may be a stabilizing figure, as he actually was in the late 1970s and early 1980, but also the expression of the opposition to a strong party dominance as he became in the late 1980s. By the same token party consolidation explains well a conflictual democracy, with all the specifics of the Italian case. In Greece, the strong role of a leader, fairly developed party structures, a controlled civil society, that is, the main characteristics of that consolidation, account very well for a strongly majoritarianism.

This analysis also raises another key question: how can the impact of different rules on consolidation and, more generally, on stability and change be evaluated? Are there differences among the countries in this direction? In political research several authors paid an enormous amount of attention to constitutional rules as well as other institutional aspects. For example, Linz (1994) emphasized how a parliamentarian arrangement characterized by higher flexibility is much better in achieving consolidation than a presidential system, which is on the contrary characterized by higher rigidity and consequent conflictuality. Stepan and Skach (1994) gave convincing empirical support to that analysis. In the perspective here put forward, the question is how institutions help the two sub-processes of consolidation. The reply is twofold. First, the recurring implementation of the same rules contributes to the formation and shaping of consensus (see Chapter 3). This seems particularly evident in the case of Italy and Portugal, which were the two countries with the lowest consensus in the first years of installation, but where the recurring implementation of electoral law, the electoral campaigns, the consequent debates, and the elections themselves create that 'habituation' mentioned by Rustow (1970), and accordingly the consensus discussed in Chapter 3. Second, the same recurring implementation of rules in the same countries meant the strengthening of the role, image, presence, and centrality of parties in the various democratic arenas and consequently in their relationship with interests, with patronage, and with other links analysed in Chapter 5.

In every consolidation, moreover, rules are a prerequisite for the development of the same process. But in some consolidations the performance of specific rules is more important than in others. The case to emphasize here is the Spanish one. An élitist consolidation with all characteristics, which were summarized in the previous section, and particularly without strong party organization and other weak anchors, is only possible with the basic combined effect of a few rules. In the Spanish case they were: an electoral system with small districts and a consequent reductive impact on the party system, the parliamentary constructive vote of no confidence to provoke a crisis and change of the cabinet, the standing orders of the Cortes that give crucial assets to the parties in general, and to the cabinet, in particular, in the approval of bills, the constitutional rules that gave a prominent position to the prime minister, the law for the public financial support of parties, but also the majoritarian internal rules of a party, such as the PSOE, which subordinates the parliamentarians to party leaders and makes that party a more cohesive body in parliamentarian activity.

In other cases where stronger anchors were shaped, the problem was the opposite, that is, how to circumvent or hold off the implementation of rules. Italy and Greece are the best example of this. As seen, in Italy the non-implementation of a few constitutional rules, such as that on the regions or on strikes, made less dangerous an exclusive legitimation; or the partial implementation of agrarian reform made easier the corporative accommodation in the agricultural sector. In Greece the maintenance of electoral law as a rule for governing, as it had been before the Colonels' regime, rather than transforming it into a 'rule of the game', contributed to PASOK dominance. In both countries not implementing the rules or circumventing them is masked by the opposite, that is, by a flood of detailed provisions in every sector of life, and this is also culturally justified by the statist values of both countries.

Finally, in all consolidations and resulting democratic regimes a few rules give to parties that gatekeeping position that was discussed in Chapter 5. Thus, in addition to aspects of party organization, such as the control of recruitment and candidacies, to the role of a leader, party cohesion, a predominant party system, and a large public economic sector, all the rules that maintain centralized decision-making at the governmental and parliamentary levels also powerfully contribute to establishing and maintaining that gatekeeping position that remains a key factor in the consolidation of the four democracies.

The Party Systems: The Seeds of Self-destruction

The empirical models of consolidation had common aspects and differences that were discussed in the first section of this chapter. The partially different outcomes of those processes were the focus of the second section. In those sections and in the previous chapters the existence of party systems with a prominent or dominant party was stressed; the extent of legitimation, the party organization, the role of party élites, the extent of clientelism, the size of the public sector were also indicated. All these aspects had intrinsically the potential for internal change. The aspects regarding the party system will be comparatively discussed in this section, the others with specific reference to each country in the following one.

		Size	
		plurality	majority
Time	5–10 years	CRITICAL PARTY	MAJORITARIAN PARTY
	more than a decade	MAIN PARTY	DOMINANT PARTY

FIG. 6.3. *Forms and degree of party dominance in multiparty democracy*

First of all, a few distinctions are useful for a clearer analysis of party systems. While the definitions of two-party systems and multiparty systems may be taken for granted (see Sartori 1976), that of predominant party systems deserves additional comment. The simplest definition of this type makes reference to two dimensions: the size of a party vis-à-vis the others and the duration of predominance. Accordingly, 'assuming that about 10 percentage points of difference between the stronger and the other parties suffice to qualify a dominant party', a predominant party system is 'a more-than-one party system in which rotation does not occur in fact . . . the same party manages to win an absolute majority of seats . . . with the exception of countries that unquestionably abide by a less-than-absolute majority principle. . .'; and in general, with regard to the time span, 'three consecutive absolute majorities can be a sufficient indication' (Sartori 1976: 193–9).[12] As apparent in Sartori's discussion, the criteria of predominance might be relaxed or made stricter. This brings to mind different forms of predominance in the party system according to the time span and size of the party.

Figure 6.3 shows those forms and degrees by referring to the *critical party*, as the weakest form, to the *majoritarian party* as a stronger one with a limited time span, to the *main party*[13] as a fairly weak form, but

[12] With reference to the literature on this topic, in addition to Sartori, see esp. Duverger (1958, part II, ch. 2), Arian and Barnes (1974), and Pempel (1990).

[13] Here, a more recurring label such as 'pivotal' (see e.g. Rémy 1975) has been discarded because it had been misleading. In fact, here the reference is not to a party that—

TABLE 6.1. *Dominant parties and predominant systems: Italy (% of seats in the Lower Chamber)*

	First party	Second party	Above/ below 50%	Interval	Bipolarization
1948	53.1 (DC)	31.9 (FDP)	+ 3.1	21.2	85.0
1953	44.6 (DC)	24.2 (PCI)	– 5.4	20.4	68.8
1958	45.8 (DC)	23.5 (PCI)	– 4.2	22.3	69.3
1963	41.3 (DC)	26.3 (PCI)	– 8.7	15.0	67.6
1968	42.2 (DC)	28.1 (PCI)	– 7.8	14.1	70.3
1972	42.2 (DC)	28.4 (PCI)	– 7.8	13.8	70.6
1976	41.7 (DC)	36.0 (PCI)	– 8.3	5.7	77.7
1979	41.6 (DC)	31.9 (PCI)	– 8.4	9.7	73.5
1983	35.7 (DC)	31.4 (PCI)	– 14.3	4.3	67.1
1987	37.1 (DC)	28.1 (PCI)	– 12.9	9.0	65.2
1992	32.7 (DC)	17.0 (PDS)	– 17.3	15.7	49.7
1994	18.6 (Lega Nord)	17.3 (PDS)	– 31.4	1.3	35.9
1996	23.8 (PDS)	18.7 (Forza Italia)	– 26.2	5.1	42.5

TABLE 6.2. *Dominant parties and predominant systems: Spain (% of seats in the Lower Chamber)*

	First party	Second party	Above/ below 50%	Interval	Bipolarization
1977	47.4 (UCD)	33.7 (PSOE)	– 2.6	13.7	81.1
1979	48.0 (UCD)	34.6 (PSOE)	– 2.0	13.4	82.6
1982	57.7 (PSOE)	30.3 (AP)	+ 7.7	27.4	88.0
1986	52.6 (PSOE)	30.0 (AP)	+ 2.6	22.6	82.6
1989	50.3 (PSOE)	30.3 (PP)	+ 0.3	20.0	80.6
1993	45.4 (PSOE)	40.3 (PP)	– 4.6	5.1	85.7
1996	44.6 (PP)	40.3 (PSOE)	– 5.4	4.3	84.9

a more durable one, and finally to a *dominant party*, as the strongest form in terms of size and time. With reference to the four countries, Tables 6.1 to 6.4 show the time and size of the principal and secondary parties, when the first party received the majority of seats, the interval between the two, and the extent of bipolarization, as an *a contrario* measure of predominance in the sense that the higher the bipolarization the lower the prospective stability of predominance. Table 6.1 suggests that in Italy the majority of seats is gained by the DC only once

whatsoever its size—maintains a 'pivotal' or key position that makes it determining in any governmental position, but to a large party that is always necessary and at the core of any such coalition.

(1948), but this party is able to maintain a plurality position for years. Consequently, it belongs to the majoritarian party in the period 1948–53, and then to the main party in a multiparty system—not to a predominant one—for a long time. The crisis of the key, central position has become apparent since 1976.

In Spain (Table 6.2) there was a classic dominant party in a predominant party system until 1993, with a shifting to a key, main party position that, however, does not make a great deal of difference in terms of the dominant role of the PSOE in the government of the country. Of course, the higher bargaining power of the Catalan CiU and the other two regional parties, which gave external support to the cabinet in the period 1993–6 (see Table 2.2), should be borne in mind. Portugal (Table 6.3) had a majoritarian party for eight years, but since 1980 that party (PSD) had been an incumbent political force, although always in coalition with others, and in 1985–7 it already had the vote and seat

TABLE 6.3. *Dominant parties and predominant systems: Portugal (% of seats)*

	First party	Second party	Above/ below 50%	Interval	Bipolarization
1976	40.7 (PS)	27.8 (PPD)	– 9.3	12.9	68.5
1979	48.4 (AD)	29.6 (PS)	– 1.6	18.8	78.0
1980	50.4 (AD)	28.4 (PS/FRS)	+ 0.4	22.0	78.8
1983	40.4 (PS)	30.0 (PSD)	– 9.6	10.4	70.4
1985	35.2 (PSD)	22.8 (PS)	– 14.8	12.4	58.0
1987	59.2 (PSD)	24.0 (PS)	+ 9.2	35.2	83.2
1991	58.7 (PSD)	31.3 (PS)	+ 8.7	27.4	90.0
1995	48.7 (PS)	38.3 (PSD)	– 1.3	10.4	87.0

TABLE 6.4. *Dominant parties and predominant systems: Greece (% of seats)*

	First party	Second party	Above/ below 50%	Interval	Bipolarization
1974	72.0 (ND)	20.3 (EK-EN)	+ 22.0	51.7	92.3
1977	56.9 (ND)	21.0 (PASOK)	+ 6.9	35.9	77.9
1981	57.3 (PASOK)	38.3 (ND)	+ 7.3	19.0	95.6
1985	53.7 (PASOK)	42.0 (ND)	+ 3.7	11.7	95.7
1989 June	48.3 (ND)	41.7 (PASOK)	– 1.7	6.6	90.0
1989 November	49.3 (ND)	42.7 (PASOK)	– 0.7	6.6	92.0
1990	50.0 (ND)	41.0 (PASOK)	0	9.0	91.0
1993	56.7 (PASOK)	36.7 (ND)	+ 6.7	20.0	93.4
1996	54.0 (PASOK)	36.0 (ND)	+ 4.0	18.0	90.0

plurality with more than a 10 per cent difference with the PS. Thus, Portugal came very close to a dominant situation, however, it had a quasi-predominant party system for the 1987–95 period. It is worth noting that despite the interval of strength between Social Democrats and Socialists, the PS was not only present in local administration, but it also gained the head of state, who had been the main oppositional institution to the dominance of the PSD since 1986. And in fact some decline of dominance is seen by putting together the decline in the interval (8 points less between 1987 and 1991) and the growth of bipolarization, which is seven points higher. Finally, in Greece (Table 6.4) ND had been a majoritarian party for seven years and PASOK was also majoritarian for eight years. Again PASOK comes close to being a dominant party, but the high bipolarization shows how unstable that position was.

In Figure 6.4, the empirical cases are put in their proper cells. What is evident at this point is that there are dominant or other kinds of prominent parties, but not always predominant party systems. The problem is in understanding the conditions that may assure a party a position of dominance or prominence for a longer time. This means drawing a difference between the more apparent prominence of the party in terms of its electoral size vis-à-vis the other parties and the aspects that allow the maintenance or strengthening of a dominant position in the relationship with society, because of a few institutional and other aspects.

		Size	
		plurality	majority
		CRITICAL PARTY	MAJORITARIAN PARTY
Time	5–10 years	Portugal2 (1995–) Spain3 (1996–)	Italy1 (1948–53) Portugal1 (1987–95) Greece1 (1981–9) Greece2 (1993–)
		MAIN PARTY	DOMINANT PARTY
	more than a decade	Italy2 (1953–94) Spain2 (1993–6)	Spain1 (1982–93)

FIG. 6.4. *Forms and degree of party dominance: Southern Europe*

In Figure 6.5 the conditions for and against party dominance are summarized. Among the core conditions there are the presence of a divided opposition, which may perpetuate the prominence of the party: in different ways this happens in all four countries where the positions of the DC, PSOE, PSD, and PASOK are challenged by more than one party that belongs to different sides of the left–right continuum; a limited legitimation of sectors of the opposition, such as that concerning the Communists and Neo-fascists in Italy, Alianza Popular, then Partido Popular in Spain, again the Communists in Greece and in Portugal; stable links with unions and other interest groups, as happened in Italy more than in Portugal, but not in Spain, where the links were looser and looser, or in Greece, where the links with the interest groups were disputed by the three main parties. The other features, indicated in Figure 6.5, also give assets to the prominent party in the country that has them. They, however, are not always present in all four countries. For example, as already said, Spain is not a unitarian state.

For	Against
A. Institutions	
PR elextoral system with threshold	polarity or bipolarizing majoritarian
no partners in cabinet	minor partners in cabinet
parliamentarian	presidential or semi-presidential
unitarian state	decentralized state
large public sector	small public sector
fusion of constitutional powers	strong role of judiciary
B. Intermediation Structures	
strong, pragmatic leadership	weak, non-prominent rigid leadership
developed party organization	light parties
stable links with unions or other interest groups	changing links or no links with interest groups
fragmented opposition	unified opposition
C. Civil Society	
Limited legitimation of opposition	full legitimation of all public actors
frozen moderate electorate for domestic/international reasons	electoral 'freedom'
weak independency of media	strong, independent media
low or declining dissatisfaction	growing dissatisfaction in the moderate middle class

FIG. 6.5. *Conditions for and against party dominance*

A. Institutions

long incumbency
no alternation in office
no partners in cabinet
unitarian state

B. Intermediation Structures

developed party organizations
strong party links with interest groups

C. Civil Society

'frozen' moderate electorate
no signs of dissatisfaction in the moderate groups

FIG. 6.6. *The critical elements of self-destruction and change*

Where then are the seeds of self-destruction or those that may bring about a deeper change in those party systems? They are basically embedded in all elements that cause either the internal erosion of legitimacy or rigidity, and that encourage continuity and resistance rather than gradual adaptation. With regard to the internal self-destruction, the very long duration of incumbency sows the seeds for change: this is the well-known 'fatigue' of incumbency that also concerns the politicians in power and brings the erosion of consensus or support for the governing party that is always taken as responsible for the probable emergence of problems that remain unsolved. When the elements of rigidity that impede or slow down the adaptation disappear for some reason, the change is greater and deeper. Figure 6.6 enumerates a few elements of this sort. On an institutional level, in addition to long incumbency the first feature is the lack of partners in the cabinet that do not compel the dominant party to bargain its policy choices. In Spain, Portugal, and Greece the three incumbent parties had no partners for years; and the non-bargained choices of leaders were present in all three cases. Centralized decision-making with only one incumbent party is the second element of potential rigidity, and for the same reason. The strong party organization, as in Italy, and vigorous links with interest groups, as in Italy, Portugal, and Greece, are two other factors of resistance and continuity. When they disappear the change may be a greater one just because of the previous resistance to the adaptation.

A 'frozen' electorate, which artificially supports the dominant or prominent party, is the result of a low level of competition because of the presence of non-integrated opposition(s). This again gives the leaders in office the illusion of non-political responsibility and a high sense of autonomy and omnipotence. Such élite attitudes and feelings are even more accentuated if there is no alternation in office, as in Italy for more than forty years or in Spain for eleven years. But in a democratic regime it is not possible to openly control the competition, if it is not a violent or subversive one, and on the contrary there is a 'natural' tendency to increment it. Accordingly, as in Italy and Spain, the 'freezing' is bound to end and problems of legitimation disappear, but meanwhile resistance increases and with it the potential for deeper change. A passive society that may not openly express a profound dissatisfaction for years until it becomes manifest all of a sudden when other aspects are added, as in Italy, is another aspect. Of course, the higher the number of critical elements the greater the possibility of self-destruction and change, with Italy largely outnumbering the other countries in this.

Another important element may be mentioned here despite not being indicated in Figure 6.6. During installation and consolidation the parties perform a role of office-seeking and vote-seeking (see Strom 1990), and other roles in establishing their own identities and gaining the identification of sectors of civil society, or also as integrative institutions. Later on, when all has become 'business as usual' and there are no alternatives to the democratic institutions, another role of party actors enters and becomes a prevailing one, that of policy-seeking and above all of problem-solving. This means political actors that are able to cope with challenges and problems, and in this they show some degree of decisional efficacy. But if there are consolidations that were built on the conscious acceptance of inefficacy as a cost for maintaining democracy, then an additional important seed of self-destruction becomes evident later on. This is particularly so in the case of Italy. Given the limited legitimation its decision-making process was necessarily grounded on the pragmatic search for agreements in parliament and in other arenas among the main prominent party (DC) and its junior partners (Liberals, Republicans, Social Democrats, and later Socialists) or also with the Communists. This meant an always difficult decision-making process with a low or very low efficacy once the DC lost its majority in parliament. But this situation became unacceptable when the legitimation became much larger with the transformation of Communists during the 1980s and at the end of that decade and the Neo-fascists later.[14]

On the whole, the key point to recall is that the predominant party system or, as in Italy, the main, central party emerges from a problem

---

[14] This point is also developed in the last section of this chapter.

of limited legitimation. More precisely, the exclusion or the weakness of the extreme right because of its involvement in the authoritarian past, and of the extreme left because of its refusal to espouse democratic institutions, partially led to the prominence of the Christian Democrats in Italy, the Socialists in Spain, and the Social Democrats in Portugal. All three parties have been enjoying an asset in terms of competition, as moderate opinion was not open to changing their vote in favour of a right that was not considered fully legitimated. In Greece the right was never delegitimated and on the contrary was the main actor in the phase of installation and later, up to 1981 (see also Chapter 3). As already discussed, the attempt at dominance was played on the grounds of the control of civil society.

What Potential for Change in Each Country

The analysis of party systems emphasizes a few aspects, but does not take into account others, which are better understood if each country is seen by itself. With respect to Italy, the exclusive legitimation has a first problem, which was mentioned above. There is, however, a second important point that works as a potential for self-change. This is very close to the over-institutionalization, suggested by Schedler (1995): the limited exclusive legitimation meant that the party control of civil society was a key aspect of that consolidation. This also meant that in Italy the consolidation of democracy was necessarily the consolidation of that specific democratic regime, not of democracy *per se*. The over-institutionalization derives from this. When the conditions of additional legitimation are laid, then democracy by itself no longer runs any risk, and the main characteristics of the consolidation model on which that democracy was founded are bound to change, as actually happened (see the next section).

In Spain, the main element of weakness and possible intrinsic change in the process of consolidation is found in its main characteristics. There is no high rigidity, as in Italy, and only some of the aspects mentioned in Figure 6.6, such as the incumbent party without minor partner(s) in the cabinet until 1993, or a partially 'frozen' electorate for a few years and a rather passive society.[15] But there is a specific role performed by élites at the party level, in the unions, and in the corporative agreements. This implies the existence of oligarchical tendencies and a wider gap with civil society that is not filled by the existing patronage. Thus, on the whole, Spain had a consolidation that was

---

[15] But see also the next chapter.

more open to absorbing the external challenges and to adapting to the change, but at the same time all this was grounded on the capability of élites in keeping informal communication channels to understanding their society. Moreover, as also mentioned in a previous section, another important aspect of the Spanish process was a cohesive incumbent party with strong internal discipline. In this case the seeds of self-change may be sown as party-organized factions emerge. This is possible after a few years of government and if external challenges are not present or perceived, but it lays the basis for changing the consolidation formula.

Again in Greece the main characteristics of consolidation lay the basis for potential internal change. Only three of them need to be mentioned. First, the central role performed by Karamanlis earlier and Papandreu later with all the included personalistic elements means that where the leader is involved in some problem or accident of other sort, such as if he is under prosecution by an independent judge, then the entire network of relationships as the basis of consolidation is in danger. Second, a strong manipulative electoral law has a reductive impact on the party system and as it happens in Greece the voter also reacts to that by casting a useful vote and in so doing by incrementing that reductive effect.[16] Consequently, there is a strong tendency for party bipolarization (see Table 6.4) and a potential undermining of all attempts to establish a dominant position by a party. This was actually the case of PASOK, as will be seen below. The third element worth stressing regards the channels and forms of representation. As noted by Mavrogordatos (1988; and Chapter 5 in this volume), party dominance was so strong that the representative functions were almost totally sacrificed. If the point made by Herring (1940: vii) and more recently by Lindblom (1959: 85) according to which 'a system works if each important value or interest has its watch dog' is valid, then much higher possibilities of change are present. Of course, this is so if some growth of civil society takes place.

With reference to Portugal—and to Greece, as well—another key characteristic of consolidation should be mentioned among the aspects with a potential for change. This is the existence of a large public sector. What if this sector shrinks as a consequence of privatization policies which the government was compelled to enact because of the urgency of cutting the public debt and the yearly deficit, and as it tries to maintain or strengthen the possibilities of staying in the European Union? In this vein, a sort of internal irony of consolidation may be noticed: Portugal carried out a process where the state played a crucial

[16] This may be seen by the lower and lower gap in Greece between the percentage of seats and of votes for each party from 1974 up to 1996.

role, but the leader and party that were at the core of that process had liberal and pro-market tenets. Consequently, if they had decided to be consistent with themselves, the entire network of relationships established during consolidation could have been dynamited. Moreover, in Portugal, too, there was a problem of a party (PSD), at the beginning a divided one and with an élite of local 'barons', which a strong leader (Cavaco Silva) was able to unify and discipline. The weakening of this leader for some accidental reasons would have revitalized the old internal divisions creating another source of instability and change.

Finally, participation in the European Union since the early (Greece) or the mid-1980s (Spain and Portugal) was a factor of democratic stabilization (see Pridham 1991, Whitehead 1991, and Chapter 2), but at the same time it might become an external source of internal change. In fact, if the participation in the European Community implied that there were no longer any fears for democratic stability, then the political arena was open to the expression of protest and dissatisfaction, also because of policies imposed by the European Union.

Therefore, the potentials for crisis are, first of all, built into the specific ways that consolidation takes place. Exclusive legitimation and the various forms of controlling civil society impose rigidities that may be at the origin and development of subsequent crises. More precisely, if an external event or a chain of events takes place the very same aspects that characterized the processes of consolidation in terms of limited legitimation and control of society contribute to the unfolding and characterization of the possible crises and changes.

Why is this so? The basic reason is that limits of legitimation and anchors of control create distortions, resistance, and a lower capability for adaptation; distortions, in terms of administrative inefficiency, particularism, and decisional stalemate; resistance of vested interests developed by that consolidation. When that legitimation grows and/or the anchors fade away or break, the costs of consolidation appear unbearable, and reactions to them are obvious and the crisis is deeper. This is the paradox of consolidation: as a tendency, in the long run a stronger consolidation (with low legitimation) may be at the origins of a deeper crisis. Accordingly, such a deeper crisis unfolded in Italy with the highest resistance, while more limited crises took place in Greece and Portugal and even a minor one occurred in Spain.

Which Crises? Parties, Interests, and the State

What actually happened in the four countries after the consolidation? Since the end of the 1980s Italy has entered a phase of crisis, which may culminate in a transformation of the previous democracy, but which, however, has already deeply transformed the model of consolidation. The expected depth of the crisis and the consequent change deserve a longer analysis, which will be developed in the next section. In Spain, there has been a crisis of the predominant party system, already apparent in 1993, and a consequent change of party system with the Partido Popular, which won the 1996 election. In Portugal too the predominant party system was revealed to be of much shorter duration and the PSD lost its majoritarian position in the 1995 election. Again this is a crisis of the party system and a consequent change toward party bipolarization. Finally, the Greek crisis took place at the end of the decade; the dominance of PASOK was halted and again a bipolarization was more clearly established. In all three cases the crisis is partial, and it only implies the destructuration of competitive patterns and the transformation of the main party in each country. On the grounds of what has been argued in this and previous chapters, even an apparently limited crisis and change means change of respective models of consolidations, and, first of all, change of the relationships among parties, the state, and organized and unorganized interests. That is, even those partial crises may conceal a more serious change, and perhaps even the beginning of a path towards societal reconsolidation (see Figure 6.2). The point not to take for granted is the direction of causality: is it the crisis and the change of party system which brings about the crisis of consolidation formulas, or vice versa? A comparison between Greece, on the one hand, and Portugal and Spain, on the other hand, gives some indications about this question.[17]

In Greece, the crisis became apparent with the elections of June 1989, October 1989, and then April 1990, when ND won a barely sufficient parliamentary majority to form a cabinet with the external support of a minor partner (Diana). The reasons for the crisis were fairly obvious: the attempt of PASOK to gain a dominant position in the polity and society had been vigorously contested by ND, that in its turn was present in civil society with the help of a bipolarizing electoral law. As already seen, a stronger penetration of civil society had been the result in terms of consolidation. When the PASOK government had to decide on a few austerity measures (see Merkel 1995: 304 ff.) popular dissatisfaction, the internal reactions of Socialist sectors, and some

---

[17] In these three countries, a crisis of clientelist mechanisms is not apparent. Despite the fact that some of the possible factors of this crisis are present, such as fewer economic resources, shrinking of the public sector, alternation in incumbency, others are not (change of political élites, also at a local level; breakdown of traditional parties). And on the whole the most recent ongoing research (Cazorla, Jerez, and Montabes 1997, Hopkin 1997, Mavrogordatos 1997, and Papadopoulos 1997) would confirm the persistence of these mechanisms.

weak protest by unions paved the way for the crisis. At the same time Papandreu was also involved in several cases of corruption, particularly but not exclusively the Koskotas affair with the Bank of Crete illegally financing PASOK officials (see next chapter and Koutsoukis 1995).[18] Consequently, the reasons for the delegitimation of the leader and people around him were numerous and increasing, and the consequent crisis of the party system became unavoidable. Let it be added that charges of corruption amongst PASOK leaders, Papandreu included, and a consequent televised trial dominated the political scene in 1991, but this episode was virtually forgotten later, when there was the 1993 election and PASOK again won and came back to power. Again, corruption and scandals have a political impact when they become an additional factor to discontent or similar, but not alone.

In the Greek case, however, the partial change of the consolidation formula came later, after the crisis of 1989–90, as a result of this first change in the pattern of competition. In fact, after the June 1989 election it was impossible to form a cabinet with the delegitimated PASOK. Consequently, the Communist KKE, which was already partially integrated into the present regime, made the last step by entering a coalition 'against nature' with the conservative ND; and later, after the inconclusive November election it participated in an all-party coalition. Thus, the inclusiveness became complete: there was no longer virtually any challenge to the legitimacy of Greek democracy.

During those governments and later with the new ND cabinet new legislation was approved to weaken state–party relationships, such as the law that broke the state TV monopoly by allowing private channels or that on the magistracy to give judges increased independence (see e.g. Pridham and Verney 1991: 58), and to give much higher autonomy to unions vis-à-vis the parties, such as a new voluntary system of conciliation or the abolition of state subsidies to unions (see Kritsantonis 1992: 615–21). At the same time agreements between entrepreneurs and unions were inaugurated (see Diamandouros 1993: 25), and with Simitis's government in 1996–7 'social dialogue' assemblies were created with the participation of government, employers and employees' representatives to discuss important economic and social issues, such as those related to welfare institutions and employment. Furthermore, a slow, contradictory process of financial liberalization and of privatization was undertaken by the conservative prime minister Mitsotakis,

---

[18] Given the high personalization of Greek politics, the divorce of Papandreu and his marriage to a much younger hostess of Olympic Airways also became a political affair. Besides, in those years there were other cases of corruption, such as the Mirage 2000 (the payment of 40 Mirage aircraft at higher prices because of bribery), Yugoslavian corn (export of Yugoslavian corn to Belgium as if it was Greek), and the illegal wire-tapping of important political persons.

and followed by the Socialist Simitis (see OECD-Greece 1994, 1995, 1996). Particularly regarding privatization, also with Simitis's governments the pace had been necessarily slow: there was the concrete risk of bankruptcy for the just privatized firms with the consequent growth of unemployment. In fact, in 1994–5, ten enterprises which did not offer public services were privatized, but in two cases the Greek Institute for Industrial Recovery (IRO) had to intervene again with a takeover; in 1996–7 there was only one important privatization, that of Greek Telecommunications (OTE). Finally, during these years, controls on debt and cutting inflation and responding to the economic constraints imposed by the European Union also brought about a limited crisis of patronage practices (see Diamandouros 1997: 30–1).

This analysis suggests that the consolidation formula changed in one specific aspect (competitive patterns) for internal (strong bipolarizing competition) and external (corruption was unveiled and trials were held) reasons. And such a change is additionally recorded by the strong internal divisions of all parties and the consequent splits in the whole party spectrum: in the right with the creation of POLAN, in the extreme left with the division and the autonomization of KKE from Synapsismos, and in the centre-left with the emergence of DIKKI out of PASOK. This additionally brings about other changes in a continuous process of adaptation, but until the main pillar (the role of the state in the economic and social life) of that formula is removed, the model of consolidation is still the same and the crisis has to be considered as a very partial one. This contradicts what could have been expected, that is, a deeper crisis. Two important reasons, however, explain the limited scope of the crisis and change. First of all, it was an earlier, anticipated crisis for which a weak resistance (three consecutive elections) was unfolded: an actual bipolarization was already present in the 1980s, as shown by the high penetration of ND into the society and its reorganization (see Chapters 4 and 5). Second, dismantling the public sector of the economy, as in Portugal (see below), would have had serious human costs in terms of unemployment and poverty that no responsible government would have easily accepted, be it conservative and pro-market or socialist, but constrained by European obligations.

For Spain and Portugal, the growth of legitimation in the late 1980s and particularly after 1989 is a first relevant element. In contrast to Italy, the quasi-inclusive legitimacy already enjoyed by those democracies in the mid-1980s or even earlier allowed a consolidation that was not basically conditioned or had constraints due to the exclusive legitimation. In Spain, for the right the opportunity of showing pro-democratic attitudes came out in early 1981, just after the attempted *coup d'état*. Actually, the full democratic integration and the 'unfreezing' of a moderate electorate that saw the possibility of an alternative to the Socialists emerged much later, in the early 1990s (see below). Thus, when after 1993 the leaders of the Popular Party saw the possibility of winning the next election, that party adapted to a moderate, governmental programme even quicker. In Portugal the Communist integration was much slower, but the CGTP-IN, the pro-communist union, began participating in the concertation committee since 1987; the Communists went on declining and their integration was no longer a relevant issue after 1989. Beside, the Portuguese right had already participated in cabinets in the years of instability at the end of the 1970s (see Chapter 2), and since then gained integration.

With regard to the anchors of consolidation in Portugal, the main aspect to point out regards the transformation of the role of the state, that had been, as seen above, a key aspect in that process. The point of departure of that change is the second constitutional revision of 1989, which created a much larger space for private enterprise and laid the bases to put an end to a few previous nationalizations. The main aspects of the revision were the repeal of a few ideological declarations[19] and of the reference to nationalizations and the agrarian reform, the introduction of the possibility of reprivatization of the means of production or small and middle enterprises, which had previously been nationalized,[20] and the introduction of limits and rules for public intervention into the management of private entreprises.[21] That is, on the whole, the change of economic principles toward a pluralistic economic order with a market and private property was very evident.

During the period 1989–94 Cavaco Silva consistent with his beliefs and political programme carried out an impressive set of 19 privatizations in the banking, insurance, and cement sectors (see OECD-Portugal 1995: 100). At the end there were more than 35 operations. To this the liberalization of telecommunications, the deregulation of public utilities and of financial markets, the strengthening of competition opportunities, and the liberalization of retail trade and of the housing market (see OECD-Portugal 1994) can be added. In fact, among the 'radical privatizers' (Wright 1996),[22] only in Great Britain and New Zealand was a more profound policy of privatization and liberalization carried out. And in a scholarly essay (1994: 515) the economist (and prime minister) Cavaco Silva may proudly affirm: 'the Portuguese

[19] For example, in art. 1 the reference to 'a society without classes', in art. 2 to the 'transition toward socialism', and in art. 9 to 'the socialization of the main production means' were left out. See Gomes Canotilho and Moreira (1991) or Miranda (1990).

[20] See art. 85 of the new Constitutional Chart.

[21] See art. 87 of the same constitution.

[22] Among the European radical privatizers, Wright (1996: 6) includes Germany, Portugal, France, and the United Kingdom.

experience in carrying out the policy of stabilization has been a unique case in Europe with regard to the depth of changes that took place in a short span of time.' As a matter of fact in about six years Cavaco had changed the very basis of the model of consolidation he had contributed to building.

The consequences of that are very important, but not spectacular. Democracy *per se* had been largely consolidated. In this sense, the change of the formula with a secondary role for the state was relevant for the actual democratic functioning, but not a matter that attracted the attention of the media. Besides, from the point of view of the population, the very choice between Social Democrats and Socialists was limited as the two parties were very close in terms of economic policies. The PS gave greater attention to social aspects, but the parliamentary compromises between the two parties had been recurrent. Therefore, the choice of citizens was rather between different political personalities and between political continuity or some limited change, with the change of party system as a side-effect, if electors had chosen Guterres and the PS, as they did.

Let us explore this point further with reference to the other anchors of consolidation and some additional characteristics of that process in Portugal. The role of parties has been weakened. In these years there was a change of leadership in all the main parties, but the party organizations remained basically the same and in some cases, as happened to PS with the new leadership of Guterres, party centralization even increased (see Braga da Cruz 1995: 146). For example, despite the emergence of a new leading generation with the young secretary Monteiro and the reintroduction of a typically conservative and nationalistic programme, the CDS showed all its organizational weaknesses at the local level in terms of militants and structures.[23]

However, in the attempt to gain political space and electors, the extreme left formed a stable alliance with the Greens; the CDS changed its leadership and its name to the Popular Party in the party congress of February 1995, and adapted its programme. But the undermining of PSD dominance had already begun. Allegations of corruption and dissatisfaction, because of economic policies and the 1992–3 recession with high unemployment, immediately led to social-democratic defeat in the 1993 local election and the 1994 European election. Particularly in 1994 and 1995, a few episodes of corruption came out with the dismissal of the Intelligence Security Service (SIS) chief for misuse of European Funds, and illegal tapping of telephone calls, also by the SIS. In such scandals, members of the government were also involved. In

---

[23] In his analysis of the 1995 election Corkill (1996: 406) also stresses this point.

fact, the Employment and Training Minister had to resign for misuse of European Social Funds, and the forthcoming leader of the PSD, Nogueira, was also accused in connection with the sale of weapons to Angola, despite the existing embargo, and to unlawful repairs to Indonesian helicopters. Finally, even union officials were accused of misusing European funds. Within this critical picture, the decision by the PSD leader, Cavaco, not to run in the 1995 election additionally created many problems for the party, by refuelling the old internal divisions.

Consequently, on the whole, some of the characteristics of consolidation turned into weaknesses and together with popular dissatisfaction and protest became the basic reasons for the crisis of the quasi-predominant party system, and at the same time, the explanation of Guterres's electoral victory. Of course, other aspects of the regime did not change, especially the key role of parties in this democracy. Although the alliance between the two main unions, CGTP-IN and UGT (see Taborda Barreto 1991: 465 ff.), had some weakening impact on the role of parties, the unions suffered a decline in membership and organization (see Ribeiro, Leitão, and Granjo 1994; Stoleroff and Naumann 1993; Stoleroff 1995). Thus, what emerged as the most important aspects were the decisions of élites, in terms of economic policies to cut debt and deficit, and to participate in the European Union, and the reaction of the population in terms of dissatisfaction and protest.

In Spain the anchors of consolidation were weak. Consequently, greater attention should be placed on the unfreezing of the moderate electorate (see above), in connection with the reorganization of the right; conversely, the additional weakening of those anchors must also be explored more closely. With the lapse of time, the consolidation of democracy as such, and the growth of dissatisfaction (see below), the emergence of the rightist alternative became obvious: people began to think that it was also possible to vote for a rightist party. Of course, this appeared when the dissatisfaction was higher and at the same time the right has changed its image and leadership. According to survey research (see Gómez Yáñez 1994: 35) this took place in mid-1994.

At the end of the previous decade, however, the Partido Popular had changed its name and leadership with Aznar and a group of people that substituted the old top leaders, who were close to Fraga, had forgotten the Francoist heritage and absorbed the centrist CDS, a party formed by Adolfo Suárez after the breakdown of the UCD in 1983; had changed its political position by becoming (and being perceived as) a neo-liberal, pro-market party with some attention even to social aspects: for example, on a 10-point scale, in 1986 its ideological placement was 8.45 and in 1993

7.9 (see López Pintor 1994: 643); transformed its internal organization into a more efficient catch-all 'machine', which also attracted young people, students, and the unemployed and not only the higher social classes (see Gómez Yáñez 1994, Table 11; and Wert 1995: 42), but with a presidential structure that was similar to the previous one even after the new statutes of 1993 (see also García-Gueretua Rodríguez 1996).

The emergence of the internal divisions within the PSOE transformed a key element in the Spanish consolidation. The cohesive, disciplined party at the core of the predominant party system is no longer the same: with the passing of the years and the policies carried out by the incumbent ministers sectors of the party are more and more in open opposition to the 'governing party'. The most important internal opponents were the 'guerristas', led by the vice-secretary of the party and its organizational 'mind', Alfonso Guerra. But in 1991 an internal, sympathetic analysis of the party showed the existence of at least four different 'sensibilities' that divide that party (see Escudero 1991: 19–30). In March 1994, Guerra and his group were on the losing side at the 33rd Congress with a third of seats in the 36-member central committee and the image of a divided party became apparent. This factionalism heavily affected policy-making by greatly reducing the legislative productivity of Socialist cabinets since 1990 (see Gillespie 1992).[24]

The internal problems of the Socialists brought to light the élitist feature of consolidation already mentioned above, and that did not only concern parties. The consensus is declining for them (see López Pintor 1994: 648; and Gómez Yáñez 1995, Table 1), and all the main leaders (see Gómez Yáñez 1994, Table 6 and Gómez Yáñez 1995, Table 2), but increasing disillusion and delegitimation of democratic institutions also came out with a lower and lower consensus about democratic institutions (see Chapter 3): from 80 per cent in 1990 to 73 per cent in 1993 (Gómez Yáñez 1994: 37).

Within this context it is not at all surprising that the already loose ties between the UGT and the Socialists broke down, the neo-corporatist pacts were not renovated, and the impact of scandals was stronger than at other moments. Under the competitive pressure of Comisiones Obreras, the UGT can no longer accept the kind of austerity and restrictive policies carried out by the supposed 'friendly' cabinet: several decisions by the cabinet were intended to meet the programme of economic convergence within the Maastricht Treaty and were carried out without the agreement of the unions. The famous general strike of 14 December 1988 (see Aguilar and Roca 1989; and

---

[24] On the internal tensions of the Socialists see also Pérez Díaz (1996: 169–72). On these divisions, together with the impact of scandals and the negative effects of long incumbency, Maravall (1995: 125) also places emphasis.

Espina 1991: 191 ff.), and other strikes, such as in 1992, 1993, and 1994,[25] show the different conflictual positions taken by unions with the leading support of the UGT. The changed position of unions toward cabinet and employers, who had become closer to the Socialists, was already stressed by the end of the neo-corporatist pacts after 1986. The whole network of consultative bodies, which should have developed a sort of 'Norwegian' participative, organized democracy revealed its problems in the very ways that participation was carried out: those organs were actually packed with 'strong', defined interests, but without the participation of general citizen interests, and they were fused and confused with the other different consultive bodies inside the bureacratic apparatuses (see again Gómez Yáñez 1995: 44–7).

The unveiling of scandals and episodes of corruption is also a piece of this picture, on which the media put very much stress. Most of them, and particularly the three best known, involved members of the cabinet, González included: the Roldán case concerning the Director of Police and his dishonest management of the Ministry of Interior funds; the GAL case, on illegal anti-terrorist activities of the Internal Security Forces; and the CESID case with the illegal recording of telephone calls, ministers, journalists, and the king included, by the Army Intelligence Service.[26] For years each day the media had largely been covering these and other scandals, and also building an important political role for a few prosecutors, such as Baltasar Garzón, who was elected in 1993, was appointed to the General Direction for fighting the drug trade, but returned to the magistracy one year later. The impact of scandals, recorded by the surveys conducted during the early 1990s up to 1995, can be better understood only within the picture of detachment and dissatisfaction mentioned above.[27] In fact, during the previous years or even during Francoism, corruption was apparent. Why did it not have the profound impact that it seems to have now? As for the other countries, Italy included, the reply is that only in the years under scrutiny do scandals and corruption emerge in a context of detachment, dissatisfaction, and negative attitudes toward the present political moment and the parties;[28] and for this reason the media are able to magnify the impact.[29]

[25] For the precise data on the strike see next chapter. Here, it may be recalled that the general strike of 14 Dec. 1988 with the participation of about 8,000,000 workers was the first one since 1934.

[26] For an analysis of other cases of corruption see Heywood (1995*b*). A vivid pro-Socialist account is given by Cotarelo (1995).

[27] Luckily in Spain the Centro de Investigaciones Sociológicas in Madrid has carried out numerous surveys on these topics which show that impact.

[28] The anti-party sentiments are attitudes largely widespread in Western Europe, not only in these countries. See Poguntke and Scarrow (1996), and the next chapter.

[29] On scandals and their political impact see also Pérez Díaz (1996, ch. 3).

The critical picture can be completed with a reference to the economic recession of 1992–3, to high unemployment, and also to the likely crisis of party patronage that further weakens the links of the parties with civil society. Thus, all considered the electoral decline of the PSOE, and in this respect the gradual crisis of the predominant party system may be seen very well with the decreasing number of votes cast for the party from 1982 to 1993, when it lost the majority of seats, to 1996 when it lost the majority votes in favour of the PP. But there are intermediate steps, such as the 1991 local election with its negative results, the 1994 European election when the party lost the majority, and the 1995 local election, which confirmed the negative trend.

The decline of the PSOE also meant the gradual change in the logic of the party system. The Socialist crisis and the other events just described meant a gradual bipolarization of patterns of competition, and in this sense a crisis of party dominance. But inferring from this only an establishment of bipolarization would be wrong. Following the complexities and specificities that are so recurrent in political life, the crisis of Socialist dominance also left room for the regional parties, which since the beginning were helped by the electoral law.[30] This actually means that the two main parties at the national level are complemented by regional parties that were already relevant in the *comunidades autónomas* (see Montabes 1994), and later acquired a growing policy salience again at the national level. As a matter of fact, in 1993 PSOE had to govern with the help of the Catalan CiU and the Basque PNV (and the Canarian CC) and since 1996 PP needed the support of the same parties (see Table 2.2). That meant a much greater role for regional demands and an increasing decentralization of Spanish policy-making, also if the end of concertation at the national level and the development of regional bargaining and agreements[31] are additionally considered.

Analysis of the three partial crises suggests a few comparative considerations. The main Greek moments of crisis took place earlier than some basic changes of consolidation: more precisely, the crisis of Socialist dominance came earlier and, as a result of it, the choice of élites later changed some other aspect of consolidation. The Spanish and Portuguese crises were more gradual, particularly with reference to the party systems. In Portugal the change was a more basic one than

[30] The small electoral districts of Spanish electoral law favour the parties with local, concentrated roots much more than parties with widespread votes in several districts, such as Socialists or Populars.

[31] For example, in Catalonia a regional social macro-agreement was reached in March 1993 (on this see Fernández-Castro 1993).

in Spain. The fact is that in Spain the only seeds of self-destruction were the length of incumbency and the 'frozen' electorate, but in general consolidation had been more flexible, and even when the PSOE lost its plurality in the 1996 election, it gained in some districts (see Wert 1996; Amodia 1996). However, the key point is that in both countries the greater or minor changes are basically the result of élite decisions. Thus, in Portugal, Cavaco's policies and then his decision against running in the 1995 election were important elements of the crisis and change; in Spain the Socialist policies and the ability of Jordi Pujol, the Catalan leader of CiU, are at the basis of the crisis and the kind of change where at the same time two larger parties, rather than one, emerge along with smaller regional parties (CiU and PNV) with greater salience in the national decision-making process. In this vein, there is a trend toward party bipolarization since at least 1991 and a later trend toward greater pluralism: in Table 6.2 the measure of bipolarization is lower in 1996 vis-à-vis 1993.

These considerations and the previous more detailed analysis also indicate a second key element in all three cases: the dissatisfaction, the negative reactions, and the perceived inefficacy by the people of those countries with its timing and content. These aspects in their attitudinal and behavioural dimensions deserve to be explored in a closer way to explain those crises and changes, as interactions between élite choices and popular reactions.

The Italian 'Earthquake': An Excursus

To be sure, more specific and detailed attention must be given to the Italian transformation. For years the Italian crisis has been at the core of the scholarly debate (see e.g. Graziano and Tarrow 1979). The empirical indicators illustrated in Chapter 2 confirm how long the crisis has lasted. The limits of legitimation and different forms of protest emerged at the end of the 1960s. The following decade had been one of partial political realignment, but also of blocking of any change: the incompletely solved legitimation of both extreme sides of the political spectrum and the total freezing of any change during the years of terrorism may account for the long crisis.

In the early 1990s and later, there is no longer a problem of legitimation of democracy, but a serious delegitimation of the specifically existing democracy. Thus, following a process inaugurated for the left in 1973 with the strategy of 'historical compromise', the integration of traditional extreme parties had been fully accomplished by 1995. The transformation of the PCI into the PDS in February 1991, and of the

MSI or MSI-AN into the National Alliance (AN) in January 1995, are the points of arrival of this integration. Even the more radical and left-ist Communist Refoundation cannot help but recognize democratic institutions, which in the late 1990s had been in existence for half a century. Therefore, the anti-system parties[32] that have characterized the Italian party system for decades no longer exist. Bilateral opposi-tions have also disappeared. For the first time the right, represented by the MSI-AN, was in office in the Berlusconi cabinet and the opposition came from the centre and the left. To be sure, the coalitional capacity of the PDS may also be taken for granted, not only because it gave cru-cial support to the cabinets in the difficult years of terrorism in 1976–9, but its very short participation in the Ciampi cabinet,[33] the support it gave to the Dini cabinet, formed at the end of January 1995, and then its central role in the Prodi cabinet, formed after the 1996 election.

However, a new anti-system party has emerged. In fact, the Northern League (NL) may be considered fairly radical, anti-fascist, but basically within the existing democracy up to December 1994, when the NL brought about the crisis of Berlusconi's cabinet; later, a process of additional radicalization began. The most probable reasons for that are: the split in the League and the consequent need to restate its hegemony and identity within the centre-periphery conflict vis-à-vis the new splinter parties; the competition with the moderate, conserva-tive Forza Italia (FI) in northern regions; and also the deliberate strategy of attracting dissatisfaction and protest, which are very wide-spread in the northern regions for economic reasons. The result is that Bossi supports secession from Italy and has developed his anti-system politics as much as possible on the extreme edge of legality.

The other key aspects in the unfolding of crisis regard the changes in the anchors of consolidation: there is not only a problem of crisis of par-ties, but a wider and deeper phenomenon. After more than fifteen years of delayed, covert crisis (see Morlino 1984 and 1985), in the early 1990s the crisis eventually erupted with the transformation of all main link-ages that characterized the consolidation process, but also maintaining curious continuities at the party system level (see also Chapter 2).

With regard to party organization,[34] the first feature to stress is the

[32] The definition of an anti-system party is that suggested by Sartori (1976: 133): a party which 'undermines the legitimacy of the regime it opposes', and 'would not change—if it could—the government, but the very system of government.'

[33] They changed their minds within a few hours, perhaps because they were afraid of internal criticism and attacks from the extreme left.

[34] The following discussion is based upon research conducted by a group under the direction of Leonardo Morlino. Preliminary (pre-1992) results of this research have been published in Katz and Mair (1994). A more complete report, which will also cover the period 1992–6, will be published in a series of books (see Morlino forthcoming).

sustained decline in the presence and diffusion of parties in civil society. During the 1970s and 1980s the partisan élites were still the main actors in Italian politics, characterized by patronage in the allocation of resources. At the same time, the need and opportunity for maintaining a large party membership declined mainly because of a deradicalization among the main parties (DC and PCI), a related de-ideologization, and the development of the political role of television after 1983, when for the first time the private TV networks played a role in an electoral campaign. Thus, this phenomenon, already stressed by Kirchheimer many years ago (1966), was enormously accentuated, from the beginning of the deradicalization years (1976) and even more so after 1983. The sustained decline in the total estimated rate of membership (TERM),[35] presents strong evidence for this. Moreover, the data for each party confirm it (see Table 6.5).

The presence of parties in civil society has not only enormously declined, but has also become fundamentally different.[36] If the figures for each party are considered, a basic difference between traditional parties (e.g. PCI and MSI) or their successors (PDS and AN) and new parties emerges. In fact, on the one hand, the membership of the traditional parties has radically declined: for example, the specific membership rate[37] of the PCI was 0.21 in 1963, but that of the successor PDS 0.09 in 1994; on the other hand, the membership of new parties no longer has the same meaning as for old mass parties. The new parties are not mass parties. Thus, for the League, the member is a militant co-opted from above, and the result is rather close to a new cadre party with very strong leadership; for Forza Italia, the member belongs to a local electoral committee, instructed from above and with no role to play during the non-electoral years.

A second element to be stressed is the continuous coexistence of different organizational models. Not only are elements of both the professional-electoral party (Panebianco 1988), except in the expertise of Publitalia for Forza Italia, and the cartel party (Katz and Mair 1995) hard to see in these parties, but above all it is impossible to see only one emergent organizational model in the party system: as in the past, they are more than only one. Thus, since the late 1940s a mass integration party, such as the PCI, had always cohabited with a denominational

[35] See Figure 4.1.

[36] This important element is only mentioned here, but it deserves to be discussed in greater depth. The key point is that since at least 1983 the presence of *mass* parties in civil society has been gradually replaced by the role of TV. For example, Ricolfi (1995) shows how in the 1994 elections a relevant percentage of the vote shifted toward the centre-right alliance because of the influence of television.

[37] This is the measure suggested by Duverger (1958): the ratio between the membership of a party and the votes won by the same party in the electoral year.

TABLE 6.5. *Membership of main Italian parties, 1984–1996*

	RC	PCI/PDS	DC/PPI	Lega	FI	MSI/AN
1984		1,619,940	1,408,208			180,688
1985		1,595,281	1,444,592			141,623
1986		1,551,576	1,395,239			156,520
1987		1,508,140	1,812,201			165,427
1988		1,462,281	1,887,615			151,444
1989		1,417,182	1,862,426			166,162
1990		1,319,305	2,109,670			142,344
1991	112,278	989,708	1,390,918			150,147
1992	119,094	769,944	—	140,000		181,243
1993	121,055	690,414	813,753			202,715
1994	120,000	700,000	233,377		300,000	355,000
1995	115,984	661,162	172,711	60,000		467,539
1996	127,734	675,114	172,000	100,000	300,000	486,911

Notes: Figures for the PDS begin in 1991; for PPI in 1994. With regard to Christian Democracy, in 1991 the data of 14 provinces were not considered; in 1992 there are no figures as at the end of that year the secretary, Martinazzoli, erased all membership because the data had been artificially inflated for reasons of internal competition among party factions; in 1993 the data of two regions (Sicily and Sardinia) and three other provinces were lacking. As for the members of the two other splinter parties from CD, CDU, and CCD, both of them belonging to the Polo, CDU members are 200,000 (1995) and 140,000 (1996), while CCD members are 125,000 in 1996 and there are no data for 1995. Both figures of Forza Italia (FI) are an estimate suggested by the party officials, grounded on the 6,500 clubs of FI with approximately 40–50 people per club; to them 5,112 members of the party should be added for 1994. In the last figure of MSI/AN, 250,000 members belong to the Movimento Sociale Italiano and 105,000 to the 1,300 clubs of Alleanza Nazionale. The figures for this party are very much inflated.

Sources: Official party data.

and catch-all party, such as the DC, or opinion parties (Republicans, Liberals, or Social Democrats) (see Bardi and Morlino 1994). In the 1990s, a variety of other models are also present, in spite of the elapsed time and of the hypothesis on the homogenizing impact of political competition.

The PDS and Rifondazione managed to preserve the structures of the former PCI, especially in Emilia Romagna, Tuscany, and Umbria. The PCI's heritage of offices and militants did not disappear, even though the PDS had decided, even prior to 1991, to reduce the number of party officials and rely on a leaner organization. It should be noted that all traditional parties implemented similar policies of sacking party functionaries and reducing the size of the party organization, given their respective financial difficulties. As a result, in July 1993 parliament passed a law that allowed party functionaries to be pensioned off early. Thus, on the whole, the PDS maintained some of the elements of the old mass integration party, becoming a sort of post-mass integration party looking for a new model.

In contrast with the 'light' party structure of the democratic left, the League developed a small but strong organization manned by voluntary workers—many of them young—from a variety of social backgrounds. It emerged as a markedly hierarchical party with a highly prominent leader and a central office controlling finances, electoral campaigns, and party policy. As much as possible—and even with reference to its patterns of recruitment—the party organization is managed with the efficiency criteria which are typical of a private business or firm. Different organizational tenets, however, are present in the League: it is a charismatic party, a cadre party, and also a party-movement. In addition, since 1990 it has moved from being a protest party to becoming a governmental party, and then again a radical, extremist party. The impact of governmental experience had important consequences. In fact, an organization solidly rooted at the local level, but with low institutionalization at the national level, was unable to bear and overcome the strains and pressures of internal dissent. The leadership of Bossi was itself challenged, especially on the issue of participating in the Berlusconi cabinet. At the end of 1994, on two occasions a group of MPs split away and a strong group opposed Bossi from within the party. The most important turning point came in February–March when Bossi regained full control of the organization, and turned it once again into a protest and movement party. The regional and local elections of April 1995 strengthened its leadership by showing how Bossi was correct in his position: despite the various splits and the formation of a new small party (Federalisti), all in all the League lost only a limited part of the electorate, that is, more precisely, less than one-third (2.7 per cent) of its previous electoral strength (from 9.1 in 1994 to 6.4 in 1995). It increased to 10.1 in the election of 1996.

Some of the organizational aspects concerning the League reveal how deeply the values of entrepreneurship, efficiency, and the free market have penetrated into Italian political culture, especially in all northern areas, as a reaction against bureaucratic inefficiency and the poor quality of public services. The same is suggested by the organization of Forza Italia (FI). The plans for such a party were carefully laid during the second half of 1993. The party was launched and its organization openly built up in late January–March 1994, before and also during the electoral campaign for the March elections. The key organizational role was performed by the staff of Publitalia, a company that is part of Fininvest (the conglomerate owned by Berlusconi) and which is a leading advertising firm at the national level. In a few days, between February and March 1994, they were able to set up about 13,000–14,000 clubs all over Italy with about 80 people per club. According to official party data, they numbered 6,500 in December 1994 with about 40–50 people per club, and still numbered 300,000 in late 1996 (see Table 6.5). The clubs are vertically connected to a national association of clubs (ANFI), which are expected to suggest their political line. In an organizational sense, FI is very difficult to define, partly because of its binary organization: the clubs, on the one hand, and the party with its tiny membership (all in all, 5,112 members),[38] on the other. If the focus is on its recent genesis, FI is a sort of firm-party, given the key role performed by Publitalia, and the role of Berlusconi remained crucial. In the late 1990s it is trying to establish itself by maintaining all its previous sets of structures, its parliamentary party, its governmental position, and a strong, undisputed leader. However, in this poorly institutionalized party the experience of being in office and the conflicts with its coalition partners have brought about internal dissent and clearly distinguishable groups, though not factions. As an additional consequence, the MPs became key figures in this organization in linking the centralized undisputed leadership with the local level of the clubs. On the whole, however, the party structures are still fluid and the organizational debate regarding the future is still open.

The new Partito Popolare Italiano (PPI), a direct successor to Christian Democracy, cannot any longer depend on the political unity of the Catholic vote, since this was divided among five main groups of the left, centre, and right (see Chapter 2). Nonetheless, despite the substantial process of secularization that had taken place in Italy over the preceding twenty-five years and a more limited possibility of influence, the PPI still relied on support from sectors of the Church hierarchy, the Catholic Associations (AC), another Catholic group named Comunione e Liberazione (CL), and some sectors of the Catholic worker association (ACLI) (see also Cartocci 1994). From this perspective, the PPI was a candidate to be considered a new neo-denominational party. But in 1995 the split of this party in two also implied a further division of the Catholic support in favour of both new formations.[39]

---

[38] But in June a much debated project of internal reform was proposed by Milanese leaders to give a higher role to the members and membership, and to overcome the internal inconsistencies of the organization.

[39] It is also worth mentioning the organizational change of the Socialist Party, which placed the party entirely in the hands of its leader, Craxi, during the 1980s. Eventually, this change was one of the causes in the abrupt breakdown of the party when Craxi was involved in 'Mani Pulite'. See Di Virgilio (forthcoming).

The far-reaching effects of internal change are also apparent when the enormous turnover of party élites is examined, above all with reference to the patterns of recruitment, their socio-economic backgrounds, and some characteristics of their behaviour. Since in almost all contemporary democracies the core party élites sit in parliament, the data on MPs elected in 1992–6 are essential to deal with these problems. First, whereas the newly elected deputies made up 27 per cent in 1979, 32.1 per cent in 1983, and 28.2 per cent in 1987, they become 42.9 per cent in 1992 and 71.3 per cent in 1994 (63.2 per cent in the PR seats) (Verzichelli 1995). Actually, in only a few years there is an almost complete turnover of the parliamentary élites: in the present Chamber of Deputies 88.6 per cent (558 out of 630) are MPs elected for the first time in 1992 or 1994; 5.6 per cent were also elected in 1987; only 5.9 per cent, that is 37 people out of 630, has a longer legislative experience.

The turnover is very high for each party, but it is clearly higher for the new parties: 90.4 per cent newly elected in FI versus 61.5 per cent in the PDS. At the same time, the newly elected are also numerous whenever a party increases its vote: the newly elected are 77.5 per cent in the MSI-AN (Verzichelli 1995: 717).[40] The extent of the turnover explains why previous experience in politics or trade unions is less frequent for deputies, who are usually younger than in previous legislatures. In this case, too, candidates with previous political experience in local administrations or as party leaders are more frequent in the traditional parties than in FI or the League (see Verzichelli 1997 and Lanza 1995). If the analysis stops at this point, nothing really new would emerge in terms of party change. The most relevant conclusion would be that the patterns of party recruitment—especially parliamentary recruitment—are enriched by a successful appeal to people without previous political experience, above all in the new parties (League and FI).[41] Of course, this is only a temporary phenomenon, as in the 1996 election the turnover partially declined again (see Verzichelli 1997). Thus, for FI and even more so for the League, the newcomers decreased.

[40] Note that these data refer to the majoritarian seats; with regard to the PR seats, the newly elected are 54.1 per cent in PDS, 85.7 per cent in Forza Italia, and 59.1 per cent in MSI-AN. This suggests that the proportional lists were also used to save the old leaders.

[41] The negative side of this is that a high turnover usually implies a new élite with poor knowledge of the actual working of institutions and, at the same time, of the problems that need to be solved. This is especially relevant in the Italian case given the high salience of the parliamentary committees in the decisional arenas. Consequences of this may be high decisional inefficacy and radicalization. Both elements occurred after March 1994.

When socio-economic variables concerning MPs are analysed, more interesting elements appear. First of all, there is a steady increase in MPs coming from the private sector: from 25.7 per cent (1987) to 34.6 per cent (1992), 44.4 per cent (1994), and 40.5 per cent (1996). Consistent with these figures, in the League in 1992–6 and in FI in 1994–6 the presence of people coming from different interest associations or also more specific interests is strong: 34.4 per cent in FI in 1994, with 14 MPs coming from Publitalia and Fininvest, as well as industrial entrepreneurs, landowners, and tradesmen (Lanza 1995, Figs. 13 and 21–2).[42] This aspect is also evident if a sample of all candidacies is considered: 23 per cent of FI candidates are entrepreneurs and 19 per cent are managers, tradesmen, or people from the private tertiary sector; 7 per cent of the candidates of the League are also entrepreneurs and 36 per cent belong to the other three sectors (Mattina 1995: 581).[43] Similar figures may be confirmed for 1996: for example, 34.2 and 23.4 per cent are entrepreneurs and managers among respectively, deputies and senators of FI. That is, in addition to and in partial substitution of the traditional lawyers or civil servants, private interests decide to enter the political arena directly. This means that the choice made by Berlusconi was not an isolated phenomenon; and to say the least it was imitated. The uncertainty of these years, the anti-party sentiments or also—as in the case of Berlusconi—the links with the previous political élite encouraged people with relevant personal interests to enter politics.[44] The serious possibility of an electoral victory of the 'hated Communists' made unthinkable for Berlusconi and other entrepreneurs the maintenance of a position of neutrality.[45] If such an attitude is maintained even when the uncertainties of the political transition are over, then there is actually something new in the patterns of party recruitment.

This gives additional empirical evidence to a new phenomenon gradually emerging in the previous years but clearly evident since 1992: the entrepreneurs who directly or through their association, the Confindustria, play a direct role in politics and prefer direct access where their autonomy is vigorously stated. And even more, industrial

[42] Almost 11% of MPs belonging to the Popular Party are members of Catholic organizations. This confirms the support of the Church for the PPI and lends greater justification to its definition as a neo-denominational party (see above).

[43] Mattina (1995) also stresses that the interest organizations are officially neutral in the electoral contest.

[44] Socio-economic status is very relevant for 73% of the MPs of Forza Italia (Lanza 1995, Table 14).

[45] The national association of entrepreneurs (*Confindustria*), however, did not openly give Berlusconi support and maintained an official position of neutrality. This support for him was more manifest at the rank-and-file level, and above all, at the post-electoral meetings of the entrepreneur association.

leaders, such as Abete and Fossa, the last two presidents of Confindustria, maintain the opinion that the interest associations are much more important than parties in the policy-making process, and they may even substitute them with greater efficiency, knowledge of the problems and solutions, and less corruption and clientelism.[46]

The positions of entrepreneurs are complemented by the acquired autonomy of unions vis-à-vis their parties of reference: if the so-called Triplice, that is, the alliance of CISL, close to DC, UIL (PRI and PSI), and CGIL (PSI and PCI) begin with the worker and student mobilization of the 'hot autumn' in 1968, and if the bases for union autonomy are laid at that moment, the process of union autonomization unfolded in the following years and particularly during the 1980s with the project of a new unity. But it is in the early 1990s, when the same traditional parties linked to unions disappeared or were transformed, that the autonomy is actually achieved.[47] Consequently, one may see the CGIL and the other unions that may oppose, even vigorously, the governmental policies when they do not correspond to worker interests as perceived by unions. This is so also when for the first time in democratic Italian history the government is supported by a leftist coalition because of a sort of alternation worked out after the 1996 elections.

Another feature of these new relationships among parties and interests emerges out of the agreements bargained by the cabinets, since that presided by over Amato (see Table 2.10)—and, except for Berlusconi's period—with entrepreneurial associations and unions (see Alacevich 1996). That is, despite the fragmentation of associations, the agreements on wages and pensions were discussed and concluded by the three main actors and also implemented with very little protest. At the same time, in 1994 when Berlusconi's cabinet made the attempt at passing a new law to cut the expenses on pensions without the agreement of unions, protests and demonstrations were very vocal and eventually at the basis of the crisis and fall of that cabinet.

In the agricultural sector the previous quasi-corporative situation changed completely. A key institution such as the Consorzi Agrari was in bankruptcy at the end of the 1980s, and policies were determined by European financial aid managed by the Ministry of Agriculture and regional governments. Although the Coldiretti and Confagricoltura are still powerful associations, other associations emerged, and above all the previous links with parties were openly cut. This happened

---

[46] Public declarations and interviews of those leaders, published by the press, support this point.

[47] On Italian industrial relations see the excellent work by Alacevich (1996); and specifically on the trade unions Accornero (1992) and Carrieri (1995).

particularly for the Coldiretti in early 1994, a few days before the formation of the new Popular Party.[48]

In the industrial and agricultural sectors, and also that of banks,
there is also a clear, apparent retreat of the state. Although Italy has
to be defined as a middle-range privatizer (see Wright 1996) and during 1995–6 there has been a halt to this, the partial privatization of
important banks and insurance companies, such as Credito Italiano,
Banca Commerciale Italiana, and INA, and the selling of a few techno-
logically advanced industrial firms (Nuovo Pignone, and several
others) in the period 1992–4 witnessed such a retreat, but above all the
basic change of political élite attitudes toward the public economic sector: despite debates and oppositon from Rifondazione and also the
rightist AN, the belief in the necessity of such a retreat is widespread.

The crisis of traditional parties (see Chapter 2) and of its organizations, compounded by the economic crisis, the policies of privatization,
and the impossibility of continuing the waste of public resources, also
brought about the crisis of the whole system of patronage, that also
became the object of the attention of a few prosecutors in Southern
Italy with consequent judicial inquiries and trials. It may be recalled
that such a system of patronage compensated for the disequilibria of
representative functions and, although it led to the growth of a *sottogoverno*, it also allowed the political-administrative machine to function to a certain extent. Consequently, when the system broke down, it
is not curious to note that particularly—but not only—in the small
provinces of Southern Italy many people were left without the institutional references and those forms of particularistic representation that
had persisted for almost half a century, that is, for the entire lifetime
of most people. Deep feelings of new uncertainty and dissatisfaction are
obvious consequences, if the partisan mobilizational traditions of fascism are recalled. And the reasons why in those areas the heirs of
Christian Democracy (PPI, CDU, CCD) still persist are also obvious,
but patronage is largely over, and only a mix of personalistic and new
partisan links partly survives, or is reshaped again. Also in these
areas, however, the direct political presence of interests and associations has become more apparent than earlier.

On the whole, the entire model of Italian consolidation, implemented
in the 1950s, that had resisted for decades in a sort of 'freezing', has
been deeply changed. With some difference among different domains of
policies, during the 1980s the gatekeeping role of parties has gradually
faded away (see Cotta and Isernia 1996: esp. 421–32). Gatekeeping is
actually restricted to a system of kickbacks to finance the expensive

---

[48] From a different perspective, which pays particular attention to policies, the crisis
of Italian party government has also been analysed by Cotta and Isernia (1996).

party organizations and augment the personal income of some leaders, as a few judicial enquiries demonstrated (see below). The formula 'the lower legitimacy, the higher party control' no longer has any meaning. Modern society is breaking those links.

A few ironic features, however, emerged. All traditional parties disappeared or changed. A few systemic aspects, such as the main, central position of a party (DC) or the lack of alternation also faded away. But, at the same time, the party system as a whole did not change in other key aspects: the high number of parties—still at least nine formations; the existence of an anti-regime party, which is now the League, unopposed to democracy as such, but opposed to the existing centralized democracy and advocating the division of Italy to create a new country in Northern Italy; the crucial salience of the centrist formation for electoral results as well as for policies; the persistence of centrifugal drives with the electoral growth in 1996 of most radical parties, such as the Social Movement-Fiamma Tricolore (MS-FT), a splinter party from the old MSI (see Chapter 2), the same Alleanza Nazionale (AN), the main heir of MSI, and on the extreme left, the Communist Refoundation; and finally the low resulting decisional efficacy in the coalitional and heterogeneous cabinets and in the strong role of parliament vis-à-vis the government. This and the activation of the new centre-periphery cleavage bring us to speak of a neo-polarized pluralism with reference to the Italian party system and the old definition provided by Sartori many years ago (1976).

Moreover, and this is the other ironical feature to stress, as implicitly suggested above, the unions and other interest associations, which were the main actors of protest, riots, and demonstrations at the end of the 1960s and 1970s, twenty years later became the most moderate and responsible actors that helped Italy to recover during the economic crisis, to fight the enormous public debt, and to cut the huge deficits. If this was not a new corporatism, however, moderation and agreements were implemented and very positive economic results came out of them.

Toward the Third Dimension

The transformations of legitimation, the weakening of anchors of consolidation, and the emergence of some new phenomenon or of specific, contingent events are all factors at the grassroots of partial or more encompassing crises in the four countries. In Italy, however, the dissatisfaction because of the policies that were decided and carried out by political élites, the perceptions of inefficacy, and the different forms of protest are the at the core of the crisis. As stated in Chapter 1, despite the connections with legitimacy and consensus as well as with the top-down dimensions of consolidation, the hypothesis here affirmed is that dissatisfaction and protest are a third important dimension of the analysis. Whereas such a dimension is not totally irrelevant during consolidation, it becomes even more important in the long run when the impact of policies is known and the population has perceived that impact and reacted to it. In other words, more apparent interactions between the élites and the population have emerged.

This hypothesis is not very far away from the view of Schmitter (1992: 425) when he states: 'in the short run the consolidation of democracy depends on actors' and citizens' ability to come up with a solution to their intrinsic conflicts over rules; in the long run, it will depend on the extrinsic impact that policies made under rules will have on social groups.' But as seen above, in the long run crises unfolded in the four countries. Thus, attitudinal and behavioural reactions to policies necessarily concern the unfolding of the crisis. Let us now turn to those reactions as a way of explaining how those crises take place, and how the anchors of consolidation are undermined.

7

Features and Explanations of Crises

The Impact of Policies

Decisions and the implementation of related policies affect relationships between civil society and regime institutions. How and why this happens is a key aspect of this analysis, but it is also one of the thorniest and most embarrassing problems in political science: it is very difficult, if not impossible, to empirically prove something that appears obvious. There is a very large literature about the empirical solution to such a problem, but with unsatisfactory, incomplete results. For example, the notion of political performance is often adopted (see e.g. Wilson 1996), but it leaves unsolved or open to speculation the crux of the matter, that is, the impact of policies on civil society and their reactions.

In this chapter, the purpose is not to solve the problem mentioned above, but, within a more limited perspective, to catch the core elements in the change in relationships between civil society and regime institutions as a consequence of policies carried out. In this vein, first of all, looking at the negative side of the phenomenon seems more profitable: the basic reason for this, already mentioned in Chapter 1, is that the absence of negative reactions appears more relevant than the presence of the positive ones in the kind of relationships to be explored, and in reference to both consolidation and crisis. Second, as also suggested by Dahl over twenty-five years ago (1971), in this domain the perception of the reality is more relevant than checking what has actually taken place. This means taking for granted the intervention-mediation, and the related attention, paid by the media and by political and cultural élites to decisions and their implementation.

Another aspect to consider is that policies have an impact on common people and élites or organized associations at the same time. However, the connection between consensus or legitimacy and efficacy or dissatisfaction has been proved to be a weak or very weak one (see Chapter 3). This is so because a long chain of links should be analysed between the moment when a policy is formulated, the subsequent related decisions, the following implementation, the outcomes, the perception of them. At each link or step there are other intervening factors that one should also take into account. The connections, then, are completely blurred. All this implies that another path must be followed. This is so, above all, when after the first years of consolidation the problem no longer concerns consensus or legitimacy, but more simply the perception that important issues are not being solved or that negative decisions are being made. Such issues or decisions have an impact on the personal lives of citizens, and the reactions of people against party leaders and decisions made by them are the most important aspects to examine. Besides, to confirm the opportunity of looking at the reactions of people, it may be recalled that at an élite level the impact of policies is already indirectly considered when the anchors of consolidation or the subsequent weakening of those anchors in case of crisis are scrutinized.

The result of this reasoning is that the negative reactions of people should be explored, above all in the analysis of crisis, because consensus or the legitimacy of democracy is no longer a problem when there has been consolidation and the crisis is a partial one or it is a crisis that does not affect democracy *per se*, as in the four cases analysed here. The negative reactions to consider are the regime inefficacy perceived by people and the consequent dissatisfaction that brings them to change political identities, party sympathies, and accordingly traditional parties, party systems, patterns of competition, and in some cases even more. Inefficacy and dissatisfaction can be examined with regard to attitudes, perceptions, and behaviour. Here also the research is problematic. Attitudes, detected through surveys, display the well-known problem of surveys in terms of reliability and fluidity of responses. From a positive point of view, there are surveys analysed here that are repeated over several years, in all four countries, and notably in Italy for more than two decades. The perceptions and behaviours will be examined through the only source that is available in the four countries above all when the problem is also the perception of the issues, that is, the press.[1] It should not be forgotten here that some of the common problems of this type of source, such as reliability and insufficient related information (see Franzosi 1987; Tarrow 1989) are present, and it is important to be conscious of them.

Given these problems, not only is it useful to explore attitudes, perceptions, and behaviour, but also the possible inconsistency between

---

[1] The protocols at the origin of the data set and the related data are available for consultation and analysis to everyone who is interested. The scrutinized newspapers were: for Italy, *Corriere della Sera* (1981–95); Spain, *El País* (1982–95); Portugal, *Diario das noticias* (1982–95) and *Publico* (1990–5); and Greece, *Hi Icathimerini* and *Eleftherotypia* (both 1981–95).

the two sets of data should be explained. At the same time attitudes, perceptions, and behaviour with surveys and the press as sources need to be complemented by other data. And a few other data, strikes included, will be presented and discussed. Accordingly, the next section will analyse the available survey data on dissatisfaction; then the perceptions of some specific issues will be presented; the fourth section will discuss the negative reactions emerging in the press, combined with other data; the last section will try to explain the different crises by complementing the data and hypotheses of this chapter with the analysis developed in Chapter 6.

Which Type of Dissatisfaction? The Attitudes

To evaluate political dissatisfaction in the four countries the classic Eurobarometer question 'Are you satisfied with the way democracy works?' was considered.[2] Of course, measurement using a single indicator has its own limits. Moreover, this question is as an 'unspecific' indicator, where cognitive and affective elements are present at the same time (see Kuechler 1991: 280–1). However, its main asset is that it has been replicated for more than twenty years for Italy (since 1973), for more than fifteen for Greece (since 1980), and for more than a decade for Spain and Portugal (since 1985). Accordingly, some trend may possibly be discerned with relative ease, and an analysis developed.

On the grounds of existing research, it can be taken for granted that this indicator also points to personal aspects, such as the perception of political efficacy, but it mainly concerns other elements, such as attitudes toward the incumbent authorities, policy dissatisfaction, and political responsiveness (see Farah, Barnes, and Heunks 1979: 409 ff.). Moreover, extrapolating from Di Palma (1970: 30 ff.), it would also be possible to conceive at least two forms of dissatisfaction: a pragmatic dissatisfaction, that is, an immediate, more concrete expression of discontent on the working of democratic institutions and reaction against the implemented policies or the negative economic moment, probably concerning a moderate opinion in many ways linked to governmental and centrist parties; and a more radical and deeply rooted ideological dissatisfaction, related and consequent to a disaffection, more dangerous for regime stability because of its connection with alternative

---

[2] The precise wording of this question in the Eurobarometer survey is: 'On the whole, are you very satisfied, fairly satisfied, not very satisfied or not at all satisfied with the way democracy works in (OUR COUNTRY)?' The last two answers refer to dissatisfaction and the corresponding people will be labelled 'rather dissatisfied' and 'very dissatisfied'. Also the wording of the question in Italian makes this negative translation preferable.

cultural values, at least until the early 1980s (see Chapter 2) or simply related to the personal adherence to the opposition party or parties and in this vein an a-priori dissatisfaction.

On the whole, the analysis will suggest that several dimensions that cannot be precisely disentangled are involved in this indicator. First of all, it is not possible to prove that pragmatic dissatisfaction, mainly concerning governmental policies, is completely expressed by the rather dissatisfied people. At the same time, this is an empirically reasonable hypothesis: the declining relevance of very dissatisfied people vis-à-vis the rather dissatisfied is evident even among the voters of extreme parties, who are more and more democratically integrated. Indirectly, this might suggest the growing salience of pragmatic dissatisfaction and a more limited meaning of ideological dissatisfaction that no longer implies deep disaffection or danger for the democratic regime (see also below).

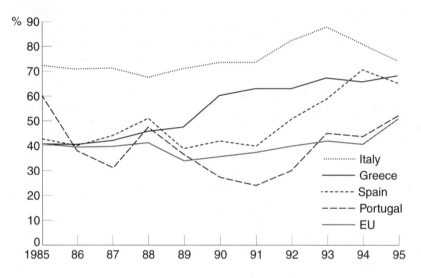

Fɪɢ. 7.1. *Dissatisfaction with democracy, 1985–1995*
Source: Eurobarometer surveys.

A first look at the data of Figure 7.1 immediately gives some important information in connection with the democratic crises. In Italy, the number of people who openly claimed dissatisfaction with the working of democracy is very high, and in addition considerably higher than in all other countries of the EU. If the rather dissatisfied and the very dissatisfied are added, the gap between the percentage of dissatisfied people in Italy and that of the other EU countries never fell below 24 per cent (in 1988), and rose to 40 per cent in 1977, a year characterized by intense terrorist activity and trouble in several universities (see Morlino and Tarchi 1996).[3] Moreover, there is a similar growth in dissatisfaction between 1991 and 1993, that is, at the moment of the highest disparity between people and democratic parties and when other indicators of crisis also exist (see Chapters 2 and 6).

In the other three countries, the level of dissatisfaction is almost always higher than in all other European countries.[4] But above all the salient growth of it takes place during the years already defined as critical periods. In fact, in Greece the highest growth with almost 15 points is between 1989 and 1990, although it is worth stressing that dissatisfaction also increases later on.[5] In Portugal, the growth has been continuous between 1991 and 1995, when it reached 28 points more than four years earlier, and the dissatisfied have more than doubled. In Spain, the steady growth is consistent from 1991 to 1994, when there were 31.2 per cent more dissatisfied people than three years earlier. In the last two countries the growth parallels the crisis and weakening of the quasi-dominant or dominant parties, already mentioned in Chapter 6. About the turning point of dissatisfaction: in Italy it coincides with the 1994 election, Berlusconi's new cabinet and the change of the incumbent parties;[6] and in Spain, with the 1995 local election and the impending 1996 election with the expected victory of the Popular Party. But in Greece and Portugal there are no apparent turning points: in the latter this is probably due to the time of the 1995 survey (April–May), before the autumn election; in Greece, there is a strong decline in the very dissatisfied in 1990 with the change of government, but this is apparently cancelled later on by a stronger growth of the rather dissatisfied.

If the distinction between rather dissatisfied and very dissatisfied is more thoroughly analysed, with the just-mentioned Greek exception there are no basic differences between the trends, but a few other features deserve to be noticed. First, except for Italy in 1993, the rather dissatisfied are always higher than the very dissatisfied. This is also true of Greece, where, during the end of the 1980s, the more radical very dissatisfied are very close in percentage to the rather dissatisfied,

[3] Setting aside the period 1992–3, which coincides with the soaring popular indignation caused by the corruption scandals.

[4] This analysis takes for granted the phenomenon of dissatisfaction and distrust in democratic institutions, that is widespread in several European countries and is recorded by a few surveys, in addition to the Eurobarometer (see e.g. Dogan 1996); and looks for the specific factors of such attitudes in the four Southern European countries.

[5] On this, the analysis will return later.

[6] Note that in Italy the survey was conducted by Doxa at the end of 1994 and the election was in March of that year.

and this at least shows deeper negative—a priori, ideological—attitudes during those years. In Portugal and Spain the steady growth and the largest part of dissatisfaction concerned the rather dissatisfied: from 18.1 per cent in 1991 to 40.5 in 1995 in Portugal; and from 30.2 per cent in 1991 to 45.2 in 1995 in Spain. In the same two countries, the very dissatisfied were much lower, but they doubled over the same period: from 5 per cent to 10.6 per cent and from 9 per cent to 19.8 per cent, respectively. At higher levels, the differences between rather dissatisfied and very dissatisfied in Italy are also in the range of about 10–20 points: 45–7 per cent of rather dissatisfied vis-à-vis 26–37 per cent of very dissatisfied. For a better understanding of this analysis, two aspects should be borne in mind. First, levels and trends of dissatisfaction actually become increasingly related when dissatisfaction rises: in fact, when dissatisfaction either becomes or is very high, then the trend becomes less evident as the possible growth is necessarily lower. Italy with its highest levels demonstrates this. Second, while the levels of dissatisfaction are not irrelevant, the trends and the moment when they appear, however, are more salient for the purposes here pursued. Consequently, in this section a greater attention will be paid to the trends and in this sense the reference will mainly concern the whole set of dissatisfied without difference of degree.

The key problem remains how to explain that widespread and in some cases growing dissatisfaction. First, the individual component of dissatisfaction may be demonstrated to be marginal or very marginal in that explanation, and even more so when only the trends are considered. This becomes more evident when two kinds of dissatisfaction are compared, that with democracy and that with 'life in general', concerning how people live and evaluate their life. The government can always be blamed for personal reasons, but on the whole this second kind of dissatisfaction has various personal components, such as the satisfaction with family life (see Campbell, Converse, and Rodgers 1976), and 'much personal dissatisfaction has no tie at all with politics' (Barnes, Farah, and Heunks 1979: 395). In fact, when the two kinds of dissatisfaction are controlled in all four countries, different levels and trends appear. This is strongly so in Italy (see Morlino and Tarchi 1996) and Spain, and largely so in Portugal. With regard to Greece, however, Figure 7.2 shows a difference in the levels, but a parallel trend, particularly between 1989 and 1990, indicating a deeper malaise concerning the whole Greek society, and not only the political aspects.

The higher levels for all four countries vis-à-vis the European averages also suggest the salience of an idiosyncratic factor concerning the whole region. This is the 'statism' that characterizes the political culture of all four countries and is expressed in the famous Italian proverb

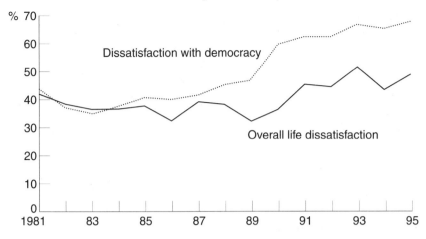

FIG. 7.2. *Different kinds of dissatisfaction: Greece, 1981–1995*
Source: Eurobarometer surveys.

'piove, governo ladro' ('it's raining, you thief of a government').[7] This factor is common to societies that had integration problems and where the public institutions are distant from, and above, civil society. In this context the solution of any problem is expected of the political institutions, and a consequently pervasive role of the government is accepted and even requested. If there is such a conception and simultaneously, for several reasons (economic, bureaucratic, or others), the existing problems are not solved, a gap between demands and outcomes is clearly perceived and dissatisfaction is the most obvious consequence.[8]

If dissatisfaction were so deep and radical that an ideological alienation from the regime results, then it would be compounded by an equally radical thrust toward change. When the dissatisfaction is controlled with the attitude toward change[9] the revolutionary perspective

[7] In other words, the government is held responsible even for natural, unavoidable events. In his 'Fragmentation, Isolation, Alienation', La Palombara also quotes this proverb (1965: 282). See also Ch. 3.

[8] The hypothesis suggested by Sani and Segatti (1995) on the impact of Catholic doctrine and the socialist-communist belief system in accounting for such a high level of dissatisfaction in Italy is less convincing. In fact, if there is a difference between the high expectations created by these doctrines and the reality, and the consequence of this is the reason for dissatisfaction, then such a phenomenon should be present also in other countries, such as Spain, with both a strong Catholic and socialist culture. In other words, the hypothesis only concerns Italy and in this way is less useful in the four cases. Of course, a certain Catholic doctrine and a socialist system of beliefs, related to other aspects of Italian culture, are at the core of the statist political culture mentioned in the text.

[9] The question was 'On this card (SHOW CARD) are three basic kinds of attitudes vis-à-vis the society we live in. Please choose the one which best describes your own opinion. 1. The entire way our society is organized must be radically changed by revolutionary

appears to be very minor in all four countries up to the point that, after 1990, the question is no longer present in the Eurobarometer surveys. It had become meaningless. In addition, in Italy the defeat of terrorism between 1976 and 1980 had left out almost any possibility of political alternative; and the same can be affirmed for Spain, despite continued though sporadic ETA terrorist action (see also below), and for the other two countries (see Chapter 2). Consequently, in all four countries the choice of gradual change and in this sense of the reformist alternative is very popular and grows with the lapse of time, and consciously even higher than the European attitudes. Finally, despite doubts manifested by Kuechler (1991)[10] the choice of 'defending society against subversive forces' is very low and declining. In Italy, for example, it goes from the mean of 28.02 per cent in the 1977–81 period to 18.42 per cent in 1986–90. In other words, the effect of moderation emerges even in the third choice, in spite of its lower consistency with the other two.[11]

If the difference suggested above is recalled, the dissatisfaction seems largely pragmatic and the existing ideological dissatisfaction is at least much less radical than twenty years earlier.[12] This means that there is: (i) an obvious overlap of democratic choice and deep dissatisfaction; and also (ii) a possible overlap between the same democratic choice and ideological dissatisfaction. At this point the reasons for dissatisfaction, even pragmatic ones, may be exaggerated by the 'statism' mentioned above, but they can only be basically related to: (i) more or less strong malaise because of a negative economic situation (unemployment, inflation, economic decline, contraction of per head consumption); (ii) a negative evaluation of different policies (on welfare protection, fiscal policies, education, or others); (iii) discontent for the scandals and corruption, that the media reported and emphasized; (iv) an a-priori negative reaction against the incumbent party in terms of values and beliefs. Thus, the question: what are the reasons for each country?

A step forward may be made by identifying more clearly who the dissatisfied are in the four countries. To begin, the most common socio-economic variables may be taken, such as age, region or area of living,

action. 2. Our society must be gradually improved by reforms. 3. Our present society must be valiantly defended against all subversive forces.'

[10] According to him (1991: 277) the third possibility, 'fight to preserve the society against subversive forces' is inconsistent with the other two attitudes, as it refers to another dimension.

[11] About the data on Italy see Morlino and Tarchi (1996); on the other countries the figures are so evident and the reformist choice so high that they can be taken for granted.

[12] Of course, only for Italy is it possible to go back to the 1970s. For the other countries the data are only available from the 1980s (since 1980 for Greece and 1985 for Spain and Portugal).

gender, religion, occupation, income, and education. The main common finding is that the highest and deepest dissatisfaction comes from the weakest and most uncertain sectors of the four societies: youth between 19 and 24 years, but particularly with reference to Portugal and in Greece (in the 1980s) also those between the ages of 25 and 30;[13] housewives, who are not protected or are largely ignored by Southern European welfare states (see Trifiletti 1996; Ferrera 1996; and below); retired people who appear among the dissatisfied in Italy since the early 1980s, in Portugal since the end of the 1980s, in Greece in the early 1990s and later; and finally people at the lowest educational levels. Such dissatisfaction seems to point to loopholes and defects in the forms of social protection and this will be analysed below. However, also among these social groups no one appears to bear a consistent and accentuated dissatisfaction.[14]

Switching to factors that are relevant in one country and not in another, a geographical distribution of dissatisfaction can be seen. As for Italy, many scholars have interpreted the success of autonomist and federalist leagues in the northern regions as an electoral manifestation of discontent by small businessmen and professionals in the industrial North and North-East. According to such an interpretation, their protest is oriented against state bureaucracies and the high costs of an overgrown welfare system, accused of being exclusively oriented to the 'parasitic' development of the South (Diamanti 1995). As a support of this hypothesis, the harsh punishment inflicted by northern voters on the parties of the 'First Republic' is frequently mentioned.

The regional disaggregation of Eurobarometer survey data does not corroborate this hypothesis. Apparently, if very dissatisfied and rather dissatisfied are analysed separately or together, the electoral analyses which consider the South and the Islands as the core of the Italian protest vote (Caciagli and Spreafico 1975) are strengthened. The peaks of dissatisfaction always emerge in the South and the Islands, with the exception of 1988, when a dissatisfaction emerges in the Centre. Particularly, during the whole period 1973–92, both north-western and

---

[13] Going beyond the evidence of the survey, on the basis of the empirical indicators of participation to protest actions, it can be added that young generations, even when not expressing the highest rates of dissatisfaction, show the strongest inclination to an anti-establishment mobilization. In Italy, it has been the case not only for the protest cycle of the late 1960s, but also for the 'dramatization' of the fall of the old ruling class involved in the judiciary inquiries on administrative corruption and illegal financing of political parties.

[14] A recent analysis of satisfaction with democracy goes in an only partially similar direction. In fact, on the basis of a European sample, Fuchs, Guidorossi, and Svensson (1995: 322–53) found the most satisfied among post-materialists, young people, and the better educated. The only relevant difference with my findings is that in Southern Europe young people are also among the most dissatisfied. See the text.

north-eastern regions show figures higher than the national average on only three occasions (see Morlino and Tarchi 1996). The fact is that on the whole the regional presence of dissatisfaction is completely blurred in Italy by the overlapping of different reasons: dissatisfied people are present in the North as well as in the South, although they have certain reasons in northern regions and others in the South. The additional aspect has been already mentioned (see Chapter 2): the centre–periphery cleavage is becoming more and more active and it is growing in the North, as the electoral results of the League show.

With respect to the other countries, in Spain the 'regional' dissatisfaction appeared at the end of the 1980s, but it mainly concerned Catalonia, whereas contrary to possible expectations it is virtually absent in Basque countries or elsewhere. In this sense it seems linked to the political mobilization that is at the grassroots of the CiU's success. In Greece regional discontent emerged with the nationalist issue against Skopje particularly in Macedonia, but also in this case a peripheral dissatisfaction seems to be present. No clear signs in this direction are expressed in Portugal, despite the fact that the debate on regionalization has been present in past years, but still not perceived as a crucial issue in 1995.

In terms of occupation, the emergence of relevant and perceived issues seems to explain the appearance of those negative attitudes. This is clearly so in Spain with the unemployed since 1992, in Greece with the manual workers between 1980 and 1984, in Portugal for the white collars at the end of 1980s and in the early 1990s. As for income, in addition to what has been affirmed above, in Italy it is sometimes even possible to find high dissatisfaction among the highest income, but this result is too random and not common enough to support any serious hypothesis. Finally, religion is never a distinguishing factor for these attitudes.

A careful analysis of these results suggests that the more continuous and consistent dissatisfaction, such as that of housewives or young people, should be left out of the picture. This is part of the *noyau dur* of dissatisfaction, but to explain the crisis and change the conjunctural factors are much more relevant. Furthermore, the data seem to make reference to the emergence of very specific problems that are not sufficient to account for the growth that is evident in Figure 7.1. The characteristics and meaning of dissatisfaction begin to be better clarified when left–right self-placement and party vote are considered.

With reference to left–right self-placement, the first point concerns the continuity in the spread of self-placement: if in Italy there is a 5-point difference among the centrists between 1973 (35.6) and 1980 (40.2), since 1985 the centrists have been the larger groups with more or less the same percentages in the subsequent decade. Thus, between 1985 and 1995, in Italy the average of centrists is 40.7 per cent, in Spain 34.2 per cent always with a strong and consistent centre-left (33.4 per cent), in Greece 41.7 per cent, and in Portugal 46.0 per cent and the highest percentage of all four countries. The variance is low or very low in all four countries and the percentages of extremists are similarly low and again without fluctuations that are worthy of attention. On the whole, a process of moderation has not been taking place because in the mid-1980s and later, the centrists are already the most consistent group. When there is a decline in this group, as in Italy in 1994–5, this is easily explained by the confrontation of the two alliances, that of the centre-left and the other of the centre-right, in the election (1994) and later.[15]

Of greater interest is the high dissatisfaction shown in the centre by moderate respondents (see Figure 7.3). The dissatisfied are high or very high in both sheer numbers and percentages, and there is no surprise if among them the centrists are also high. The more relevant aspect is to notice the centrist dissatisfaction that goes on growing during the years up until 1994 in Italy; the growth of similar dissatisfaction in Spain with a subsequent decline and a new upsurge in 1995;

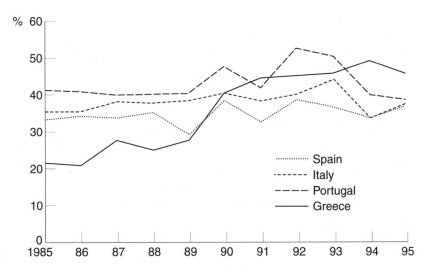

FIG. 7.3. *Dissatisfaction with democracy and centre self-placement, 1985–1995*
Source: Eurobarometer surveys.

[15] And in fact there is a corresponding growth of centre-left and centre-right people.

a large, salient growth in Greece; and ups and downs during the relevant years (1989–95) in Portugal. These are people who both did and do not raise doubts about democracy, but express criticisms—probably more pragmatic ones—against the present political institutions.

Of course, these trends are connected to the parties and their position in office or in opposition. For example, in Greece the growth of centrist dissatisfaction is paralleled after 1989 by the decline of the centre-rightist equivalent, which in its turn had gone up after 1981. In the other cases the centrist growth of dissatisfaction might be related to an internal detachment of the same sympathizers of Christian Democracy and the Socialist Party for Italy, of the PSOE for Spain and PSD for Portugal. From this perspective, dissatisfaction and vote for the different parties must be explored.

The connection between attitudes of strong pragmatic criticism, because of a negative evaluation of democratic performance and institutions, and the preferences for traditional opposition forces is also confirmed by the analysis of the voting intentions for specific parties, when the rather dissatisfied and the very dissatisfied are distinct. In Italy, the highest degree of dissatisfaction has been expressed on eight occasions by extreme leftist voters (Proletarian Democracy and Communist Refoundation), on seven occasions by the extreme right MSI, twice by those of the Radical Party, that is the libertarian left, and of PCI.[16] In the following years dissatisfaction declined considerably and stabilized around medium/high values, rising only during the period of the Tangentopoli[17] scandal for the communist or ex-communist left. Of course, for a lot of communist sympathizers criticism of the defects of the capitalist system remains distinct from their judgement on institutions. The 'national solidarity' experience of 1977–9 had a remarkable influence on such attitudes. With regard to the MSI, its voters maintain a very negative opinion of the Italian model of democracy, with precise ideological implications. In the mid-1970s the evaluation of MSI voters became even more negative (see Morlino and Tarchi 1996, Figure 8*b*). On the whole, however, the trend of the two extremist voters is similar: decline of very dissatisfied and growth of rather dissatisfied.

As expected, deeper dissatisfaction is relatively lower among the supporters of traditional governmental parties (DC and PSI) (see Morlino and Tarchi 1996, Figures 8*c* and 8*d*). Thus, interestingly enough, the trend among the two lines of dissatisfied is convergent among the

[16] The PCI figures reached their apex only in 1975–6 (see Morlino and Tarchi 1996, Figure 8*a*). These were years of highly competitive elections and of a direct confrontation with the governments, which sharpened the ideological polarization in the country.

[17] The Italian media used this term to designate the cases of political corruption discovered in the early 1990s.

extreme voters and divergent among the moderate voters (Morlino and Tarchi 1996, Figures 8*a*, 8*b*, 8*c*, and 8*d*). It is also not surprising that in 17 out of 19 cases the lowest percentage of negative attitudes have been expressed by Christian Democratic voters. The relevant share of discontent among the followers of the DC and its coalition partners (PSI, PSDI, PRI), although heavily reduced in the course of the 1980s, is another indicator of the characteristics of the Italian crisis. Here, it should be stressed that the dissatisfaction in both forms, the milder one and the more radical, increases strongly after 1991; they are the very moderate and governmental voters that express higher dissatisfaction (see Figures 7.4*a–d*).

In Spain the dissatisfaction of Popular Party sympathizers can be taken for granted. Here, too, it is interesting to realize that both forms of dissatisfaction were declining until 1991, but later they quickly grew, and the more radical dissatisfaction much more than the milder form of dissatisfaction. A strong growth of such negative attitudes during the same years can be seen among the Communist and United Left. Here, again the most interesting aspect is the enormous growth of both forms of dissatisfaction, which however reflect a different timing. The rather dissatisfied, formed by the traditional centre-leftist socialist sympathizers, began growing after 1990, the very dissatisfied after 1993 (see Figure 7.4*b*). There was a likely shift of rather dissatisfied toward a deeper negative feeling and a more gradual switching of the satisfied toward dissatisfaction. In any case, the most telling aspect is that growing negative evaluation of Socialist policies as the criticism comes from inside and a consistency of values between the dissatisfied Socialists and the government can be reasonably supposed. These aspects are also confirmed by other surveys that additionally stress the growing gap between parties and people (see e.g. Wert 1995).

In Greece, the dissatisfaction of PASOK voters began rising after 1986, and here the overlapping with the austere economic decisions seems revealing: it continues until 1989. Later on, it is true that the dissatisfaction is even higher. But after 1990 there is a new Nea Dimokratia government. Consequently, the discontent is much more physiological and easy to understand in a civil society that is squeezed by partisan bipolarism. To confirm this, after 1993 when PASOK again won the election, the discontent of its sympathizers reached a turning point (see Figure 7.4*c*). An analysis of the trend of Nea Dimokratia voters basically shows a similar trend, characterized by the a-priori negative evaluation of democracy when the interviewed are closer to the opposition party. In this case, however, there is also a growth of dissatisfaction amongst Nea Dimokratia voters when this party is the incumbent one between 1991 and 1993. Furthermore, such dissatisfac-

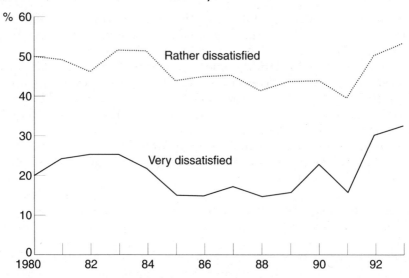

FIG. 7.4a. *Dissatisfaction with democracy of DC and PSI voters, Italy, 1980–1993*
Source: Eurobarometer surveys.

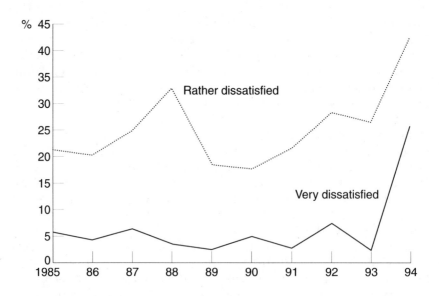

FIG. 7.4b. *Dissatisfaction with democracy of PSOE voters, Spain, 1985–1994*
Source: Eurobarometer surveys.

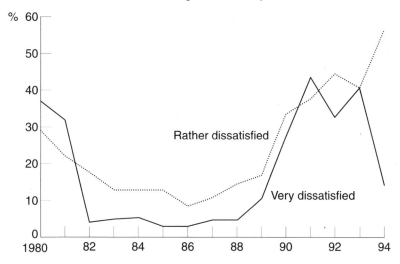

FIG. 7.4c. *Dissatisfaction with democracy of PASOK voters, Greece, 1980–1994*
Source: Eurobarometer surveys.

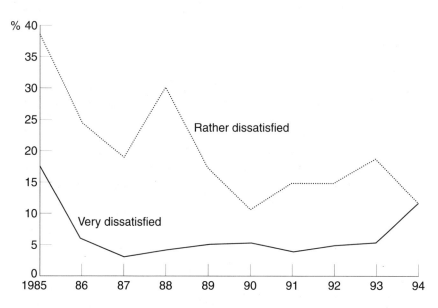

FIG. 7.4d. *Dissatisfaction with democracy of PSD voters, Portugal, 1985–1994*
Source: Eurobarometer surveys.

tion anticipated the electoral results that gave PASOK victory in 1993, and the subsequent change of cabinet formed by PASOK.

The Portuguese case displays a more moderate opinion, which also reacts according to the lines of interweaving between the sympathizers of the opposition party and those of the governmental party, who can also be dissatisfied, and within this last hypothesis these attitudes are more revealing and probably more pragmatic and related to specific issues and policies. Consequently, Socialist dissatisfaction grows after 1987, but then there is decline and acceptance of Social Democrat quasi-dominance. After 1991 the more obvious positions of discontent against the working of democracy are evident: the Socialist opinion that is readier to react negatively is the more moderate one, probably belonging to rather satisfied. The Social Democrat discontent against democracy governed by its own party also grows after 1990 and up to 1993 for the rather dissatisfied. But in 1993 the very dissatisfied went up much more, contrary to the rather dissatisfied: the opposite trends suggest a switching toward the more radical position that is not filled by a similar shifting of the satisfied to a milder dissatisfaction (see Figure 7.4*d*).

The whole picture that has been sketched up to now is useful for giving the direction in which to search for the explanation of the dissatisfaction in all four countries. The pragmatic aspects and the ideological ones, but always within democratic choice, are at the basis of those attitudes. But what are the more precise reasons for these reactions, and what are the differences among the four countries? Economic malaise, growth of fiscal pressure, cuts in public debt, the reshaping of welfare benefits, a-priori negative evaluation of the incumbent authorities, and consequently anti-establishment attitudes, or negative reactions to scandals? Or all of these reasons together? To begin providing a reply to these questions, some simple quantitative analysis may give indications that will help us to propose more precise hypotheses.

The first questions concern the economic aspects, and more precisely to what extent economic malaise, growth of fiscal pressure, and the public debt may contribute to explaining dissatisfaction. Economic malaise can be measured by the index of economic misery, suggested by Kitschelt (1994: 78), where annual inflation is added to the percentage of unemployment and subtracted from the growth of Gross Domestic Product.[18] To the classic measure of discomfort, composed of inflation plus unemployment, Kitschelt rightly added the real growth of GDP. A

---

[18] To calculate the index, the three sets of figures were standardized. It can be assumed that Kitschelt did the same, but in the four cases standardizing is essential otherwise unemployment becomes much more relevant in the total index. See the data in Appendix, Tables 7.A1, 7.A2, 7.A3. An index of inflation and unemployment is adopted

correlation[19] between this index and dissatisfaction suggests that in Greece and Italy the index explains little or nothing (r^2 is 0.18 for Greece and 0.02 for Italy) whereas in Spain (0.36) and in Portugal (0.47) it is much more relevant. Accordingly, the first important indication is that in Spain and Portugal the weakening of incumbent parties and the consequent crisis of party systems is partly accounted for by an interweaving of statism, according to which a negative economic situation is ascribed to the government ('piove, governo ladro'), and governmental economic policies that were unable to fight the negative economic phase. Conversely, in Italy and Greece the reasons for dissatisfaction point more openly to the political domain with both ideological and pragmatic elements. From this perspective, objective economic inefficacy seems to be imputed to Spanish and Portuguese governments more than to Italian and Greek ones.[20]

The possible growth of fiscal pressure and the cut in expenditure on social protection are the other two candidate variables which explain the growth of discontent. Actually, as suggested by Table 7.A4 in all four countries there was a basic growth of tax revenue, measured in percentage of GDP, but only in Greece a relevant correlation of 0.44 emerges, whereas in the other three countries the correlation is insignificant: for Italy, it is 0.08; for Spain 0.01; for Portugal 0.07. Hence, the second indication is that Italy again seems to make reference to more political reasons, whilst in Greece the fiscal policies are a basic part of the explanation, that becomes even more evident when the jump of fiscal pressure between 1989 and 1991 is taken into consideration (see Table 7.A4).

Besides, in Greece a strong positive correlation (0.80) emerges with the public debt, in Spain a much weaker one (0.18), and in the other two countries no correlation. But if the European experience of the 1970s is

by several authors. At the same time, the effects of economic conditions on democratic satisfaction have been the object of attention of a few other authors. See e.g. Clarke, Dutt, Kornberg (1993).

[19] Note that the low number of observations on the dependent variable (10–15 per country) and the possible high number of explanatory variables do not allow a reliable implementation of more sophisticated techniques.

[20] This simple finding indirectly does not confirm an intriguing hypothesis suggested by Anderson (1995) on Britain and Germany (1960–90). According to this author, 'the greater the effective number of parties in a system, the stronger the effects of macroeconomic performance on support for the government.' In fact, if this hypothesis had been confirmed, then in Italy dissatisfaction would have been more sensitive to economic malaise. The main economic variables of Anderson are inflation and unemployment; his political variables are, on the one hand, the effective number of parties (ENP) (see Ch. 2) and the support for the governing party as collected through survey analysis, on the other hand. Here, the economic variables are the same ones, plus real growth, and the political ones, in addition to ENP, the democratic dissatisfaction, that is the dependent variable. An attempt with the dissatisfaction of governing party voters was also made with similar negative results.

recalled, in Greece and Spain the direction of causality is the opposite one to that which is of interest here. The government often reacts with a growth of expenses to try to soften the dissatisfaction, and this seems to be the explanation here when attention is paid to the fact that the correlation is a positive one.

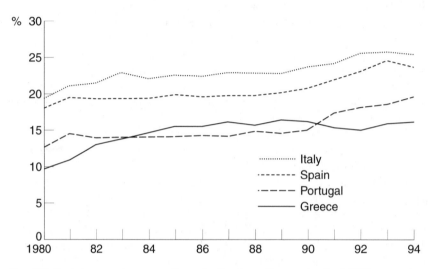

FIG. 7.5. *Social protection expenditure in Southern Europe (as % of GDP at market prices)*
Source: See Table 7.A6.

As regards social protection, the current expenditures per head in PPS[21] (see Table 7.A6) show that actually there is no shrinking of expenditure during the years that are considered here. Basically, in all four countries the governments recently tried to maintain the welfare state at the same level with only some decisions aimed at cutting the most evident waste of resources. When the trends after 1980 are analysed, a decline of expenditure becomes apparent in Greece between 1989 and 1992, a stronger decline in Spain after 1993, some cuts in Italy after 1993, but a growth in Portugal. If at this point the trends of dissatisfaction are recalled (see Figure 7.1), with the Italian decline after 1993, the Spanish decline in 1994, and the Portuguese and Greek growth, a third indication can be suggested: there is no connection between growth of dissatisfaction and welfare expenditures.[22]

[21] Purchasing Power Standard specific to private consumption.
[22] Characteristics and problems of Southern European welfare states are not the content of this analysis. However, on this there are already some good appraisals and

In this specific perspective very low correlations for all four countries confirm the non-salience of this variable in accounting for dissatisfaction (see Table 7.1). However, it has to be added that in his Euro-barometer Survey of 1992 Ferrera (1993: 34–6) found a widespread discontent of Southern European people with social protection schemes: 70 per cent in Greece, 67 in Portugal, 51 in Spain, and 40 in Italy vis-à-vis a total average (South Europe included) of 33 per cent. This is a specific pragmatic dissatisfaction that distinguishes these four countries from the other European ones: Spain, Portugal, and Greece are also the countries where attitudes of discontent and want for welfare continuity are more widespread and stronger than all other European countries, with Italy where the parallel high discontent is complemented by the different acceptance of welfare retrenchment. Such a discontent is detected in one year only. Consequently, it is impossible to relate it to the other data on dissatisfaction, but some consistency is apparent with those data as well as a pragmatic dissatisfaction on this issue, that is present in all four countries to a different extent: higher in Greece and Portugal than in Italy.

Of course, a more obvious hypothesis concerns the general stabilizing impact of welfare institutions, which may begin in the years of consolidation and then reduce the levels of dissatisfaction, and protest, later in the years that are examined now. Although very difficult to evaluate and measure, such an impact may be taken for granted and better explored in the ways that were done here (see previous chapters) with reference to the anchors and to its changes.

A different hypothesis could be the following: despite the lack of actual change, a more negative conjunctural evaluation of the socio-economic situation may cause a worsening evaluation of welfare services, and in this sense some dissatisfaction. This seems to be a concrete possibility in the Portuguese case where the evaluation of equality in existing welfare services worsened very greatly between 1991 and 1994: in 1991, the negative evaluation is declared by 27 per cent of interviewed people, but in 1994 56 per cent gave a negative evaluation (see Villaverde Cabral 1995: 25). Such a negative evaluation mainly concerned the lower socio-economic strata, and this makes the hypothesis above a more plausible one. Although there are data for one year only, the negative evaluation of welfare services, and particularly of health care, is confirmed by Ferrera (1993: 14) in all four countries with specific reference to the quality and efficiency of services: on both

research. See, among others, on Southern Europe, Maravall (1992), Castles (1993), Ferrera (1996); on Italy, Ferrera (1984); on Portugal and Spain, Esping-Andersen (1993); on Spain, Ayala (1994); on Portugal, Mozzicafreddo (1992); on Greece, Katrougalos (1996), but also Petmesidou (1991).

features the negative attitudes of people from all four Southern European countries largely outnumbered those of all other countries. In addition, a recurring debate in the press about the necessities of cutting welfare expenditure and reducing the related services may bring about growing dissatisfaction to some extent, even if at the end there is no actual cut in those expenditures. In fact, in any case it would mark a turning point after a fairly short phase of expansion, as it was connected to democratic installation. The emergence of dissatisfaction among the retired (see above) seems to give some empirical support to such a hypothesis. But if it is so, additional data picked up through the press would be needed (see below).

A temporary conclusion of this analysis allows me to point out that for Italy the political reasons of crisis seem the prevailing ones, such as reaction of people against revealed corruption or some kind of policy dissatisfaction that impinges upon the incumbent parties (DC and PSI); for Spain and Portugal, the economic reasons—welfare issues included—are strong, but also other political motives should be added; for Greece, certain economic policies—especially, fiscal policy (and welfare policies in the early 1990s)—are very important, but also for this country other explanations are needed. What is the additional empirical source that could help in this analysis?

Manifest Inefficacy: The Perceptions

In an attempt to shed light upon value-loaded policies or other reasons mentioned in the previous section, the press is another important source to exploit. With the necessary caution and the consciousness of the limits of this source (see Franzosi 1987 and Tarrow 1989) an important contribution can, however, be introduced into the analysis. First of all, it is possible to see what the most clearly perceived problems in the country are. Of course, the implicit assumption is that newspapers are a fairly reliable record of those problems and at the same time they bring attention to and make people more conscious of them.

The first phenomenon that attracts attention concerns corruption, and above all its coverage by the press, and often by the television too, making such phenomena widely known. Figure 7.6 gives strong empirical evidence of time overlapping between the dissatisfaction and revealing of corruption: in Italy, after a few previous episodes the higher growth is after 1992 with the inquiry of 'Mani Pulite'; in Greece, enormous attention is paid to four cases of corruption or mismanagement, such as the Koskotas affair, where Papandreu and other Socialist ministers were involved and prosecuted, but also Mirage 2000,

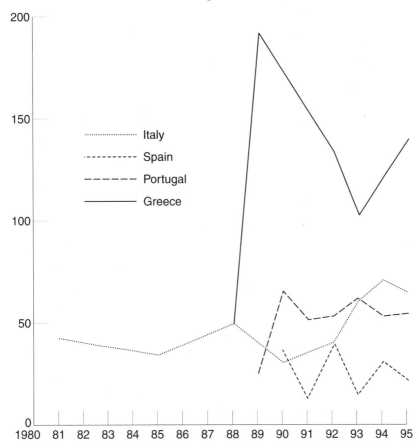

Fɪɢ. 7.6. *Coverage of corruption in Southern Europe, 1980–1995*
Source: Data from the press collected by the author.

Yugoslavian corn, and wire-tapping.[23] The attention and negative
reactions are recorded in the jump in the line between 1989 and 1990,[24]
but later (1993–4) there is an increase in both dissatisfaction and the
news on corruption with the Aget-Iraklis scandal, and subsequently on
illegal wire-tapping. In both countries the consistency between the
trend of dissatisfaction and the extent of coverage of corruption is very
strong. For example, after 1994 in Italy there is a descending line in

[23] See also the previous chapter on this.
[24] A survey conducted in Athens at the end of 1990 confirms the fairly strong impact
of Koskotas's affair on PASOK voters.

both trends. Simple correlations of 0.30 for Greece and 0.27 for Italy give additional support to the relevance of these political reasons for the crisis.

In Portugal and Spain, news on corruption also overlaps dissatisfaction, but rather they coincide with the slow decline of the main incumbent party and there is no precise moment as in the Greek case. Moreover, in Spain, fluctuations can be explained by the prosecutions of different scandals (see Chapter 6). In Portugal the very low coverage of corruption in 1988, when this kind of news is almost absent from the press, and the much higher coverage in 1989 or 1990, when there is the highest 'jump' (see Figure 7.6) are not consistent with the growth of dissatisfaction that becomes more evident after 1991. Here again, the low Portuguese correlation between coverage of corruption and dissatisfaction (0.11) and the little, but meaningful higher Spanish figure (0.20) confirms the analysis of trends. Consequently, the fourth indication that comes from these data is that coverage of corruption accounts for dissatisfaction in Italy and in Greece more than in Portugal and Spain, and Portugal is the country where it has the lower political impact. In this sense, there is a political inefficacy that is felt in a stronger way in the former two countries.

To better understand this phenomenon one should remember that corruption is revealed when there is serious, effective police activity in this direction. In Southern Europe this mainly implies not only the obvious existence of few or several episodes of corruption, but above all the more or less intense activity of prosecutors and judges. As has been particularly evident in Italy (see also Chapter 2) the combined, continuous activity of magistracy, which at some point seemed to become an alternative channel of representation, complemented by a strong role of the press, is an important explanation of the uncovering of the scandals and possible consequent dissatisfaction. In Greece and Spain too, this sort of alliance was also established between magistracy and press with the consequences examined in this chapter.

During the last decade, the Southern Europeans have been constantly and heavily bombarded with news on decisions concerning attempts to improve the economic situation, more specifically concerning wages, containment of public debt, fiscal policies, inflation, unemployment, education, pensions, health services, and so on. For brevity's sake, they can be labelled 'austerity measures'. The onslaught has been so continuous that it would be wrong to establish any connection either with the additional problems raised by the Maastricht Treaty and European Union, or with the growth of dissatisfaction. The data collected from the press are unambiguous on this. However, in Portugal and Greece the coverage of these items seems to have some impact on dissatisfaction (see Table 7.1). The point is that these are the two countries where a high sensitivity to economic malaise (Portugal) and fiscal pressure (Greece) was already detected. Consequently, it would be wiser to look at this attention to austerity measures as a way of confirming the salience of the two other variables.

As mentioned in the previous section, a debate on welfare services and the consequent possible fear of losing recently established benefits might explain an increase of dissatisfaction despite no real change taking place. In Italy, during 1994–6, there is actually a cut in health expenditures and a discussion about this, the crisis of Berlusconi's cabinet on a bill concerning pensions, a subsequent law on this topic with the agreement of the unions, and again another debate on the necessity of cutting pension spending, that is, in a sector where the Italian government has the highest expenses in Western Europe. However, this does not coincide with the growth of dissatisfaction, which declines after the 1994 election. In Greece, a slight increase of discontent overlapped with the discussion of and protests against a new bill approved in 1992 on a social security system (IKA). IKA was facing financial bankruptcy, and the Nea Dimokratia government had to change the amount of contributions by both employers and employees, but the amount of pensions was not touched. On the contrary, in 1995 there was a slight increase in the pensions. In Spain and Portugal, welfare benefits are not seriously discussed. On the contrary, in the latter in 1990 and 1995, there is an improvement in pensions; and in Spain there was a cut in expenditures on a less important aspect regarding the abolition of temporary invalidity. On the whole, there is no serious connection between dissatisfaction and discussion on welfare cuts because in Italy the trend goes in the opposite direction; in Greece, if there is a reaction in terms of attitudes this is a minor one; and in Spain and Portugal, because no one seriously cast doubts on welfare institutions as they were.

The lines of this section and of the previous one on the possible explanations of dissatisfaction can be drawn up. The review of the press sources gives strong empirical support to the relevance of news on corruption for the growth of dissatisfaction. This is an important factor of perceived, political inefficacy in Italy and Greece—and for this second country this is so when the period 1988–9 is considered, but also with regards to the subsequent years. In the case of Greece, also the growth of fiscal pressure is important and when the 1985–95 period is considered, this is more important than corruption.[25] For Spain, reactions to economic malaise come first, and in the background there is the other

[25] With the limits of available data, a stepwise regression indicates fiscal pressure as the strongest explanatory factor.

most relevant reason, the reactions against corruption. Finally, for Portugal, economic malaise and reactions to the coverage of austerity measures, but not corruption, are the reasons to consider. Table 7.1 summarizes these points. The previous analysis of parties also suggested that ideological reasons such as the a-priori opposition to the incumbent party are relevant in both Greece and Italy. No doubt this analysis does not fully explain the deeper Italian crisis and the partial ones in the other countries. To do so, attention must be devoted to other features.

TABLE 7.1. *Correlations (r²) between dissatisfaction and certain variables in Southern Europe*

	Italy	Spain	Portugal	Greece
Index of misery	0.02	0.36	0.47	0.18
Fiscal pressure	0.08	0.01	0.07	0.44
Public debt	0.00	0.18	0.00	0.80
Austerity measures	0.04	0.01	0.28	0.36
Social expenditure	0.09	0.00	0.02	0.09
Corruption	0.27	0.20	0.11	0.30

Sources: Eurobarometer Surveys and see Appendix 7A.

Dissatisfaction and Protest: The Behaviour

'Tra il dire e il fare c'è di mezzo il mare.' This other well-known Italian proverb serves as a reminder that between simple declarations and the actions there is a world of difference. If not for other reasons, this alone would be sufficient to justify an analysis of the behaviour that could suggest an existing crisis and the extent of it, in addition to the dissatisfied attitudes and possible perceptions, reviewed in the two previous sections. Moreover, the behaviour may better clarify the reasons for those same attitudes.

Negative reactions against the government or different forms of protest, related to governmental decisions or hot issues, may be translated into electoral behaviours that punish the incumbent party. In some specific cases, however, there may be dissatisfaction and protest, but not changes in voting behaviours. This happened in the Italian case and has to be taken into account to better explain that crisis.[26] When there are strong anchors, as in Greece, the translation may be limited

[26] The next section will return to this.

and only take place after three close, subsequent elections. In Spain or Portugal,[27] 400,000 people or more profited from the electoral opportunity to express their discontent against the incumbent party, and changed their vote. In all four cases, the characteristics and origins of that discontent have still to be explained by the analysis of behaviours.

Before reviewing the data, it should be mentioned that the analysis of negative reactions can insert a systematic error in the explanation of crises. In fact, in the end, most negative reactions are the result of opposition, that is, of opposition parties and unions or other political organizations. This implies that once more civil society is not analysed *per se*, but as organized and directed by political society. There is an element of truth in this possible criticism. A way of circumventing the problem is to consider the behaviours, to check the consistency with attitudes mentioned in the previous sections, and above all to point out the trend in those manifestations. In fact, a growing trend in the protest implies a civil society that follows élites and organizations in its protest activity or other kinds of initiatives. However, autonomous organizations that are in a position to promote recurrent and continuous protest are usually backed by sectors of civil society.

Moreover, two other considerations are useful to understand the data. In Italy and Greece the tradition of participation and protest is stronger than in Portugal or Spain. This means that from a comparative perspective, the internal trend is again more relevant. In other words, the comparison should analyse above all the amount of growth or decline to check more correctly the depth of crisis. Second, a growth of negative reactions in a democracy where a more consensual political climate is the rule is more worrying in terms of crisis than a similar growth in a more conflictual climate. This is relevant for all four countries where such a growth at least denotes the corresponding decline of party dominance in those countries.

The first set of relevant data concerns all negative reactions related to salary, working conditions, economic malaise, and protest that may have a political or partisan component and are expressed in the strikes. Figure 7.7 gives the data on the four countries since 1981 and a few salient indications. As for Italy the main political explanation of the crisis is indirectly confirmed: in the early 1980s, at the end of the difficult period of 'national solidarity' there is more strike activity, but when the crisis really emerges, autonomous unions act in a very cautious way and during some transitional cabinets, such as Amato's and Ciampi's, there are even corporatist agreements among unions, the employer associations and the government. The serious economic problems,

---

[27] On the Spanish 1996 elections see Wert (1996); on the Portuguese 1995 election and the change of voting behaviour see *Expresso* (14 Oct. 1995, 29–41).

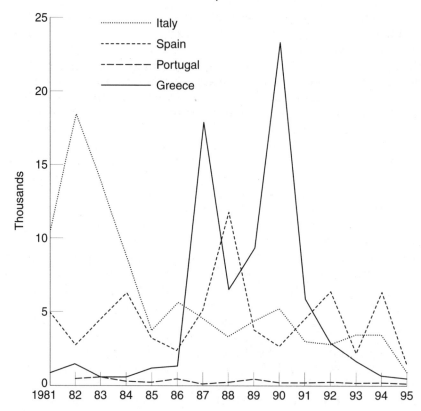

FIG. 7.7. *Trends of strikes in Southern Europe, 1981–1995*
Note: The strikes are indicated in thousands of lost days.
Sources: ILO *Yearbook of Labour Statistics*, various issues.

related to public debt and consequent necessities of reshaping the welfare state, are solved consensually, and when this is not so the unions are able to impose their positions by emerging as the key actors during the crisis of traditional parties, their organizations included.

In Greece the growth of strikes during 1987–90 with a peak in 1990 suggests that the crisis had also an economic component, but later the decline is not compounded by a parallel decline in dissatisfaction. Actually, in Greece there are a few components to disentangle and this is only possible through a qualitative analysis of the press. Such an analysis suggests, first, that in strike activity the partisan component is very strong: in a situation of inflation and economic malaise strike activity until 1989 is the result of socialist, leftist components of GSEE and other unions and of the communist component of the same unions. Inside the unions there is also a PASOK sector that is always against striking. The peak in 1990 is explained by the incumbency of Conservative government since April, that again brings together on the same side the main worker unions.

Second, the existence of strikes during that period suggests that the reasons of crisis is not only provided by scandals and corruption, and the beginning of mobilization for the *katharsis* (the cleaning from corruption) by opposition parties (Communists and Nea Dimokratia). These are very much relevant (see above), but they strengthen the widespread negative evaluation of PASOK government and its mismanagement. All this takes place in a society that feels the insecurity of inflation, fights for the adjustment of salaries to meet price increases (and the adjustments will be three in 1987, three in 1988, and three in 1989), asks for maintaining the control of house rents and the prices of basic foods, such as bread, and vigorously refuses the dismissal of workers in a welfare state that protects very badly against unemployment.

The third observation concerns the growing gap between the increasing attitudinal dissatisfaction with democracy and overall life, above all between 1992 and 1993 (see Figure 7.2), and the decline of strikes in the early, mid-1990s during the conservative cabinet and later with PASOK. Consequently, there is an attitudinal dissatisfaction that the civil society is not able—or unwilling—to translate into behaviours. There is also an additional decline after 1993, when PASOK came back into office, that can again be accounted for by strongly party-penetrated unions, and society as well. However, on the whole, the quantitative decline of strikes covers an intense activity of a civil society where the unions are very much present and party penetrated, but that actively fights against privatizations, worker dismissals, the 1992 reform of Social Security System, the freezing of wages, and for a better education, the protection of pensions or even for maintaining the possibility of tax evasion by protesting against the approval of 'objective' criteria for taxation. This controlled but active society is formed by students, middle and lower class associations, and unions of lawyers, doctors, tradesmen, artisans, farmers, that all ask conservative and socialist cabinets for an improvement of their living conditions, which governments are unable to provide. In this situation the true question is why neither a serious crisis nor a stronger political translation emerged in mid-1996, the Socialists are confirmed in the cabinet after the 1996 election, and the more serious indicators of political uneasiness are the deepening of internal party division and the consequent growth of effective parties.[28]

[28] For more analysis, see Chs. 2 and 6.

In Portugal, the lowest number of strikes among the four countries shows a moderate, basically passive society, that only had upsurges of mobilization in the most difficult years during the end of the 1970s and the early 1980s. In this country, however, the growth of dissatisfaction and the changes in the electoral behaviours with the consequent crisis of party systems are mirrored by a qualitative analysis, and again the press source is very useful for illustrating the protests and demonstrations of public employees for better wages, the activities of the farmer's union (CAP) and other sectoral unions for an improvement of governmental agricultural policies and a better defence of Portuguese interests in Brussels, the protest and riots of students against new university fees, and massive criticisms and protest against the privatizations that immediately caused worker dismissals. Such an economic uneasiness was also illustrated by threats of police strikes and army protest for better wages still in 1991. From this perspective, negative behavioural reactions in terms of criticisms and various forms of protest in 1991 and 1992 are consistently complemented by the growth of attitudinal dissatisfaction in the same years (see Figure 7.1), which are also the years of major privatizations. The protest and the growth of dissatisfaction are both lower in 1993–5, but as will be seen, in addition to scandals and corruption (see above), other factors intervene to establish bipolarization, and consequent change.

The Spanish strikes show a more active society where the unions even became part of the opposition while the Socialist Party was still in office (see Chapter 6). That is, to the political and ideological opposition of the Popular Party on one side of the political spectrum, another political opposition on the other side is provided by the allied unions, UGT and CCOO. This emerges in the strike activism, which remained at a relatively high level after the peak of 1988, a year that also marked the turning point in the relationships between PSOE and UGT. However, there is no full consistency between attitudinal dissatisfaction and strikes: the trend of the former steadily grows from 1991 through 1994 whereas strikes go up then down in the same years.

Again, for the explanation of dissatisfaction and a better understanding of negative reactions other data are needed. Table 7.2 is very telling: it groups all demonstrations and forms of protest held during the last decade according to the reasons for them. Such a table is also partially consistent with the growth of dissatisfaction. In fact, it can be easily seen that there is a jump in protest between 1989 and 1990 and later the level of negative reactions is high, and growing from 1992 to 1994. Once the years when educational reform was in the spotlight had elapsed, economy and economic policies were the main explanatory factors for the dissatisfaction and protest or, by and large, negative reac-

TABLE 7.2. *Demonstrations and protest in Spain, 1985–1994*

Years	Total	Economy[a]	Autonomy[a]	Education[a]
1985	5,248	49.8	4.6	9.5
1986	5,148	35.1	6.6	14.9
1987	8,144	38.6	7.2	19.7
1988	6,666	38.4	6.2	9.1
1989	6,393	38.4	8.6	8.0
1990	9,460	36.1	10.3	7.4
1991	11,815	36.0	7.5	4.8
1992	9,455	44.6	11.7	7.3
1993	9,711	35.6	15.3	9.6
1994	10,902	36.9	13.5	7.1

[a] The numbers are percentages of demonstrations according to three main reasons, organized by unions, *comités de empresa*, simple workers, employer associations, employers; by independentist groups and parties; and in the third case by teachers and their associations.

Source: The data were collected by Mellizo-Soto from the Ministries of Justice and the Interior.

tions. But from both Table 7.2 and the qualitative analysis of the press, in addition to reaction to corruption (see above and Figure 7.6), the issue of autonomy appears the second more important reason of discontent. And this is again consistent with the decisions made and the role taken by this issue during the last years of crisis of PSOE dominance and later, in 1996 when the Popular Party was not able to gain the parliamentary majority.

With regards to negative reactions a different analysis must be accorded to violent activities. They were an important part of Italian politics during the 1970s, and particularly at the end of the decade when Red Brigades were able to kidnap and then kill the influential leader, then President of Christian Democracy, Aldo Moro. At that moment this terrorist group provoked a strong defensive reaction of parties, the formation of the cabinet of National Solidarity, inaugurated just the day of Moro's kidnapping (16 March 1978), and the virtual block of any possible deeper political change at mass level, as well. In Greece and Spain, the two countries where this form of more radical protest existed during the last two decades, violence had a different political impact. Basically, people were able to live with it by acquiring a perverse habituation.

In Spain since 1985 the major terrorist actions were conducted by the well-known independentist organization, the ETA. Figure 7.8 records that activity. GRAPO performed a much more limited number

Facets of Crisis

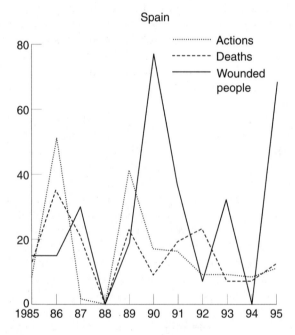

FIG. 7.8. *Major terrorist activities in Spain and Greece, 1985–1995*
Sources: See press and for Spain also Associación Victimas del Terrorismo.

of actions: it was present in 1990 with 9 main actions and 1993 with 4, which may be added to ETA actions for the total.[29] The terrorism of ETA is very much related to the political problem of Basque indepen- dentism, but not to dissatisfaction and protest. The societal habitua- tion to ETA actions made it basically impossible to compel the whole Spanish society to cope with that problem. As in Italy for a few years, that activity seems to go on because of inertia and the sympathies that the group enjoy in Basque regions.

Greek terrorist violence has different characteristics. It can be imputed to two main radical, leftist groups, '17 November' and ELA (Revolutionary Popular Struggle). Most actions are performed by '17 November' and are curiously related to the real issues of the moment: growth of salaries, corruption, tax increases, and so on. It seems a sort of political discourse developed with bombs and small rockets. Their goals are neither the unreal, maximalist goals of Italian and even Spanish terrorism nor linked to grand tenets. On the contrary, they are strictly embedded in everyday politics. More generally, the actions of 17 November and ELA have to be seen as the extreme example of a more radical society than the Spanish or Portuguese ones. In such a society, which remains deeply penetrated by parties and ideologies as well, there are also anarchists, the so-called 'autonomous' groups, and radical students, who are ready to clash with police. There is, in other words, the kind of availability to ideological and violent political behav- iour that was a recurrent feature of Italian society during the 1970s. From this perspective a proximity, although not mechanical consis- tency, with the activity of non-violent protest mentioned above, is fairly evident.

As a way of completing the analysis grounded on the same sources a profile of each country with more specific reference to the critical years may be developed with reference to the negative reactions in terms of issues, actors, and specific modes of protest. As for the issues, each country has mixed reasons for protest, but such a mix is a different one in each country: in Italy the economic issues are important, but cor- ruption and scandals and at the same time the protest to affirm basic rights illustrate again the political characteristics of crisis. In Greece too, economic issues are very much present in the key years of 1988–90, but during this period scandals and the initiatives for *katharsis* are the most relevant features. In Greece, however, above all during the 1990s, two other issues acquired relevance. The first one concerns education and the related vocal student protest, and this issue is present also in Portugal and still in Spain (see also Table 7.1). The second issue is

[29] There are also two other groups with episodic presence: GAL (see Ch. 6) and EGPGC.

related to the domestic impact of the peripheral geopolitical position of Greece. Accordingly, relations with Turkey, the problem of Macedonia-Skopje, the presence of a Muslim minority, and relationships with the European Union are also objects of protest and the creation of a climate of uncertainties that is part of the uneasiness that is emerging from these data, and from those on dissatisfaction too.[30] In the Portuguese and Spanish profiles economic issues are at the centre of protest. But for Spain reactions to corruption and protest for an additional affirmation of autonomy are also main features of the profile; for Portugal the above-mentioned student protest, but also the problem stemming from the European Union and in this way a peripheral syndrome, which is similar, but more attenuated than in Greece, have to be included.

As expected, there is strong consistency between actors of negative reactions and their modes, and here the differences in profiles are more pronounced, and in this sense more meaningful. In Italy unions and strikes, and also demonstrations, mass protest and clashes with police, but at the same time and with the same salience, criticisms and protest of various interest associations are at the core of political debate and of the existing crisis. In a second rank the parties come out, and a fairly relevant position acquired by the head of state, as vocal interpreter of popular discontent and demands. The anomaly in an institutional framework where the president of the Republic is supposed to have limited, formal powers is evident. But this point complements and is perfectly consistent with what has been stressed in Chapter 2 with reference to the extraordinary intervention of this office (see Chapter 2). In this country the presence of the protest of the general population additionally illustrates an active civil society that is ready and available for mobilization and participation. This feature has no parallel in the other three countries.

In Spain the negative reactions are also hegemonized by active unions and several interest associations. Parties are more present than in Italy, but again the most distinctive feature concerns the presence of local and regional authorities in political discourse and decision-making, also concerning economic issues such as fiscal policy. In Portugal the presence of interest associations is compounded by serious criticisms of opposition parties, and above all by the head of state. In a more obvious and legitimate way than in Italy because of the semi-presidential institution (see Chapter 2), the Portuguese president played an authentic role in political opposition, and these data would clearly suggest the contribution he gave to the crisis of the quasi-dominant party system. In terms of the autonomy of civil society, this is

---

[30] But this is an important point that will be developed in the next section.

more evident in Spain than in Portugal, mainly because on the one hand the anti-party role performed by UGT and CCOO in Spain and on the other, the partisan links with the Socialist Party of Portuguese President Soares. According to this analysis and the categories suggested in Chapter 1, semi-autonomy and semi-control would respectively be the models that better suit Spain and Portugal.

Actors and modes of protest confirm a radical, value-loaded, party-penetrated society in Greece. In fact, the internal division of the main worker peak organization, GSEE, with the Socialist left and Communists in favour of striking and mass demonstration openly comes out. In addition, the authors of the greater number of criticisms are institutional actors, and again they are mainly MPs belonging to opposition parties, dissenting ministers, local authorities who usually express partisan and limited views. In addition, it is confirmed that different forms of violent behaviours are a major part of negative reactions and in this vein of the political debate. It could be objected that the adopted source is biased on this point because it 'naturally' emphasizes the more radical and extreme behaviours. If so, radicalism should result as a recurrent characteristic of the other three countries. Actually, it is very partially present in Italy, and it is perfectly consistent with also the recent tradition of this country, but it is relatively marginal in the Spanish political arena with the specifications given on ETA activity, and very marginal in Portugal.

Disanchoring, Constraints, and Incentives

The analysis of the previous sections develops and deepens observations that were already mentioned in the second part of the previous chapter. There, other observations and details were also provided. At this point the whole process of larger or partial crises and changes can be better reconstructed and explained. The key point is to explain why a change of party systems was achieved at different moments in the three southern countries with the partial change of aspects in its consolidation, and why to a greater extent the whole model of consolidation was changed in Italy, despite elements of apparent continuity. Here again, an ironic aspect may be emphasized: while the apparently weak Italian formula of consolidation had persisted for three decades, again despite marginal changes, the other three consolidations were transformed in a few years. Moreover, while in Italy the change has been very profound in several aspects, in the other countries it has been smaller, but important: the only transformation from predominant or quasi-predominant party system to bipolarism is enough to account for a change in the present and future relationships with interests and the potential growing autonomy of civil society.

An effective and profound disanchoring takes place only in Italy. As mainly seen in the previous chapter, party organization, the possibilities of gatekeeping, and the same clientelist structure are transformed or disappear at least partially. In the other three countries there are changes, such as in Portugal with the great change of the presence of the public sector in the economy, but on the whole the disanchoring is a minor phenomenon that has an impact on the party system alone. The basic explanation I offer for these crises and the changes described above is grounded on the disappearance of constraints and emergence of incentives that élites and citizens exploit.

Thus, for Italy the hypothesis (see also Morlino and Tarchi 1996) is that in the early 1990s a 'window of opportunity' for the behavioural manifestation of discontent and protest was opened when a few constraints disappeared and other facilitating conditions emerged.[31] To put it in historical terms, the first constraining factor to fade away was the already mentioned collective memory of fascism and the war (see Chapter 3). For a long time, memories of fascism have prevented people from acting against democratic institutions. Hence the manifestation of dissatisfaction by moderate people has been blocked: the perceived inefficacy of institutions in fulfilling basic demands was kept on ice by that memory of worse moments in recent Italian history. During the 1970s and above all in the following decade, in spite of the emergence of a small, young neo-authoritarian component, the memory of the past was basically fading away as one generation succeeded another (see Morlino and Mattei 1992). Fascism was no longer an impending danger from any point of view.

Related to this memory, the anti-communist role of moderate parties was also itself slowly disappearing as can be seen in the declarations by leaders of those parties, notably among Christian Democrats. The defeat of terrorism in the early 1980s was a first step in this direction, but the integration of the left was the second more important moment. Therefore, when a new international set-up emerged from the breakdown of Eastern European Socialist regimes, in a highly symbolic moment the Communists felt obliged to form a new party, the PDS (see Chapter 2). The old fears within moderate opinion disappeared as well, and moderate voters became free to express their dislike for those same parties for which they had felt 'compelled' to vote in the past, while 'holding their noses'. They did this by shifting their consent to new parties and movements.

[31] We may recall the moderate attitudes shown by trade unions in the agreements signed with both Amato's cabinet and Ciampi's cabinet in 1992 and 1993.

Along with the secularization of society, the de-ideologization of politics—two widespread phenomena to be observed throughout Western Europe—the consequent disintegration of Catholic subcultures, and the diminishing polarization of conflicts, the fading away of those constraints account for the weakening of the links of partisanship, party attachment included, and the other anchors described in previous chapters (see Chapters 4 and 5). Whilst the organizational structures were gradually disappearing, the bases for an expression of dissatisfaction were laid. But this was not yet enough to transform a latent crisis into an open one. In a situation of deadlock the emergence of various incentives has also been decisive in creating the moment when the open crisis and change took place.

The incentives which emerged at the very beginning of 1990 are of a different sort, but they can be reduced to three: the delegitimating impact of the inquiry called 'Mani Pulite', the economic crisis, the Referendum of April 1993, and the subsequent change of electoral laws for parliament. First, scandals and corruption have been recurring in Italy since the 1950s: the front pages of all newspapers have given great emphasis to all these episodes of corruption, but without political consequences until the early 1990s, because earlier the mentioned constraints were still at work. On the contrary, in recent years the public prosecutors were very conscious of popular support, which gave them a greater autonomy vis-à-vis the executive power, and this was an important factor in enlarging the field of prosecutions. But from 1992 onwards, the news of widespread corruption in every sector of public life[32] and, above all, the impact of one specific trial, broadcast by a public TV channel every evening for almost two months,[33] this time provoked a strong delegitimation of all DC and PSI leaders.[34] To realize the impact of 'Mani Pulite', one may note that by the end of 1996 about 2,000 people had been prosecuted and about one-third had already been sentenced.[35] Other inquiries were undertaken in a few other towns, such as Rome, Perugia, La Spezia, Naples, Brescia, and Salerno. They stress how widespread the corruption was. Briefly, the action of a 'neutral power', such as the magistracy, gave the dissatisfied groups of

[32] Actually, it had become a way of expressing interest. On this aspect of Italian democracy see Morlino (1991*a*).

[33] The trial was because of a few instances of kickbacks (*tangenti*) in the selling of an important company in the chemical industry. Actually, it became a trial against the entire governmental class, and the programme had enormous success.

[34] In the elections of 1994 there were more than 70% of deputies elected for the first time (see Verzichelli 1995).

[35] These data were given by the office of the public prosecutor in Milan and published by newspapers (see e.g. *Corriere della Sera*, 9 Feb. 1996).

citizens the additional stimulus to cut their links with traditional parties.[36]

Secondly, it should not be forgotten that for decades the traditional decisional inefficacy of Italian institutions has been counterbalanced by efficiency at the micro- and local level (see Chapter 5). In the new context, the prolonged economic crisis and the impossibility of continuing with the same patronage system emphasized the unbearable costs of the protracted partisan occupation of the state. At this point, corruption, exacerbated partisanship, the inefficiency of the civil service, and even collusion between institutional powers and organized crime could become the main targets for the mobilizing controversies of old and new political leaders and associations of protest with some chance of success. In fact, the regional Leagues, La Rete, Segni's movement in favour of referenda, the Greens, the neo-communists, the plethora of single-issue lists had all emerged since the 1990 local elections. It should again be stressed that, with the exception of Uomo Qualunque in 1946[37] for at least two decades discontent led only to modest gains of the vote for extremist parties and no mass movement was born until the early 1990s.

Third, the April 1993 referendum, prepared by some of the old traditional leaders—particularly, the Christian Democrat Mario Segni—expressed the citizen demand for a change in the electoral laws towards a majority system, with the manifest purpose of achieving a higher efficacy in parliamentary decision-making. The approval of new electoral laws for the Senate and Lower Chamber (see Chapter 2) is an additional incentive for change. But, as already mentioned, at the grassroots of everything there is the dissatisfaction, the perceived inefficacy, and since 1990 the actual possibility of translating attitudinal discontent into electoral behaviours.

For the other three countries the interplay of constraints and incentives unfolded in only a few years and other factors have to be stressed. As pointed out by the previous analysis, the interest of the Greek case lies in the evident necessity of distinguishing two key periods. The first one, which has been at the centre of attention, encompasses the 1989–90 years when there is the definite crisis of PASOK dominance and of its pervasive anchoring in civil society. The second moment comes later, and above all after 1993.

The reasons for the 1989–90 crisis should be clear at this point. In a context of economic malaise and disappearance of political constraints

---

[36] It also provoked the rapid growth of that same dissatisfaction.

[37] In that year the Fronte dell'Uomo Qualunque, which campaigned against both fascism and anti-fascist parties, collected 5.3% of the votes and 30 seats in the elections for the first post-war democratic parliament.

because of the largely inclusive legitimation, but also because information improved with the creation of the first private radio and TV channels since 1987–8, two main incentives emerged: on the one hand, the attempt of an until then populist leader and government to rescue the bad economic situation with several 'austerity measures' and the uncovering of widespread corruption, on the other. The negative reactions to the policies gave a sense of an existing gap between earlier satisfied but subsequently disappointed citizens and a populist leader and government that had necessarily to cope with a troublesome economic situation. The news on corruption and scandals, and the mobilization of opposition on this issue with the *katharsis*, became at this point a determining element in delegitimating personalized governments and consequently partially weakening the existing anchors. Finally, the elections gave the opportunity to change the party system. But this was done step by step with the three consecutive elections, and PASOK came back into office at the next electoral occasion. The popular unwillingness to accept a restrictive political economy encouraged the new change of incumbency in 1993.

The second moment came after 1993. Here, the question is the most salient one: how is it possible that a growing dissatisfaction, which has a behavioural translation into criticisms and protest, is not complemented by a change of electoral preferences when in 1996 there is the possibility of doing that, and the most relevant aspects that emerge are deeper intra-party conflicts and subsequent party splits and higher effective number of parties? In a situation where there are no longer specific incentives for change, there are no strong scandals, and the death of Papandreu in June 1996 eliminated the protest against his personalized leadership, the old partisan anchors seems to be re-established. No doubt the very mechanisms of bipolarization, where— it should be recalled—the electoral law still plays an important role, contribute to that outcome, but there is also the simple fact that the economic problems are the most relevant ones, and discontented people cannot trust the rightist Nea Dimokratia to solve them. In other words, the peculiarities of the unsolved problems help maintain the previous anchors: in a situation of dissatisfaction and discontent of an economic kind where the welfare state has to be defended as much as possible, only a technocratic left represented at its best by Simitis can cope with those problems. In 1996–7 Simitis showed a great deal of caution in implementing a major programme of privatization. Consequently, a basic change in the consolidation formula will come out gradually , and a possible weakening of all anchors, clientelism included, will take place very slowly, only under the spur of European Union policy constraints.

In Portugal and Spain, more than in Greece, the analysis developed in the previous and current chapters had to be maintained within the lines of a crisis of the party systems alone. In both countries the key point, however, is to understand why and how the dominant or quasi-dominant party lost its position and consequently a new bipolarization became established. As seen in the previous chapter, in Portugal there were no longer specific constraints. On the one hand, in the 1990s the marginalized Communist Party or an integrated small right could not have been an obstacle to bipolarization. On the other hand, the deep change in the model of consolidation brought about by Cavaco Silva partially weakened the partisan and clientelistic anchors of consolidation. In this vein, the interaction between an élite decision to cope with the existing problems, i.e. the privatizations, and the discontent at mass level are at the grassroots of the outcome.

The incentive for change came from three main sources: reactions to corruption, economic malaise, and the role of the president of the Republic. The delegitimating impact of episodes of corruption, however, seems very marginal, and in any case not central in the public debate. The two other factors are much more crucial in accounting for the result. The first one, very powerful, is the economic malaise compounded by the fear of unemployment caused by those same policies of privatization. The second one is the actual role of institutional opposition performed by the Socialist President Soares, who profited from every occasion to take the central public role, often by containing the government. Here again, the opportunity given to people is the electoral one, and they are pushed to profit from it. As in Greece, when there are economic problems and the necessity of defending a young, imperfect, and dissatisfying welfare state, leftist parties are seen as best suited to coping with these problems and defending a moderate middle class of civil servants and workers threatened with dismissal. In Portugal, Socialists were ready to cash both cheques: one indirectly offered by the president and the other by the fear of more drastic measures by a centre-right party without Cavaco and with a tough 'curriculum' of austerity.

As for Spain, the changes are even more limited, basically along the lines of 'business as usual'. In this country, survey analyses and also press sources showed the gradual emergence of the potential for alternation once the Popular Party was considered completely integrated, thanks also to its changes at the end of the 1980s (see Chapter 6). In this way, a moderate electorate became fully 'unfrozen'. Something very similar to the Italian case took place, although it concerned the right and not the left and the extent of the phenomenon is largely different. The kind of constraint, however, that faded away is the same:

no fear of switching his vote to a party that has become fully democratic, the lapse of time, and a new generation that no longer remembers the traces of Francoism.

As basically emerged in the previous analysis, economic problems in a 'statist culture' at a mass level, the economic policies of the Socialist government, even against the union positions, and the persisting presence of scandals and corruption in everyday political debate are the three incentives to insert into the picture. The opportunities were offered by the local and national votes, and given the relatively weak and indirect anchoring that characterized the consolidation in that country, the outcome is even easier to explain.

The limited Spanish crisis would be misunderstood if the ongoing demand for decentralization and autonomy were not adequately considered as an additional incentive for change. It is well known how historically important and regionally different the Spanish ethnic cleavage was, how it became the symbol of the deep crisis of the Second Republic during the final months of its existence in 1936, how the authoritarian Francoism made even more profound and politically salient such a cleavage by trying to suppress it. An electoral law with small electoral constituencies, which gives an advantage to parties with a local, concentrated distribution of the vote, contributed to the growing weight of regional parties, with regionalized interest groups as well, and consequently to a deepening of that cleavage. As pointed out in Chapter 2, despite the institutional, electoral, party and élite consolidation, this cleavage never became completely settled: on the contrary, the crisis of Socialist dominance refuelled it by accentuating the allocation of decision-making processes toward the different regional centres. The pivotal position of regional parties at a parliamentary level also allows an even higher autonomy.

As a concluding remark, the kind of crisis that took place in all four countries can be specified. When, as has been done here, the relationships among civil society, parties, and government institutions are at the core of internal democratic crisis, then the key features concern the representative system. Thus, in Italy there is a crisis of the whole system of representation with all the features that have been described in this and previous chapters; a partial crisis of party dominance, concerning the Socialists, and the change to multiparty bipolarism took place in Spain. In between there are the Portuguese and Greek experiences. In Portugal the crisis of Social-democratic shorter dominance and the establishment of bipolarism is complemented by the change of another basic element of consolidation formula with the squeezing of the public sector; in Greece the crisis of the socialist attempt to establish its dominance and the definite affirmation of bipolarism is followed by a latent dissatisfaction without strong consequences in terms of anchoring. In all four cases crisis has not to be considered a threat to democracy, as in earlier times. A new notion of it should be kept in mind as a first indication that in the representative network some aspect may change to a greater or lesser extent. To be sure this is also so because the four countries are definitely part of the European Union with a thick network of political, social, and economic links.

Appendix

TABLE 7.A1. *Consumer price indices in national currency (1985 = 100)*

	Italy	Greece	Spain	Portugal
1980	52.5	39.1	65.0	35.2
1981	61.9	48.7	72.9	42.2
1982	72.1	58.9	79.2	51.7
1983	82.7	70.8	86.2	64.8
1984	91.6	83.8	93.1	83.8
1985	100.0	100.0	100.0	100.0
1986	105.9	123.1	104.2	111.7
1987	110.9	143.2	108.6	122.2
1988	116.5	162.6	112.6	133.9
1989	123.8	184.9	120.0	151.0
1990	131.8	222.6	127.4	170.9
1991	140.0	266.0	132.8	189.6
1992	147.3	308.1	136.7	206.7
1993	153.8	352.6	139.7	220.0
1994	160.0	391.1	141.2	231.5

Source: Eurostat, *Social Protection Expenditure and Receipts 1980–1994* (1996).

TABLE 7.A2. *Unemployment rates (%)*

	Italy	Greece	Spain	Portugal
1980	5.6	2.8	11.5	8.0
1981	6.3	4.0	14.3	7.7
1982	6.9	5.8	16.4	7.5
1983	7.7	7.9	18.2	7.8
1984	8.5	8.1	20.1	8.6
1985	8.6	7.8	21.5	8.7
1986	9.9	7.4	21.0	8.6
1987	10.2	7.4	20.5	7.1
1988	10.5	7.7	19.5	5.8

	Italy	Greece	Spain	Portugal
1989	10.2	7.5	17.3	5.1
1990	9.1	7.0	16.3	4.7
1991	8.6	7.7	16.3	4.2
1992	8.8	8.7	18.4	4.1
1993	10.2	9.7	22.7	5.6
1994	11.3	9.6	24.2	6.9
1995	12.0	10.0	22.9	7.2

Source: OECD, *Economic Outlook*, 59 (June 1996).

TABLE 7.A3. *Real GDP*

	Italy	Greece	Spain	Portugal
1980	879.69	70.26	365.97	50.18
1981	884.54	70.30	365.33	50.99
1982	886.43	70.58	371.05	52.08
1983	895.01	70.86	379.28	51.99
1984	919.09	72.81	384.85	51.01
1985	942.95	75.08	394.90	52.44
1986	970.50	76.30	407.54	54.61
1987	1,000.93	75.95	430.53	57.64
1988	1,041.62	79.33	452.75	60.98
1989	1,072.24	82.53	474.20	64.48
1990	1,095.12	81.84	491.94	67.24
1991	1,108.27	84.70	503.10	68.68
1992	1,116.37	85.04	506.46	69.43
1993	1,103.22	84.26	500.56	68.63
1994	1,127.23	85.49	511.10	69.15

Source: OECD, *National Accounts*, vol. I (1996).

TABLE 7.A4. *Total tax revenue as percentage of GDP*

	Italy	Greece	Spain	Portugal
1980	30.2	29.4	24.1	25.2
1981	31.4	29.6	25.4	26.7
1982	33.7	33.4	25.6	27.4
1983	35.8	33.9	27.5	28.9
1984	34.9	34.9	28.8	28.4
1985	34.5	35.1	28.8	27.8
1986	36.0	36.9	30.6	29.4
1987	36.1	37.2	32.5	27.6

TABLE 7.A4. *cont.*

	Italy	Greece	Spain	Portugal
1988	36.7	34.9	32.8	30.1
1989	37.9	34.6	34.6	30.8
1990	39.1	37.5	34.4	31.0
1991	39.7	39.0	34.7	31.7
1992	42.1	40.8	36.0	33.4
1993	43.8	41.2	35.0	31.4
1994	41.7	42.5	35.8	33.0

Source: OECD, *Revenue Statistics of OECD Member Countries 1965–1995* (1996).

TABLE 7.A5. *General government gross financial liabilities*[a]

	Italy	Greece	Spain	Portugal
1980	53.0	22.9	6.1	33.0
1981	56.4	27.1	9.2	41.6
1982	62.6	29.8	13.0	44.6
1983	67.4	34.0	18.5	49.7
1984	73.0	40.9	22.0	55.4
1985	80.0	47.8	27.5	58.5
1986	84.3	48.4	30.1	68.7
1987	88.5	53.3	30.7	66.2
1988	90.9	63.5	31.4	67.1
1989	93.9	66.6	30.9	65.1
1990	84.4	90.2	31.7	65.5
1991	89.4	92.4	33.4	70.2
1992	95.7	99.3	35.1	62.4
1993	103.7	111.8	42.0	67.3
1994	109.1	110.4	45.9	69.6
1995	107.5	111.8	48.7	71.7

Note: [a] This table previously appeared under the title Gross Public Debit.

Source: OECD, *Economic Outlook*, 60 (1996).

TABLE 7A6. *Social protection current expenditure per head in PPS*[a]

	Italy	Greece	Spain	Portugal
1980	1,414.7	435.6	914.9	524.0
1981	1,698.1	529.1	1,073.6	659.9
1982	1,876.6	684.8	1,159.5	691.5
1983	2,116.1	761.5	1,243.5	729.5
1984	2,210.1	870.4	1,325.1	755.0
1985	2,432.2	991.2	1,464.2	814.8
1986	2,569.0	1,039.7	1,533.3	886.0

	Italy	Greece	Spain	Portugal
1987	2,765.9	1,096.8	1,656.7	950.4
1988	3,001.2	1,162.6	1,821.1	1,099.6
1989	3,224.8	1,340.3	2,036.3	1,197.5
1990	3,581.2	1,358.7	2,269.9	1,306.2
1991	3,907.4	1,385.8	2,625.8	1,659.4
1992	4,270.4	1,434.5	2,801.7	1,856.9
1993	4,223.8	1,574.7	3,020.4	1,995.8
1994	4,311.7	1,644.9	3,019.7	2,162.4

Note: ᵃ PPS is the Purchasing Power Standard specific to private consumption.

Source: Eurostat, *Social Protection Expenditure and Receipts 1980–1994* (1996).

Conclusions: A Theory of Anchoring?

Theory may be understood in a traditional, orthodox way as a set of related generalizations and explanations that are also predictions (see e.g. Kaplan 1963). It may also have a more realistic meaning as 'local theory' (Boudon 1984). In macro-politics this is characterized by a few broad hypotheses about a precise geopolitical area, in a specific historical period, with a definite socio-economic background and political tradition. The analysis developed in the previous seven chapters has sketched out something very close to such a theory with reference to the four countries of Southern Europe, after the Second World War, and given the characteristics of countries with authoritarian experiences. The 'export' of such a theory is surely possible by emphasizing and integrating the main variables and processes that are involved with all the other elements suggested by the politico-cultural traditions and socio-economic background of the other countries, such as those in Latin America or Eastern Europe, that are confronted with similar problems.

This 'theory of anchoring' suggests that democratic consolidation and crisis can be explained by the diverse and changing connections between legitimation and a few precise anchors. The main related conclusions may be simplified and summarized in the following propositions:

1. To detect and measure consolidation and crisis, a few aspects concerning the institutional, electoral, party, and élite domains must be explored, but the main attention should be paid to parties and their connections with civil society.
2. The two basic processes of consolidation and crisis are characterized by a bottom-up phenomenon—legitimation—and a top-down phenomenon—the anchoring of civil society.
3. Legitimation is always formed by two distinct aspects that are intertwined, consensus at a mass level and support at an élite level.
4. The development of legitimation may be distinctively detected, although a precise quantitative analysis of it is not always possible.

5. The anchors are shaped during the first years after the installation and to a greater or lesser extent are weakened or transformed during the crisis.
6. The main anchors are party organization, the function of gatekeeping, clientelist ties, and neo-corporatist arrangements.
7. To achieve consolidation, the more exclusive the legitimacy, the stronger and more developed the anchors.
8. To achieve consolidation, alternatively, the more inclusive the legitimacy, the weaker the anchors may be.
9. Anchors, however, are always very important to understand better which types of consolidation and democracy emerge.
10. The 'formulas' of consolidation are defined by the actors in the different mix of the two sub-processes.
11. These 'formulas' are party consolidation, state consolidation, and élite consolidation.
12. The outcomes of those processes are different models of democracies where institutional aspects, party systems, and the relationships among parties and civil society are considered.
13. Consolidation formulas contain the seeds of their own self-destruction, such as long incumbency, no alternation in office, no partners in cabinet, an unitarian state, overdeveloped party organizations, strong party links with interest groups, a 'frozen' moderate electorate, and no signs of dissatisfaction in the moderate groups.
14. Crises are related to the previous consolidation formulas. They are the result of interactions between élites and citizens that affect the existing anchors in different ways and to a different extent.
15. At a mass level, attitudes, perceptions of inefficacy, and negative reactions are the most crucial aspects to explore for analysing the crisis.
16. Crisis is mainly explained by weakening of anchors, together with fading constraints and emerging incentives.

In an effort at simplification it can be affirmed that the propositions sketched above basically point to the strong connection between levels and dimensions of legitimation and forms of anchoring. The main, apparently paradoxical, result is that consolidation is also achieved with low legitimacy. If so, however, strong anchoring is needed. The consequent, successful consolidation brings about a subsequent, more and more inclusive legitimation. Consequently, strong anchoring is superfluous, and its costs more evident and unbearable. The road to crisis is paved, and the counter-intuitive connection between consolidation and crisis clarified. Within this perspective a phase of crisis is not at all necessary. It is not bound to take place after consolidation. But it is more probable when additional legitimation unfolds, while a strong anchoring remains. Even more, its depth depends on the strength of anchoring. Thus, when legitimacy becomes a more inclusive one, and in addition specific problems and related dissatisfaction grow, the four modes of anchoring (see proposition 6) are undermined, and a process of change unfolds.

The four cases also show that the point of arrival of such a process is also dependent on the choices made by political élites: more conservative élites, like the Italian ones, or more open to innovation, as the Portuguese ones. The first, the Italian ones,[1] were more conservative as they felt more threatened and strove for achieving some continuity; the others were more innovative as they felt safer, although they eventually lost the 1995 election. In any case, these propositions give a central role to actors and particularly to parties and party élites and their interactions with civil society. This is so even in the case of an apparently weaker anchoring, namely in Spain. The combination of a fairly manipulative electoral system, internal party discipline, rules of parliamentary standing order in favour of parties, constitutional rules that support the dominance of cabinet over parliament, the very role assigned by democracy and elections to parties, a strong socialist leadership—all these account for the key position of parties in Spanish consolidation and crisis. Consequently, the anchors may be comparatively weak, but they work effectively as they are helped by the other mentioned aspects (see Chapter 6).

The analysis developed in the previous chapters stressed that parties and party élites are even more crucial in the other three countries. Moreover, the 'statist' conception, which is strongly present in Southern European cultures, and at the same time the serious economic problems of those countries with an inactive civil society and fairly recent[2] and limited welfare states put the demand for solutions to problems even more into the hands of party élites—or rather, they at least made those élites the crucial ones in the mediation between highly conflictual interests in a context of scarce or diminishing resources.

In this sense, the research cannot join the large literature that affirms the lower, declining role of parties. Those authors often point to the widespread delegimating attitudes and low sympathy toward parties,[3] but this is actually an imputation of responsibility to them for the

---

[1] Although they are basically substituted. See the data on élite turnover in Ch. 2.

[2] In three cases out of four.

[3] Specifically on anti-party sentiments, see the excellent contribution by Poguntke (1996).

existing problems, and this confirms their crucial salience. The four countries point to a *de facto* similar direction that may be synthesized by 'we despise them, but we need them', a maxim already discussed in Chapter 3. On the whole, with the disappearance of parties as structures of integration and legitimation, these same actors increasingly take on another, even stronger, pivotal role as problem solvers or at least as institutions to which people look at to solve collective problems. In this vein, the strong centrality of leaders and parties with light organizations is perfectly understandable.

To parties and party organizations, as key elements of anchoring and dis-anchoring, the other basic anchors have to be added and emphasized. The varieties of gatekeeping, the reproduction of patronage, the emergence of neo-corporatist agreements may be—or become—even more important than party organizations for consolidation. But this is not the crucial point. The crucial point is rather in the self-reinforcing and overlapping mix of the anchors, in the fact that such a mix differs from one case to another, and finally that it is buttressed by various few institutional rules, as shown above for Spain and already mentioned for all cases in Chapter 6. In other words, the problem is not how to build or maintain strong party organizations, as has been stated for years. This is simply impossible in a number of cases for several reasons, such as past traditions, recent experiences, or de-ideologization of the civil society. Instead the problem is finding the best possible mix to accommodate the varieties of interests, as suggested even earlier by Lindblom (1959). On the ground of this empirical research, such a mix seems an unavoidable element of democracy. The simplest explanation is that one or more forms of anchoring are necessarily favoured by the very democratic rules, and wanted by political élites. Anchoring also means continuity and resistance to change, and several, additional negative features may be added in terms of democratic ideals. However, they not only characterize democracy, but also introduce stability and efficacy related to policies enacted for a longer time. And this is a goal pursued by élites, but it also has objective advantages at least for different sectors of population.

Moreover, such a mix of anchoring accounts not only for the consolidation or crisis, but also for the specific implemented consolidation and the partial crisis. With reference to the crisis, this may be partial as it only involves an anchor or a single aspect of it, but is however relevant because it also affects the whole mix. As for the consolidation, the most interesting problem is not democratic consolidation *per se*. In terms of symbols, declaration and more generally visible politics, democracy is so widely accepted that the point is not to explain why a democracy has become consolidated. The more interesting and relevant problem is to describe and explain what the specific consolidation formula was. The basic reason for this is, additionally, to consider what kind of democracy emerged, also in terms of 'democratic quality', that is, with reference to the actual implementation of some democratic tenets.

The specific formulas of consolidation were revealed as of short duration in three cases out of four: on the whole, about a decade in Spain, four to five years in Greece, and about eight years in Portugal. These were inclusive or quasi-inclusive processes. Consequently, the most unstable cases were those with relatively higher democratic legitimation. Conversely, the most stable case—Italy—was the one with the lowest and exclusive legitimation. This once more confirms the freezing impact of exclusive legitimation when there is strong anchoring. In the unstable[4] cases there has been a partial crisis of the party systems, and other transformations, such as the size of the public economic sector in Portugal.

This entailed the transformation from various forms and degrees of party dominance (see Chapter 6) towards multipartism and bipolarism. In the Italian case, the one with the longest duration of consolidation formulas, crisis and change has been deeper, and bipolarism is still very weak, and only electoral. It is partially encouraged by a mixed electoral system,[5] which was a conscious decision by party élites, and more open and unconstrained electoral competition, but contrasted by high party fragmentation, the pivotal role of centrist formations in determining the electoral results, and parliamentary dominance in interactions with government.

Despite its weaknesses and all the involved requisites of information and evaluation currently at work, bipolarity is the democratic device that gives some actual content to political accountability.[6] Dahl (1971: 3) considers it an essential institutional guarantee because 'institutions for making government policies depend on votes and other expressions of preference'. In fact, institutions 'depend on votes' and political responsibility and accountability may be implemented only if there is bipolarity and alternation in government. Moreover, when

---

[4] Here the reference is to stability or instability of a specific democracy, not of the democratic regimes of those countries. This is not at all the object of any challenge.

[5] Let it be recalled that this system is actually a mixed system, and worked in a fairly proportional way in the last 1996 election. On this specific point, see Morlino (1997).

[6] Of course, it is possible to create and strengthen other forms of accountability, such as—for example—that deriving from strongly participative democracy with several committees in the ministries and at local level, or through the allocation of different decisional arenas at a local level. There is a large literature on these topics. Here, let it suffice to point out that participative democracy presupposes strongly articulated civil society. If this is not so, as in several areas of Southern Europe, then it becomes either another mode of party or bureaucratic clientelism, or arenas taken over by union leaders.

there is a civil society that is penetrated by parties or with a poor autonomous structuration, the higher actual form of accountability is only achieved through bipolarization and bipolarity, with low radicalization.[7] Accordingly, the changes in Southern Europe better implement that institutional guarantee, by also reducing the inconsistency between public opinion and policy (discussed by Brooks (1988) with reference to Spain, Portugal, and Greece in the first part of the 1980s), which characterized those consolidations.

Bipolarization may have two other positive impacts to take into account. First, as can be indirectly deduced by this analysis, it may slowly prime a process of autonomization of civil society. Interests and interest organizations may find it more convenient to assume a neutral position (see Chapter 5) vis-à-vis the party élites. This mainly implies the possibility of more autonomous unions and higher potential for protest, and employers that more openly and consistently maintain their neutrality. Second, the persistence of two moderate alternatives over a long period may be another way of anchoring, which can actually be very strong because of its high internal flexibility, complemented by various high external barriers. Within this perspective, strong party organization or other anchors would not be needed. All that would be necessary is the presence and persistence of the same two alternatives, and of them alone, without a relevant growth of radicalization. This may be achieved with electoral laws that erect high barriers against the entrance of additional actors, such as in Greece, or corporatist arrangements that in fact have the same effect. The old suggestion by Schattschneider (1942) about the strengthening impact of bipartism may be reconsidered from this perspective.

Bipolarity, alternation, an established, acknowledged role of opposition, light or very light anchoring, and greater autonomy of an active civil society would point to the achievement of such societal consolidation. Such a consolidation is also characterized by a network of institutions that allow for democratic integration, by both the representation of interests and their participation in the decision-making process, in some cases by an intermediate important regional or federal level, by large private sectors and associations of civil society that articulate their interests without party gatekeeping or patronage, and are able to influence policies that concern them (see Chapter 6). While this is an open possibility for all four countries, however, at the end of the 1990s, none of the four countries seems to be close to that result. In the

---

[7] For this distinction between bipolarization and radicalization, see Morlino (1996). In a nutshell, bipolarization with low radicalization or without it refers to situations where two parties or two political alliances are not compounded by democratic alienation, and by anti-regime positions.

Spanish bipolar reconsolidation, as well as in that of Portugal and Greece, parties are still very relevant, and civil society is not particularly autonomous. One might also wonder whether such a result would be a completely positive one in our cases. In a more pessimistic hypothesis of a very serious economic crisis with high unemployment and more radical, active protest, the partisan anchors may again perform the same precious moderating and integrative role that they did in the past; and in this not a totally abstract hypothesis, all other forms of anchoring will also become essential to defending the democratic regime.

In the Italian case, bipolarity is weak and the challenge of secession by the Northern League, based upon high economic dissatisfaction, makes the hypothesis of societal reconsolidation even more distant. In the future of this country, there are two possible different paths. The first is an institutional reform that makes parliament much closer to and directed by the government, and at the same time an electoral system with higher reductive effects vis-à-vis a highly fragmented party system. In other words, what is needed is an institutional reform that broke some key element of the exisiting continuity, such as the dominance of parliament in legislative activity and the very high party fragmentation, by making Italian institutional design much closer to that of the other three countries. Although a steep path, there is a real possibility of approval of such reforms only thanks to a strong commitment of élites in this direction. The objective elements, namely, the high numbers of actors and the consensual traditions would bring an opposite direction, and in the best outcome a rationalization of a consensual model.[8]

Consequently, the second path seems a careful, cautious, and consensual management of the economic situation with entrance into the European single currency system, whilst the weak thrust toward bipolarization, embedded in the electoral system, and a more open competition among the parties release all its effects for bipolarization, to be established at least at the electoral level. This path needs a much longer time to develop all its effects, but it is less traumatic, and more realistic. Furthermore, the consensual path can be followed without being explicitly chosen, and this makes it even more probable. Whatever the result, however, all modes of anchoring still remain essential for the present democratic regime, challenged by the well-known economic problems and the radical strategy of the Northern League.

Anchoring will also remain a basic aspect in the other three democracies. But as it has been partially for the present, even more in the

---

[8] At the end of June 1997 the outcomes of the Committee formed by representatives of parties from both Chambers and appointed with reforming purposes pointed to this direction.

future of all four countries there is the European 'framework'. The implementation of a single currency and other policies of convergence, envisaged by the Maastricht Treaty and subsequent agreements, create a general context that can be defined as 'pre-federative'. To be sure all this will have an impact on those anchors in a way that is difficult to anticipate precisely at the end of 1990s, although some of them, such as gatekeeping and patronage, appear much more vulnerable and even bound to disappear to a great extent than the others.[9]

However, these and other changes should not affect the only positive results that the democratic regimes of Southern Europe have been able to achieve in the two main directions of democratic 'quality'—bipolarity and the welfare state—despite the weak, sometimes simply poor civil societies. Both results were achieved after a long, difficult, and sometimes painful road that has also spanned the last years of this century. They are minimal results, very far away from the great expectations and the perfectionist, utopian, radical ideals that several élites have been cultivating for years, from the Second Spanish Republic to the Portuguese Revolution of Carnation. No wonder that some élites and sectors of civil society, also for selfish reasons, believe that defending and hopefully strengthening these outcomes, even through all necessary adaptations and changes, but also against the constraints coming from the European Union, is the only way to avoid becoming once again 'democracies without quality'.

[9] This analysis eventually focused upon the domestic factors, although there is no doubt that the European factor can be a source of strain and challenge to several political and economic aspects of the four countries. On this see Whitehead (1996, esp. chs. on Southern Europe).

．．．．．．．．．．．．．．

References

．．．．．．．．．．．．．．．

Note: the most relevant surname for the identification of Portuguese authors is the second. Such authors are listed in the References according to second surname, e.g. Manuel Braga da Cruz can be found under Cruz, M. Braga da.

ACCORNERO, A. (1992), *La Parabola del Sindacato* (Bologna, Il Mulino).

ACHIMASTOS, M. (1996), 'Le Mouvement Socialiste panhellénique et l'implantation de l'idéologie populiste dans un régime pluraliste', in M. Lazar (ed.), *La Gauche en Europe depuis 1945: Invariants et mutations du socialisme européen* (Paris, Presses Universitaires de France), 347–65.

AGGER, R. E., GOLDSTEIN, M. N., and PEARL, S. A. (1961), 'Political Cynicism: Measurement and Meaning', *Journal of Politics*, 23: 477–506.

AGÜERO, F. (1995), *Militares, civiles y democracia: La España postfranquista en perspectiva comparada* (Madrid, Alianza Editorial).

AGUIAR, J. (1983), *A ilusão do poder: Análise do sistema partidário português 1976–1982* (Lisbon, Publicações Dom Quixote).

—— (1994), 'Partidos, eleições, dinâmica política', *Análise social*, 29 (1/2): 171–236.

AGUILAR, S., and ROCA, J. (1989), *14-D: Economía política de una huelga* (Barcelona, Fundació Jaume Bofill).

ALACEVICH, F. (1996), *Le Relazioni industriali in Italia: Cultura e strategie* (Rome, La Nuova Italia Scientifica).

ALBERONI, F. (1967) (ed.), *L'Attivista di partito* (Bologna, Il Mulino).

ALEXAKIS, E. G. (1993), 'The Greek Right: Structure and Ideology of the New Democracy Party', Ph.D. dissertation (London, London School of Economics).

ALIVIZATOS, N. (1990), 'The Difficulties of "Rationalization" in a Polarized Political System: The Greek Chamber of Deputies', in Liebert and Cotta 1990: 131–53.

ALLUM, P. A. (1975), *Potere e società a Napoli nel dopoguerra* (Turin, Einaudi Editore).

ALMARCHA BARBADO, A. (1993) (ed.), *Spain and EC Membership Evaluated* (London, Pinter Publishers).

ALMOND, G. A., FLANAGAN, S., and MUNDT, R. J. (1973) (eds.), *Crisis, Choice and Change. Historical Studies of Political Development* (Boston, Little, Brown and Company).

—— and VERBA, S. (1963), *The Civic Culture: Political Attitudes and Democracy in Five Nations* (Princeton, Princeton University Press).

AMODIA, J. (1996), 'Spain at the Polls: The General Election of 3 March 1996', *West European Politics*, 19 (4): 813–19.

ANDERSON, C. (1995), 'Party Systems and the Dynamics of Government Support: Britain and Germany, 1960–1990', *European Journal of Political Research*, 27 (1): 93–118.

ARIAN, A., and BARNES, S. (1974), 'The Dominant Party System: A Neglected Model of Democratic Stability', *Journal of Politics*, 36 (3): 592–614.

—— and SHAMIR, M. (1983), 'The Primarily Political Functions of the Left–Right Continuum', *Comparative Politics*, 15: 139–58.

AYALA, L. (1994), 'Social Needs, Inequality and the Welfare State in Spain: Trends and Prospects', *Journal of European Social Policy*, 4 (3): 159–79.

BACALHAU, M. (1978), *Os Portugueses e a política: Quatro anos depois do 25 de abril* (Lisbon, Meseta).

BACCETTI, C. (1997), *Il PDS: Verso un nuovo modello di partito?* (Bologna, Il Mulino).

BALABANIAN, O., BOUET, G., *et al.* (1991), *Les États méditerranéens de la CEE: Espagne, Grèce, Italie, Portugal* (Paris, Masson).

BAÑÓN MARTÍNEZ, R., and BARKER, T. M. (1988) (eds.), *Armed Forces and Society in Spain. Past and Present* (New York, Columbia University Press).

BARDI, L., and MORLINO, L. (1994), 'Italy: Tracing the Roots of the Great Transformation', in R. Katz and P. Mair (eds.), *How Parties Organize. Change and Adaptation in Party Organizations in Western Democracies* (London, Sage Publications), 242–77.

BARNARD, C. J. (1938), *The Functions of the Executive* (Cambridge, Mass., Harvard University Press).

BARNES, S. (1966), 'Ideology and the Organization of Conflict: On the Relationship Between Political Thought and Behavior', *Journal of Politics*, 28: 513–30.

—— (1967), *Party Democracy: Politics in an Italian Socialist Federation* (New Haven, Yale University Press).

—— (1972), 'The Legacy of Fascism: Generational Differences in Italian Political Attitudes and Behavior', *Comparative Politics*, 5 (1): 41–57.

BARNES, S. H., FARAH, B. G., and HEUNKS, F. (1979), 'Personal Dissatisfaction', in Barnes, Kaase, *et al.* 1979: 381–407.

—— KAASE, M., *et al.* (1979) (eds.), *Political Action: Mass Participation in Five Western Democracies* (Beverly Hills, Sage Publications).

BARRETO, A. (1989), 'Reforma agrária e revolução em Portugal (1974–76)', in Coelho 1989: 453–68.

BARRETO, J. M. TABORDA (1991), 'A formação das centrais sindicais e do sindicalismo contemporâneo em Portugal', doctoral dissertation, Universidade de Lisboa.

BARROSO, A., and DE BRAGANÇA, J. V. (1988), 'El Presidente de la República: Función y poderes', *Revista de estudios políticos*, 60–1: 307–32.

BARTOLINI, S. (1983), 'The Membership of Mass Parties: The Social Democratic Experience, 1889–1978', in Daalder and Mair 1983: 177–220.

—— (1986), 'La volatilità elettorale', *Rivista italiana di scienza politica*, 16 (3): 363–400.

——and D'Alimonte, R. (1995) (eds.), *Maggioritario ma non troppo: Le elezioni politiche del 1994* (Bologna, Il Mulino).

BARTOLINI, S. and MAIR, P. (1984) (eds.), *Party Politics in Contemporary Western Europe* (London, Frank Cass).

—— —— (1990), *Identity, Competition, and Electoral Availability: The Stabilisation of European Electorates, 1885–1985* (Cambridge, Cambridge University Press).

BEBLER, A., and SEROKA, J. (1990) (eds.), *Contemporary Political Systems: Classifications and Typologies* (Boulder, Colo., Lynne Rienner).

BELOTTI, V. (1992), 'La rappresentanza politica locale delle Leghe', *Polis*, 6 (2): 281–90.

BENDIX, R. (1964), *Nation Building and Citizenship: Studies of our Changing Social Order* (New York, Wiley & Sons).

—— and BERGER, B. (1959), 'Images of Society and Problems of Concept Formation in Sociology', in L. Gross (ed.), *Symposium on Sociological Theory* (New York, Harper & Row), 92–118.

BENTLEY, A. (1908), *The Process of Government* (Chicago, The University of Chicago Press).

BERNHARD, M. (1993), 'Civil Society and Democratic Transition in East Central Europe', *Political Science Quarterly*, 108 (2): 307–26.

BINDER, L., COLEMAN, J., *et al.* (1971), *Crises and Sequences in Political Development* (Princeton, Princeton University Press).

BLONDEL, J. (1968), 'Party Systems and Patterns of Government in Western Democracies', *Canadian Journal of Political Science*, 1 (2): 180–203.

BOBBIO, N. (1984), *Il futuro della democrazia* (Turin, Einaudi Editore).

BOGDANOR, V., and BUTLER, D. (1983) (eds.), *Democracy and Elections: Electoral Systems and their Political Consequences* (Cambridge, Cambridge University Press).

BOSCO, A., in collaboration with GASPAR, C. (1997), 'Four Actors in Search of a Role: The South European Communist Parties', in N. Diamandouros and R. Gunther (eds.) (forthcoming), *Parties and Politics in Southern Europe* (Baltimore, Johns Hopkins University Press).

BOTELLA, J. (1992), 'La cultura política en la España democrática', in Cotarelo 1992: 121–36.

BOUDON, R. (1984), *La Place du désordre* (Paris, Presses Universitaires de France).

BRACHER, K. D. (1971), *Die Aufloesung der Weimarer Republik* (Villingen, Ring-Verlag).

BROOKS, J. E. (1988), 'Mediterranean Neo-democracies and the Opinion–Policy Nexus', *West European Politics*, 11 (3):127–40.

BRUNEAU, T. C. (1983), 'People Support for Democracy in Post-Revolutionary Portugal', in Graham and Wheeler 1983: 21–42.

—— (1984), 'Continuity and Change in Portuguese Politics: Ten Years after the Revolution of 25 April 1974', in Pridham 1984: 72–83.

—— and MACLEOD, A. (1986), *Politics in Contemporary Portugal: Parties and the Consolidation of Democracy* (Boulder, Colo., Lynne Rienner Publishers).

BUENO CAMPOS, E., *et al.* (1989), 'Características básicas de la empresa española: Aspectos estructurales', *Papeles de Economía Española*, 39/40.

References   349

BURTON, M., GUNTHER, R., and HIGLEY, J. (1992), 'Introduction: Elite Transformations and Democratic Regimes', in Higley and Gunther 1992: 1–37.
CABRAL, M. VILLAVERDE (1995), 'Equidade social, "estado-providência" e sistema fiscal: Atitudes e percepções da população portuguesa (1991–1994)', *Sociologia: Problemas e práticas*, 17: 9–34.
CACIAGLI, M. (1989), 'La parábola de la Unión de Centro Democrático', in Tezanos, Cotarelo, and De Blas Guerrero 1989: 389–432.
—— and SPREAFICO, A. (1975), *Un sistema politico alla prova* (Bologna, Il Mulino).
—— *et al.* (1977), *Democrazia Cristiana e potere nel Mezzogiorno: Il sistema democristiano a Catania* (Rimini, Guaraldi).
CALLIGAS, C. (1987), 'The Centre: Decline and Convergence', in Featherstone and Katsoudas 1987: 135–44.
CAMPBELL, A., *et al.* (1966), *Elections and the Political Order* (New York, Wiley & Sons).
—— CONVERSE, P. E., and RODGERS, W. L. (1976), *The Quality of American Life: Perceptions, Evaluations, and Satisfactions* (New York, Russell Sage).
CANOTILHO, J. J. GOMES, and MOREIRA, V. (1991), *Fundamentos da constituição* (Coimbra, Coimbra Editora).
CAPO GIOL, J. (1992), 'The Local Political Elite in Spain', working paper no. 62, Institut de Ciències Polítiques i Socials, Barcelona.
CARRIERI, M. (1995), *L'incerta rappresentanza* (Bologna, Il Mulino).
CARTOCCI, R. (1994), *Fra Lega e Chiesa* (Bologna, Il Mulino).
CASTLES, F. G. (1993), 'Social Security in Southern Europe: A Comparative Overview', paper presented at the conference on Southern Europe, Bielefeld.
—— and WILDENMANN, R. (1986) (eds.), *Visions and Realities of Party Government*, (Berlin, de Gruyter).
CAZORLA, J. (1992), 'Del clientelismo tradicional al clientelismo de partido: Evolución y características', working paper no. 55, Institut de Ciències Polítiques i Socials, Barcelona.
—— (1994), 'El clientelismo de partido en España ante la opinión pública: El medio rural, la administración y las empresas', working paper no. 86, Institut de Ciències Polítiques i Socials, Barcelona.
—— JEREZ, M., and MONTABES, J. (1997), 'Analysis of Political Clientelism in Spain', ECPR Joint Sessions, paper, Bern, 27 Feb.–4 Mar.
CAZZOLA, F. (1970), *Il partito come organizzazione. Studio di un caso: Il P.S.I.* (Rome, Edizioni del Tritone).
—— and MORISI, M. (1981), 'La decisione urgente: Usi e funzioni del decreto legge nel sistema politico italiano', *Rivista italiana di scienza politica*, 11 (3): 447–82.
—— —— (1996), *La mutua diffidenza: Il reciproco: controllo tra magistrati e politici nella prima Repubblica* (Milan, Feltrinelli).
CELLA, G. P. (1979), *Il movimento degli scioperi nel XX secolo* (Bologna, Il Mulino).
CHELES, L., FERGUSON, R., *et al.* (1991) (eds.), *The Far Right in Western and Eastern Europe* (London, Longman).

CHISLETT, W. (1994), *Spain at a Turning Point* (Madrid, Banco Central Hispano).

CITRIN, J., McCLOSKY, H., *et al.* (1975), 'Personal and Political Sources of Political Alienation', *British Journal of Political Science*, 5: 1–31.

CLARKE, H. D., DUTT, N., and KORNBERG, A. (1993), 'The Political Economy of Attitudes toward Polity and Society in Western European Democracies', *Journal of Politics*, 55 (4): 998–1021.

CLOGG, R. (1983), 'Greece', in Bogdanor and Butler 1983: 190–208.

—— (1987), *Parties and Elections in Greece: The Search for Legitimacy* (London, C. Hurst and Duke University Press).

—— (1993) (ed.), *Greece, 1981–89: The Populist Decade* (London, Macmillan).

COELHO, M. Baptista (1989) (ed.), *Portugal: O sistema político e constitucional 1974–1987* (Lisbon, Instituto de Ciências Sociais-Universidade de Lisboa).

COLLIER, D., and LEVITSKY, S. (1994), 'Democracy "With Adjectives": Finding Conceptual Order in Recent Comparative Research', unpublished.

COLLIER BERINS, R., and COLLIER, D. (1991), *Shaping the Political Arena: Critical Junctures, Labor Movement, and Regime Dynamics in Latin America* (Princeton, Princeton University Press).

COLOMÉ, G. (1993), 'The "Partit del Socialistes de Catalunya" ', in J. M. Maravall *et al.* (eds.), *Socialist Parties in Europe* (Barcelona, Institut de Ciències Polítiques i Socials), 35–61.

COMPSTON, H. (1995), 'Union Participation in Economic Policy Making in France, Italy, Germany and Britain, 1970–1993', *West European Politics*, 18 (2): 314–19.

CONDOMINES, J., and BARROSO, J. DURÃO (1984), 'La Dimension gauche–droite et la compétition entre les partis politiques en Europe du Sud (Portugal, Espagne, Grèce)', *Il politico*, 49: 405–38.

CONVERSE, P., and PIERCE, R. (1986), *Political Representation in France* (Cambridge, Mass., The Belknap Press of Harvard University Press).

CORKILL, D. (1993), 'The Political System and the Consolidation of Democracy in Portugal', *Parliamentary Affairs*, 46 (4): 517–33.

—— (1996) 'Portugal Votes for Change and Stability: The Election of 1995', *West European Politics*, 19 (2): 403–9.

COTARELO, R. (1989), 'El sistema de partidos', in Tezanos, Cotarelo, and De Blas Guerrero 1989: 347–88.

—— (1992), *Transición política y consolidación democrática en España (1975–1986)* (Madrid, Centro de Investigaciones Sociológicas).

—— (1995), *La conspiración: El golpe de estado difuso* (Barcelona, Ediciones B.).

COTTA, M. (1979), *Classe politica e parlamento in Italia: 1946–1976* (Bologna, Il Mulino).

—— and ISERNIA, P. (1996) (eds.), *Il gigante dai piedi di argilla* (Bologna, Il Mulino).

CRAIG, P. (1992), 'Local Party Organization and Party System Construction' (Ohio State University, unpublished).

CROZIER, M. J., HUNTINGTON, S. P., and WATANUKI, J. (1975), *The Crisis of Democracy: Report on the Governability of Democracies to the Trilateral Commission New York* (New York, New York University Press).

CRUZ, M. BRAGA DA (1988), 'Sobre o Parlamento português: Partidarização parlamentar e parlamentarização partidária', *Análise social*, 24: 97–125.

—— (1994), 'O Presidente da República na génese e evolução do sistema de governo português', *Análise social*, 29 (125–6): 237–65.

—— (1995), *Instituições políticas e processos sociais* (Venda Nova, Bertrand Editora).

—— and ANTUNES, M. LOBO (1989), 'Parlamento, partidos e governo: Acerca da institucionalização política', in Coelho 1989: 351–68.

CULLA, J. (1992), 'Unió Democrática de Catalunya: Le Parti Démocrate-Chrétien Catalan (1931–1989)', in M. Caciagli *et al.* (eds.), *Christian Democracy in Europe* (Barcelona, Institut de Ciències Polítiques i Socials), 83–110.

DAALDER, H. (1966), 'Parties, Elites and Political Developments in Western Europe', in La Palombara and Weiner 1966: 43–77.

—— and MAIR, P. (1983) (eds.), *Western European Party Systems: Continuity and Change* (London, Sage).

DAHL, R. A. (1971), *Polyarchy: Participation and Opposition* (New Haven, Yale University Press).

—— (1982), *Dilemmas of Pluralist Democracy* (London, Yale University Press).

—— (1986), 'Procedural Democracy', in R. Dahl, *Democracy, Liberty, and Equality* (Oslo, Universitetsforlaget), 191–225.

DANOPOULOS, C. (1984), 'From Military to Civilian Rule in Contemporary Greece', *Armed Forces and Society*, 10 (2): 229–50.

DE BLAS GUERRERO, A. (1992), 'Estado de las autonomías y transición política', in Cotarelo 1992: 105–19.

DE CARO BONELLA, C. (1983), 'Sviluppi della forma di governo in Portogallo dal 1958 al 1982', *Quaderni costituzionali*, 3 (2): 323–48.

DE LA FUENTE BLANCO, G. (1991), *Las organizaciones agrarias españolas: El asociacionismo sindical de los agricultores y ganaderos españoles en la perspectiva de la Unidad Europea* (Madrid, Instituto de Estudios Económicos).

DEL CAMPO GARCIA, E. (1995), 'Los grupos de interés en la transición y en la consolidación democrática', in Román Marugán 1995: 201–22.

DEL CASTILLO, P. (1985), *La financiación de partidos y candidatos en las democracias occidentales* (Madrid, Centro de Investigaciones Sociológicas).

—— (1994) (ed.), *Comportamiento político y electoral* (Madrid, Centro de Investigaciones Sociológicas).

DELLA PORTA, D., and VANNUCCI, A. (1994), *Corruzione politica e amministrazione pubblica* (Bologna, Il Mulino).

DE VERGOTTINI, G. (1977), *Le origini della Seconda Repubblica Portoghese* (Milan, Giuffré).

DIAMANDOUROS, N. (1986), 'Regime Change and the Prospects for Democracy in Greece: 1974–1983', in O'Donnell, Schmitter, and Whitehead 1986: 138–64.

—— (1991), 'PASOK and State–Society Relations in Post-authoritarian Greece (1974–1986)', in S. Vryonis (ed.), *Greece on the Road to Democracy: From the Junta to PASOK 1974–1986* (New Rochelle, NY, Caratzas Publishers).

—— (1993), 'Politics and Culture in Greece 1974–91: An Interpretation', in Clogg 1993: 1–25.

References

DIAMANDOUROS, N. (1995), 'Politics and Constitutionalism in Greece: The 1975 Constitution in Historical Perspective', in R. Gunther (ed.), *Politics, Society, and Democracy: Comparative Studies. Essays in Honor of Juan J. Linz* (Boulder, Colo., Westview Press), 279–96.

—— (1997), 'Greek Politics and Society in the 1990s', in G. T. Allison and K. Nicolaidis (eds.), *The Greek Paradox: Promise v. Performance* (Cambridge, Mass., Harvard University Press), 23–38.

DIAMANTI, I. (1992), 'La mia patria è il Veneto: I valori e la proposta politica delle Leghe', *Polis*, 6 (2): 225–56.

—— (1994), 'La politica come marketing', *Micromega*, 2: 60–77.

—— (1995), *La Lega: Geografia, storia e sociologia di un nuovo soggetto politico* (Rome, Donzelli, 2nd edn.).

DIAMOND, L. (1993), 'Three Paradoxes of Democracy', in Diamond and Plattner 1993: 95–107.

—— (1994), 'Toward Democratic Consolidation', *Journal of Democracy*, 5 (3): 4–17.

—— (1995), 'Promoting Democracy in the 1990s: Actors and Instruments, Issues and Imperatives', paper prepared for the Carnegie Commission on Preventing Deadly Conflict.

—— (1996), 'Democracy in Latin America: Degrees, Illusions, and Directions for Consolidation', in T. Farer (ed.), *Beyond Sovereignty: Collectively Defending Democracy in the Americas* (Baltimore, Johns Hopkins University Press).

—— LINZ, J. J., and LIPSET, S. M. (1989), 'Introduction: Politics, Society, and Democracy in Latin America', in L. Diamond, J. J. Linz, and S. M. Lipset (eds.), *Democracy in Developing Countries*, IV: *Latin America* (Boulder, Colo., Lynne Rienner), 1–58.

—— —— —— (1995), 'Introduction: What Makes for Democracy?', in L. Diamond, J. J. Linz, and S. M. Lipset (eds.), *Democracy in Developing Countries* (Boulder, Colo., Lynne Rienner, 2nd edn.), 1–66.

—— and PLATTNER, M. (1993) (eds.), *The Global Resurgence of Democracy* (Baltimore, Johns Hopkins University Press).

DI LORETO, P. (1991), *Togliatti e la doppiezza: Il PCI tra democrazia e insurrezione 1944–49* (Bologna, Il Mulino).

DIMITRAS, P. E. (1987), 'Changes in Public Attitudes', in Featherstone and Katsoudas 1987: 64–84.

DI PALMA, G. (1970), *Apathy and Participation: Mass Politics in Western Society* (New York, The Free Press).

—— (1984), 'Government Performance: An Issue and Three Cases in Search of Theory', in Pridham 1984: 172–87.

—— (1987), 'Parlamento-arena o Parlamento di trasformazione?', in *Rivista italiana di scienza politica*, 17 (2): 179–201.

—— (1990a), *To Craft Democracies: An Essay on Democratic Transitions* (Berkeley, University of California Press).

—— (1990b), 'Parliaments, Consolidation, Institutionalization: A Minimalist View', in Liebert and Cotta 1990: 31–51.

DI VIRGILIO, A. (forthcoming), *Dal PSI alla Diaspora* (Bologna, Il Mulino).

DOBRY, M. (1986), *Sociologie des crises politiques* (Paris, Presses de la Fondation Nationale des Sciences Politiques).

DOGAN, M. (1988) (ed.), *Comparing Pluralist Democracies: Strains on Legitimacy* (Boulder, Colo., Westview Press).

—— (1996), 'La crisi di fiducia nelle democrazie pluraliste', *Queste istituzioni*, 24 (1): 89–102.

DOWNS, A. (1957), *An Economic Theory of Democracy* (New York, Harper & Row).

DUVERGER, M. (1950), *L'Influence des systèmes électoraux sur la vie politique* (Paris, Colin).

—— (1958), *Les Partis politiques* (Paris, Colin).

—— (1980), 'A New Political System Model: Semi-Presidential Government', *European Journal of Political Research*, 8 (2): 165–87.

EASTON, D. (1965), *A System Analysis of Political Life* (New York, McGraw-Hill).

EC Report (1981), 'The Economic and Social Interest Groups of Greece', Brussels, General Secretariat.

—— (1985), 'The Economic and Social Interest Groups of Portugal', Brussels, General Secretariat.

ECKSTEIN, H. (1971), *The Evaluation of Political Performance: Problems and Dimensions* (London, Sage).

—— and GURR, T. R. (1975), *Patterns of Authority* (New York, John Wiley & Sons).

ESCUDERO, M. (1991), 'La pluralidad de sensibilidades en el PSOE', *Sistema*, 102: 19–30.

ESPINA, A. (1990), *Empleo, democracia y relaciones industriales en España* (Madrid, Ministerio de Trabajo y Seguridad Social).

—— (1991) (ed.), *Concertación social, neocorporatismo y democracia* (Madrid, Ministerio de Trabajo y Seguridad Social).

ESPING-ANDERSEN, G. (1993), 'Orçamentos e democracia: O Estado-Providência em Espanha e Portugal, 1960–1986', *Análise social*, 28 (3): 589–606.

ETZIONI, A. (1964), 'On Self-Encapsulting Conflicts', *Conflict Resolution*, 8 (3): 242–55.

ETZIONI-HALEVY, E. (1993), *The Elite Connection: Problems and Potential of Western Democracy* (Cambridge, Polity Press).

Eurobarometer Surveys (1972–95).

EVANS, J. (1996), 'Conceptualising the Left–Right Continuum as an Enduring Dimension of Political Competition', Florence, EUI Working Paper, SPS no. 96/13.

FAKIOLAS, R. (1987), 'Interest Groups: An Overview', in Featherstone and Katsoudas 1987: 174–88.

FARAH, B. G., BARNES, S. H., and HEUNKS, F. (1979), 'Political Dissatisfaction', in Barnes, Kaase, *et al.* 1979: 409–47.

FARNETI, P. (1971), *Sistema politico e società civile* (Turin, Giappichelli).

—— (1973) (ed.), *Il sistema politico italiano* (Bologna, Il Mulino).

FEATHERSTONE, K. (1987), 'PASOK and the Left', in Featherstone and Katsoudas 1987: 112–34.

FEATHERSTONE, K. (1990), 'Political Parties and Democratic Consolidation in Greece', in Pridham 1990a: 179–202.

—— and KATSOUDAS, D. K. (1987) (eds.), *Political Change in Greece* (London, Croom Helm).

FEDELE, M. (1996), 'Governo e Parlamento nella transizione', in M. Fedele and R. Leonardi (eds.), *La politica senza i partiti* (Rome, Edizioni SEAM), 145–62.

FELTRIN, P. (1991), 'Partiti e sindacati: Simbiosi o dominio?', in Morlino 1991a: 293–366.

FERNÁNDEZ-CASTRO, J. (1993), *The Role of Unions and Business Associations at the Various Stages of the Process of Political Change in Spain* (Cambridge, Mass., Center for European Studies & Real Colegio Complutense, Harvard University).

FERRARESI, F. (1984) (ed.), *La destra radicale* (Milan, Feltrinelli).

FERRERA, M. (1984), *Il Welfare State in Italia* (Bologna, Il Mulino).

—— (1993), *EC Citizens and Social Protection: Main Results from a Eurobarometer Survey* (Brussels. Division V/E/2, Cortenberg 80 2/66).

—— (1995), 'Le quattro Europe sociali tra universalismo e seletività', research paper, Università Bocconi, POLEIS.

—— (1996), 'Il modello di welfare sud europeo: Caratteristiche, genesi, prospettive', research paper, Università Bocconi, POLEIS.

FIELD, G. L., HIGLEY, J., and BURTON, M. G. (1990), 'A New Elite Framework for Political Sociology', *Revue européenne des sciences sociales: Cahiers Vilfredo Pareto*, 28: 149–82.

FINE, R., and RAI, S. (1997) (eds.), *Civil Society: Democratic Perspectives*, special issue of *Democratization*, 4 (1).

FINIFTER, A. (1970), 'Dimensions of Political Alienation', *American Political Science Review*, 64: 389–410.

—— (1972), *Alienation and the Political System* (New York, John Wiley & Sons).

FISHMAN, R. (1990), *Working-Class Organization and the Return to Democracy in Spain* (Ithaca, NY, Cornell University Press).

FLORES, M., and GALLERANO, N. (1992), *Sul PCI: Un'interpretazione storica* (Bologna, Il Mulino).

FOWERAKER, J. (1987), 'Corporatist Strategies and the Transition to Democracy in Spain', *Comparative Politics*, 20 (1): 57–72.

FRANCIONI, F. (1992) (ed.), *Italy and EC Membership Evaluated* (London, Pinter Publishers).

FRANZOSI, R. (1987), 'The Press as a Source of Socio-historical Data: Issues in the Methodology of Data Collection from Newspapers', *Historical Methods*, 20 (1): 5–16.

FRASER, J. (1971), 'Personal and Political Meaning and Correlates of Political Cynicism', *Midwest Journal of Political Science*, 15: 347–64.

FUCHS, D., GUIDOROSSI, G., and SVENSSON, P. (1995), 'Support for the Democratic System', in H.-D. Klingemann and D. Fuchs (eds.), *Citizens and the State* (Oxford, Oxford University Press), 323–53.

GALLAGHER, T. (1989), 'The Portuguese Socialist Party: The Pitfalls of Being

First', in T. Gallagher and A. M. Williams (eds.), *Southern European Socialism* (Manchester, Manchester University Press), 12–32.

GALLI, G. (1966), *Il bipartitismo imperfetto: Comunisti e Democristiani in Italia* (Bologna, Il Mulino).

GAMSON, W. A. (1968), *Power and Discontent* (Homewood, Ill., Dorsey Press).

GANGAS PEIRÓ, P. (1995), *El desarrollo organizativo de los partidos políticos españoles de implantación nacional* (Madrid, Ediciones Peninsular).

GARCIA-GUERETUA RODRÍGUEZ, E. (1996), 'The Spanish "Partido Popular": A Case Study of Intra-party Power Distribution through a Period of Party Change', paper presented at ECPR workshop, Oslo.

GASPAR, C. (1988), *Organizações de interesses e democracia em Portugal* (pre-publication draft).

—— (1990), 'Portuguese Communism since 1976: Limited Decline', *Problems of Communism*, 3: 45–63.

—— and RATO, V. (1992), *Rumo à memória: Crónicas da crise comunista* (Lisbon, Quetzal Editores).

GERMANI, G. (1975), *Autoritarismo, fascismo e classi sociali* (Bologna, Il Mulino).

GHINI, C. (1982), 'Gli iscritti al partito e alla FGCI, 1943/1979', in Ilardi and Accornero 1982: 227–92.

GILLESPIE, R. (1990), 'Regime Consolidation in Spain: Party, State and Society', in Pridham 1990*a*: 126–46.

—— (1992), 'Factionalism in the Spanish Socialist Party', working paper no. 59, Institut de Ciències Polítiques i Socials, Barcelona.

GOLDEN, M. (1986), 'Interest Representation, Party System, and the State: Italy in Comparative Perspective', *Comparative Politics*, 18 (3): 279–301.

GOMEZ YÁÑEZ, J. (1994), 'Recomposición de los espacios políticos en la España de los noventa', paper presented at AEDEMO, 7th Seminar on Political Investigations, Madrid.

—— (1995), 'La democracia y sus problemas al final del siglo XX: El caso de España', paper presented in Seminar on Political Innovation, Madrid.

GONZÁLEZ BLASCO, P., and GONZÁLEZ-ANLEO, J. (1992), *Religión y sociedad en la España de los 90* (Madrid, Fundación Santamaría).

GONZÁLEZ HERNÁNDEZ, J. C. (1989), 'El Partido Comunista de España en el proceso de transición política', in Tezanos, Cotarelo, and De Blas Guerrero 1989: 543–85.

GRAHAM, L. S. (1993), *The Portuguese Military and the State: Rethinking Transitions in Europe and Latin America* (Boulder, Colo., Westview Press).

—— and WHEELER, D. L. (1983) (eds.), *In Search of Modern Portugal: The Revolution and its Consequences* (Madison, The University of Wisconsin Press).

GRASSI, D. (1992), 'The Explanation of Strikes in the Social Sciences: A Theoretical and Empirical Survey' (mimeo, University of Chicago).

GRAZIANO, L. (1980), *Clientelismo e sistema politico: Il caso dell'Italia* (Milan, Angeli Editore).

—— and Tarrow, S. (1979), *La Crisi Italiana* (Turin, Einaudi Editore).

GROFMAN, B., and LIJPHART, A. (1986) (eds.), *Electoral Laws and their Political Consequences* (New York, Agathon Press).

GUARNIERI, C. (1992), *Magistratura e politica in Italia: Pesi senza contrappesi* (Bologna, Il Mulino).

GUIDOROSSI, G. (1984), *Gli Italiani e la politica: Valori, opinioni, atteggiamenti dal dopoguerra a oggi* (Milan, Angeli Editore).

—— and WEBER, M. (1988), 'Immagine dei partiti e antagonismo politico in Italia, Spagna, Portogallo e Grecia', *Il politico*, 53 (2): 225–59.

GUNTHER, R. (1985), 'Un análisis preliminar de las alteraciones producidas en 1982 en el sistema español de partidos', *Revista de estudios políticos (nueva epoca)*, 45: 7–41.

—— (1986*a*), 'Los partidos comunistas de España', in Linz and Montero 1986: 493–523.

—— (1986*b*), 'The Spanish Socialist Party: From Clandestine Position to Party of Government', in Payne 1986: 8–49.

—— (1986*c*), 'El colapso de UCD', in Linz and Montero 1986: 433–92.

—— (1987), 'Democratization and Party Building: The Role of Party Elites in the Spanish Transition', in R. P. Clark and M. H. Haltzel (eds.), *Spain in the 1980s: The Democratic Transition and a New International Role* (Cambridge, Mass., Ballinger), 35–66.

—— (1989), 'Electoral Laws, Party Systems and Elites: The Case of Spain', *American Political Science Review*, 83: 835–58.

—— (1992), 'Spain: The Very Model of Modern Elite Settlement', in Higley and Gunther 1992: 38–80.

—— (1993), *Politics, Society, and Democracy: The Case of Spain. Essays in Honor of Juan J. Linz* (Boulder, Colo., Westview Press).

—— DIAMANDOUROS, N. P., and PUHLE, H. J. (1995) (eds.), *The Politics of Democratic Consolidation: Southern Europe in Comparative Perspective* (Baltimore, Johns Hopkins University Press).

—— and MONTERO, J. R. (1994), 'Los anclajes del partidismo: Un análisis comparado del comportamiento electoral en cuatro democracias del sur de Europa', in Del Castillo 1994: 467–548.

—— SANI, G., and SHABAD, G. (1986), *Spain after Franco: The Making of a Competitive Party System* (Berkeley, University of California Press).

HABERMAS, J. (1975), *Legitimation Crisis* (Boston, Beacon Press).

HALL, J. A. (1993), 'Consolidations of Democracy', in D. Held (ed.), *Prospects for Democracy* (Cambridge, Polity Press), 271–90.

HEIMER, F.-W., VALA-SALVADOR, J., and LEITE VIEGAS, J. M. (1990), 'Padrões de cultura política em Portugal: Atitudes em relação à democracia', *Análise social*, 25 (105–6): 31–56.

HERRING, P. (1940), *The Politics of Democracy* (New York, W. W. Norton & Co.).

HERZ, J. H. (1982) (ed.), *From Dictatorship to Democracy: Coping with the Legacies of Authoritarianism and Totalitarianism* (Westport, Conn., Greenwood Press).

HEYWOOD, P. (1994), 'The Spanish Left: Towards a Common Home?', in M. Bull and P. Heywood (eds.), *West European Communist Parties after the Revolution of 1989* (London, Macmillan), 56–89.

—— (1995*a*), 'Dalla dittatura alla democrazia: Le mutevoli forme della corruzione in Spagna', in D. Della Porta and Y. Mény (eds.), *Corruzione e democrazia: Sette paesi a confronto* (Naples, Liguori Editore), 87–106.

—— (1995*b*), 'Sleaze in Spain', *Parliamentary Affairs*, 48 (4): 726–37.

—— (1995c), *The Government and Politics of Spain* (London, Macmillan).

HIGLEY, J., and BURTON, M. G. (1989), 'The Elite Variable in Democratic Transitions and Breakdowns', *American Sociological Review*, 54: 17–32.

—— and GUNTHER, R. (1992) (eds.), *Elites and Democratic Consolidation in Latin America and Southern Europe* (Cambridge, Cambridge University Press).

HIRSCHMAN, A. O. (1970), *Exit, Voice and Loyalty* (Cambridge, Mass., Harvard University Press).

—— (1971), *A Bias for Hope* (New Haven, Yale University Press).

—— (1987), 'Dilemmas of Democratic Consolidation in Latin America', unpublished paper.

HOPKIN, J. (1997), 'Clientelism and Party Organization in Italy and Spain: A Comparative Analysis', ECPR Joint Sessions, paper, Bern, 27 Feb.–4 Mar.

HUNEEUS, C. (1985), *La Unión de Centro Democrático y la transición a la democracia en España* (Madrid, Centro de Investigaciones Sociológicas).

HUNTINGTON, S. P. (1968), *Political Order in Changing Societies* (New Haven, Yale University Press).

—— (1989), 'The Modest Meaning of Democracy', in Pastor 1989: 11–28.

—— (1991), *The Third Wave: Democratization in the Late Twentieth Century* (Norman, University of Oklahoma Press).

IGNAZI, P. (1989), *Il polo escluso: Profilo del Movimento Sociale Italiano* (Bologna, Il Mulino).

—— (1992), *Dal PCI al PDS* (Bologna, Il Mulino).

ILARDI, M., and ACCORNERO, A. (1982) (eds.), *Il Partito Comunista Italiano: Struttura e storia dell'organizzazione 1921–1979* (Milan, Annali della Fondazione Feltrinelli).

INGLEHART, R. (1990), *Culture Shift in Advanced Industrial Society* (Princeton, Princeton University Press).

—— and KLINGEMANN, H.-D. (1976), 'Party Identification, Ideological Preference and the Left–Right Dimension among Western Mass Public', in I. Budge, I. Crewe, and D. Farlie (eds.), *Party Identification and Beyond: Representations of Voting and Party Competition* (London, John Wiley & Sons), 243–76.

JEREZ MIR, M. (1992), *Business and Politics in Spain: From Francoism to Democracy* (Barcelona, Institut de Ciències Polítiques i Socials).

JONES, M. P. (1995), 'A Guide to the Electoral Systems of the Americas', *Electoral Studies*, 14 (1): 5–21.

JORDAN, G. (1994), 'A Conceptual Analysis of "Interest Groups": Identifying the Field of Interest', paper presented at XVI World Congress of the IPSR, Berlin.

KAASE, M., and NEWTON, K. (1995), *Beliefs in Government* (Oxford, Oxford University Press).

KAPETANYANNIS, V. (1987), 'The Communists', in Featherstone and Katsoudas 1987: 145–73.

KAPETANYANNIS, V. (1991), 'Neo-Fascism in Modern Greece', in Cheles, Ferguson, *et al.* 1991: 129–44.

KAPLAN, A. (1963), *The Conduct of Inquiry: Methodology for Behavioral Science* (New York, Thoma Y. Crowell Co.).

KARL, T. L., and SCHMITTER, P. C. (1990), 'Modes of Transition and Types of Democracy in Latin America, Southern and Eastern Europe', *International Social Science Journal*, 43: 269–84.

KATROUGALOS, G. (1996), 'The Southern European Welfare Model: The Greek Welfare State in Search of an Identity', *Journal of European Social Policy*, 6 (1): 39–60.

KATSANEVAS, T. K. (1984), *Trade Unions in Greece* (Athens, National Center of Social Research).

KATSOUDAS, D. K. (1987), 'The Constitutional Framework', in Featherstone and Katsoudas 1987: 14–33.

KATZ, R. S. (1986), 'Party Government: A Rationalistic Conception', in Castles and Wildenmann 1986: 31–71.

—— and MAIR, P. (1994) (eds.), *How Parties Organize: Change and Adaptation in Party Organization in Western Democracies* (London: Sage Publications).

—— —— (1995), 'Changing Models of Party Organization and Party Democracy: The Emergence of the Cartel Party', *Party Politics*, 1 (1): 5–29.

KEANE, J. (1988) (ed.), *Civil Society and the State* (London, Verso).

KELSEN, H. (1929), *Vom Wesen und Wert der Demokratie* (Tübingen, J. C. B. Mohr).

KEY, V. O. (1955), 'A Theory of Critical Elections', *Journal of Politics*, 17: 13–18.

KIRCHHEIMER, O. (1966), 'The Transformation of the Western European Party Systems', in La Palombara and Weiner 1966: 177–200.

KITSCHELT, H. (1992), 'Political Regime Change: Structure and Process-Driven Explanations?', *American Political Science Review*, 86 (4): 1028–34.

—— (1994), *The Transformation of European Social Democracy* (Cambridge, Cambridge University Press).

KLINGEMANN, H.-D. (1979), 'Measuring Ideologic Conceptualizations', in Barnes, Kaase, *et al.* 1979: 215–54.

KÖHLER, H.-D. (1995), *El movimiento sindical en España* (Madrid, Editorial Fundamentos).

KOUKIADIS, J. (1983), 'Relazioni industriali e questione sociale', in T. Treu (ed.), *Crisi economica e mutamenti politici nell'area mediterranea* (Rome, Edizioni Lavoro), 215–35.

KOUTSOUKIS, K. S. (1994), 'Cabinet Decision Making in the Hellenic Republic 1974–1992', in M. Laver and K. A. Shepsle (eds.), *Cabinet Ministers and Parliamentary Government* (Cambridge, Cambridge University Press), 270–82.

—— (1995), 'Sleaze in Contemporary Greek Politics', *Parliamentary Affairs*, 48 (4): 688–96.

KRISTINSSON, G. H. (1996), 'Parties, States and Patronage', *West European Politics*, 19 (3): 433–52.

KRITSANTONIS, N. D. (1992), 'Greece: From State Authoritarianism to Modernization', in A. Ferner and R. Hyman (eds.), *Industrial Relations in the New Europe* (Oxford, Basil Blackwell), 1–28.

KUECHLER, M. (1991), 'The Dynamics of Mass Political Support in Western Europe: Methodological Problems and Preliminary Findings', in K. H. Reif (ed.), *Eurobarometer: The Dynamics of European Public Opinion. Essays in Honour of Jacques-René Rabier* (London, Macmillan), 275–93.

LAAKSO, M., and TAAGEPERA, R. (1979), ' "Effective" Number of Parties: A Measure with Application to Western Europe', *Comparative Political Studies*, 12 (1): 3–27.

LANDOLFI, A. (1968), *Il socialismo italiano: strutture, comportamenti e valori* (Rome, Lerici Editore).

LANZA, O. (1991), 'L'agricoltura, la Coldiretti e la DC', in Morlino 1991*a*: 41–125.

—— (1995), 'Gli eletti: Il ricambio dei Parlamentari', in G. Pasquino (ed.), *L'Alternanza inattesa* (Messina, Rubbettino), 209–53.

LA PALOMBARA, J. (1964), *Interest Groups in Italian Politics* (Princeton, Princeton University Press).

—— (1965), 'Italy: Fragmentation, Isolation, and Alienation', in L. Pye and S. Verba (eds.), *Political Culture and Political Development* (Princeton, Princeton University Press), 282–329.

—— and WATERS, J. B. (1961), 'Values, Expectations, and Political Predispositions of Italian Youth', *Midwest Journal of Political Science*, 5 (1): 39–58.

—— and WEINER, M. (1966) (eds.), *Political Parties and Political Development* (Princeton, Princeton University Press).

LAPONCE, J. (1970), 'Note on the Use of the Left–Right Dimension', *Comparative Political Studies*, 2: 480–502.

—— (1981), *Left and Right: The Topography of Political Perceptions* (Toronto, University of Toronto Press).

LAWSON, K. (1980) (ed.), *Political Party and Linkage: A Comparative Perspective* (New Haven, Yale University Press).

—— (1988), 'When Linkage Fails', in K. Lawson and P. Merkl (eds.), *When Parties Fail: Emerging Alternative Organizations* (Princeton, Princeton University Press), 13–40.

LEGUINA VILLA, J. (1982), 'Las comunidades autónomas', in E. García de Enterria and A. Predieri (eds.), *La Constitución Española de 1978* (Madrid, Editorial Civitas and Giuffré), 727–80.

LEHMBRUCH, G., and SCHMITTER, P. C. (1982) (eds.), *Patterns of Corporatist Policy-Making* (London, Sage).

LIEBERT, U., and COTTA, M. (1990) (eds.), *Parliament and Democratic Consolidation in Southern Europe* (New York, Pinter Publishers).

LIJPHART, A. (1984), *Democracies: Patterns of Majoritarian and Consensus Government in Twenty-One Countries* (London, Yale University Press).

—— (1992) (ed.), *Parliamentary vs Presidential Government* (Oxford, Oxford University Press).

—— (1994), *Electoral Systems and Party Systems: A Study of Twenty-Seven Democracies 1945–1990* (Oxford, Oxford University Press).

—— et al. (1988), 'A Mediterranean Model of Democracy? The Southern European Democracies in Comparative Perspective', *West European Politics*, 11 (1): 7–25.

LIMA, J. ÁVILA DE (1991), 'As organizacões agrícolas socioprofissionais em Portugal e a integração europeia (1974–85)', *Análise social*, 26 (110): 209–39.

LINDBLOM, C. E. (1959), 'The "Science" of Muddling Through', *Public Administration Review*, 19 (1): 79–88.

LINZ, J. J. (1964), 'An Authoritarian Regime: The Case of Spain', in E. Allardt and Y. Littunen (eds.), *Cleavages, Ideologies and Party Systems* (Helsinki, Westermarck Society), 291–342.

—— (1974*a*), *The Consolidations of Regimes: A Theoretical Problem Approach*, ISA World Congress, Toronto.

—— (1974*b*), 'La democrazia italiana di fronte al futuro', in F. L. Cavazza and S. R. Graubard (eds.), *Il caso italiano* (Milan, Garzanti), 124–62.

—— (1978), 'Crisis, Breakdown, and Reequilibration', in Linz and Stepan 1978: 3–124.

—— (1982), *The Transitions from Authoritarian Regimes to Democratic Political Systems and the Problems of Consolidation of Political Democracy*, IPSA Round Table, Tokyo.

—— (1986), *Conflicto en Euskadi* (Madrid, Espasa Calpe).

—— (1988), 'Legitimacy of Democracy and the Socio-Economic System', in Dogan 1988: 65–113.

—— (1989), 'Il rapporto tra legittimazione ed efficacia di governo', *Mondoperaio*, 3: 111–16.

—— (1990), 'Transitions to Democracy', *Washington Quarterly*, 1 (1): 143–64.

—— (1994), 'Presidential or Parliamentary Democracy: Does It Make a Difference?', in Linz and Valenzuela 1994: 3–87.

—— *et al.* (1981), *Informe Sociológico sobre el cambio político en España 1975–1981* (Madrid, Euramerica).

—— and MONTERO, J. R. (1986) (ed.), *Crisis y cambio: Electores y partidos en la España de los años ochenta* (Madrid, Centro de Estudios Constitucionales).

—— and STEPAN, A. (1978) (ed.), *The Breakdown of Democratic Regimes* (Baltimore, Johns Hopkins University Press).

—— —— (1989), 'Political Crafting of Democratic Consolidation or Destruction: Europe and South American Comparisons', in Pastor 1989: 41–61.

—— —— (1996), *Problems of Democratic Transition and Consolidation. Southern Europe, South America, and Post-Communist Europe* (Baltimore, Johns Hopkins University Press).

—— and VALENZUELA, A. (1994) (eds.), *The Failure of Presidential Democracy* (Baltimore, Johns Hopkins University Press).

LIPSET, S. M. (1959), *Political Man: The Social Bases of Politics* (Garden City, NY, Doubleday).

LLERA RAMO, F. J. (1989), 'El sistema de partidos vasco: Distancia ideológica y legitimación política', *Revista española de investigaciones sociológicas*, 28: 171–206.

—— (1992), '*Conflicto en Euskadi* Revisited', in R. Gunther, (ed.), *Politics, Society, and Democracy: The Case of Spain* (Boulder, Colo., Westview Press), 167–95.

—— (1993), 'The Construction of the Basque Polarized Pluralism', working paper, Institut de Ciències Polítiques i Socials, Barcelona.

—— (1994), 'La construcción del pluralismo polarizado vasco' in Del Castillo 1994: 275–95.

LOEWENBERG, G. (1971), 'The Influence of Parliamentary Behavior on Regime Stability', *Comparative Politics*, 3: 170–95.

LOPES, J. DA SILVA (1993) (ed.), *Portugal and EC Membership Evaluated* (London, Pinter).

LOPES, P. SANTANA (1988), 'PPD/PSD: La Dependencia del Carisma', *Revista de estudios políticos*, 60–1: 173–84.

LÓPEZ LÓPEZ, M. T., and UTRILLA DE LA HOZ, A. (1994), *Introducción al sector público español* (Madrid, Editorial Civitas).

LÓPEZ NIETO, L. (1988), *Alianza popular: Estructura y evolución electoral de un partido conservador (1976–1982)* (Madrid, Centro de Investigaciones Sociológicas).

—— (1995), 'The Spanish Popular Party', unpublished paper.

LÓPEZ PINTOR, R. (1994), 'El sistema político', in M. Juárez (ed.), *Informe sociológico sobre la situación social en España* (Madrid, Fundación Foessa), 551–650.

LUCENA, M. DE, and GASPAR, C. (1991), 'Metamorfoses corporativas? Associações de interesses económicos e institucionalização da democracia em Portugal', *Análise social*, 26 (114): 847–903.

—— —— (1992), 'Metamorfoses corporativas? Associações de interesses económicos e institucionalização da democracia em Portugal', *Análise social*, 27 (115): 135–87.

LUTTBEG, N. R. (1974) (ed.), *Public Opinion and Public Policy: Models of Political Linkage* (Ithaca, NY, F. E. Peacock).

LUZZATTO FEGIZ, P. (1956), *Il volto sconosciuto dell'Italia: Dieci anni di sondaggi doxa* (Milan, Giuffrè).

—— (1966), *Il volto sconosciuto dell'Italia: Dieci anni di sondaggi doxa* (Milan, Giuffré).

LYRINTZIS, C. (1984), 'Political Parties in Post-Junta Greece: A Case of "Bureaucratic Clientelism"', in Pridham 1984: 99–118.

—— (1989), 'Between Socialism and Populism: The Rise of the Panhellenic Socialist Movement (PASOK)', Ph.D. dissertation (London, London School of Economics).

—— (1993), 'PASOK in Power: From "Change" to Disenchantment', in Clogg 1993: 26–46.

McDONOUGH, P., BARNES, S. H., and LÓPEZ PINA, A. (1986), 'The Growth of Democratic Legitimacy in Spain', *American Political Science Review*, 80: 735–60

—— —— —— (1992), 'The Nature of Political Support and Legitimacy in Spain', paper delivered at the 8th International Conference of Europeanists, Chicago.

—— —— —— (1994), 'The Nature of Political Support and Legitimacy in Spain', *Comparative Political Studies*, 27 (3): 349–80.

MAGONE, J. M. (1995), 'Party Factionalism in New Small Southern European Democracies: Some Comparative Findings from the Greek and Portuguese

Experiences (1974–82)', in R. Gillespie, M. Waller, *et al.* (eds.), *Factional Politics and Democratization* (London, Frank Cass), 90–101.

MAINWARING, S. (1992), 'Transitions to Democracy and Democratic Consolidation: Theoretical and Comparative Issues', in S. Mainwaring, G. O'Donnell, and J. S. Valenzuela (eds.), *Issues in Democratic Consolidation* (Notre Dame, Ind., University of Notre Dame Press), 294–341.

—— and SCULLY, T. R. (1995) (eds.), *Building Democratic Institutions: Party Systems in Latin America* (Stanford, Calif., Stanford University Press).

MAIR, P. (1989), 'The Problem of Party System Change', *Journal of Theroetical Politics*, 1 (3): 251–76.

—— (1991), 'Electoral Markets and Stable States', in M. Moran and M. Wright (eds.), *The Market and the State: Studies in Interdependence* (London, Macmillan), now in P. Mair (1997), *Party System Change: Approaches and Interpretations* (Oxford, Clarendon Press), 157–74.

—— (1995), 'Political Parties, Popular Legitimacy and Public Privilege', *West European Politics*, 18: 40–57.

MALDONADO GAGO, J. (1995), 'La organización territorial del estado', in Román Marugán 1995: 53–66.

MALEFAKIS, E. (1995), 'The Political and Socio-economic Contours of Southern European History', in Gunther, Diamandouros, and Puhle 1995: 33–76.

MANNHEIMER, R. (1989a), *Capire il voto: Contributi per l'analisi del comportamento elettorale in Italia* (Milan, Angeli).

—— (1989b), 'Una componente della decisione di voto: L'identificazione di partito', in Mannheimer 1989a: 51–70.

—— (1991), *La Lega Lombarda* (Milan, Feltrinelli).

—— and SANI, G. (1987), *Il mercato elettorale: Identikit dell'elettore italiano* (Bologna, Il Mulino).

MANOUKIAN, A. (1968) (ed.), *La presenza sociale del PCI e della DC* (Bologna, Il Mulino).

MARAFFI, M. (1991), *Politica ed economia in Italia: La vicenda dell'impresa pubblica dagli anni trenta agli anni cinquanta* (Bologna, Il Mulino).

MARAVALL, J. M. (1981), *La política de la transición 1975–80* (Madrid, Taurus).

—— (1992), 'What is Left? Social Democratic Policies in Southern Europe', working paper 1992/36, Centro de Estudios Avanzados en Ciencias Sociales, Instituto Juan March, Madrid.

—— (1995), *Los resultados de la democracia: Un estudio del sur y el este de Europa* (Madrid, Alianza Editorial).

—— and SANTAMARIA, J. (1986), 'Political Change in Spain and the Prospects for Democracy', in O'Donnell, Schmitter, and Whitehead 1986: 71–108.

MARCH, J., and OLSEN, J. (1989), *Rediscovering Institutions: The Organizational Basis of Politics* (New York: Free Press).

MARTÍN ACEÑA, P., and COMÍN, F. (1991), *INI: 50 años de industrialización en España* (Madrid, Espasa-Calpe).

MARTÍNEZ, R. E. (1993), 'The Business Sector and Political Change in Spain: "Apertura", "Reforma" and Democratic Consolidation', in Gunther 1993: 113–39.

—— and PARDO AVELLANEDA, R. (1985), 'El asociacionismo empresarial español en la transición', *Papeles de economía española*, 22: 84–114.

MARTÍNEZ ALIER, J., and ROCA JUSMET, J. (1988), 'Economía política del corporativismo en el estado español: Del Franquismo al Posfranquismo', *Revista española de investigaciones sociológicas*, 41: 25–62.

MATTEI, F. (1987), 'Le dimensioni dell'efficacia politica: Aspetti metodologici', *Rivista italiana di scienza politica*, 17: 105–33.

MATTINA, L. (1991), 'La confindustria oltre la simbiosi', in Morlino 1991a: 207–91.

—— (1995), 'I Candidati', in Bartolini and D'Alimonte 1995: 233–72.

MATTOSO, J. (1994), *História de Portugal: Portugal em transe* (Lisbon, Editorial Estampa).

MAVROGORDATOS, G. T. (1983), *Rise of the Greek Sun: The Greek Election of 1981* (London, Centre for Contemporary Greek Studies, Occasional Paper).

—— (1984), 'The Greek Party System: A Case of "Limited but Polarised Pluralism"?', in Bartolini and Mair 1984: 156–69.

—— (1987), 'Downs Revisited: Spatial Models of Party Competition and Left–Right Measurements', *International Political Science Review*, 8: 333–42.

—— (1988), *From Dictatorship to Populism: Organized Interests in Greece*, unpublished manuscript.

—— (1993), 'Civil Society under Populism', in Clogg 1993: 46–64.

—— (1997), 'Party Clientelism in Greece', unpublished paper.

MAXWELL, K. (1986a), *Portugal in the 1980s: Dilemmas of Democratic Consolidation* (Westport, Conn., Greenwood Press).

—— (1986b), 'Regime Overthrow and the Prospects for Democratic Transition in Portugal', in O'Donnell, Schmitter, and Whitehead 1986: 109–37.

MAZZOLENI, G. (1992), 'Quando la pubblicità elettorale non serve', *Polis*, 6 (2): 291–304.

MECKSTROTH, T. (1975), 'Most Different Systems and Most Similar Systems: A Study in the Logic of Comparative Inquiry', *Comparative Political Studies*, 8: 132–57.

MEIRIM, J. M. (1994), *O financiamento dos partidos políticos e das campanhas eleitorais* (Lisbon, Aequitas e Editorial Notícias).

MELLA MÁRQUEZ, M. (1992), 'Los grupos de interés en la consolidación democrática', in Cotarelo 1992: 327–42.

MERKEL, W. (1992), 'Between Class and Catch-all: Is there an Electoral Dilemma for Social Democratic Parties in Western Europe?', in Merkel *et al.* 1992: 11–32.

—— (1995), *¿Final de la socialdemocracia? Recursos de poder y política de gobierno de los partidos socialdemócratas en Europa Occidental* (Valencia, Edicions Alfons el Magnànim).

—— *et al.* (1992), *Socialist Parties in Europe*, II: *Of Class, Populars, Catch-all?* (Barcelona, Institut de Ciències Polítiques i Socials).

MIGUÉLEZ LOBO, F. (1991), 'Las organizaciones sindicales', in Miguélez Lobo and Prieto 1991: 213–31.

—— and Prieto, C. (1991) (eds.), *Las relaciones laborales en España* (Madrid, Siglo XXI de España Editores).

MINNA, R. (1984), 'Il terrorismo di destra', in D. Della Porta (ed.), *Terrorismi in Italia* (Bologna, Il Mulino), 21–74.

MIRANDA, J. (1990), *Manual de direito constitucional*, vol. I (Coimbra, Coimbra Editora).

MOLINS, J. (1994), 'Los grupos de interés en España', in Papeles de la Fundación para el Análisis y los Estudios Sociales, no. 7.

MONTABES, J. (1994), 'Non-state Wide Parties within the Framework of the Spanish Party System', in L. de Winter (ed.), *Non-state Wide Parties in Europe* (Madrid, Institut de Ciències Polítiques i Socials), 117–62.

MONTERO, J. R. (1986*a*), 'El sub-triunfo de la derecha: Los apoyos electorales de AP-PDP', in Linz and Montero 1986: 345–432.

—— (1986*b*), 'Iglesia, secularización y comportamiento político en España', *Revista española de investigaciones sociológicas* , 34: 131–59.

—— (1989), 'Los fracasos políticos y electorales de la derecha política española: Alianza Popular, 1976–1987', in Tezanos, Cotarelo, and De Blas Guerrero 1989: 495–542.

—— (1990), 'Non-voting in Spain: Some Quantitative and Attitudinal Aspects', working paper no. 22, Institut de Ciències Polítiques i Socials, Barcelona.

—— (1992), 'Las elecciones legislativas', in Cotarelo 1992: 243–97.

—— LLERA, F. J., and TORCAL, M. (1992), 'Sistemas electorales en España: Una recapitulación', *Revista española de investigaciones sociológicas*, 58: 7–56.

—— and TORCAL, M. (1990), 'Autonomías y comunidades autónomas en España: Preferencias, dimensiones y orientaciones políticas', *Revista de estudios políticos (nueva epoca)*, 70: 33–91.

MORÁN, M. L. (1989), 'Un Intento de análisis de la "clase parlamentaria" española: Elementos de renovación y de permanencia (1977–1986)', *Revista española de investigaciones sociológicas*, 45: 61–84.

—— (1996), 'Renewal and Permanency of the Spanish Members of Parilament (1977–1993): Reflections on the Institutionalization of the Spanish Parliament', working paper 1996/81, Instituto Juan March.

MORISI, M. (1991), 'Il Parlamento tra partiti e interessi', in Morlino 1991*a*: 367–446.

—— (1992), *Le leggi del consenso: Partiti e interessi nei parlamenti della Prima Repubblica* (Messina, Rubbettino Editore).

—— (1994), 'La giurisdizione come "lavoro politico": Come studiare il caso italiano', *Stato e mercato*, (41): 215–48.

—— and CAZZOLA, F. (1981), 'La decisione urgente: Usi e funzioni del decreto legge nel sistema politico italiano', *Rivista italiana di scienza politica*, 11 (2): 447–82.

MORLINO, L. (1979), 'La crisi della democrazia', *Rivista italiana di scienza politica*, 9 (1): 37–70.

—— (1980), *Come cambiano i regimi politici: Strumenti di analisi* (Milan, Franco Angeli).

—— (1981), *Dalla democrazia all'autoritarismo: Il caso spagnolo in prospettiva comparata* (Bologna, Il Mulino).

—— (1984), 'The Changing Relationship between Parties and Society in Italy', in Bartolini and Mair 1984: 46–66.

—— (1985), *Como cambian los regímenes políticos* (Madrid, Centro de Estudios Constitucionales).

—— (1986*a*), 'Consolidamento democratico: Definizione e modelli', *Rivista italiana di scienza politica*, 16 (2): 197–238.

—— (1986*b*), 'Consolidamento democratico: Alcune ipotesi esplicative', *Rivista italiana di scienza politica*, 16 (3): 439–59.

—— (1987), 'Crisis autoritaria y cambio de régimen en el sur de Europa', in C. Huneeus (ed.), *Para vivir la democracia* (Santiago, Editorial Andante), 13–48.

—— (1991*a*) (ed.), *Costruire la democrazia: Gruppi e partiti in Italia* (Bologna, Il Mulino).

—— (1991*b*), *Democratic Consolidations in Southern Europe: Theoretical Guidelines for the Empirical Analysis* (Stanford, Calif., Center for European Studies, unpublished paper).

—— (1996), 'Crisis of Parties and Change of Party System in Italy', *Party Politics*, 3 (1): 5–30.

—— (1998), 'Is There an Impact? And Where Is It? Electoral Reform and Party System in Italy', *South European Society and Politics*, 2 (2).

—— (forthcoming), *Partiti e sistemi di partito in Italia: Le trasformazioni organizzative* (Bologna, Il Mulino).

—— and MATTEI, F. (1992), 'Vecchio e nuovo autoritarismo nell'Europa Mediterranea', *Rivista italiana di scienza politica*, 22 (1): 137–60.

—— and MONTERO, J. R. (1995), 'Legitimacy and Democracy in Southern Europe', in Gunther, Diamandouros, and Puhle 1995: 231–60.

—— and TARCHI, M. (1996), 'The Dissatisfied Society: Protest and Support in Italy', *European Journal of Political Research*, 30 (2): 41–63.

MOYANO ESTRADA, E. (1988), *Sindacalismo y política agrária en Europa: Las organizaciones profesionales agrárias en Francia, Italia, y Portugal* (Madrid, Ministerio de Agricultura Pesca y Alimentación).

MOZZICAFREDDO, J. (1992), 'O Estado-Providência em Portugal: Estratégias Contraditórias', *Sociologia: Problemas e práticas*, 12: 57–89.

MUJAL-LEÓN, E. (1983), *Communism and Political Change in Spain* (Bloomington, Indiana University Press).

MULLER, E. W., and JUKAM, T. O (1977), 'On the Meaning of Political Support', *American Political Science Review*, 71: 1561–95.

OBERDOFF, H. (1992) (ed.), *Les Constitutions de l'Europe des Douze* (Paris, La Documentation Française).

O'CONNOR, J. (1987), *The Meaning of Crisis* (Oxford, Basil Blackwell).

O'DONNELL, G. (1992), 'Delegative Democracy?', working paper no. 172, Kellogg Institute, Notre Dame.

—— SCHMITTER, P. C., and WHITEHEAD, L. (1986) (ed.), *Transitions from Authoritarian Rule: Southern Europe* (Baltimore, Johns Hopkins University Press).

OECD (1990–1), *Economic Surveys: Greece* (Paris, OECD).

—— (1991–2), *Economic Surveys: Greece* (Paris, OECD).

—— (1993), *Economic Surveys: Greece* (Paris, OECD).

—— (1994), *Economic Surveys: Greece* (Paris, OECD).

OECD (1995), *Economic Surveys: Greece* (Paris, OECD).
—— (1996), *Economic Surveys: Greece* (Paris, OECD).
—— (1990–1), *Economic Surveys: Portugal* (Paris, OECD).
—— (1991–2), *Economic Surveys: Portugal* (Paris, OECD).
—— (1993), *Economic Surveys: Portugal* (Paris, OECD).
—— (1994), *Economic Surveys: Portugal* (Paris, OECD).
—— (1995), *Economic Surveys: Portugal* (Paris, OECD).
—— (1991), *Economic Surveys: Spain* (Paris, OECD).
O'KANE, R. H. T. (1993), 'Against Legitimacy', *Political Studies*, 41: 471–87.
OPELLO, W. C. (1986), 'Portugal's Parliament: An Organizational Analysis of Legislative Performance', *Legislative Studies Quarterly*, 11 (3): 291–319.
PADRÓ-SOLANET, A. (1996), 'Political Parties in Spain: A Review of Literature since the Democratic Transition', *European Journal of Political Research*, 29 (4): 451–75.
PALLARÉS, F., and FONT, J. (1994), 'Las elecciones autonómicas en Cataluña (1980–1992)', in Del Castillo 1994: 221–73.
PANEBIANCO, A. (1982), *Modelli di partito* (Bologna, Il Mulino).
—— (1988), *Political Parties: Organization and Power* (Cambridge, Cambridge University Press).
PAPADOPOULOS, I. (1989), *Dynamique du discours politique et conquête du pouvoir: Le cas du PASOK, 1974–1981* (Bern, Peter Lang).
—— (1997), 'Transformations of Party Clientelism in Southern Europe in a Phase of Democratic Consolidation: An Introduction', ECPR Joint Sessions, paper, Bern, 27 Feb.–4 Mar.
Papeles de economía española (1989), *La empresa pública en España*, special issue, 38.
PAPPAS, T. (1994), ' "New Democracy": The Logic of a Conservative Party's Organization', Yale University working paper, Department of Sociology.
—— (1995), 'The Making of Party Democracy in Greece', Ph.D. dissertation, Yale University.
—— (1996), 'Grand Designs, Narrow Choices: Conservatives and Democracy in Southern Europe', European University Institute working paper, SPS 96/7.
PARTRIDGE, H. (1995), 'Can the Leopard Change its Spots? Sleaze in Italy', *Parliamentary Affairs,* 48 (4): 711–25.
PASQUINO, G. (1980), 'Italian Christian Democracy: A Party for all Seasons?', in P. Lange and S. Tarrow (eds.), *Italy in Transition: Conflict and Consensus* (London, Frank Cass), 88–109.
PASTOR, R. A. (1989) (ed.), *Democracy in the Americas: Stopping the Pendulum* (New York, Holmes & Meier).
PATRICIO, M. T., and STOLEROFF, A. (1994), 'The Portuguese Communist Party: Perestroika and its Aftermath', in M. Bull and P. Heywood (eds.), *West European Communist Parties after the Revolution of 1989* (London, Macmillan), 80–118.
PAYNE, S. G. (1986) (ed.), *The Politics of Democratic Spain* (Chicago, Council of Foreign Relations).
PEELER, J. A. (1995), *Party Dominance and Civil Society: Contradictions in the Reconstitution of Democracy in Venezuela,* paper delivered at the Conference

on 'The Challenge of Democracy in Latin America: Rethinking State–Society Relations', Rio de Janeiro, IUPERJ, 4–6 Oct..

PEMPEL, T. J. (1990) (ed.), *Uncommon Democracies. The One-Party Dominant Regimes* (Ithaca, NY, Cornell University Press).

PEREIRA, J. PACHECO (1988), 'A Case of Orthodoxy: The Communist Party of Portugal', in M. Waller and M. Fennema (eds.), *Communist Parties in Western Europe: Decline or Adaptation?* (Oxford, Basil Blackwell), 86–95.

PÉREZ DÍAZ, V. (1985), 'Los empresarios y la clase política', in *Papeles de economía española*, special issue on ' Empresarios, sindicatos y marco institucional', 2–37.

—— (1987), *El retorno de la sociedad civil: Respuestas sociales a la transición política, la crisis económica y los cambios culturales de España 1975–1985* (Madrid, Instituto de Estudios Económicos).

—— (1990), 'The Emergence of Democratic Spain and the "Invention" of the Democratic Tradition', Centro de Estudios Avanzados en Ciencias Sociales, Working Paper no. 1990/1.

—— (1993), *La primacía de la sociedad civil* (Madrid, Alianza Editorial).

—— (1996), *España puesta a prueba 1976–1996* (Madrid, Alianza Editorial).

PÉREZ YRUELA, M., and GINER, S. (1988) (eds.), *El corporativismo en España* (Barcelona, Editorial Ariel).

PERIFANAKI ROTOLO, V. (1985), 'La nuova legge elettorale e il comportamento dell'elettorato femminile in Grecia', *Il politico*, 50 (4): 669–85.

—— (1989), *L'evoluzione della forma di governo in Grecia* (Padua, CEDAM).

—— (1990), 'Il nuovo sistema elettorale e il voto di preferenza in Grecia', *Il politico*, 55 (1): 143–66.

PETERSEN, J. (1975), 'Elettorato e base sociale del fascismo italiano negli anni venti', *Studi storici*, 16 (3): 627–69 .

PETMESIDOU, M. (1991), 'Statism, Social Policy and the Middle Classes in Greece', *Journal of European Social Policy*, 1 (1): 31–48.

PINKELE, C. F. (1992), 'Plus ça change: The Interaction between the Legal System and Political Change in Francoist Spain', *International Political Science Review*, 13 (3): 285–300.

PINTO, A. Costa (1991), 'The Radical Right in Portugal', in Cheles, Ferguson, *et al.* 1991: 108–28.

PINTO, J. NOGUEIRA (1989), 'A direita e o 25 de Abril: Ideologia, estratégia, e evolução política', in Coelho 1989: 193–212.

PINTO, M. (1989), *Les Relations industrielles au Portugal* (Brussells, EEC Commission).

PIZZORNO, A. (1980), *I soggetti del pluralismo* (Bologna, Il Mulino).

POGGI, G. (1963), *Il clero di riserva* (Milan, Feltrinelli).

—— (1968) (ed.), *L'organizzazione partitica del PCI e della DC* (Bologna, Il Mulino).

—— (1975), 'La chiesa nella politica italiana dal 1945 al 1950', in S. Woolf (ed.), *Italia 1943/50: La ricostruzione* (Bari, Laterza), 255–83.

POGUNTKE, T. (1996), 'Anti-party Sentiment: Conceptual Thoughts and Empirical Evidence: Explorations into a Minefield', *European Journal of Political Research*, 29 (3): 319–44.

POGUNTKE, T. and SCARROW, S. (1996), 'Introduction', *Politics of Anti-party Sentiment: European Journal of Political Research*, special edition, 29 (3): 257–62.

POMPER, G. M. (1992), 'Concepts of Political Parties', *Journal of Theoretical Politics*, 4 (2): 143–59.

POWELL, B. G. (1982), *Contemporary Democracies: Participation, Stability and Violence* (Cambridge, Harvard University Press).

PRIDHAM, G. (1984) (ed.), *The New Mediterranean Democracies: Regime Transition in Spain, Greece and Portugal* (London, Frank Cass).

—— (1990*a*) (ed.), *Securing Democracy: Political Parties and Democratic Consolidation in Southern Europe* (London, Routledge).

—— (1990*b*), 'Political Actors, Linkages and Interactions: Democratic Consolidation in Southern Europe', *West European Politics*, 13: 103–17.

—— (1991), 'The Politics of the European Community, Transnational Networks and Democratic Transition in Southern Europe', in G. Pridham (ed.), *Encouraging Democracy: The International Context of Regime Transition in Southern Europe* (Leicester, Leicester University Press), 212–45.

—— and VERNEY, S. (1991), 'The Coalition of 1989–90 in Greece', *West European Politics*, 14 (4): 42–69.

PRZEWORSKI, A. (1985), *Capitalism and Social Democracy* (Cambridge, Cambridge University Press).

—— (1986), 'Some Problems in the Study of the Transition to Democracy', in O'Donnell, Schmitter, and Whitehead 1986: 47–63.

—— (1991), *Democracy and the Market: Political and Economic Reforms in Eastern Europe and Latin America* (Cambridge, Cambridge University Press).

—— and TEUNE, H. (1970), *The Logic of Comparative Social Inquiry* (New York, Wiley-Interscience).

PSOMIADES, H. J. (1982), 'Greece: From the Colonels' Rule to Democracy', in Herz 1982: 251–73.

PUHLE, H. J. (1986), 'El PSOE: Un partido dominante y heterogéneo', in Linz and Montero 1986: 289–344.

PUTNAM, R., with LEONARDI, R., and NANETTI, R. Y. (1993), *Making Democracy Work: Civic Traditions in Modern Italy* (Princeton, Princeton University Press).

RAE, D. W. (1971), *The Political Consequences of Electoral Laws* (New Haven, Yale University Press).

RAGIN, C. (1987), *The Comparative Method: Moving beyond Qualitative and Quantitative Methods* (Berkeley and Los Angeles, University of California Press).

REINARES, F. (1989), 'Democratización y terrorismo en el caso español', in Tezanos, Cotarelo, and De Blas Guerrero 1989: 611–44.

—— (1991), 'Sociogénesis y evolución del terrorismo en España', in VV.AA *España: Sociedad y política* (Madrid, Alianza).

RÉMY, D. (1975), 'The Pivotal Party: Definition and Measurement', *European Journal of Political Research*, 3 (3): 293–301.

RIBEIRO, J., LEITÃO, N., and GRANJO, R. (1994), *Visões do sindicalismo: Trabalhadores e dirigentes* (Lisbon, Edições Cosmos).

RICHARDSON, B. (1990), 'The Development of Partisan Commitments in Post-Franquist Spain', Department of Political Science, Ohio State University, paper.

RICOLFI, L. (1995), 'Il voto proporzionale: Il nuovo spazio politico italiano', in Bartolini and D'Alimonte 1995: 273–316.

RIGHETTINI, S. (1995), 'La politicizzazione di un potere neutrale: Magistratura e crisi italiana', *Rivista italiana di scienza politica*, 25 (2): 227–65.

RIJNEN, H. (1985), 'La CEOE como organización', *Papeles de economía española*, 22: 115–21.

ROBINSON, R. A. H. (1991–2), 'The Evolution of the Portuguese Socialist Party, 1973–86, in International Perspective', *Portuguese Studies Review*, 1 (1): 6–26.

ROMÁN MARUGÁN, P. (1987), *El Partido Socialista Obrero Español en la transición española: Organización y ideología (1975–1982)* (Madrid, Departamento de Ciencia Política y de la Administración).

—— (1995) (ed.), *Sistema político español* (Madrid, McGraw-Hill).

ROSE, R. (1969), 'The Variability of Party Government: A Theoretical and Empirical Critique', *Political Studies*, 17: 413–45.

—— and MISHLER, W. (1996), 'Testing the Churchill Hypothesis: Popular Support for Democracy and its Alternatives', *Journal of Public Policy*, 16 (1): 29–58.

ROSSI, M. (1979), 'Un partito di "anime morte"? Il tesseramento democristiano tra mito e realtà', in A. Parisi (ed.), *Democristiani* (Bologna, Il Mulino), 13–60.

ROTH, G. (1963), *The Social Democrats in Imperial Germany* (Totowa, NJ, The Bedminster Press).

RUBINSTEIN, J. C. (1995), *Reflexiones en torno a la sociedad civil* (La Plata, Editorial de la Universidad Nacional de La Plata).

RUSTOW, D. (1970), 'Transition to Democracy: Toward a Dynamic Model', *Comparative Politics*, 2: 337–63.

SÁNCHEZ DE DIOS, M. (1995), 'El poder judicial y la jurisdicción constitucional', in Román Marugán 1995: 129–57.

SANI, G. (1974), 'A Test of Least-Distance Model of Voting Choice: Italy 1972', *Comparative Political Studies*, 7: 193–208.

—— (1980), 'The Political Culture of Italy: Continuity and Change', in G. A. Almond and S. Verba (eds.), *The Civic Culture Revisited* (Boston, Little, Brown & Co.).

—— (1981), 'Partiti e atteggiamenti di massa in Spagna e Italia', *Rivista italiana di scienza politica*, 11: 235–80.

—— and MONTERO, J. R. (1986), 'El espectro político: Izquierda, derecha y centro', in Linz and Montero 1986: 155–200.

—— and SEGATTI, P. (1995), 'AntiParty Politics in Italy: Old or New?', unpublished paper.

SANTANA LOPES, P. (1988), 'PPD/PSD: La dependencia del carisma', *Revista de estudios políticos (nueva época)*, 60–1: 173.

SANTOS, B. DE SOUSA (1986), 'Social Crisis and the State', in Maxwell 1986a: 167–95.

SARTORI, G. (1965), *Democratic Theory* (New York, Praeger).

—— (1975), 'The Tower of Babel', in G. Sartori, F. Riggs, and H. Teune, *Tower of Babel: On the Definition and Analysis of Concepts in Social Sciences*, International Studies Occasional Paper no. 6, University of Pittsburgh.

—— (1976), *Parties and Party Systems: A Framework for Analysis* (Cambridge, Cambridge University Press).

—— (1987), *The Theory of Democracy Revisited* (Chatham, NJ, Chatham House).

—— (1993), *Democrazia: Cosa è* (Milan, Rizzoli).

—— (1994), *Comparative Constitutional Engineering* (London, Macmillan).

SATRÚSTEGUI, M. (1992), 'PSOE: A New Catch-all Party', in Merkel *et al.* 1992: 33–48.

SCARPARI, U. (1977), *La democrazia cristiana e le leggi eccezionali 1950–53* (Milan, Feltrinelli).

SCHAAR, J. (1981) (ed.), *Legitimacy in the Modern State* (New Brunswick, NJ, Transaction Books).

SCHATTSCHNEIDER, E. E. (1942), *Party Government* (New York, Rinehart & Winston).

SCHEDLER, A. (1995), 'Under- and Overinstitutionalization: Some Ideal Typical Propositions Concerning New and Old Party Systems', working paper no. 213, Kellogg Institute, Notre Dame, Ind.

—— (1997a), 'Concepts of Democratic Consolidation', paper delivered at 1997 LASA Meeting, Guadalajara, 17–19 Apr.

—— (1997b) 'Expected Stability: Defining and Measuring Democratic Consolidation', unpublished paper, Vienna, Institute for Advanced Studies, Apr.

SCHMITT, H. (1989), 'On Party Attachment in Western Europe and the Utility of Eurobarometer Data', *West European Politics*, 12: 122–39.

—— (1990), 'Party Attachment and Party Choice in the European Election of June 1989', *International Journal of Public Opinion Research*, 2: 169–81.

—— and MANNHEIMER, R. (1991), 'About Voting and Non-voting in the European Elections of June 1989', *European Journal of Political Research*, 19 (1): 31–54.

SCHMITTER, P. C. (1985), 'The Consolidation of Political Democracy in Southern Europe', Florence, European University Institute and Stanford, Stanford University, rev. edn., mimeo, unpublished.

—— (1988), *The Consolidation of Political Democracy in Southern Europe*, mimeo, 2nd. rev. edn., Stanford University.

—— (1992), 'The Consolidation of Democracy and Representation of Social Groups', *American Behavioral Scientist*, 35 (4/5): 422–49.

—— (1993), 'Some Propositions about Civil Society and the Consolidation of Democracy', unpublished.

—— (1995), 'Organized Interests and Democratic Consolidation in Southern Europe', in Gunther, Diamandouros, and Puhle 1995: 284–314.

—— and KARL, T. (1993), 'What Democracy Is . . . and Is Not', in L. Diamond and M. Plattner (eds.), *The Global Resurgence of Democracy* (Baltimore, Johns Hopkins University Press), 39–52.

SCHUMPETER, J. (1954), *Capitalism, Socialism and Democracy* (London, Allen & Unwin).

SCHWARTZ, D. C. (1973), *Political Alienation and Political Behavior* (Chicago, Aldine).

SCOPPOLA, P. (1977), *La proposta politica di De Gasperi* (Bologna, Il Mulino).

SEFERIADES, S. (1986), 'Polarizzazione partitica e non proporzionalità elettorale in Grecia', *Rivista italiana di scienza politica*, 16: 401–37.

SEGATTI, P. (1992), 'L'offerta politica e i candidati della Lega alle elezioni amministrative del 1990', *Polis*, 6 (2): 257–80.

SHABAD, G. (1986), 'After Autonomy: The Dynamics of Regionalism in Spain', in Payne 1986: 111–80.

SHARE, D. (1989), *Dilemmas of Social Democracy: The Spanish Socialist Workers Party in the 1980s* (Westport, Conn., Greenwood Press).

SHILS, E. (1991), 'The Virtue of Civil Society', *Government and Opposition*, 26 (1): 3–20.

SHIN, D. C. (1994), 'On the Third Wave of Democratization: A Synthesis and Evaluation of Recent Theory and Research', *World Politics*, 47 (1): 135–70.

SILVA, A. Cavaco (1994), 'Combinação de políticas de estabilização num quadro de integração: A experiência portuguesa', *Brotéria*, 138: 493–515.

SJÖBLOM, G. (1994), *Notes on the Concept of 'Institution'*, IPSA XVIth World Congress, Berlin.

SOTIROPOULOS, D. A. (1991), 'State and Party: The Greek State Bureaucracy and Panhellenic Socialist Movement (PASOK), 1981–1989', Ph.D. dissertation, Yale University, New Haven.

—— (1994), 'Bureaucracy and Civil Society in Contemporary Greece', paper presented at XVIth World Congress of IPSA, Berlin.

SOUSA, V. ALVES DA COSTA E (1983), 'O Partido Comunista Português (subsídios para um estudo sobre os seus adeptos)', *Estudos políticos e sociais*, 11: 495–543.

SPINI, V., and MATTANA, S. (1981), *I quadri del PSI* (Firenze, Quaderni del Circolo Rosselli, Nuova Guaraldi).

SPOURDALAKIS, M. (1988), *The Rise of the Greek Socialist Party* (London, Routledge).

—— (1992), 'A Petty Bourgeois Party with a Populist Ideology and Catch-All Party Structure: PASOK', in Merkel *et al.* 1992: 97–122.

—— (1996), 'Securing Democracy in Post-authoritarian Greece: The Role of Political Parties', in G. Pridham, and P. G. Lewis (eds.), *Stabilising Fragile Democracies* (London, Routledge), 167–85.

SPREAFICO, A. (1963), 'Orientamento politico e identificazione partitica', in A. Spreafico, and J. La Palombara (eds.), *Elezioni e comportamento politico in Italia* (Milan, Edizioni di Comunità), 689–731.

STEPAN, A. (1978), *The State and Society: Peru in Comparative Perspective* (Princeton, Princeton University Press).

—— (1988), *Rethinking Military Politics: Brazil and the Southern Cone* (Princeton, Princeton University Press).

—— and SKACH, C. (1994), 'Presidentialism and Parliamentarianism in Comparative Perspective', in Linz and Valenzuela 1994: 119–36.

STOCK, M. J. (1985), 'O centrismo político em Portugal: Evolução do sistema de partidos, génese do "Bloco Central" e análise dos dois parceiros da coligação', *Análise social*, 21 (85): 45–82.

—— (1986), *Os partidos do poder dez anos depois do '25 de April'* (Évora, Universidade de Évora).

—— (1988), 'El centrismo político y los partidos del poder en Portugal', *Revista de estudios políticos*, 60–1: 139–72.

STOLEROFF, A. (1988), 'Sindicalismo e relações industriais em Portugal', *Sociologia: Problemas e práticas*, 4: 147–64.

—— (1990), 'Reflexões sobre a evolução do sindicalismo e do movimento operário na era dos governos Cavaco Silva', *Vértice*, 31: 45–55.

—— (1995), 'Elementos do padrão emergente de relações industriais em Portugal', *Organizações e trabalho*, 13: 11–42.

—— and NAUMANN, R. (1993), 'A Sindicalização em Portugal: A sua medida e a sua distribuição', *Sociologia: Problemas e práticas*, 14: 19–47.

STROM, K. (1989), 'Inter-party Competition in Advanced Democracies', *Journal of Theoretical Politics*, 1 (3): 277–300.

—— (1990), 'A Behavioural Model of Competitive Political Parties', *American Journal of Political Science*, 34: 565–98.

—— (1992), 'Democracy as Political Competition', in G. Marks and L. Diamond (eds.), *Reexamining Democracy: Essays in Honor of Seymour Martin Lipset* (London, Sage Publications), 27–46.

SVENSSON, P. (1986), 'Stability, Crisis and Breakdown: Some Notes on the Concept of Crisis in Political Analysis', *Scandinavian Political Studies*, 9 (2): 129–39.

TAAGEPERA, R., and SHUGART, M. S. (1989), *Seats and Votes: The Effects and Determinants of Electoral Systems* (New Haven, Yale University Press).

TARCHI, M. (1997), *Dal MSI ad AN* (Bologna, Il Mulino).

TARROW, S. (1967), *Peasant Communism in Southern Italy* (New Haven, Yale University Press).

—— (1982), 'Transforming Enemies into Allies: Non-ruling Communist Parties in Multiparty Coalitions', *Journal of Politics*, 4: 924–54.

—— (1989), *Democracy and Disorder: Protest and Politics in Italy 1965–1975* (Oxford, Clarendon Press).

—— (1995), 'Mass Mobilization and Regime Change: Pacts, Reform and Popular Power in Italy (1918–1922) and Spain (1975–1978)', in Gunther, Diamandouros, and Puhle 1995: 204–30.

TATE, N. C., and VALLINDER, T. (1995), *The Global Expansion of Judicial Power* (New York, New York University Press).

TEZANOS, J. F. (1983), *Sociología del socialismo español* (Madrid, Tecnos).

—— (1989), 'Continuidad y cambio en el socialismo español: El PSOE durante la transición democrática', in Tezanos, Cotarelo, and De Blas Guerrero 1989: 433–93.

—— COTARELO, R., and DE BLAS GUERRERO, A. (1989) (eds.), *La transición democrática española* (Madrid, Editorial Sistema).

THEOFANIDES, S. (1989) (ed.), *Greece and EC Membership Evaluated* (London, Pinter Publishers).

THOMAS, P. (1994), *Civil Society and the Preconditions of Democracy*, IPSA XVIth World Congress, Berlin.

TILLY, C. (1975), *The Formation of National States in Western Europe* (Princeton, Princeton University Press).

—— (1978), *From Mobilization to Revolution* (Reading, Mass., Addison-Wesley Publishing).

TORCAL, M., and CHIBBER, P. (1995), 'Elites, cleavages y sistema de partidos en una democracia consolidada: España (1986–1992)', *Revista española de investigaciones sociológicas*, 69: 7–38.

TRIFILETTI, R. (1996), 'Southern European Welfare Regimes and the Worsening Position of Women', paper presented at conference on 'Social Research and Social Policy in Southern Europe', Athens.

TSATSOS, C. D. (1988), 'Making the Constitution of Greece', in R. Goldwin and A. Kaufman (eds.), *Constitution Makers and Constitution Making: The Experience of Eight Nations* (Washington, American Enterprise Institute for Public Policy Research), 69–93.

VALENZUELA, S. J. (1992), 'Democratic Consolidation in Post-transitional Settings: Notion, Process, and Facilitating Conditions', in S. Mainwaring, G. O'Donnell, *et al.* (eds.), *Issues in Democratic Consolidation: The New South American Democracies in Comparative Perspective* (Notre Dame, Ind., University of Notre Dame Press), 57–104.

VALLAURI, C. (1981) (ed.), *L'arcipelago democratico: Organizzazione e struttura dei partiti italiani negli anni del centrismo (1949–1958)* (Rome, Bulzoni Editore).

VALLINDER, T. (1994), 'The Judicialization of Politics', *International Political Science Review*, special issue, 15 (2): 91–108.

VAN DER EIJK, C., and NIEMOELLER, B. (1983), 'Theoretical and Methodological Considerations in the Use of Left–Right Scales', paper presented at ECPR joint sessions, Salzburg.

VARELA-GUINOT, H. (1990), 'The Legalization of the Spanish Communist Party: Elites, Public Opinion and Symbols in the Spanish Political Transition', working paper 1990/8, Instituto Juan March, Madrid.

VASCONCELOS, A. de (1990), 'Sociedade, partidos e estado em Portugal', unpublished paper.

VASILEIOU, I. (1991), 'Profile of the Left', *Anti-B*, 28 June: 22–5 (in Greek).

VEGLERIS, P. (1981), 'Greek Electoral Law', in H. R. Penniman (ed.), *Greece at Polls: The National Elections of 1974 and 1977* (Washington, American Enterprise Institute for Public Policy Research), 21–48.

VEREMIS, T. (1987), 'The Military', in Featherstone and Katsoudas 1987: 214–29.

VERNEY, S. (1994), 'Central state–local government relations', in P. Kazakos and P. C. Ioakimidis (eds.), *Greece and EC Membership Evaluated* (London, Pinter), 166–80.

VERZICHELLI, L. (1995), 'Gli eletti', in Bartolini and D'Alimonte 1995: 401–25.

—— (1997), 'La classe politica della transizione', in R. D'Alimonte and S. Bartolini (eds.), *Maggioritario per caso: Le elezioni politiche del 1996* (Bologna, Il Mulino), 309–50.

VILA, D., and GÓMEZ REINO, M. (1980), 'El proceso de cambio político en el electorado (1973–1980)', paper delivered at the Seminar on 'Electoral Surveys and Electoral Behavior', Madrid.

WARE, A. (1992), 'Liberal Democracy: One Form or Many?', *Political Studies*, 40: 130–45.

—— (1996), *Political Parties and Party Systems* (Oxford, Oxford University Press).

WEATHERFORD, M. S. (1991), 'Mapping the Ties that Bind: Legitimacy, Representation and Alienation', *Western Political Quarterly*, 44 (2): 251–76.

—— (1992), 'Measuring Political Legitimacy', *American Political Science Review*, 86 (1): 149–66.

WEIL, F. (1989), 'The Sources and Structure of Legitimation in Western Democracies: A Consolidated Model Tested with Time-Series Data in Six Countries Since World War II', *American Sociological Review*, 54: 682–706.

WEINBERG, L. (1995), *The Transformation of Italian Communism* (New Brunswick, Transaction Publishers).

WERT, J. I. (1995), 'Sobre cultura política: Legitimidad, desafección y malestar', unpublished paper.

—— (1996), 'Las elecciones legislativas del 3–M: Paisaje después de la batalla', *Claves de razón práctica*, 61: 36–44.

WHITEHEAD, L. (1989), 'The Consolidation of Fragile Democracies: A Discussion with Illustrations', in Pastor 1989: 76–95.

—— (1991), 'Democracy by Convergence and Southern Europe: A Comparative Politics Perspective', in Pridham 1991: 45–61.

—— (1995), 'An Elusive Transition: The Slow Motion Demise of Authoritarian Dominant Party Rule in Mexico', *Democratization*, 2 (3): 246–69.

—— (1996) (ed.), *The International Dimensions of Democratization. Europe and the Americas* (Oxford, Oxford University Press).

—— (1997), 'The Vexed Issue of the Meaning of "Democracy"', unpublished paper, Oxford, Nuffield College.

WILDENMANN, R. (1986) (ed.), *The Future of Party Government* (Berlin, De Gruyter).

WILSON, F. L. (1996), *Concepts and Issues in Comparative Politics* (Upper Saddle River, NJ, Prentice Hall).

WRIGHT, J. D. (1976), *The Dissent of the Governed: Alienation and Democracy in America* (New York, Academic Press).

WRIGHT, V. (1996), 'Industrial and Banking Privatization in Western Europe: Some Public Policy Paradoxes', unpublished paper.

YRUELA, M. P., and GINER, S. (1988) (eds.), *El corporatismo en España* (Barcelona, Editorial Ariel).

ZANGRANDI, R. (1962), *Il lungo viaggio attraverso il fascismo* (Milan, Feltrinelli).

ZARAGOZA, A. (1988) (ed.), *Pactos sociales, sindicatos y patronal en España* (Madrid, Siglo Veintiuno de España Editores).

ZARISKI, R. (1986), 'The Legitimacy of Opposition Parties in Democratic Political Systems: A New Use for an Old Concept', *Western Political Quarterly*, 39 (1): 29–47.

ZIMMERMANN, E. (1983), *Political Violence, Crisis, and Revolutions: Theory and Research* (Boston, G. K. Hall/Schenkman).

—— (1985), 'The 1930s World Economic Crisis in Six European Countries: A First Report on Causes of Political Instability and Reactions to Crisis', in P. Johnson and W. Thompson (eds.), *Rhythms in Politics and Economics* (New York, Praeger), 84–127.

ZOHLNHOFER, W. (1969), 'Party Identification in the Federal Republic of Germany', in K. Shell (ed.), *The Democratic Political Process* (Waltham, Blaisdell Publ. Co.).

ZUCKERMAN, A. (1979), *The Politics of Faction: Christian Democratic Rule in Italy* (New Haven, Yale University Press).

Index

Abete, L. 291
AC (Italy) 288
ACLI (Italy) 288
Accornero, A. 182 n., 291 n.
accountability 1, 6
Achimastos, M. 200 n.
AD (Portugal) 60, 266
adaptation 2, 5, 14, 14 n., 16, 18, 20, 24, 34, 49, 53–5, 276
ADEDY (Portugal) 236 n., 237
AEM (Portugal) 237
Aget-Iraklis 315
Agger, R. E. 126 n.
Agüero, F. 71 n., 74, 75 n., 76 n.
Aguiar, J. 195 n., 198 n.
Aguilar, S. 280
AIP (Portugal) 229–30, 242
Alacevich, F. 291, 291 n.
Alberoni, F. 182, 207
Alentejo 195
Alexakis, E. G. 204 n.
Alianza Popular, see AP
Alivizatos, N. 67 n., 68 n., 103 n.
Alleanza Contadini (Italy) 216
Alleanza Democratica (Italy) 97, 99
Alleanza Nazionale, see AN
Alleanza Progressista (Italy) 97
Allum, S. 153
Allum, Percy A. 220 n.
Almarcha Barbado, A. 82 n.
Almond, G. A. 13, 26, 113–14, 117, 126, 126 n., 138
Amato, G. 59, 291, 319, 328
Amodia, J. 283
AN (Italy) 58, 98, 98 n., 99–100, 284–6, 289, 289 n., 292–3
anchoring 34–5, 41, 169–70, 205–6, 213, 226, 242, 245–6, 277, 279, 284, 293, 296, 330–3, 338–45
anchors of consolidation, see anchoring
Anderson, C. 311 n.
Andreotti, G. 58–9, 96 n., 97, 154
ANFI (Italy) 288
Angola 279

anti-party sentiments 281 n., 290
anti-regime and anti-system parties 50, 251–2, 254, 256, 284, 284 n., 293
Antunes, M. Lobo 67, 68 n., 224 n.
AP (Spain) 95, 151, 158–60, 174–5, 177, 189, 190 n., 210, 222–3, 265, 268
Arian, A. 133 n., 264 n.
Arias Navarro, C. 60
army, political role of 11, 12, 18–19, 30–1, 45, 52–5, 55–6, 62, 71–6, 83–4, 154, 162, 166
Athens 80 n., 155, 204
authoritarianism 1, 19, 22 n.
   breakdown of 19, 21, 27
   consolidation of 13 n.
   establishment of 21, 49
   experience with 118 n., 121, 160, 221, 338
   installation of 9 n.
   preference for 119–21, 127–8, 136–48, 161
   transition from 73, 122–3
   transition to 16
   see also crisis, of authoritarian regimes
Averoff, G. 203
Ayala, L. 313 n.
Azevedo, Pinheiro de 60
Aznar, J. M. 60, 190, 279

Bacalhau, M. 117 n., 135 n.
Baccetti, C. 96
Bad Godesberg conference 152
Balabanian, O. 232
Balsemao, Pinto 60
Banca Commerciale Italiana 292
Bañón Martínez, R. 76 n.
Bardi, L. 286
Barker, T. M. 76 n.
Barnard, C. J. 15 n.
Barnes, S. H. 3, 28, 115, 128, 130, 132 n., 207, 207 n., 264 n., 297, 300

Index